# Collaboration in Performance Practice

## Premises, Workings and Failures

Edited by

Noyale Colin
*University of Winchester, Hampshire, UK*

and

Stefanie Sachsenmaier
*Middlesex University, London, UK*

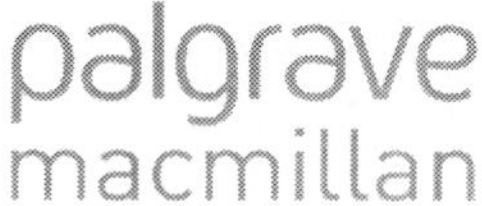


UNIVERSITY OF WINCHESTER
LIBRARY

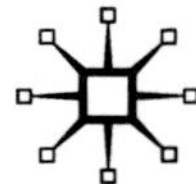

Introduction, selection and editorial matter © Noyale Colin and Stefanie Sachsenmaier 2016
Individual chapters © Contributors 2016

All rights reserved. No reproduction, copy or transmission of this publication may be made without written permission.

No portion of this publication may be reproduced, copied or transmitted save with written permission or in accordance with the provisions of the Copyright, Designs and Patents Act 1988, or under the terms of any licence permitting limited copying issued by the Copyright Licensing Agency, Saffron House, 6–10 Kirby Street, London EC1N 8TS.

Any person who does any unauthorized act in relation to this publication may be liable to criminal prosecution and civil claims for damages.

The authors have asserted their rights to be identified as the authors of this work in accordance with the Copyright, Designs and Patents Act 1988.

First published 2016 by
PALGRAVE MACMILLAN

Palgrave Macmillan in the UK is an imprint of Macmillan Publishers Limited, registered in England, company number 785998, of Houndmills, Basingstoke, Hampshire RG21 6XS.

Palgrave Macmillan in the US is a division of St Martin's Press LLC, 175 Fifth Avenue, New York, NY 10010.

Palgrave Macmillan is the global academic imprint of the above companies and has companies and representatives throughout the world.

Palgrave® and Macmillan® are registered trademarks in the United States, the United Kingdom, Europe and other countries.

ISBN 978–1–137–46245–9

This book is printed on paper suitable for recycling and made from fully managed and sustained forest sources. Logging, pulping and manufacturing processes are expected to conform to the environmental regulations of the country of origin.

A catalogue record for this book is available from the British Library.

A catalog record for this book is available from the Library of Congress.

Typeset by MPS Limited, Chennai, India.

UNIVERSITY OF WINCHESTER

*To Susan Melrose*

*With thanks*

*From our hearts*

# Contents

# List of Illustrations

## Chapter 9



## Chapter 10



## Chapter 12

## Chapter 13



## Chapter 14

# Acknowledgements

The initial steps that eventually led towards this publication can in hindsight be traced back in time to our decision to organize the first Symposium on Collaboration in 2012 at Middlesex University, which had a particular emphasis on memory, time and place. The overwhelming number of stimulating proposals, presentation of papers as well as instances of performance practice shared on the day, as well as the debates that unfolded at the event amongst contributors and delegates, led us to organize a follow-up event a year later, with a specific focus on the politics of collaboration. We would like to thank the many contributors that have been involved in these symposia, as well as Middlesex University and University Campus Suffolk for their invaluable support.

Further, certain individuals have helped us along the process of drawing this publication together. We would like to thank Josephine Machon for guidance and advice through the editing process. We are grateful to Tim Fletcher for his generous assistance in preparing the manuscript and his continuous encouragement throughout the development of the volume. Susan Melrose has provided us with invaluable comments on the writing of our introductory chapter.

We would moreover particularly like to thank artists Ewan Forster and Chris Heighes for providing us with a wonderful cover photograph. Our thanks also go to Agat Film for authorizing the reproduction of stills from the film *Au Soleil même la nuit*. Furthermore, we are extremely grateful to the photographers who have kindly provided us with their permissions to reproduce their images in this publication. Our thank you extends to all performance-makers involved in the works discussed in these pages.

We would also like to acknowledge the wonderful support and guidance we have received through the publishing team at Palgrave Macmillan. We specifically would like to thank Paula Kennedy, whom we were sad to see leave her position as publisher mid-way through our writing process and would like to thank her for her enthusiasm and warm support during the crucial initial stages leading to this publication. Peter Cary, Linda Auld, Daniel Willcocks and Jenny McCall have provided us with a steady continuation of her work.

*Noyale Colin and Steffi Sachsenmaier*
*London, 2015*

# Notes on Contributors

**Caroline Bowditch** is an Australian-born but now Glasgow-based performance artist and choreographer. She is a founder member of Weave Movement Theatre (Melbourne) and The FATHoM Project (Newcastle). In 2007 she received a Wellcome Trust Arts Award to create *Proband,* which uses her genetic mutation as the basis for the choreography and music. From April 2008 to March 2012, Caroline held the role as Scottish Dance Theatre's Dance Agent for Change. In December 2010 she received an Unlimited Commission to create her most ambitious work to date, *Leaving Limbo Landing,* as part of the Cultural Olympiad for the London 2012 Olympics.

**David Bower** is a Deaf performer and is Artistic Director at the Signdance Collective International. He has worked on numerous company productions as a performer, filmmaker, director and set builder. David has also undertaken roles in film, television, repertory theatre and is a regular on BBC Radio drama. Productions include *Rapid Intervention, Four Weddings and a Funeral, Travelog, Little voices, Titus Andronicus, Children of the Lesser God, The Hunchback of Notre Dame*. David is an associate artist at Carovana SMI (Sardinia). He is also a Director on the NDACA (National Disability Arts Collection and Archive) panel.

**Carol Brown** is a choreographer and an Associate Professor at the University of Auckland New Zealand where she also directs Choreographic Research Aoteaora. Her work evolves through dialogue, experimentation and creative research in response to contemporary issues of space and corporeality. After completing a practice-led PhD (University of Surrey), Carol was invited to be Choreographer in Residence at the Place Theatre London where she developed Carol Brown Dances. Her dance theatre and performance installation works have toured internationally, and she has received commissions for large-scale urban works in Barcelona, Athens, Perth, Prague and Auckland.

**Emilyn Claid** is an independent dance artist, professor of choreographic practices at Roehampton University (London) and a Gestalt psychotherapist. Throughout the 1970s and 80s she was at the forefront of the UK experimental dance scene and in the 1990s she worked as an independent choreographer. In 1997 Emilyn was awarded a PhD and published

*Yes? No! Maybe... Seductive Ambiguity in Dance Theatre Performance* (2006). Between 2003 and 2013 Emilyn directed Choreography at Dartington College of Arts. Choreographic research projects have taken her to Auckland, Hong Kong, Singapore, Berlin, Helsinki, Melbourne and Beirut. Alongside a professorship at Roehampton Emilyn has a private psychotherapy practice in London.

**Noyale Colin** is Senior Lecturer in Choreography and Dance at the University of Winchester. Noyale studied dance and music at the Conservatoire National of Nantes and the Conservatoire Supérieur de Lyon, before working as a performer and choreographer in the United States and Europe. In 2009 she received a Research Studentship in Performing Arts at Middlesex University, where she obtained a PhD which examines the politics of co-working in contemporary performance making. With Stefanie Sachsenmaier, Noyale has co-organized the Symposia On Collaboration held at Middlesex University in 2012 and 2013.

**Laura Cull Ó Maoilearca** is Head of the Department of Theatre & Dance at the University of Surrey, UK. Her most recent books are *Theatres of Immanence: Deleuze and the Ethics of Performance* (2012) and *Encounters in Performance Philosophy* (2014) co-edited with Alice Lagaay. Her other publications include *Deleuze and Performance* (2009) and *Manifesto Now! Instructions for Performance, Philosophy, Politics* (2013) co-edited with Will Daddario. She is core convener of Performance Philosophy and joint series editor of the Performance Philosophy book series with Palgrave.

**Pedro de Senna** is a theatre practitioner and academic. He is a Senior Lecturer in Contemporary Theatre, and Programme Leader for the BA Theatre Arts (Theatre Directing) at Middlesex University. His research and publications focus on translation and adaptation, the relationship between directing and dramaturgy, and disability aesthetics. Pedro is a member of the executive committee of SCUDD, where he convenes the Diversity in the Discipline Working Group. His play *A tragédia de Ismene, princesa de Tebas* won the first Seleção Brasil em Cena, a national award for new writing, and is published by Móbile Editorial.

**Ewan Forster** and **Christopher Heighes** studied theatre at Dartington College of Arts in Devon and in 1993 formed an artistic partnership creating performance and installation works for unusual and often neglected architectural sites.

Their numerous site-specific projects are diverse in nature and have been commissioned for a wide variety of locations both in the United

Kingdom and abroad including Mary Ward House in Bloomsbury for LIFT in London and the Hufeisensiedlung for HAU in Berlin. Their first gallery installation, *'Plant Science',* was commissioned by Kings Cultural Institute and the Performance Foundation for the Inigo Rooms at Somerset House in 2013. They both hold Creative Research Fellowships at The University of Roehampton.

**Tim Jeeves** is an artist and writer, currently in the final stages of a PhD, 'Towards Economies of Generosity in Contemporary Performance', at Lancaster University that examines issues around arts funding, artistic labour and organ transplantation.

Since 2011 he has produced the *Giving in to Gift* festival in Liverpool where he lives, whilst recent performance work includes 'The Kindness of Strangers'; an exploration of Tim's relationship with the anonymous donor of the bone marrow transplant he received in 1998, and Blanche Dubois, the tragic protagonist of Tennessee Williams' *A Streetcar Named Desire*, a play Tim studied for his A-Levels in 1997.

**Alexandra Kolb** is Associate Professor in Dance at Middlesex University, London. Following her doctorate at Cambridge University, she also held positions as head of Academic Studies at the Northern School of Contemporary Dance in Leeds, and chair of Dance Studies at Otago University in New Zealand. She is the author of *Performing Femininity: Dance and Literature in German Modernism* (2009), editor of *Dance and Politics* (2011), and contributor to a wide range of international dance and arts journals. She is recipient of the Gertrude Lippincott Award for the best English-language article published in dance studies (2014) and a Harry Ransom Fellowship at the University of Texas at Austin (2013).

**Erin Manning** holds a University Research Chair in Relational Art and Philosophy in the Faculty of Fine Arts at Concordia University (Montreal, Canada). She is the director of the SenseLab (www.senselab.ca). Her current art practice is centred on large-scale participatory installations that facilitate emergent collectivities. Her publications include *Always More Than One: Individuation's Dance* (2013), *Relationscapes: Movement, Art, Philosophy* (2009) and, with Brian Massumi, *Thought in the Act: Passages in the Ecology of Experience* (2014). Forthcoming book projects include a translation of Fernand Deligny's *Les détours de l'agir ou le moindre geste* and a monograph titled *The Minor Gesture*.

**Susan Melrose** is Professor of Performance Arts at Middlesex University. She is author of *A Semiotics of the Dramatic Text* (Macmillan, 1994) and editor, with British choreographer and researcher Rosemary Butcher, of *Rosemary Butcher: Choreography, Collisions and Collaborations* (2005). Other writing relating in particular to expert or professional creative decision-making in performance is available or cited on her website at www.sfmelrose.org.uk.

**Simon Murray** teaches Theatre and Performance at the University of Glasgow. He has been a professional theatre maker and performer and trained in Paris in the 1980s with Philippe Gaulier and Monika Pagneux, amongst others. Before moving to Glasgow he was Director of Theatre at Dartington College of Arts. Simon is originally a sociologist 'by trade' and spent 15 years working in adult and workers' education in the 1970s and 1980s. In recent years he has written on Jacques Lecoq, physical theatres, lightness, W.G. Sebald and contemporary performance and is currently researching for a book on ruins and performance. He is co-founder and co-editor with Jonathan Pitches of the journal *Theatre Dance and Performance Training*.

**Moana Nepia** is a Māori visual and performing artist, choreographer, curator, video artist, writer, and Assistant Professor in The Center for Pacific Islands Studies at the University of Hawai'i at Mānoa, where he is developing new courses with a focus on visual and performing arts in the Pacific Islands. Having trained in Dance at the VCA in Melbourne, Moana had a career in ballet and contemporary dance in New Zealand and Europe before retraining as a visual artist at Chelsea and Wimbledon Schools of Art in London. His Practice-led PhD from AUT University in Auckland investigated *Te Kore*, the Māori concept of void.

**Martina Ruhsam** is a choreographer, performer and writer. From October 2008 to March 2009 she was head of the theorycentre in Tanzquartier Wien. She is the author of *Kollaborative Praxis: Choreographie* (2011). Her artistic works and collaborations have been presented at numerous venues and festivals in Europe. She is a member of the editorial board of *Maska, Performing Arts Journal* and she has published essays in several publications dedicated to the performing arts. Currently she is completing her doctorate at the Justus Liebig University in Gießen.

**Stefanie Sachsenmaier** (PhD Middlesex University, DEA Sorbonne Nlle, MA Goldsmiths) is Senior Lecturer in Theatre Arts at Middlesex University. She has a background as a performer and trains and teaches tai chi at Wu's Tai Chi Chuan Academy London, Bethnal Green. Her research interests and publications relate to the processual in creative practice. She has published several articles related to her ongoing research with choreographer Rosemary Butcher and has contributed to the *Laban Sourcebook* (ed. Dick McCaw, 2011). Together with Noyale Colin she has organized two Symposia On Collaboration at Middlesex University, London, in 2012 and 2013.

**Kris Salata** is an artist-scholar and Associate Professor of Performance in the School of Theatre at Florida State University. He teaches performance, directing, devised theatre, and critical theory courses in the BA, MA, MFA, and Ph.D. programs. He focuses his research on phenomenological, ontological, and epistemological aspects of theatre practice with emphasis on Performance as Research. He has published articles and book chapters on Konstantin Stanislavsky, Polish theatre laboratories, Jerzy Grotowski, and the Workcenter of Jerzy Grotowski and Thomas Richards. With his recent book, *The Unwritten Grotowski: Theory and Practice of the Encounter*, he takes on a new approach to Grotowski's legacy and pursues an interdisciplinary field of study of the encounter.

# Collaborative Performance-Making in Context

*Noyale Colin and Stefanie Sachsenmaier*

'Collaboration in the arts', according to historian Charles Green (2001: x), became 'a crucial element in the transition from modernist to postmodernist art' and it continues to be a key component of creative processes in Western arts contexts. Although performative art forms can be seen to have an inherent collaborative aspect, it is only recently that an emphasis has been placed on problematizing processes of co-labouring in the disciplines of the performing arts. The recognition and exploration of creativity as 'social' and frequently 'an explicitly collaborative endeavour' has opened new avenues for research across diverse disciplines in the early twenty-first century (Littleton and Miell, 2004: 1). With specific reference to the performing arts, Kathryn Syssoyeva (2013: 2) similarly suggests that scholarly interest in 'collective creation' has only recently gathered pace. This collection of writing contributes to this growing area of scholarly interest in its examination of the role and place of collaboration in contemporary performance-making. Critically evaluating issues around the politics and ethics of collaborative work, it foregrounds the notion of creativity in performance as 'social', presenting an analysis of both the social and cultural conditions and the artistic processes that shape contemporary collaboration.

In order to investigate these social aspects of performance-making, the essays in this volume explore different modes of collaborative working; and they include case studies examining interdisciplinary and cross-disciplinary collaborations, cross-cultural collaborations, and collaboration between disabled and non-disabled artists. The volume seeks to raise and debate issues that emerge directly from the practice of collaborative performance-making. Within the narratives of modernism and postmodernism, collaborative methods of working in performance during the twentieth century have been recurrently assimilated to radical artistic gestures challenging dominant modes of socio-political structures. However, in the 1990s a surge of artistic concerns with collectivity and collaboration in advanced capitalist societies has invited a re-consideration of their modern historical development.

In what follows we offer a brief historical contextualization of the changing terminology, ideas and methods of collaborative creativity; these provide a critical framework for this volume's engagement with contemporary performance practices. We seek to establish a historical and theoretical ground from which to examine the shifting and unstable nature of 'co-labouring' in the arts, and address questions in particular of the relationships between the methods of co-working of the Modernist avant-garde, as compared to those associated with the collective spirit of the 1960s and those of the contemporary era. This initial enquiry reveals themes of central importance to collaborative performance-making, illustrating the recurring centrality of the themes of individual and collective authorship, the place of political resistance, the impact of social developments (including technological change) on modes of working, and the construction of artistic identities.

## Historical perspectives

In terms of historical writing on collective creation in theatre, Syssoyeva observes that a broader framing of analysis has emerged in recent scholarship (Syssoyeva, 2013). She challenges what she identifies as an ongoing scholarly tendency to root collective creation in the leftist political rebellions of the 1960s, noting that contemporary discourse is still permeated by ideologically-informed readings which prioritize New Left ideas of consensual decision-making and leaderlessness over those that entertain a more richly textured set of practices in radical collective work (2013: 3). Syssoyeva offers a chronological reading of three phases in the evolution of the practice of Western collective creation. The first unfolds during the first half of the twentieth century and is characterized by the impact of 'often contradictory' aesthetic, social, and political influences. This phase encompasses Total Art and a modernist interest in popular theatre, but also involves divergent political aspirations (nationalism, communism and antifascism). A second phase spanning the 1950s to the 1980s encompasses the idealism and participatory cultures of the 1960s. The third phase is located in the early 1980s and continues into the twenty-first century and is marked by a veering away from ideological towards ethical imperatives. Syssoyeva (2013: 8) defines this period as a 'postutopic' time, marked by the search for 'ethical leadership' which foregrounds the performer as creator. This historicization of collective creation in theatre indicates the diversity of conditions and forms of collaboration, and provides a broader framework within which idealized constructs of collective work can be re-assessed with reference to specific socio-political contexts and a more varied set of creative practices.

In the first phase of collective creation, the call for interdisciplinary engagement in the arts was marked by the development of the idea of Total Art as a reaction against the authority of specialized arts forms which had reached a critical point at the end of the nineteenth century. Divisions within artistic productions reflected wider social and economic circumstances. Following the industrial revolution, the specialization of production aimed at increasing productivity by reducing its cost. While the English economist William Petty first observed the concept of the division of labour at the end of the eighteenth century,[1] it was subsequently developed by Marx (and later in Taylorism). As art historian David Roberts (2011) notes, a number of artists associated with the historical avant-garde challenged insular methods of artistic labour and embraced a decompartmentalizing vision of artistic work crossing music, theatre, dance practices and visual arts. From the legacy of Richard Wagner's seminal synthesis of art (his 'Gesamtkunstwerk') to Serge Diaghilev's collaborative enterprise with the Ballets Russes, or from Antonin Artaud's scenographic expansion of theatrical language in his 'Theatre of Alchemy' to the collective works of art of the Bauhaus, collaboration in the early twentieth century was adopted as a creative remedy for any narrowing over-specialization in the arts.

In his analysis of European Total Art, Roberts argues (2011: 2) that the Wagnerian vision is often understood as the union of the arts into one piece of artwork, and this vision is linked to the desire to rehabilitate and renew the public function of art. Modernism in Europe was fundamentally concerned with 'a social function that goes beyond the limits of autonomous art' (2011: 5). His insights on Total Art stand in contrast to the widely held assumption that the aesthetics of modernism are based on the separation and autonomy of the arts. For example, Clement Greenberg's application of his notion of 'pure art' (Burt 2006: 7) requires the elimination of the influence of any other art form, and 'thereby each art would be rendered "pure", and in its "purity" find the guarantee of its standards of quality as well as of its independence'. In contrast, Roberts demonstrates the existence of an intrinsic relationship between Total Art and the avant-garde movements of the early twentieth century. In the first Futurist Manifesto (1909) and in the work of the Surrealists at the end of the 1930s, Roberts sees this relationship as underpinned by the artistic desire to respond to the combined crisis of autonomous art and the instabilities then characterizing European politics (Roberts, 2011: 2).

While dance historian Lynn Garafola in her study of the Ballets Russes (Garafola, 1998: 45) recognizes the influence of Wagner's Gesamtkunstwerk on Diaghilev's ballets, she observes that the ballets rarely followed a collaborative process, but that 'far more than collaboration' the strength of the work resided in 'the community of values to which their contributing artists subscribed'. Garafola argues that the achievement of the company rested on a 'social imperative'; with the initial not-for-profit ethos of Diaghilev – combined with the value placed on the individual within a democratized structure – constituting the basis of the collective framework of the Ballets Russes. However, Garafola observes that Diaghilev's 'collaborative eden' did not last long. The socio-economic climate resulted in economic pressures distorting relations within the group, creating a different division of labour as the collective framework depicted earlier shifted into 'a contractual arrangement' (Garafola, 1998: 199).

A shared quest for spirituality, Roberts notes, provides another connection between the interdisciplinarity of Total Art and the collaborative ethos of the avant-garde. At the end of the nineteenth century, the radical reforms undertaken by theatre theorists and practitioners – from Adolphe Appia to Antonin Artaud – led to a regeneration of the sacred in performance through the reintegration of art, religion, and politics (Roberts, 2011: 165–68). Influenced by the spirituality of the Balinese theatre, Artaud's ambition to give back to the theatre its magical power is a clear example of the application of ideas of totality to theatre. Artaud argued that:

> to link the theatre to the expressive possibilities of forms, to everything in the domain of gestures, noises, colours, movements, etc., is to restore it to its original direction, to reinstate it in its religious and metaphysical aspect, is to reconcile it with the universe.
>
> (Artaud, 1958: 70)

The unification of art training at the Bauhaus into a collective work of art similarly embraced a search for spirituality in art. Walter Gropius described 'the idea of a universal unity in which all opposing forces exist in a state of absolute balance', adding that 'only work which is the product of inner compulsion can have spiritual meaning' (Gropius, in Harrison and Wood, 2011: 309).

Yet, Roberts highlights an 'undeniable *affinity*' (Roberts, 2011: 10) between the utopian dream of the total work of art and the social and ideological reforms proposed by the totalizing political movements which marked the whole period of modernism from the French Revolution to the Bolshevik and Fascist revolutions.[2] If the idea of interdisciplinarity and spirituality encompassed in the collaborative work of the early modernist avant-garde was based, Roberts notes (2011:6), on a refusal to compartmentalize artistic and intellectual labour, its alienation by totalitarianism 'reveals a perversion latent in the hubris of political and aesthetic modernism'.

A particularly negative idea of collaboration is associated with the 1940 Vichy Regime in France.[3] If, in the contemporary context, the term has lost its pejorative connotations, one might argue that its promise remains bound to what Florian Schneider (2006) refers to as the 'darker side of the multitude'. In the aftermath of the Second World War, cooperation became a persuasive political term to describe the solidarity necessary for global reconstruction. This is evident in the fostering of European economic cooperation,[4] and in post-war calls for 'multiethnic cooperation' in North America (Smith, 2004). On the other hand, the establishment of a post-war order led to new and deep divisions between countries in the age of Cold War; which along with the stirrings of decolonization contributed to the maintaining of a destabilized and fragmented international community.[5] A number of intellectuals in Europe engaged in a rethinking of the idea of community. For example, the French philosopher George Bataille argued against the religious and utilitarian conception of community used by totalitarian regimes, proposing an open concept of community as a 'community of those who have no community' (Bataille, 2001: xi). Bataille's controversial ideas became an influential source for the reframing of the notion of community. As Benjamin Noys observes, in the work of Jean-Luc Nancy community is understood as 'a fusion or communion' (Noys, 2000: 54) and as 'the heart of fraternity' (Noys, 2000: 56) in Maurice Blanchot's *The Unavowable Community* (1984). Equally, community is a critical topic of discussion in Jacques Derrida's *The Politics of Friendship* (1994). Such developments account for a shift in attitudes towards the idea of community after the Second World War, which was reflected in the experimental work of the collectives of the 1960s.

Charles Green (2001) has made a leading contribution to the study of collaboration in post-1960s artistic practice (although without specific reference to performance-making). In his analysis of a number of case studies, Green proposes that collaboration entails a deliberate choice by the artist away from 'individual identity to composite subjectivity', and that the 'proliferation of teamwork in post-1960s art challenged not only the terms by which artistic identity was conceived but also the "frame" – the discursive boundary between the "inside" and the "outside" of a work of art' (Green, 2001: x). Modes of collaboration located within the evolution of 1960s conceptualism came to be based on innovative models of authorship. However, the rise of postmodern theory, with its emphasis upon the limits of the 'author' might not, he notes, capture the subtleties of these shifts (2001: xi).

According to dance critic Sally Banes (1983) the modes and influence of the collectives of the 1960s have excited considerable interest. In her account of the work of the Judson Church Dance Theatre Group, Banes has argued that 'the great collective' discovered a democratizing practice based on cooperative methods (Banes, 1983: xi). Theatre director and performance studies theorist Richard Schechner similarly highlights what appeared to be the unlimited possibilities of emancipation and creativity of the era: 'there was such wild, fecund intercourse among theatre people, visual artists, musicians, dancers, social activists, theorists that we believed we could renew the world' (Schechner, 1981: 49). David Williams, in his study of the collectivist practices of Ariane Mnouchkine's Théâtre du Soleil, also speaks of a theatre caught up in critical reinventions of democracy, motivated by a desire for 'ethical change and the possibility of renewal through a processual fashioning of self-relation' (Williams, 1999: xix).

More recently, a re-emergence of interest in artistic collaborations has led to critical reassessments of the ways in which artists work together. In the field of theatre, a number of scholarly works have challenged idealized constructs of theatrical collaboration. In the specific context of devised performance, Deirdre Heddon and Jane Milling's analysis of the history of devised theatre (2005) links a range of international performance works from the 1950s to contemporary practices through the lens of collaborative creation. Alex Mermikides and Jackie Smart's examination of contemporary British devising companies' collective process (2010) highlights its lineage with avant-garde traditions. Other recent writings have focused on analyses of the working and the structures of collaborative theatre, including Tim Etchells' account of the devising process of his company Forced Entertainment (1999), Susan Melrose's ongoing inquiry into expertise and signature in performance-making (2005), and Duška Radosavljević's study of contemporary ensemble work (2013). These different approaches are indicative of an increasing concern around the status of co-working in the contemporary performing arts.

The emergence of a number of artist-driven performance networks and initiatives over the last decade has signalled a shift in the ways in which artists seem to articulate notions of embodiment, authorship and subjectivity. According to Katherine Hayles Hayles (1999), the development of digital technologies has raised questions around the construction of contemporary subjectivity. From a posthuman perspective, the entwinement of technology with the formation of the subject can be traced in the range of terms associated with collaborative works and the rhetoric of computer sciences. This is evident, for example, in the use of terms such as 'network' rather than 'group', or 'self-organised' rather than 'organisation'. We might speculate that digital technologies offer enhanced possibilities for remote collaboration across time and space and could lead to a redefinition of collective identities as networks of affinities which encompass separate identities, hybridity and expanded authorship. On the one hand, these tendencies point to the ways in which collaborative participants' bodies and actions might be understood as part of a dynamic and inter-relational system. Indeed, development of digital technologies might even allow collaborating artists to facilitate global change in a movement of networked resistance (Holmes, 2007). On the other hand, these findings might account for a tension between self and other or, in cultural theorist Brian Rotman's terms, a sense of 'besideness' in performance-making (Rotman, 2008). Indeed, this tension might be seen as symptomatic of the 'digitally hybridized' or 'nomadic' subjectivities as constructed in contemporary collaboration. The contemporary emphasis on difference over similitude takes us some distance away from the idea of the collective group work of the 1960s. In dance, as social theorist Rudi Laermans highlights, 'the once influential and romantic rhetoric of moving together freely has been replaced by the idea of "doing a project with others"' (Laermans, 2012, 94). Based more on shared interests than shared methodologies, the success of these artistic collaborations rests upon what Laermans terms 'the potentialities of cooperation itself' (Laermans, 2012, 94).

Recent cultural and socio-political shifts have led to a renewed questioning of the possibilities for politicized, experimental modes of collaboration which might be of relevance against a backdrop of economic globalization. Concerns have been expressed by art theorists in regard to the mimetic characteristics between the new dominant type of labour produced by the advanced capitalist society and artistic practices. The 'project-driven' nature of collaboration and the new status of the director/choreographer as facilitator rather than author represents a key characteristic of processes of performance work in the early twenty-first century. Concurrently, Gabriele Klein and Bojana Kunst (2012) observe the necessity for the contemporary artist to adopt a wide range of roles and skills including being a mobile entrepreneur, to participate in the presentation and dissemination of one's own production, to network, and to respond to the internationalization of work. This not only leaves the artist with limited scope for other types of activities, but as Kunst further stresses, may alienate the artist to 'the temporal totality of capitalism' (Klein and Kunst, 2012, 122).

Meanwhile, from a wider political perspective, Erin Manning and Brian Massumi have evaluated the changing conditions under which research and creative activities are pursued against the backdrop of 'the rise of an increasingly speculative, high-turnover, innovation-driven "knowledge economy"' (Manning and Massumi, 2014: 84). They observe that the new economy, described in terms of 'creative capital' and 'immaterial labour', offers challenges to the traditional division between theory ('pure research') and practice ('applied research'). Alongside this are a set of opportunities and threats to consider:

> What is new, in our context, is the extent to which policies intended to facilitate collaboration across the divides have been prioritized in government cultural and academic policy and in university structures. The way this has been done has created real opportunities – but also highly troubling alignments with the neoliberal economy.
>
> (Manning and Massumi, 2014, 84)

Collaboration can therefore be seen as Janus-faced. It is variously understood as a process which can enable artists to expand their fields of possibilities and resources, but carries with it the potential for uncontrolled compromises.

## Collaborative performance-making in the present

Collaborative modes of working in performance-making in the simplest of terms are process-specific, and might be aligned with performance works in dance and theatre that are described as 'experimental' or 'devised'. Crucially such ways of making performances tend to be characterized by a significant input on behalf of the performers to the creation of the performance material; in order to capture the ways of working at stake in such processes and on the basis of this focus on the processual, rather than product, and on shared creation, rather than single-authoring we propose in what follows to define such processes more specifically as 'inventive'. We would argue that the outcome of such inventive modes or ways of making is likely to retain the mark of collaborative process and shared authorship, bringing about different kinds of engagement for a spectator.

How might we theorize collaborative processes and shared invention? When Erin Manning in her publication *Relationscapes: Art, Movement, Philosophy* (2009) observes that '[t]echniques for invention cannot be captured, [as w]hen they are, they become redundant, [since] you cannot recompose with something that has already been spoken for', she goes on to note that inventive techniques 'must remain on the plane of composition' (Manning, 2009: 10). Inventive techniques themselves, then, are virtual, rather than reiterable as such, and what such techniques enable practitioners to invent similarly cannot be foreseen – or guaranteed. Inventive techniques are likely to be strongly informed by contingent factors – the immediate context or contexts of practice, the particular mix of expertise in the collaborative group, what is 'in the air', in the media, 'on the mind'. In these sorts of terms, Manning's work seems to suggest, such techniques must be invented anew, in each instance of collaborative process, by the practitioners involved, if their work, in turn, is to lay claim to innovation or originality.

Where is the 'plane', in the Deleuzian sense of the term,[6] of composition, and who has access to it? In Melrose's terms,[7] understandings of performance compositional methods is a key aspect of practitioner expertise; and while techniques of invention may very well be context and group-dependent, 'ways to make new work', in terms of performance composition, are likely to intervene in the times and sites of invention. The performance *set-up* (taken from the French *dispositif*) that might be understood as a 'higher', organizing plane of performance-making, is likely to intervene at key moments or stages in the making, to contain and indeed to control the times and places of invention.

Which practitioners have access to this particular set-up? We would argue that even in collaborative or collective processes, where shared performance authorship plays its role, access to that set-up or performance *dispositif* is unequally shared, and that an energetic investment in that mechanism, sufficient to bring new work into being, is similarly likely to be unequally shared. In terms of a theoretical account of collaborative practice, then, we might need to bring into play a range of theoretical writing, and a number of theoretical notions. One such is provided by the work of Jean-François Lyotard who in 'Painting as a Libidinal Set-up (Genre: Improvised Speech)', makes an important connection between 'process', in the making, and 'repetition'.[8] Interestingly Lyotard's work in the 1970s leads us to a focus on a system, set-up or *dispositif*, which involves repetition, in compositional terms, yet *through which energy is transformed and metamorphosed*, to produce something 'new'.

Recent debates by researchers at two Symposia on Collaboration at Middlesex University, London (held in 2012 and 2013),[9] established a sense of existing trends within the professional or expert performing arts context with regard to the use of 'collaboration' as a politicizing factor in defining performance work – even though it emerged, in the proceedings, that less democratic structures are actually at work in certain practitioners' processes. The perceived tendency to associate collaborative ways of working with collective authorship remains acute, and 'collective decision-making' seems to be constitutive of collaborative performance-making processes in their most radical application. Yet here again we find what Melrose has called a 'constitutive ambiguity' (Melrose, 2006) – a tension between the shared and the singular, each vital to collaborative or collective making. Political issues around 'freedom' and 'agency' with regard to the creative input of each collaborator plainly come into the equation here.

In order for this account or accounts of collaborative or collective practices to reach beyond particular instances of performance practice that look mainly at a finished product, seemingly 'brushing over' practitioner-centred issues at stake in the making processes themselves, several voices gathered in this volume present issues emerging from the practitioner-researcher's perspective. The first-hand engagement in the practice of performance-making of practitioners and practitioner-researchers allows us to begin to establish a theorization of collaborative practice from a practitioner's point of view. Of key interest to the 'workings' of collaborative or collective performance-making is the term 'collective or shared responsibility', taken from the Social Sciences. The work of social and political philosopher Marion Smiley is key here. Smiley points out that negative as well as positive associations are at stake in shared or collaborative undertakings: the notion of a collective or shared *responsibility* comes into play in all such set-ups. Issues such as 'fairness' and 'agency' (in the case here, in the making) remain problematic and ambiguous within debates in the social and political sciences that are concerned with group behaviour (Smiley, 2011: n.p.), and we would argue that issues of agency and fairness are no less important in collaborative performance-making. The euphoria of collective invention that 'works' can conceal resentment and feelings of non-inclusion or a loss of effective agency in some participants. Yet in research terms, it is difficult to identify and gather pertinent data relating to these sorts of experiences, precisely, perhaps, because outside of the collaborative set-up itself, researchers are likely to have to deal with the feelings but also the reticence of individual performance-makers or artists.

Smiley points out that the German sociologist and philosopher Max Weber (1864–1920), has claimed, however, that the idea of 'collective responsibility' is nonsensical, since 'genuine collective actions' cannot be 'isolated' (Smiley, 2011: n.p.). In collaborative performance-making, indeed, not least where compositional decision-making is concerned, it is unlikely that practitioners would want to entertain the notion of a 'group identity', such as we find in the social sciences, that might overtake notions of individual identity and agency. The notion of 'identical actions of many individuals', from Weber, below, might be a compositional choice, in set-ups specific to collaborative performance-making, rather than the basis for a theorization of performance-making practices. In her discussion of Max Weber's argument, Smiley further explains that according to this view:

> collective responsibility makes no sense both because we cannot isolate genuinely collective actions, as distinct from identical actions of many persons, and because groups, unlike the individuals who belong to them, cannot think as groups or formulate intentions of the kind normally thought to be necessary to actions.
>
> (Smiley, 2011: n.p.)

What comes into focus then in the present context is 'intentionality', in any given performance-making action, and more specifically 'collective intention', which in the case of collaborative performance-making will have a certain role to play, at least in the creation of an artistic agenda, ethos and vision for a given performance work. Once again, however, the notion of 'collective intention' reveals a degree of ambiguity: it is unlikely that 'collective intention' can be arrived at, and clearly articulated, without the intervention of the stronger or more experienced member or members of the group. If any action begins with intention – which is how 'action' and 'behaviour' are differentiated – the actions of the performance-making group are likely, at any moment, to overrule the intentions of certain members of that same group. Nonetheless, 'group intentions' are a necessary defining element of collective responsibility, as a different school of thought within the social sciences debate asserts. Here, Smiley makes a distinction between 'collective action' and 'collective behaviour'. Smiley refers to J. Angelo Corlett's definition as exemplary in this debate:

> [a] collective (intentional) action is an action the subject of which is a collective intentional agent. A collective *behavior* is a doing or behavior that is the result of a collective, though not the result of its intentions. A *collective action* is caused by the beliefs and desires (wants) of the collective itself, whether or not such beliefs and desires can be accounted for or explained in individualistic terms.
>
> (Corlett, 2001 cited in Smiley, 2011: n.p.)

To interrogate collaborative or collective performance-making from what is in fact a single example from the social sciences is useful precisely because some of the key terms from collaborative performance-making can be found in the contexts of the social sciences; yet it is clear that some of the ways these terms are used in those contexts fail to achieve empirical fit with understandings in collaborative performance-making. 'Collective' has often been used as an equivalent to the term 'collaborative', and from this perspective the artistic implication of 'collective action' is the existence of a collective intentional agent. However it is difficult to define group intentions, as Smiley proceeds to argue, because 'intentions are mental states and hence not the kinds of things that are normally thought to be shareable' (Smiley, 2011: n.p.). A question arises here, specifically with regard to collaborative performance-making: in what ways might an engagement with collective intentions be at stake, and how, in research terms and in the discourses specific to performance research, might these be identified, tested and verified?

Given the present concern with collaborative performance-making that seeks to work inventively (see Manning above), collective intention might be understood to figure, on a certain plane, in many performance set-ups; that intention can be further described as 'meta-structural', referring to choices relating to the overall organization of individuals into what one may or may not call a 'group', as well as a structuring of a creative mechanism. Access to the 'meta-structural' plane supposes a considerable expertise and an explicit acknowledgement of systems and possible options available to the making, which suggests, once again, the need to bring a clear differentiation between collaborators into play. Further aspects that we might find in operation at this plane of 'meta-practice' are a commitment to shared sensibilities and ways of seeing; yet many practitioners, in our experience, prefer not to entertain notions of meta-practice. Nonetheless, few would refuse to acknowledge the importance of the notion, within the context of collaborative performance-making, of *ways of relating* to the 'other'. Political philosopher Larry May usefully defines collective actions *relationally*, based on situations in which individuals are enabled 'to act in ways that they could not manage on their own'; some individuals, indeed, are likely to benefit from the opportunity to represent their own actions as the actions of a given group (May in Smiley, 2011: n.p.).

A further useful parallel might be drawn from the social sciences to collaborative processes of performance-making: the set-up can support an interest in maintaining the individual identities of each collaborator, while also providing opportunities for the development of those practitioner identities. In the specific context of cross-disciplinary collaborations, which might bring together artists, musicians and performers, it is the action of working with other expert practitioners from their different disciplines that may well allow each to better understand her or his own disciplinary identity. While each is likely to operate according to her or his own expert judgment (Melrose, 2009), taking the interests of the 'whole' into account, and seeking to progress it, tends to mean that the competence of the individual practitioner is both tempered and extended. In such cross-disciplinary performance practices and experiments it is the metaphorical 'meeting' of different discipline-specific actions that creates 'the work'. What are apparently individual actions, in this context, are in the event modulated, modified, relationally-determined and other. Each collaborator's work advances according to its own logic, yet in response to the evolvement of the others' input, and hence expansively, 'in ways that they could not manage on their own' (May in Smiley, 2011).

How might we understand the 'other' who is collaborator in the same event, yet also an 'other' in terms of a disciplinary expertise? The work of philosopher Martin Heidegger (1889–1976) is of considerable interest here, and we note in particular his discussion of the concept of the 'other' in his work *Sein und Zeit* (translated as *Being and Time*):

> By 'Others' we do not mean everyone else but me—those over against whom the 'I' stands out. They are rather those from whom, for the most part, one does not distinguish oneself—those among whom one is too. [...] By reason of this *with-like* Being-in-the-world, the world is always the one that I share with Others. The world of Dasein is a *with-world* [*Mitwelt*]. Being-in is *Being-with* [*Mitsein*] Others. Their Being-in-themselves within-the-world is Dasein-with [*Mitdasein*].
>
> (Heidegger, 1962: 154–55)

According to Davis and Steinbock (2011), philosopher Max Scheler (1847–1928) similarly does not conceive of the 'other' as problematic in any sense. Any experience, in Scheler's terms, involves what he calls a *Miteinander-Erleben* – an 'experiencing with another' – rather than a distance between individuals that must be confronted and crossed, and on this basis he identifies different types of 'co-feeling' (Davis and Steinbock, 2011: n.p.). The practice of 'co-laborating' in cross-disciplinary collaborative performance-making might, in these sorts of terms, be usefully defined as involving a disciplinary 'co-feeling' of the 'other' in the Heideggerian sense. Each is engaged in what is specific to her or his disciplinary experience and expectations, yet, equally works inventively in collaboration according to a collective intention at the level of the set-up. This sensibility towards the 'other', as noted above, allows for developments of practice that would not otherwise have occurred – a vital characteristic of inventive practice.

An engagement with the 'other' in collaborative performance-making enables us to examine issues of collective and individual responsibility. However, the feeling of 'otherness' resulting from such processes is far from guaranteed to be universally understood as a constructive element in a given collaborative practice. What constitutes 'failure' or 'success' in performance is obviously a slippery question. 'Failure is the hallmark of performance', observe Róisín O'Gorman and Margaret Werry (2012: 2) in an insightful assessment of the subject which draws attention to a multiplicity of ways in which 'failing' can be seen as integral to creating. They note, for example, that performance practitioners are continually rehearsing the *performance of failure* through creative processes of experimentation, improvisation and repetition in order for new work to emerge. As a site of resistance, 'failure rehearsals' can be seen to offer the potential to critically rebalance a dominant rhetoric of success and outcomes. As O'Gorman and Werry remind us, failure is also the 'innate ontological condition: its defining liveness and ephemerality marks performance's ultimate failure to perpetuate itself. It becomes itself (to bowdlerize Peggy Phelan) through failing' (Gorman and Werry, 2012: 2).

Social theorists have drawn attention to the ways in which attempts to manage 'failure' became characteristic of postmodernity. The German sociologist Ulrich Beck (1992) in his conception of the 'risk society', for example, suggests that the creation of new ecological and economic risks – inherent to the development of modernity – resulted in political transformations which aimed to come to terms with a new age of uncertainty and anxiety. In place of determining the distribution of goods, the identification, measurement and avoidance of risk assumes ever-increasing importance. Within this framework, the position of the expert gains significance, yet societal fear of systemic failure concurrently erodes the social authority of these same experts. Beck's position suggests that failure is not only a logical consequence of modernity and thus integral to late capitalism, but that failure remains a negative force whose social meanings generate conflict.

We might want to ask whether the social authority of expert judgment is eroded in Beck's risk society in the face of failure, with implications for the role of the expert performance-maker identified by Melrose (above). Can alternative understandings of the relationship between expert judgment and the significance of risk be advanced from the perspective of the performance practitioner? Failure might be the 'hallmark of performance' with a willingness to take risks integral to inventive practice. Even if the basis for the reaching of expert judgments between performance practitioners, as Melrose (2009) observes, remains infrequently articulated, we might assume that shared understandings of the potential gains of embracing uncertainty or otherness will be of significance for collaborative participants. Uncertainty in 'risk society' may lead to loss, but it is something, we would argue, that runs with the grain of professional performance mastery, with broader implications as to how expert compromise or agreement may or may not be reached without loss of status.

Collaborative ways of working might then be usefully understood as approaches to performance-making that embrace the unknowable at its outset, in that they entail encounters with any given 'others', which are inherently productive in creative terms. Melrose (2007) identifies this relative unknowing as *disciplined* in the sense that one aspect of practitioner expertise comprises practitioners continually surprising themselves in the making of their work. An active embracing of the unknown entails an inherent premise of the accidental, the contingent and chance, in art-making at least. James Austin, in the publication *Chase, Chance and Creativity: The Lucky Art of Novelty*, refers to the etymology of 'chance', which relates to the Latin word 'cadere', to fall, suggesting that 'it is in the nature of things to fall, settle out, or happen by themselves.' He makes the following observation:

> Chance is unintentional, it is capricious, but we needn't conclude that chance is immune from human interventions. However, one must be careful not to read any unconsciously purposeful intent into 'interventions.' All such interactions [...] are to be viewed as accidental, unwilled, inadvertent and unforeseeable. Indeed, chance plays several distinct roles when humans interact with one another and with their environment.
>
> (Austin, 2003: 70)

In performance-specific terms, when one proceeds to pursue something, over time, in a specific 'set-up', the likelihood grows that unexpected occurrences will happen, that are judged to be appropriate or inappropriate to the task in hand, and recognized as such. Austin suggests that qualities that are at stake in such processes are 'persistent curiosity about many things coupled with an energetic willingness to experiment and explore' (Austin, 2003: 75). This way of seeing recalls Gregory Ulmer's theoretician as tourist, who explores the unknown and the contingent.[10] Austin further refers to a 'kinetic' principle, which suggests that '[w]hen someone, *anyone*, does swing into motion and keeps on going, he or she will increase the number of collisions between events' (Austin, 2003: 72).

The centrality of the consequences of such collisions is illustrated by a number of contributors to this collection, revealing the ways collaborative performance-making processes are driven by the exercise of opinion of a particular group of practitioners, working towards something they cannot foresee before its occurrence, while however fostering a certain qualitative 'sense' of *something new*, which, despite the play of accident, otherness and contingency, is guided and controlled by judgment and decision-making.

## The scope of this publication

Part One, entitled *Premises*, is concerned with examining the ways in which collaborative practice in contemporary performance-making might be modelled in the context of post-industrial capitalism and globalization. The chapters in this part set up a contextualization of the notion of collaboration within the performing arts while considering wider political, economic and social contexts. Critically reviewing definitions of the term, this group of essays investigates the relationships between earlier models of collaboration with current creative strategies deployed by contemporary collaborative artists. Part One also focuses upon the impact of collaboration on contemporary subjectivities by relating ideas of politics and philosophy to the process of performance-making. Taken together, the chapters in this part establish a theoretical framework within which to consider how collaborative practices might be considered to be 'radical', 'democratic' and 'creative'.

In the first chapter, entitled 'Contemporary Collaborations and Cautionary Tales', Simon Murray sets out by critically reflecting upon the aspirations, languages and vocabularies of collaboration in view of its proliferation over the past decade. He does so in dealing with the specific area of the performing arts, and in adopting a perspective that encompasses trends in the wider economic landscape and its current managerial practices, thus examining questions around practices of partnership and collective labour. Murray sets out by closely examining the etymology and usage of the term 'collaboration', and establishes a focus on the arts as a site of cultural production within the context of his discussion of collaboration in the cultural industries. He proceeds to review collaborative practices within the areas of devised, immersive and site-specific performance-making, and discusses how more contemporary utilitarian and pragmatic conceptions of collaboration may co-exist with or still allow space for more utopian spaces within which 'generative, generous and progressive' qualities can flourish.

From a historical perspective, Alexandra Kolb investigates the tension in the ways that models of collaboration have 'mirrored certain forms of social and political organization', but have also been propelled by optimistic visions of the future. Her chapter, 'Collaboration, Democracy and the Total Artwork', constitutes in part an appraisal of the relevance of composer Richard Wagner's conception of the 'Gesamtkunstwerk' or 'total art work' to contemporary collaborative choreographic practices. In specifically highlighting the particularities of the role of art within nineteenth-century German society, Kolb applies the interrelation between politics and arts to later developments in performance practice, with reference to the collaboration between John Cage and Merce Cunningham, as well as the works of Yvonne Rainer and Pina Bausch, amongst other significant practitioners. In this respect she critically investigates issues around the application of varying democratic ideologies in collaborative choreography-making.

In the next chapter, Martina Ruhsam considers the influence and relevance of models of co-working established in the 1960s and early 1970s, but argues that a shift has taken place away from shared utopian ideals towards processes that negotiate collectivity in terms of the heterogeneity of the participating artists. Ruhsam provides a historical appraisal of the ethico-political aspect of working collaboratively, looking at changes in artistic practice from the Second World War onwards, with a particular emphasis on the conception of 'being-with' as set out by Nancy (2000). Specifically discussing the characteristics of the neoliberal economic environment, she investigates the challenges posed to contemporary conceptions of collaboration, as well as the function of notions of complicity, cooperation and the collective.

Delving into the nature of the collaborative author, Laura Cull Ó Maoilearca's chapter, 'Since each of us was several: collaboration in the context of the differential self', redefines collaborations as 'a continuum of activities by individual authors, as well as groups'. She examines the relationship between 'collaborative and individualist tendencies' that emerge from performance practice. Drawing on the work of the North American performance company Goat Island and the philosophy of Deleuze and Guattari, Cull Ó Maoilearca argues that the self is 'preceded and ceaselessly (re)constituted by its relations'. Connecting philosophical thinking and performance processes, she illustrates that both disciplines can be conceived 'as productions of subjectivities, plural', and seeks to 'extend the concept of collaboration to include individual practice and [...] the ways we work with nonhuman others'.

In the last chapter of Part One, 'Collaboration as a Mode of Labour', Noyale Colin discusses the shifting context of artistic labour within the contemporary digital economy and its potential for 'remote collaboration' and 'expanded authorship'. Reflecting on theoretical notions of co-labour, Colin problematizes the emancipatory potential credited to contemporary labour – and its association with the notion of the immaterial – by theorists including the Italian autonomists. She demonstrates the ways in which recent artistic initiatives, including in the field of European choreographic practices, promote differing structures of collaborative practices which centre on the development of co-working conditions that aim at enabling individualized qualitative transformations. Colin argues that it is the capacity of contemporary collaborative processes to enable such transformations which creates an expansion of performance practice.

Part Two, entitled *Workings*, presents a series of writings that deal with ways of practising and conceiving collaborative performance-making. The chapters in this section examine a series of conceptual approaches to collaboration, covering a range of works including case studies drawn from professional collaborative practice and collaborative research experiments. The contributions of this section raise key questions concerning the ethical workings and processes of collaborative performance-making, in that the case studies reveal how cultural boundaries and power relations might be navigated in collaborative contexts.

Erin Manning's opening to this section offers a distinct way of writing about collaboration. Her manifesto 'Ten Propositions for Research Creation' adopts a creative and conceptual approach to address issues at stake in collective experimentation. Bringing together philosophical and artistic practices, Manning proposes a way of thinking about collaborative processes that moves beyond what is still – in the university at least – the dominant division between theory and practice. Drawing on a range of innovative techniques of relation that she has been involved in developing and experimenting with as part of a decade-long series of international events curated under the umbrella of Manning and Massumi's 'SenseLab', Manning's propositions suggest a way to celebrate the internal connections between art and philosophy. She offers us a philosophical score exploring the conditions necessary for collective events to flourish, including an emphasis on processes of 'emergent relations' and 'metamodelling' over 'pre-existing modes of existence'. Manning thus demonstrates the general importance of resisting any pre-modelled form of collaboration.

The contribution of Ewan Forster and Christopher Heighes, entitled 'Double Vision in Performance and Architecture', constitutes an adaptation of a performance score in which the site-specific artists reflect on their experience of collaborating over the past twenty years. In combining graphic symbols, text and images, Forster and Heighes present a visual chapter in which they thematize issues of working in partnership since their training at Dartington College in the 1980s. A second part of their contribution is set in the form of a comic strip, which presents a narrative of an imaginary journey of the artists by boat towards Cologne – a place they never seem to reach, but on the journey towards which they make new discoveries – illustrating how Forster and Heighes relate to each other in processes of negotiation, when constantly asking what to do next.

Tim Jeeves considers collaboration in relation to the gift economy as a 'practice of authorship'. He offers an account of his experimental approach as practised in his performance series *The Horse's Teeth*. Having developed a series of six works, Jeeves then gifted their authorship to six other artists in a deliberate distortion of the prioritized status of the individual artist/author or, for that matter, the collective in contemporary art production. Jeeves illustrates the ways in which contemporary performers are searching for alternative models of (collaborative) authorship, which challenge what he defines as the reductive 'modes of possession' that arise in the formation of discrete identity.

Kris Salata's chapter proposes a perspective on collaboration as 'meeting through work'. In this rigorous analysis of Jerzy Growtoski's collaborative processes, Salata offers a genealogy of the Polish theatre director's approach to the notion of encounter in theatre. After introducing the successive phases of Grotowski's artistic research, Salata proceeds by outlining the different natures of the director's collaborations including critical dialogues, self-discovery, collective creations, and intercultural exchanges. And yet, 'on behalf of Grotowski' Salata suggests that collaboration can be understood as a unique 'meeting between two individuals, even in a group.'

The politics of difference in collaborative work is a theme which informs many of the contributions to this volume, but is explicitly addressed by Carol Brown and Moana Nepia, who reflect on their exploration of cultural differences in duet practices. Brown and Nepia have placed the potentiality inherent in the uncertainty of the duet as central to their collaboration, recognizing an affinity between the Māori concept of *Te Kore* and the energy of two performers off-balance. They write of being suspended with doubt in the act of dancing, as they seek reciprocity as creative performers whose work is inspired by their differing ancestral histories and experiences of different landscapes.

The opportunity for 'alliances' across boundaries is also addressed by Caroline Bowditch, David Bower and Pedro de Senna's trialogue on issues of collaboration between disabled and non-disabled artists, including the politics of visibility, aesthetics and leadership. As the conversation unfolds, it becomes apparent that co-working in the context of the disability arts movement remains a field layered with both opportunity and tension.

Part Three, entitled *Failures,* focuses on aspects of failure – or compromise – in collaborative performance-making. It thematizes joyousness versus misery and pain in the experience of the performance-makers, things that go wrong, productive materials that come out of processes where misapprehensions, misunderstandings and accidents are at stake. It further deals with notions of recurring tensions between the individual voice within a collective, as well as processes that never lead to their intended outcome.

Susan Melrose, in 'Positive Negatives – or the subtle arts of compromise', discusses the role of failure and loss in collaborative practice, which she conceives of as being tied to professional risk on behalf of the expert practitioners involved. She focuses on the role of compromise that is at stake amongst expert performance practitioners and in particular addresses the establishing of signature practices in which the figure of the director takes the lead in terms of decision-making in working with a collective. Melrose examines the development of expertise in collaborative practice, proposing to understand 'expert collaboration' as tied to 'ways of coping'. Discussing the work of the Théâtre du Soleil and Ariane Mnouchkine, Melrose argues that a 'fracturing of the self' is constitutive of (expert) identity in the collaborative practitioner.

Emilyn Claid's chapter 'Messy Bits' presumes that collaboratively devised performance inevitably entails failure in its process. Written from a practitioner perspective, she reflects on her experience of being co-director of the performance *Grace & Glitter* by Extemporary Dance Theatre (1987). Claid presents a close analysis of a section of the performance that had been cut after the opening night, and investigates how failure might be conceived as resistant to contemporary performance culture functioning within neo-liberalist structures. In particular, Claid engages with feminist and racial issues, in contextualizing her discussion of Extemporary with experiences drawn from her participation in a 2014 artist symposium in London.

Issues around practitioner identity in performance practice are thematized by Stefanie Sachsenmaier who focuses on the collaborative project entitled Artscross, which saw choreographers from the cities of Beijing, London and Taipei create work inspired by the theme *Leaving Home, Being Elsewhere* with dancers from each place in open rehearsals attended by academics. In a quest to challenge ways of thinking in terms of an East/West binary that the project set up, she addresses how the collaborative encounters can be understood as productive in the sense of being transformative to each individual engaged, and also formative in terms of the works that have arisen as part of this process. Sachsenmaier suggests that the concept of what 'dance' or what a 'dancer' is has been renegotiated in this 'zone of encounter', which she understands as a zone of contestation and re-negotiation.

The purpose of this publication has been to draw together a variety of voices from a range of perspectives that might give insights into the unstable and precarious nature of collaborative ways of working within the performing arts. Yet it needs to be stressed that at the basis of this project has been a bias towards a preoccupation with practitioner-centred issues within a larger overall research quest as to how performance practice might be articulated. The majority of the contributions included here hence explicitly deal with questions emerging *from* practice, rather than *about* practice (as for instance from the critic's perspective), which is mirrored in this volume by the representation of perspectives established by what might be called 'practitioner researchers'. The actual involvement of the different authors in the various practices discussed here varies, from performance-makers offering first-person accounts to researchers whose sensibilities and foci are on the processes of performance-making, rather than exclusively on the finished products. The publication thus engages directly with the wider established 'practice-as-research' research culture.

## Notes

1. Petty demonstrates the usefulness of dividing work tasks in his practical study of Dutch Shipyards (Petty, 1690).
2. As Roberts observes, after the 1848–49 revolutions, the legacy of the 1789 revolution fractured into 'increasingly hostile camps of socialism and nationalism attaining their extreme expression in the rival totalitarian movements that emerged from World War I' (Roberts, 2011: 5).
3. Philippe Pétain in a radio speech called upon the French population to collaborate with the German occupiers.
4. See the emphasis on the term solidarity in the full text of the Schuman Declaration delivered on 9th May 1950, available at: http://europa.eu/about-eu/basic-information/symbols/europe-day/schuman-declaration/index_en.htm, [accessed August 2014].
5. For a discussion of European post-war distributions of power, see *The Oxford Handbook of Postwar European History* (Stone, 2012).
6. See Deleuze and Guattari (1997).
7. See indicatively Melrose (2009b).
8. For a discussion of Lyotard's concept of the *dispositif* in a similar context enquiring into the processual in performance-making, see for instance Sachsenmaier (2013).
9. Both symposia were co-convened by Noyale Colin and Stefanie Sachsenmaier: Symposium on Collaboration I with a specific focus on the notions of

'memory', 'place' and 'time' (Middlesex University, London, 2012) and Symposium on Collaboration II on the politics of collaboration in performance-making (Middlesex University, London 2013). For documentation see: http://mdxoncollaboration.blogspot.co.uk/ (Accessed 2013).
10. See Ulmer (1994).

## Bibliography


Austin, J. H. (2003) *Chase, Chance, and Creativity: The Lucky Art of Novelty.* (Cambridge, Massachusetts and London: The Massachusetts Institute of Technology Press).

Banes, S. (1983) *Democracy's Body: Judson Dance Theater, 1962–1964.* (Ann Arbor Michigan: University of Michigan Research Press).

Bataille, G. (2004), *The Unfinished System on Nonknowledge,* in Kendall, S. (ed). (Minneapolis: University of Minnesota Press).

Beck, U. (1992) *Risk Society: Towards a New Modernity.* Translated by M. Ritter. (London: Sage).

Burt R. (2006) *Judson Dance Theater: Performative Traces.* (Abingdon and New York: Routledge).

Cvejić, B. (2005) *Collectivity? You mean Collaboration?,* URL: http://eipcp.net/transversal/1204/cvejic/en [Accessed December 2014]

Davis, Z. and Steinbock, A. (2011) 'Max Scheler' in E. Zalta (ed.) *The Stanford Encyclopedia of Philosophy,* URL: http://plato.stanford.edu/archives/win2011/entries/scheler/ [Accessed December 2014]

Deleuze, G. and Guattari, F. (1987) *A Thousand Plateaus.* Translated by Brian Massumi. (Minneapolis: University of Minnesota Press).

Filewod, A. (2008) 'Collective Creation: Process, Politics and Poetics', in Barton, B. (ed.) *Collective Creation, Collaboration and Devising.* (Toronto: Playwrights Canada Press).

Garafola, L. (1998) *Diaghilev's Ballets Russes.* (New York: Da Capro Press).

Green, C. (2001) *The Third Hand: Collaboration in Art from Conceptualism to Postmodernism.* (Sydney: University of New South Wales Press).

Gropius, W. (2011) 'The Theory and Organization of the Bauhaus', in Harrison, C. and Wood, P. *Art in Theory 1900–2000: An Anthology of Changing Ideas.* (Oxford: Blackwell Publishing).

Hayles, K. (1999) *How We Became Posthuman: Virtual bodies in cybernetics, literature and informatics.* (Chicago: University of Chicago Press).

Heidegger, M. (1962) *Being and Time.* Translated by J. Macquarrie and E. Robinson. 1st edn. Published in 1927 (Oxford: Blackwell Publishing).

Holmes, B. (2007) 'The revenge of the concept: Artistic exchanges, networked resistance', in Bradley, W. & Esche, C. (eds) *Art and Social Change.* (London: Tate Publishing & Afterall), 350–68.

Klein, G. and Kunst, B. (2012) 'Introduction: Labour and Performance', *Performance Research: A Journal of the Performing Arts,* 17:6, 1–3.

Kunst, B. (2012) 'Art and Labour: On consumption, laziness and less work', *Performance Research: A Journal of the Performing Arts,* 17:6, 116–25.

Laermans, R. (2012) '"Being in common": Theorizing artistic collaboration', *Performance Research: A Journal of the Performing Arts,* 17:6, 94–102.

Manning, E. (2009) *Relationscapes: Movement, Art, Philosophy.* (Cambridge Massachusetts and London: The Massachusetts Institute of Technology Press).

———. and Massumi, B. (2014) *Thought in the Act: Passages in the Ecology of Experience* (Minneapolis: University of Minnesota Press).

Melrose, S. (2005) '"Out of Words"'. Presented as a keynote address at the Centre for the History and Analysis of Recorded Music (CHARM) Symposium.

———. (2006) '"Constitutive Ambiguities": Writing Professional or Expert Performance Practices, and the Théâtre du Soleil' in Kelleher, J. and Ridout, N. (eds), *Contemporary Theatre in Europe: A Critical Companion.* (London and New York: Routledge), pp. 120–35.

———. (2009a) 'Signs of Life, Signs of the Times: and if all artists are semioticians?', ADSA Conference Keynote, *Boom or Bust: Economies of Production and Exchange in Theatre, Performance and Culture,* Edith Cowan University, Curtin University and Murdoch University, Western Australia, Australia, URL: https://eprints.mdx.ac.uk/3068/1/presentationADSA2009.pdf [Accessed December 2014]

———. (2009b) 'Expert-intuitive processing and the logics of production: struggles in (the wording of) creative decision-making in dance', in Butterworth, J. and Wildschut, L. (eds) *Contemporary Choreography: A Critical Reader.* (London and New York: Routledge), pp. 23–37.

Nancy, J. (2000) *Being Singular Plural.* (California: Stanford University Press).

Noys, B. (2000), *George Bataille: A Critical Introduction.* (London: Pluto Press).

O'Gorman, R. and Werry, M. (2012) 'On Failure (On Pedagogy): Editorial Introduction', *Performance Research: A Journal of the Performing Arts,* 17:1, 1–8.

Petty, W. (1690), *Political Arithmetick,* URL: http://www.marxists.org/reference/subject/economics/petty/index.htm [Accessed November 2014].

Roberts, D. (2011), *The Total Work of Art in European Modernism.* (Ithaca: Cornwell University Press).

Rotman, B. (2008) *Becoming Beside Ourselves: The Alphabet, Ghosts, and Distributed Human Being.* (Durham and London: Duke University Press).

Sachsenmaier, S. (2013) 'Beyond Allan Kaprow: An Interview with Rosemary Butcher', *Journal of Dance & Somatic Practices,* 4: 2, 267–81.

Smiley, M. (2011) 'Collective Responsibility', *The Stanford Encyclopedia of Philosophy, Fall 2011 Edition,* URL: http://plato.stanford.edu/entries/collective-responsibility [accessed December 2014].

Schechner, R. (1981) 'Fall of the American Avant-Garde', *Performing Art Journal* 5: 2, 48–63.

Schneider, F. (2006) 'The Darker Side of the Multitude', Theory Kit, URL: http://kit.kein.org/node/1 [Accessed January 2015].

Smith, E. (2004) *Visions of Belonging: Family Stories, Popular Culture and Postwar Democracy.* (New York: Columbia University Press).

Stone, D. (ed.), (2012) *The Oxford Handbook of Postwar European History.* (Oxford: Oxford University Press).

Syssoyeva, K. and Proudfit, S. (eds), (2013), *A History of Collective Creation.* (New York: Palgrave Macmillan).

Ulmer, G. (1994) *Heuretics: The Logic of Invention.* (Baltimore: Johns Hopkins University Press).

Williams, D. (1999), 'Introduction: A grain of sand in the works: continuity and change at the Théâtre du Soleil' in Williams, D. (ed.) *Collaborative Theatre: The Théâtre du Soleil Sourcebook* (London and New York: Routledge).

# Part I

# Premises – Modelling Collaborative Performance-Making

# 1

# Contemporary Collaborations and Cautionary Tales

*Simon Murray*

> ***collaboration ... association ... ensemble ... contamination ... cooperation ...complicité ... teamwork ... partnership ... corruption ... relationship ... alliance ... working together ... infection ... negotiation ... common ... commons ... betrayal ... quisling ... union ... commonwealth ... commonweal ... contagion ... mutuality ... comradeship***

This chapter draws upon a keynote presentation given at the second Symposium on Collaboration at Middlesex University in May 2013. What propelled the direction of this paper, and as I began to research its contents, was a growing and rather uneasy sense that the passionate and poetic panegyric I imagined offering in praise of collaboration – based on thirty years engagement with devised theatre practices – was not good enough. Collaboration both as principle and practice became more complex, nuanced and (sometimes) murky the more I read around the subject. Consequently, as I constructed the paper, my intention – rather than complacently (re)state the obvious attractions of collaboration – became instead, and remains now, an opportunity to reflect critically and quizzically on the various practices of collaboration within and beyond the fields of cultural production and in theatre, dance, and performance in particular.

As rhetoric, aspiration, organizing strategy, political structure and relational principle collaboration has become ubiquitous over the last decade. Of what does this proliferation speak and what wider story does it tell? I pose these questions since I believe that even tentative responses suggest that as artists, practitioners, academics and makers we would do well to heed – and understand – the varying motives at work when collaboration is proposed or claimed. To shed light on the disparate ways that collaboration is invoked within the cultural industries I initially consider the various (and often contradictory) meanings ascribed to the term and then reflect briefly on how collaboration – sometimes blandly called 'team work' – is increasingly proposed as a managerial strategy across all forms of material and immaterial production. Recognizing who argues for collaboration, how it might be positioned within the wider context of neo-liberal[1] socio-economic regimes – and in whose interests – should make us pause for a moment of productive and critical reflection before we embark on projects propelled, funded and/or sanctified in the name of collaboration. The chapter concludes by glancing at what I believe are some inspirational and generative models of collaborative practice in the arts, whilst also considering those qualities in collaboration that we would most like to propose and defend. I finish with a poem entitled 'We'.

As I think through the articulation of any argument which largely employs the lens of art as cultural production I regularly ask myself how the novelist and cultural theorist Raymond Williams (1921–88) might have written about the issue, in this case collaboration. At the end of his lecture 'Drama in a Dramatised Society' Williams says:

> I learned something from analysing drama which seemed to me to be effective not only as a way of seeing certain aspects of society, but as a way of getting through to some of the fundamental conventions which we group as society itself. These in their turn made some of the problems of drama quite newly active.
>
> (Williams in O'Connor, 1989: 11)

So, following Williams, this chapter considers how collaboration in the arts is currently being expressed and how this articulation connects with a range of managerial practices in the wider economy. Alongside the lens Williams might employ on this subject I shall repetitively summon up, as kind of choric mantra, a question my friend and ex-Dartington colleague, John Hall (currently Professor of Performance Writing at the University of Falmouth) would often insert into dialogue and conversations, both academic and more socially informal. 'But, who are the "we" in all this?' John would regularly interject, thereby prompting – indeed, demanding – a pause for (self-)critical reflection on the often lazy assumptions lying behind the claim of the plural 'we', and of whom the 'we' actually spoke.

## Collaboration: etymology and usage

At its most obvious and fundamental, 'collaboration' means working with one or more people to undertake a task and to achieve shared goals. It also, as the online *Free Dictionary* reminds me, implies 'to cooperate treasonably, as with an enemy occupation force in one's country' (http://www.thefreedictionary.com/collaboration). I return to this more troubling usage below. The first and most regular convention is perhaps equally unsettling, although probably less treasonable. Here, there is hardly any human endeavor which cannot be considered collaborative. I collaborate regularly, but briefly, with the supermarket checkout operator as I present and then pay for the goods in my shopping trolley. Whatever I may privately feel about the politics of food production or packaging, and most retailers' role within this ethical minefield, I 'collaborate' with the lowly paid employee at the checkout over a 'contract' implicitly agreed by my presence in the store. I place my groceries in a trolley and then pay a supermarket for the pleasure of removing them from the building to my home. I collaborate, more or less willingly, with the checkout operative in this transaction. Perhaps, in this example the two usages of collaboration identified above begin to bleed uneasily into each other.

Moving from the supermarket into the theatre it also becomes blindingly obvious that all performance-making is hard-wired to be collaborative. It cannot help but be collaborative if, at its most basic, we understand collaboration to mean a process whereby two or more people come together to make and show something. And, of course, film-making is even more obviously a collaborative process as the lengthy list of credits illustrate at the close of any feature film or documentary. Making theatre necessitates collaboration between director, actors, writer, scenographer, technical workers, administrators, choreographers, musicians and often others outwith the creative process itself. This, of course, speaks nothing of the act of collaboration that is entailed in the reception and reading of any work. I will return to this later.

Although within the arts, and in particular political contexts, many of us will invest an ethical and political aspiration into our collaborations, at root collaboration is a relatively neutral term. In itself it reveals very little about process, about purpose and objective, and particularly about the motives which have propelled the collaboration to be established and pursued in the first place. But, of course, if theatre is indeed hard-wired to be collaborative that tells us next to nothing about the experience of that collaboration. It discloses nothing of power relations, about the nature or the purpose of the exchange between participants and other art forms or disciplines; it says nothing about whether such a process was pleasurably productive, or toxically draining, creatively and innovatively generative, or enervatingly and mind/body-numbingly reductive, unchallenging and trivial.

My short-lived Panglossian perspective on collaboration (admitted above) was further problematised as I was reminded that in many political, industrial and military conflicts the verb 'to collaborate' or the abstract noun 'collaboration' speaks of treachery, betrayal and – literally or metaphorically – of 'sleeping with the enemy'. So, collaboration as perfidious cooperation with an enemy extends our reading of the term not simply to the leaders and active protagonists of Vichy France between 1940 and 1944, but also, for example, to a Marxist analysis of industrial relations where workers and their trade unions 'collaborate' – against their own 'deep' interests – with management and capital.[2] Certainly in 2014 this is a rarely articulated discourse, but in the 1970s and 1980s it was a commonplace critique from the Marxist left and particularly leveled against those who were unwilling to take up the struggle, or who signed weak and unpropitious agreements with managements on behalf of a workforce.[3] Of course, this is complex territory and the line between collaboration and resistance is often blurred and shifting. And what is the relationship between collaboration and collusion? Furthermore, in the hands of Simon McBurney, Artistic Director of Complicite, the negative and treacherous connotations of collusion are turned on their head when, in searching for a definition of *complicité*, Michael Ratcliffe, author of a programme note for *The Three Lives of Lucy Cabrol,* writes of a 'collusion between celebrants' (Ratcliffe, 1994) and, by implication, of the roguish and creatively transgressive qualities of collaboration and collusion between actor, writer, designer and director when making work. For McBurney and Ratcliffe this 'collusion between celebrants' is also a texture and condition of a successful communicative relationship between a theatre performance and its spectators.

Thus, even before we consider the practices of collaboration within the arts, the term upon examination rapidly loses much sense of definition, or a clear and unified ethical grounding. At best it is elastic and porous, at worst anodyne, almost meaningless and counter-productive for the processes and goals of the individuals involved.

## Collaboration within business and the cultural industries

Whilst the language, strategies and rhetoric of collaboration have regularly been employed in the fields of arts and political activity, throughout the twentieth century collaboration has also been invoked as a desirable force field within management economics, business studies and industrial relations. Before turning attention to the arts it is productive to consider how collaboration has been invoked and extolled within labour relations and contemporary managerial thinking. Rudi Laermans' essay entitled 'Being in Common: Theorizing artistic collaboration' (2012: 94–102), Florian Schneider's 'Collaboration: the Dark side of the Multitude' (2006) and Bojana Kunst's 'Prognosis on Collaboration' (2010) all examine current usage of the term and together they make for fascinating reading as the authors position collaboration, and the processes it describes, primarily within the territory of industrial relations. Schneider says:

> Collaboration [...] is widely used to describe new forms of labour relations [...] In contrast to cooperation, collaboration is driven by complex realities rather than romantic notions of a common ground or communality.
>
> (Schneider, 2006, n.p.)

Both Kunst and Schneider note that in the West's post-Fordist era of industrial production the old relations of authority typified by highly stratified and authoritarian layers of management ending down the line with supervisors and foremen have been replaced by a degree of enforced, but at least notionally self-regulating collaboration between workers. *Fordism* is an epithet derived, of course, from Henry T. Ford and speaks of a particular mode of division of labour, standardized systems of mass production and the economic and social systems that frame them.[4] This Post-Fordist self-regulating collaboration is driven by bonus targets, rewards, penalties and ever more sophisticated and incorporating forms of productivity management. Here it is understood that in a teamwork environment workers are expected to grasp that thinking, planning, decision-making and actions are more productive when carried out in cooperation with others. And Schneider quotes nineteenth-century steel tycoon and philanthropist Andrew Carnegie who espoused collaboration as the:

> [...] ability to work together toward a common vision, the ability to direct individual accomplishments toward organizational objectives. It is the fuel that allows common people to attain uncommon results.
>
> (Carnegie, quoted in Schneider, 2006, n.p.)

In this global economic landscape of neo-liberal principles and practices, collaboration is a means to further ends: a means to manage time more productively, to enable difficult decisions (for example, around redeployment and spatial relocation) to be made more swiftly and with minimal conflict, a means to manage (and justify) labour mobility more smoothly and a strategy to secure employee loyalty to the corporate brand. Paradoxically, too, given an apparently shared language of commonality, cooperation and solidarity, the ethos of collaboration as a managerial strategy to engender regulatory self-control of behaviour and productivity, runs counter to the belief in trade union membership as the most effective form of protecting workers rights and conditions. Here the collaborative solidarity of joining fellow workers through the organizational agency of a union is replaced by injunctions and systems obliging collaboration between employees to fulfill production targets and to self-regulate their own behaviours and needs to this end. Schneider argues that 'against the background of a postmodern control society collaborations are all about exchanging knowledge secretly [...] the concept of individual rights has vanished ...' (Schneider, 2006, n.p.)

*Who are the 'we' in all this?*

### Some randomly selected titles (from Amazon) of contemporary Business and Management Studies with their glosses

***Collaboration: How Leaders Avoid the Traps, Build Common Ground, and Reap Big Results* by Morten T Hansen (2009)**
In *Collaboration,* author Morten Hansen takes aim at what many leaders inherently know: in today's competitive environment, companywide collaboration is an imperative for successful

strategy execution... How can managers avoid the costly traps of collaboration and instead start getting the results they need? In this book, Hansen shows managers how to get collaboration right through 'disciplined collaboration'.

***Radical Collaboration* by James W. Tamm (2006)**
Radical Collaboration is a how-to-manual for anyone who wants to create trusting, collaborative environments, and transform groups into motivated and empowered teams. It is an eye-opener for leaders, managers, HR professionals, agents, trainers, and consultants who are seeking constructive ways of getting the results they want.

***Nice Companies Finish First: Why Cutthroat Management Is Over--and Collaboration Is In* (2013) Peter Shankman**
The era of authoritarian cowboy CEOs like Jack Welch and Lee Iacocca is over. In an age of increasing transparency and access, it just doesn't pay to be a jerk. In *Nice Companies Finish First*, Shankman, a pioneer in modern PR, marketing, advertising, social media, and customer service, profiles the famously nice executives, entrepreneurs, and companies that are setting the standard for success in this new collaborative world.

This boxed vignette epitomizing contemporary management thinking is instructive since it indicates with great clarity that collaboration as a practice can – self-evidently – serve different ends and purposes. I present these examples, not necessarily because collaboration within industry is inherently pernicious and regressive, but so as to prompt a series of questions it might be productive to ask any theatre or arts practitioner when faced with the prospect of a collaborative project.

- What are the explicit (or unstated) goals and objectives of this collaboration?
- What are the rules of engagement and who defines these rules and protocols?
- For whose benefit is this collaboration being proposed?
- Who is excluded from this collaboration?
- How is power practised within collaboration?
- What are the long-term consequences of this collaboration?

It should be clear, therefore, that 'collaboration' emerges as a slippery term: a practice whose shape and purpose remains endlessly negotiable and in flux, a highly ideological practice and – like most interesting terms – a site of dispute and contestation. I find interesting parallels here between collaboration and how Raymond Williams explores the term 'community' in his seminal book, *Keywords; a vocabulary of culture and society*. Williams writes:

> Community can be the warmly persuasive word to describe an existing set of relationships, or the warmly persuasive word to describe an alternative set of relationships. What is most important, perhaps, is that unlike all other terms of social organization (*state, nation, society* etc.) it seems never to be used unfavourably, and never to be given any positive opposing or distinguishing term.
>
> (Williams 2014: 74)

## The force fields of collaboration

I would like now to reflect on the range of force fields – cultural, artistic, political and economic – which in present times might be propelling or seeding this movement towards collaboration. A range of paradigms inform the conceptual contours of collaborative practices. Sometimes these are mutually reinforcing, but at other times are in a sharply contestatory relationship with each other. Locating these forces may help us to understand a little of the why, how and what of collaboration. Whilst in the creative landscape of arts practices, motives to collaborate may appear to be largely utopian, creative and constructed upon the desire to innovate, experiment and take risks, it is, I would suggest, naïve and simplistic to believe that all collaboration is driven by such dispositions. Moreover, even if collaboration seems to be ethically honorable, as we all know, its actual and unfolding practice remains rocky and unpredictable.

I would propose that collaboration as an emerging political, creative and organizational sensibility may be understood through a number of lenses and that these are not necessarily mutually exclusive:

- Collaboration as a form of economic and labour relations whose primary driving impulse is to enhance productivity, and hence surplus or profit. Here collaboration is an instrumental and utilitarian practice harnessed to highly ideological aims and objectives. In such circumstances cost savings, efficiency and higher productivity may be achieved through collective peer pressure, managerial 'carrot and stick' injunctions, self-regulation and shared self-identity.

- Collaboration as sites of mutuality, transformation, exchange and of a radical reclaiming of the experience of being in 'common'. Here the drivers come from impulses to understand and construct art-making as a radical, transformative and social practice with ***affects*** not only on spectators but on participants themselves. Here there may be dual routes (or roots) into such positions. One of these may be traced to the utopian energies of the 1960s and their lingering, though complex, contested and messy legacies to the present day. Here, art-making becomes a way of life: a domestic, social, economic and political practice as much as a cultural or aesthetic one. The other of these routes has its provenance – connectedly of course – in the Socialist and Labour movement where the only form of non-exploitative labour is a collaborative one in which the means of production and exchange are owned and controlled collectively by those who toil within the enterprise. In this context collaboration and comradeship are both means and ends, and in this context I enjoy Sukhdev Sandhu's description of John Berger as a one-man personification of collaboration in *Here is Where We Meet: A Season in London* (2005)[5]. Sandhu writes:

  A one-man hyper text, making links and connections between radically disparate times and places, he has managed to create a dialogue – no: seen the inextricability – of the poetic and the political, the local and the international, the past, present and future.

  (Berger, 2005: 15)

- As a consequence of our changed and changing understanding of identity and artistic subjectivity, collaboration becomes almost 'hard-wired' as it were into both the reception process of any art and also our construction as human beings. From Roland Barthes (1967) through various structuralist and postructuralist critiques of authorship, the subjectivity of the artist is no longer understood as singular, unitary and romantically heroic. Being in collaboration de-subjectivises the artistic process. Reception Theory (see Bennett, 1990) has also taught us that the reading of a work of art – whether dance, theatre, live art, sculpture, installation, music or whatever – is not a one-way passage from the foundational art object to the receptively passive spectator. Spectatorship, as we know, resides in a complex matrix of relationships which *collaborate* or compete to construct the sense and multiple meanings we take from experiencing a work of art.

- In relation to these challenges around strongly held beliefs about the singularity of the artist as subject, Charles Green in his book, *Collaboration in Art* (2001), argues that collaboration becomes signaled in the transition from modernist to postmodern art and is exemplified by the proliferation of teamwork in the 1960s. Whilst Green's book focuses on models of collaboration in the visual arts since the 1960s, the creative processes of theatre and performance have never been quite so suffused with the paradigm of the heroic, lone and ineffable artistic originator. Here the picture is more complex, problematizing and complicating the singular force of the originary play text by directorial and dramaturgical intervention, and through its live realization on stage by a gang of performers whose words, behaviours and actions can never be totally fixed, predictable and circumscribed.
- In parallel with critique of the singularity of creative subjectivity, the dynamics of collaboration also serve to challenge and re-appraise the boundaries of both art forms and intellectual disciplines. The will to collaboration is both cause and consequence of the urge towards inter- or cross-disciplinary practice in both the arts and in the wider landscape of higher education. Cross-disciplinarity is omnipresent in the vernacular of academic discourse and today a commonplace, if (largely) rhetorical aspiration. Of course, interdisciplinary projects are inherently collaborative – in the most basic sense of the term – and collaboration is often (but not automatically) interdisciplinary, since the 'inter' of interdisciplinarity takes us firmly into the territory of collaboration. Here we are talking of the relational, of a force field where two of more people, practices, groups or organizations 'meet' to create an outcome (known or unknown) which, it is imagined, will be different from the one to be produced if there had been no collaboration. It is the spatial and dialectical 'betweenness' of collaboration, whether it be interdisciplinary or not, which is crucial to mark in this context. Significantly, the suppleness of what inter-disciplinarity may mean as practice shadows similar elasticity in the multiple projects of collaboration. Just as collaboration has now become the mantra of an innovative capitalism ever seeking new markets and to enhance productivity and profit, so too has interdisciplinarity been colonized and incorporated. Joe Moran's exploration of interdisciplinarity (2002) concludes with a chapter

which offers a health warning for those who would uncritically support any project or practice which proudly proclaims its interdisciplinary credentials. Citing Bill Readings' book, *The University in Ruins* (1996), Moran notes that the contemporary western university has become a 'transnational bureaucratic corporation' and when universities advocate interdisciplinarity it is as much to do with managing budgets and being flexible to the demands of the marketplace as it is with intellectual dialogue and cooperation. In North America advocacy and implementation of interdisciplinary programmes have been accompanied by the shrinking of Arts and Humanities departments. In this context interdisciplinarity has been propelled by cost saving and apparent cost-effectiveness. Of course, I am not proposing anything as trite as saying that all the impulses towards interdisciplinary collaboration are simply a managerial conspiracy, but merely proposing that we check out the drivers behind such moves.

*Who are the 'we' in all this?*

## Collaboration in devising

As I noted at the beginning of this chapter, it is almost impossible to imagine theatre practices which are not collaborative. Even in productions that adhere slavishly to the authorial play text and which are directed in a manner that brooks little creative input from actors, the work is still collaborative in the sense that its realization in front of an audience requires countless 'micro' acts of collaboration both within the creative process (between text, director, actors, designers, sound and lighting technicians, carpenters, choreographers, dramaturgs etc.) and beyond it. Moreover, no theatre is ever performed without the conscious or implicit collaboration of the box office, cleaners, janitors and those with administrative, financial, marketing and other behind-the-scenes roles. However, for the purposes of this chapter I shall consider some models of a more avowedly and explicitly collaborative practice beyond the 'taken for granted' relationships identified immediately above.

The growth of devised performance within the landscape of western theatre, having been hidden from history and largely unnoticed for several decades, has more recently been much analyzed and documented (for example, Oddey 1996, Williams [ed] 1999, Heddon and Milling 2006, Murray and Keefe 2007, Graham and Hoggett 2009, Mermikedes and Smart 2010, Harvie and Lavender 2010). Moreover, in the last two years, books (Britton [ed.] 2013 and Radosavljevic [ed.] 2013) on the rewards and tribulations of working as an ensemble have documented the vicissitudes of collaboration by focusing on artists and companies, all of whom aspire to forge working relationships in the toil of making theatre which are different from the commercial and pragmatic model of hiring the creative team only for the duration of one production. John Britton quotes Robert Cohen thus: '[...] ensemble is a long-term relationship: a day-in, day-out *collaboration* in shared living, thinking and creating' (my italics) (Cohen in Britton, 2011: 16–17). When framing the purpose of *Collaborative Theatre: The Theatre du Soleil Sourcebook* (1999), and echoing questions posed earlier in this essay, editor David Williams asks: 'How does one collaborate with ethical and political integrity? What processes disperse and multiply creativity and power within a collective?' (Williams 1999: xi). In the same book Ariane Mnouchkine herself foregrounds the importance of collaboration in her company:

> Remember that the (theatre) director has already achieved the greatest degree of power he has ever had in history. And our aim is to move beyond that situation by creating a form of theatre where it will be possible for everyone to collaborate without there being directors, technicians, and so on, in the old sense.
>
> (Mnouchkine quoted in Williams, 1999: 1)

So, within the territory of devised theatre there are many different orders of collaboration operating at various levels of thought and action and with diverse rules and expectations. Heddon and Milling make very clear in their book that what we might call 'utopian' collaboration, where participants equally share all the roles, is rarely to be found in twenty-first century practices. Instead, there is an acceptance of some division of labour in the creative process and of different levels of skill and expertise. Forced Entertainment's website announces that 'We are committed to collective practice' (www.forcedentertainment.com). The Sheffield-based collective which celebrated its thirtieth anniversary in 2014 is an example of a collaborative practice where, for example, co-founder Tim Etchells is clearly signed as director and Richard Loudon as 'designer and performer'. Whilst Etchells also leads on assembling the spoken texts, this is far from the process of the 'auteur' handing down an unchallengeable play text for the company to deliver without question or alteration. Complicite claims that the only aspect of the company that has stayed the same throughout its history is that 'everything changes. Each production is different from the last.' (http://www.complicite.org). However, the website also goes on to state that the principle of working collaboratively is a constant in their approach to making work. Moreover, were we to unpick the weave of Complicite's collaborative process we might see divisions of labour nuanced very differently from, for example, Forced Entertainment. Whilst Complicite actors collaborate in generating material there would appear to be far greater directorial control in the hands of McBurney than there is with Etchells and Forced Entertainment.

Clearly, in contemporary devised collaborations the manner in which decisions and choices are configured, negotiated and ultimately controlled varies considerably. Today, what collaboration might mean within devising practices seems at best to be a productive preoccupation and creatively contested. Submerging individual identities into a common gestalt is no longer the hegemonic model of practice in the way it might have been in the 1970s and 1980s. The acquisition of a shared vocabulary and grammar of compositional dramaturgy where seamlessly undifferentiated voices and bodies speak with a common tongue often now gives way to collaborative practices where difference becomes a dramaturgical driver and remains both visible and celebrated. Mariella Greil and Martina Ruhsam in their abstract for the 'Symposium on Collaboration II' (Middlesex University, 2013) articulate this alternative model with two questions:

> Which kind of 'We' emerges if people collaborate without subordinating themselves to a common identity? What is happening if they do not merely become representatives of what they have in common? Collaboration undecides regimes of identity, production and representation.
>
> (Middlesex University Symposium on Collaboration II, Greil and Ruhsam 2013: 14)

The pleasing (and political) notion of 'undeciding' also seems to be a feature of the collaborations between disabled and non-disabled artists described by Bowditch, Bower and de Senna in their Middlesex symposium paper and where 'quite apart from the issues of authorship and ownership that any collaboration might give rise to, these collaborations offer the opportunity for "alliances" to borrow a term from Feminist criticism' (Middlesex University Symposium on Collaboration II, (Abstract) Bowditch, Bower and de Senna 2013: 10). Whether the articulation of difference through collaboration is any less utopian than other models is highly questionable.

## Immersive and site-specific collaboration

Alongside this shifting of ground within the territory of devising we can also note that developments in immersive and site-specific theatre offer to stretch collaborative partnership even further and particularly to reconfigure the role of the spectator as collaborating 'co-worker' in the dramaturgy of the work. In *Fair Play: Art, Performance and Neoliberalism* (2013) Jen Harvie insightfully maps key developments in performance practices over the last two decades and within the economic and political context of neo-liberalism. Harvie notes the 'recent proliferation of performance and art practices that engage audiences *socially* – by inviting those audiences to participate, act, work and create together' (Harvie: 1). In such work the performer-audience relationship – always elementally collaborative in the production of sense and meaning – becomes more complex as spectators are granted (or claim) degrees of agency in shaping or interrupting the direction, tempo and composition of the work in question, although almost always within clearly prescribed limits. The growth of immersive theatre usually offers audiences the opportunity of moving around and within the production, thus offering spectators a degree of control over their spatial relationship with the performance. In addition to changing the normal 'contract' between performer and audience, such practices oblige audiences to interact socially with each other in a manner proscribed or made difficult in the proscenium arch theatre or black box studio. Harvie also notes that within much immersive and socially engaged theatre there is often a degree of 'delegation' (Harvie 2013: 36) to other non-artists and workers both in the pre-performance (setting up) phase and during the production itself. Setting up many immersive or site-specific performances often requires multiple collaborations with different agencies (police, local authorities, owners of buildings etc.) or individuals such as engineers, builders, electricians, park workers and so on. In 'Turning Tourists into Performers' Wrights and Sites performer Phil Smith tells of various 'Mis-guides' the company have constructed over the years, dramaturgies, he says, of 'counter tourism' (Smith, 2013: 110). A critical dimension of these Mis-guides is to enable or produce 'the agentive tourist' who is 'more immersed and engaged than either a passive gazing or a voluntarist, aggressive "intervention"' (Smith 2013: 109). A visceral and humorous example of such collaborative agency (although certainly a doomed one) is represented in a photograph with the following caption:

> Testing the resistance of an artifact. Members of Phil Smith's volunteer panel 'attempting' to push a Victorian lamp(post) into the River Exe.
>
> (Smith, 2013: 108)

## Collaboration for utility and pragmatism

Beyond and alongside these modalities of collaboration today other more pragmatic and utilitarian forces may be at work. Rudi Laermans (2012) notes the proliferation of temporary collaborative projects since the mid 1990s in the world of western dance, projects bringing together not only choreographers and dancers but also sound-makers, visual artists, dramaturgs, critics, producers and academics. Laermans suggests that although these collaborations sometimes recall the practices of the Judson Church Dance Theater collective:

> [t]he utopian longing for a united 'we' marked by a harmonious togetherness that informed 1960's dance avant-gardism no longer predominates [...] these days collaborators will assemble for a usually well defined period of time, during which two or more artists network their interests, desires and capacities on the basis of their shared interest in the common exploration of a topic or issue.
>
> (Laermans, 2012: 94)

In addition, Laermans notes other salient points from the world of dance-based collaborations: the downplaying of romantic rhetoric of moving together freely and the quest for what he calls 'social authenticity', the emphasis upon and emphatic signing of 'research' as a coda for creative invention, and a sense that the 'value added' has to be realised in the here and now of the studio space and not simply of rewards 'yet to come'. Overall, Laermans suggests that whilst collaboration still has utopian overtones of a social and not merely an art practice, in the flinty world of twenty-first century market place economic realities, it is the utilitarian rewards of collaboration which frame and propel many practices. Nonetheless, notwithstanding Laermans' sanguinity about the cold realities of contemporary collaboration, he argues that all artistic production with multiple participants tests, and has no choice but to confront the 'politics of commonalism' in so far as the process of making insistently poses such questions as:

> How to organize work? What has value? How to go on with topic X or issue Y? Which materials will be finally included in the planned performance according to what sort of choreographic logic? And how to agree when disagreeing?
>
> (Laermans, 2012: 101)

Another mode of collaboration which is spurred largely for economic and financial reasons – though often with the promise of enhanced and embellished creative outcomes – is the organizational practice of co-production. In recent years funding bodies (e.g. Arts Council England) often specifically encourage collaborative projects: 'the current strategic touring fund is designed to encourage collaboration between organisations' (Arts Council England, 2014). Here, the bringing together of – say – two theatre companies to construct a new production has become a relatively common feature of cultural production for middle- to large-scale companies. Joint artistic directors of Paines Plough (the UK's 'national theatre of new plays' [Paines Plough, 2011]) James Grieve and George Perrin, responding to *Guardian* critic, Lynn Gardner's blog where she wrote that '[e]very bit of theatre is now reliant on collaboration' (Gardner, 2011) continue enthusiastically:

> We can collaborate more and we should. Not only to make public subsidy stretch further, but because partnerships are so creatively rewarding [...] If collaboration is rooted in shared taste and clearly articulated objectives then the more people at the table the better. Collaborating means constructive arguments as well as agreements.
>
> (Paines Plough, 2011)

Grieve and Perrin cite some examples of what they believe to have been successful recent collaborations within the UK: for example, the work of Plymouth's Drum Theatre with the Royal Court and the Lyric Hammersmith. Complicite's *A Disappearing Number* opened after rehearsal in Plymouth and was billed as a collaboration or joint production between the company, the National Theatre and Plymouth's Theatre Royal. Other examples of joint productions over the last two decades include: Warwick Arts Centre's co-productions with other UK and international partners; Glasgow Citizens Theatre's co-production of *Dr Faustus* with the West Yorkshire Playhouse; Northern Stage's co-production of *The Noise* with Unlimited Theatre; and Punchdrunk and the National Theatre.

And there are many more. One of the issues which emerge from these accounts and narratives is that 'co-production' regularly becomes elided and synonymous with 'collaboration'. I know little of the details, of the warp and weft of these 'collaborations', but most of these are driven – as Gardner, Grieve and Perrin acknowledge – initially at least by financial imperatives. This is, of course, neither dishonorable nor *a priori* suspect, but it leaves me wanting to know more about how such collaborations actually worked, how they were experienced by the participants, whether new creative ground was trodden, and – perhaps most importantly – what were the unplanned and unintended consequences of their conjoining.

A question which particularly presents itself around co-productions as models of collaboration is that of *time*. One of the often-attested features of experiments in collaboration between different artists and performance makers is that it takes time – more time – to establish the methods, protocols, understandings and 'undecidings' of the shared practice in question. Laermans, citing Kunst (2010), points out that:

> [...] (t)emporal restrictions are probably the most limiting, if not the most crushing, constraint when it comes to artistic collaboration in general. Indeed they vastly hinder the creation and exploration of an always particular 'common wealth'.
>
> (Laermans, 2012: 100)

When joint productions are driven by the imperative to save money, or to make reduced budgets stretch further – in a different context one might use the term 'economies of scale' – time will be at a premium and the *slow cooking* of a sensitive, critical and generous construction of the project is likely to be under threat. It would be arrogant to argue that co-productions should be opposed on these grounds, but the growth of these couplings, forged largely through economic imperatives, deserves to be researched and reflected upon through a cautious and quizzical lens.

UNIVERSITY OF WINCHESTER
LIBRARY

## Collaboration and utopia

Finally, having explored the range of (sometimes highly questionable) motivations, interests and forms of collaboration which seem to lie behind the current ubiquity of the term, and the claims behind it, I wish to consider how aspects of the original 'utopianism' and radicalism of collaboration are being practiced in the contemporary landscape of theatre, dance and performance. Although, as we have established, collaboration describes simply enough a working relationship between two or more people from within the same art form or discipline, it is the encounters over time between people whose working, intellectual and aesthetic practices are different – sometimes hugely so – which sign the most ambitious, risk-laden and generative forms of collaboration. In these, I would argue, 'risk-laden' implies lack of certainty about outcomes, a not-knowing about the endgame, an inherent playfulness about process, a relational lightness and a critical generosity between the collaborative players involved. Entering a collaborative project with these dispositions in mind – and managing to sustain them throughout the inevitable tribulations of the process – might helpfully define at least part of a contemporary collaborative utopianism.

It seems important, too, to acknowledge that whilst collaboration between players from varying artistic or disciplinary backgrounds always implies an accretion of know-how, skill and creativity towards some kind of yet-to-be-known end product, a place where the whole is more than the sum of the parts, there will always be loss involved as well. A genuinely radical and utopian collaboration must of necessity, I would argue, possess a willingness to make strange, destabilize and possibly jettison entirely, existing habits, practices and knowledges. Here, that most difficult of practices, the subversion of ego and the giving up of dearly-held beliefs and behaviours has always to be a very present possibility. It is perhaps not too fanciful here to see such collaboration as a kind of productive betrayal, a healthy and generative *contamination*. Collaboration always engages with the politics of interaction and relation – it cannot help but do this – and at the centre of this must lie a refusal to ignore or erase difference, and an ever-present awareness of the dangers of a fictional consensus. And at the other end of the scale from the unsettlement of dealing with difference lie the pitfalls of coziness and satisfaction. A productive and utopian collaboration requires its players to be able to nose out the critical difference between a state of flourishing (Eagleton, 2003: 124–30) and feeling good, being happy.

**Some models of recent and contemporary collaboration which might lay claim to a productive but grounded utopianism ... collaborations between partners marked by difference and distinction in skill, discipline, art form, age, culture, (dis)ability, ethnicity, faith or location:**

- Lone Twin's *Boat Project* (2012)
- Artists, Minty Donald and Nick Millar's 'Bridging' collaboration with Off Shore Workboats Ltd which involved a huge rope being woven eleven times across the Clyde in Glasgow (2010)
- Dee Heddon's collaborative walking projects (2000–)
- Collaboration between architect turned visual artist, Chris Crickmay, and dancer Miranda Tuffnell (1980's–)
- The West-Eastern Divan Orchestra set up by Daniel Barenboim and Edward Said in 1999
- Merce Cuningham and John Cage (1942–92)
- Robert Wilson, Tom Waits and William Burroughs working together on *The Black Rider* (1990)
- John Berger working with Simon McBurney and Complicite on *Lucy Cabrol* (1994), *The Vertical Line* (1999), *To the Wedding* (1997), and *Vanishing Points* (2005)
- John Berger's collaboration with photographer Jean Mohr (1960's–); Forced Entertainment's collaboration with photographer Hugo Glendinning (1984–)
- John Berger (1926–) and WG Sebald (1944–2001) – writers whose dramaturgies of writing are a collaboration of forms, registers and voices
- *The Choreography and Cognition Project* (2003–04) – a collaboration between arts researcher Scott deLahunta, choreographer and dancer Wayne McGregor and Cambridge University's Crucible Computer Laboratory
- *The Wall of Death* – National Theatre of Scotland's collaboration with visual artist Stephen Skrynka and the Ken Fox Troupe (2010)
- Places of collaboration and learning like Black Mountain College (1933–57) or Dartington College of Arts (1961–2008)

In this chapter I have identified and briefly explored different contexts and rationales for contemporary collaborations both within and beyond the work of theatre, dance and performance. I have suggested that within the ubiquitousness of current calls to collaborate, there often lies a murky and questionable politics. Models of collaboration are multiple, overlapping and rarely represent categorical and mutually exclusive modes of operation or practice. In current times the motivation to collaborate in order to make unknown discoveries, to take risks and to establish new ways of working by deepening personal relationships and friendships can easily become compromised by economic and financial constraints. Such constraints may simply mean the absence of cash resource to allow the *slow cooking* of a genuinely productive exercise in collaboration to take place, but equally they may be the result of limitations and conditions attached to funding, and an increasingly instrumental and commodified culture which values art-making largely in terms of economic or social value added. Quietly utopian and progressive models of collaboration remain, of course, in our midst and I identify some of the qualities of these above. Such models try to resist many conventional and quotidian expectations and behaviours, but particularly the excessive commodification of time, representing a stubborn refusal to 'speed up' artistic processes with a celebration of slowness, uncertainty and *undeciding*.

## Afterwords I

The models I have identified in the box above deserve a little elaboration and contextualization. Each of these merit being written up into a full-length case study in its own right, but this essay had a different purpose, namely to offer an overview of how contemporary collaboration is invoked and justified in many different cultural, economic and social spaces. Of course, these examples are amongst many I could have selected, but they were chosen to exemplify what I feel to be enduring qualities of a generative, generous and progressive collaboration. As this essay has argued, there are many different 'orders' of collaboration, but all these examples, except perhaps for the West-Eastern Divan Orchestra, speak of a model collaboration which takes the initiating artists outside and beyond their own discipline and art form. Sometimes these are collaborations *between* artists: choreographer and dancer Cunningham with composer Cage; theatre-maker Wilson with writer Burroughs and singer/composer Waits; architect-turned-artist Crickmay with dancer/choreographer Tufnell; theatre director and actor McBurney with writer and visual artist Berger; theatre company Forced Entertainment with photographer Glendinning; and so on. Other collaborations take the partnerships *outwith* the sphere of the arts: visual artist and performance maker

Donald with marine workers employed by Off Shore Workboats Ltd on the Clyde; performance maker Lone Twin's extraordinary 'collaboration' with hundreds of members of the public who contributed artifacts to the building of the boat; Heddon's performative walking encounters with many colleagues, friends and strangers; the National Theatre of Scotland with the circus entertainers, the Ken Fox Troupe (and visual artist Skrynka) in the *Wall of Death*; and academic deLahunta's research collaborations with choreographer and dancer McGregor and computer engineers and software designers from Cambridge University. Dartington College of Arts and Black Mountain College are included here as highly unusual institutions (now, sadly, no longer in existence) which practised collaboration and experimentation across and between art forms. Both places have an illustrious list of alumni who have populated contemporary arts practices over the last fifty years. All these examples articulate a complex and sometimes passionate politics of collaboration, but perhaps none more so than the West-Eastern Divan Orchestra, established by conductor Daniel Barenboim and political activist and writer Edward Said[6]. The orchestra particularly draws upon Palestinian and Israeli musicians who play side by side, offering a glimpse of what a future peaceful co-existence might look like between these two countries.

## Afterwords II: poem

***We***
Who we?
Who I?
Why we?
Why I?
Where's we?
Where's I?
Who's not we?
Why not those we?
Can we?
Should we?
Could we?
Would we?
What if we?
If not we, who?
How can we?
Where do we stop?

How do we start?
Do we continue being we?
When do we stop being we?
Are we in common?
What have we in common?
Are we for we?
Are we against we?
Who are the 'we' in all this?

## Notes

1. By 'neo-liberal' I am referring to the dominant economic and political regimes in the West over the last three decades which have privileged the rule of the market, cutting public expenditure on social services, deregulation, privatisation and an attempt to eliminate the concepts and practices of 'public good' and 'community'.
2. A Marxist, or indeed many socialist analyses of industrial relations argue that there is a fundamental division of interest between Capital (owners) and Labour (workers/employees). Capital, in order to maximize profits, must forever seek to enhance productivity and reduce costs, at the centre of which are labour costs. Workers, and the unions which represent them, can never fundamentally escape this conflict of interests even when struggles are lost and pragmatic compromises have to be made.
3. *The British Journal of Industrial Relations* has carried essays which articulate a Marxist perspective on industrial relations. Other key texts on this subject include: Allen (1971), Braverman (1974) and Hyman (1975). Hyman in particular has written prolifically from this standpoint.
4. Jessop (1992) and De Grazia (2005) both write about industrial systems of production in the post-Fordist era. Aldous Huxley's dystopian novel, *Brave New World* (2007), first published in 1931, imagines an automated future in the year 2540.
5. 'Here is where we meet' was a pioneering season of events in 2005, designed around the work of writer John Berger. It was intended to explore and celebrate cultural collaboration and creative / political commitment. The event was marked by a book of essays in which Sandhu writes.
6. West-Eastern Divan Orchestra is a youth orchestra based in Seville, Spain, consisting of musicians from countries in the Middle East, of Egyptian, Iranian, Israeli, Jordanian, Lebanese, Palestinian, Syrian and Spanish background. The Argentine-Israeli conductor Daniel Barenboim and the late Palestinian-American academic Edward Said founded the orchestra in 1999, and named the ensemble after an anthology of poems by Johann Wolfgang von Goethe.

## Bibliography

Allen, Victor (1971), *The Sociology of Industrial Relations: Studies in Method*. Harlow: Longman.

Arts Council England website: <http://www.artscouncil.org.uk/>

Barthes, Roland (1967), 'The Death of the Author' in *Aspen*, No 5–6. New York: Aspen.

Bennett, Susan (1990), *Theatre Audiences: a Theory of Production and Reception*. New York: Routledge.

Berger, John (2005), *A Season in London*. London: Art Events.

Bowditch, Caroline, Bower, David & de Senna, Pedro (2013), 'Nothing about us without us: collaborations between disabled and non-disabled practitioners' in Middlesex University (2013). *Symposium on Collaboration II*. London: Middlesex University.

Braverman, Harry (1974), *Labour and Monopoly Capital: the Degredation of Work in the Twentieth Century*. New York: Monthly Review Press.

*British Journal of Industrial Relations*. London: London School of Economics.

Britton, John (2013), Encountering Ensemble. London: Bloomsbury.

Complicite website: <http://www.complicite.org/>

De Grazia, Victoria (2005), *Irresistible Empire: America's Advance Through 20th-Century Europe*, Cambridge: Belknap Press of Harvard University Press.

Eagleton, Terry (2003), *After Theory*. London: Allen Lane Penguin Press.

Forced Entertainment website: <www.forcedentertainment.com>

Free Dictionary online: <http://www.thefreedictionary.com/collaboration>

Gardner, Lyn (2011), Blog. Website: <http://www.theguardian.com/stage/2011/apr/01/what-to-see-theatre-shared-experience-bronte>

Green, Charles (2001), *The Third Hand, Collaboration in Art from Modernism to Postmodernism*. Sydney: University of New South Wales Press.

Greil, Mariella & Ruhsam, Martina (2013) 'Postconsual Collaboration' in Middlesex University (2013), *Symposium on Collaboration II*. London: Middlesex University.

Harvie Jen & Lavender, Andy (2010), *Making Contemporary Theatre*. Manchester: Manchester University Press

Harvie, Jen (2013), *Fair Play: Art, Performance and Neoliberalism*. London: Palgrave Macmillan.

Heddon, Deirdre & Milling, Jane (2006), *Devising Performance: a Critical History*. London: Palgrave Macmillan.

Hoggart, Stephen & Graham, Scott (2009), *The Frantic Assembly Book of Devising Theatre*. Abingdon: Routledge.

Huxley, Aldous (2007), *Brave New World*. London: Vintage Classics.

Hyman, Richard (1975), *Industrial Relations: a Marxist Perspective*. Basingstoke: Macmillan.

Jessop, Bob (1992), 'Fordism and post-fordism: A critical reformulation', in Storper, M; Scott, A J, *Pathways to industrialization and regional development*, London: Routledge, pp. 42–62.

Kunst, Bojana (2010), 'Prognosis on Collaboration' in *How to do things by theory*, online journal at <http://www.howtodothingsbytheory.info/2010/05/13/bojana-kunst-prognosis-on-collaboration/>

Laermans, Rudi (2012). '"Being in common": Theorising artistic collaboration' in *Performance Research*, Volume 17, No 6, December. Abingdon: Routledge.

Mermikides, Alex & Smart, Jackie (2010), *Devising in Process*. London: Palgrave Macmillan.

Moran, Joe (2002). *Interdisciplinarity*. London: Routledge.

Murray, Simon & Keefe, John (2007), *Physical Theatres: a Critical Introduction*. Abingdon: Routledge.

Oddey, Alison (1996), *Devising Theatre: a Practical and Theoretical Handbook.* London: Routledge.

Paines Plough website (2011): <http://www.theguardian.com/stage/2011/apr/01/what-to-see-theatre-shared-experience-bronte>

Radosavljevic, Duska (Ed.) (2013), *The Contemporary Ensemble: interviews with theatre-makers.* Abingdon: Routledge.

Readings, Bill (1996), *The University in Ruins.* Massachusetts: Harvard University Press.

Schneider, Florian (2006), 'Collaboration: the Dark Side of the Multitude' in *Theory Kit,* online journal at <http://kit.kein.org/node/1>

Smith, Phil (2013), 'Turning Tourists into Performers' in *Performance Research,* Volume 18, No 2, April. Abingdon: Routledge.

Theatre de Complicité (2006), *The Three Lives of Lucy Cabrol* (Programme Notes by Michael Ratcliffe). Oxford: Berg 3PL.

Williams, David (Ed.) (1999), *Collaborative Theatre: the Theatre du Soleil Sourcebook.* London: Routledge.

Williams, Raymond in O'Connor, Alan (1989), *Raymond Williams on Television, Selected Writings.* London: Routledge.

Williams, Raymond (2014), *Keywords.* London: Fourth Estate.

# 2

# Collaboration, Democracy and the Total Artwork

*Alexandra Kolb*

'The idea of *Gesamtkunstwerk* – a German word for "total art-work" – has long since gone the way of all nineteenth-century Romantic ideals, into the trash-heap of history' – or so announced the American architect and visual artist Lebbeus Woods in 2010. Woods (1940–2012), whose work addressed political and societal issues, believed that art had by the twenty-first century degenerated into a 'commodity', broken down 'into salable [sic] units', and advocated a 'reunification of the arts, in the service of both public and private life' (Woods 2010).

In the light of Woods' uncompromising metaphor, I shall attempt to perform the role of a rubbish sifter by rescuing the concept from its proclaimed oblivion. This chapter sets out to demonstrate how Richard Wagner's mid-nineteenth-century landmark writings on the role of art in society and the reform of opera, and specifically his embrace of the 'collective Art-work' (Wagner, 2012, 58) or *Gesamtkunstwerk*, sympathetically elucidate and have significantly shaped later twentieth-century collaborative practices and discourses in the performing arts (notably dance).

Much scholarly research has been dedicated to the enactment of Wagner's visions of the total artwork in modernism, such as the Bauhaus theatre and Diaghilev's *Ballets Russes* (see for instance Koss 2010). This chapter, however, will examine how Wagner's objectives can be usefully extended to, and take form in, postmodern dance, tracing a critical genealogy from Wagner through Bertolt Brecht and the Cunningham-Cage collaboration, to the postmodern work of Yvonne Rainer and Pina Bausch. Centering my discussion on artists operating in Germany and the US – two countries which are intimately associated with developments of the *Gesamtkunstwerk* – I seek to shed particular light on how Wagner's thought opened the way for differentiated views on the relationship between collaborative performance practices and political aspirations. Critical attention will be given throughout the chapter to calls for dance to reflect, and indeed enact, different conceptions of democracy through collaborative means.[1]

## Richard Wagner and the Gesamtkunstwerk's collaborative unity

Taking Richard Wagner's notion of total artwork as the basis for a discussion of contemporary models of collaboration might appear odd, if not positively misconceived, given his frequent association with Third Reich aesthetics and anti-Semitism. Yet there is little doubt that his theoretical writings, which expound on his notion of the *Gesamtkunstwerk*, mark a central reference point for later collaborations in performance. Wagner advocated a synthesis of the arts in the *Gesamtkunstwerk*, positing what he deemed the original desirable unity of art forms – foremost among the three 'sister-arts' (Wagner 2012, 67) of music, poetry and dance – in the tragedies conceived and performed in the democratic Athenian *polis*. Wagner stressed that 'each separate art can only bare its utmost secret to their common public through a mutual parleying with the other arts' (Wagner 2012, 65). In other words, each art only comes to full fruition by interaction with others, meaning that the individual benefits of the arts are transcended to achieve a totality which is greater than the sum of its parts.

Wagner also advocated a *'Fellowship of all the Artists'* (2012, 69, emphasis in original), projecting the *Gesamtkunstwerk* as a collective artistic pursuit which unites its participants in harmonious relations. In the realisation of his music-dramas, however, Wagner himself relied little on genuine artistic collaboration. He was an omni-talented creator who wrote his own libretti ('poems') as well as musical compositions, and as Katherine Syer (2009, 3) notes, expanded his sphere of influence to control virtually every aspect of bringing an opera to stage. Hence, if by collaboration one understands a process of joint creation between participants of equal standing, his work could hardly be so called. The *Gesamtkunstwerk* rests instead on a notion of collaboration as a formal aesthetic pursuit of synthesising art forms, in the sense suggested by Thomas Hines in his book *Collaborative Form*, which examines a heterogeneous range of works combining two or more artistic genres. Hines writes that collaboration can refer to the formal combinative integration 'of the contributing arts', and not only to the collaborative working processes between performance-makers (Hines 1991, 4). Wagner's pursuit thus consisted of a collaboration in the former sense: a combining of art forms though correlating on-stage action, musical gesture, text and set to achieve an organic unity.

This correlation of artistic elements in the *Gesamtkunstwerk*, as well as the *leitmotif* technique – a recurring melodic theme or passage which accompanies the (re)appearance of certain characters or themes (such as the River Rhine) – were designed to avoid the structural and aesthetic incongruities of conventional operatic format. Wagner harshly criticised traditional operas, lamenting the arbitrary juxtaposition of art forms and the fact that rather than promoting mental engagement through coherent dramaturgy, they offered sensationalism to placate the superficial demands of audiences. In 1850 he wrote:

> There are even many of our most popular artists who do not in the least conceal the fact, that they have no other ambition than to satisfy this shallow audience. They are wise in their generation; for when the prince leaves a heavy dinner, the banker a fatiguing financial operation, the working man a weary day of toil, and go to the theatre: they ask for rest, distraction, and amusement, and are in no mood for renewed effort and fresh expenditure of force. This argument is so convincing, that we can only reply by saying: it would be more decorous to employ for this purpose any other thing in the wide world, but not the body and soul of Art.
>
> (Wagner 2012, 19)

In order to avoid audience 'distraction', Wagner rejected the common practice of keeping house lights on during performances, which had allowed spectators to meander around and socialise, and was the first consistently to darken the auditorium in his own Festspielhaus in Bayreuth (see for instance DiGaetani 2014, 162).

Marked by a deep unease over the employment of art as light entertainment, or as a form of paid business (which Wagner terms 'industry' and 'commerce', 2012, 18), his perspective may be seen as offering a critique of middle- or upper-class consumerism; which was linked to a more general concern, as Matthew Wilson Smith (2007, 20) notes, over industrialisation in the wake of technological advances. Wagner's mid-nineteenth-century writings indeed coincided with the transition years between the First and Second Industrial Revolutions and the acceleration of technology, including the large-scale manufacture of machines. Wagner's yearning for organic unity and the recovery of a social community as expressed in the *Gesamtkunstwerk* – born of a resistance to the fragmentation of the human being through division of labour and mechanisation – anticipated, as Smith (2007, 20) maintains, Guy Debord's critique of the society of the spectacle. Debord, as I shall discuss in detail below, complained of the 'alienated consumption' and 'commodification' which came with the advent of the Second Industrial Revolution (Debord, 1994, thesis 42).

The *Gesamtkunstwerk*, therefore, did not purely revolve around aesthetic issues and the relation between different art forms, but was intimately linked to socio-political concerns. It sought to express the 'people's consciousness' (Wagner 2012, 20) and a free nation which were both conditions for its successful realisation and expressions of it: a united art work was deemed to be both the cause and consequence of a united community. Ancient Athens provided a suitable, if imperfect historical precedent, whose principles Wagner sought to develop further into a new model of the ideal democratic state. The fact that he located his notion of the working *Gesamtkunstwerk* within a democracy is by no means coincidental. As a consequence of Wagner's twentieth-century association with fascism (the result of his 1850 anti-Semitic text 'Jewishness in Music'; the acquaintance of his daughter-in-law, the English-born Winifred, with Adolf Hitler; and Hitler's promotion of Wagner's compositions at Nazi events), his early pro-democratic political aspirations and affinity with revolutionary, progressive causes are easily overlooked.

It is undisputable, however, that Wagner received significant impulses from democratically-minded figures, among others the socialist August Röckel (himself a composer) who convinced Wagner of the necessity of founding a national Republic as an alternative to the despotism of monarchical power. The 1848 revolution in the German States, part of a wider movement within Europe, rejected traditional authoritarian political structures and called instead for greater democracy: freedom of the press, freedom of assembly, liberal state policies, more participation in government and national unity.[2] The defeat of the democratic movement by the conservative aristocracy at the hands of the Prussian and Austrian military forced many revolutionaries into exile; including Wagner himself who had taken active part in the Dresden upheaval in May 1849, both by writing supportive articles and reportedly by procuring hand grenades (Lippert 2012, in particular 215; Jansen 2013).

An immediate upshot of his embroilment in this revolution, which significantly impacted on his thought as a young man, were his lengthy essays 'Art and Revolution' (1849), 'The Art-Work of the Future' (1850), and 'Opera and Drama' (1852). In these works, which were written in exile in Zurich, Wagner noted the reciprocal influence of forms of society and forms of art; whereby a specific social structure will produce a certain kind of art, and conversely art has an impetus back on society. He traces the '*severance* of the arts' (Wagner 1893, 72; emphasis in original), which he so deplores, back to the abolition of (Athenian) democracy:

> Hand-in-hand with the dissolution of the Athenian State marched the downfall of Tragedy. As the spirit of *community* split itself along a thousand lines of egoistic cleavage, so was the great united work of Tragedy disintegrated into its individual factors.
>
> (Wagner 2012, 16)

Wagner expected the revolution to bring about a rebirth of art, a new music and model of society. It was his endeavour to place his artistic vision in the context of a progressive political programme, in particular a plea for democracy: a legacy that was to determine many future discourses about artistic collaboration, whether based on formal aesthetic features or genuinely joint creation. Political unity *qua* democracy was the precondition for a working *Gesamtkunstwerk*, which had a utopian character in that it was accompanied by a new idea of humanity rooted in the common people. Wagner seemed to understand unity, firstly in a political sense to mean a society that eschews egoistic aspirations and where people work together towards a common cause; and secondly in an artistic context to mean that spectators unite as an audience – although in neither case are the individual identities of citizens or audience members entirely conceded.

Importantly, Wagner's call for a greater sense of community should not be understood as advocating the predominance of the state. He did not deny the value of individuality, and indeed challenged the curtailment of individual liberties and imposition of norms by governments: 'The State is [...] a stiff, dogmatic, fettering and domineering might; which lays down for the individual in advance, "So shalt thou think and deal I"' (Wagner 1893, 104). Wagner's scepticism towards the state, and the influence he took from the Russian revolutionary anarchist Mikhail Bakunin, have incited some commentators to term his early ideas anarchic, or even (following Jansen) 'anti-political' radicalism (Jansen 2013). Although diffuse, his aspirations to impact on society were serious. As Barry Millington first pointed out, 'the reuniting of the constituent parts in the *Gesamtkunstwerk* mirrored the socialist aim of restoring integrity to a fragmented, divided society' (1992, 397). More specifically, Wagner's aesthetic project of *Gesamtkunstwerk* was targeted, politically, at the building of a modern nation-state.

In his rejection of self-interest in favour of a collective cause – claiming for instance that the *Gesamtkunstwerk* involves the 'passing over of egoism into communism' (Wagner 1993, 78) – Wagner anticipated in many respects the rhetoric of work on collaboration published between the 1970s and early 1990s in an array of subject areas: from business studies (Schrage 1990) to the visual arts (Hobbs 1984). The art historian Robert Hobbs, for example, wrote that collaboration 'does not make the ego the subject but instead is attuned to some function outside the individual, isolated self' (1984, 79). The collaborative ethos of this era supported group dynamics and shared understanding, rejecting the talented but isolated ego as the mainstay of business and creativity. In contrast with Wagner who sought the artistic equivalent of a united nation, the socio-political motivations for postmodern artistic collaborations, according to Henry Sayre (1989, 101), stemmed from the feminist movement which offered collaborative activity as an alternative to traditional, male-connoted modes of production. Whilst seemingly far removed from Wagner's political aims, they echoed his quest for striving for the collective good and a fairer distribution of power within society.

Wagner was keen for art to express the identity and cultural aspirations of an entire people rather than being an aristocratic pastime that excludes the majority. His projected new art had a public character: he interchangeably uses the terms *Kunstwerk des Gesamtvolkes* ('art work of the entire people'), *das gemeinsame Kunstwerk* ('common art work' – i.e. that which is either produced or owned together), and *Gesamtkunstwerk*. At various points in the *Art-Work of the Future*, he makes disparaging observations that 'in our superior theatres, loll only the affluent classes' (Wagner 2012, 20), and that 'art has become the private property of an artist-caste' (Wagner 2012, 64). Even a cursory glance at proclamations of Wagner's contemporaries shows that this perspective was by no means commonplace. The young poet Stéphane Mallarmé, for example, made no bones about his elitist stance when writing in 1862:

> Let man be democratic; the artist must separate and remain an aristocrat [...]. If there is a popularization [vulgarization], let us make sure that it is a popularization of the good, not of the beautiful [art]; that your efforts do not tend – and I trust that they have not tended in that direction – to make you a *worker's poet*, which would be grotesque, if it were not pitiful, for the truly superior artist.
>
> (Mallarmé 1965 [1862], 207)

By contrast, Wagner's view of art was shaped by what we might today regard as a call for greater accessibility:

> If, however, we were to ask the Artist whether the great majority of art's amateurs are able to understand him in his best endeavours, he could only answer with a deep-drawn sigh. But if he ponders on the infinitely greater mass of those who are perforce shut out on every side by the evils of your present social system from both the understanding and the tasting of the sweets of modern art, then must the artist of to-day grow conscious that his whole art-doings are, at bottom, but an egoistic, self-concerning business; that his art, in the light of public life, is nothing else than luxury and superfluity, a self-amusing pastime.
>
> (Wagner 2012, 64)

Additionally, he supported a closure of the gap between art and life, pointing to the relevance of art to everyday concerns, for which it is important that artworks originate from the foundations of society and are thus 'grown up from below' (Wagner 2012, 64).

## Wagner's critical reception in modernism

While Wagner's writings promote a non-hierarchical collaboration of art forms, the shift from page to stage is less conclusive. The musical element of his own works often predominated at the expense of other arts. There was, in particular, a notable shortage of dance, which featured prominently in just three operas: *Tannhäuser* (Bachanale scene), *Meistersinger* (Festwiese) and *Parsifal* (Blumenmädchen scene). And while Wagner used the most innovative stage technology then available, including mechanical machines to evoke the Rhinemaidens' swimming in *Rheingold* (1876) and landscape paintings for his sets (see Smith 2007, 26 & 33), nineteenth-century staging possibilities were obviously limited in comparison with today's digital projections and computer technology. Wagner's view of the aesthetic experience achieved through his music-dramas was in fact somewhat ambivalent: 'Oh! I am seized with horror at the idea of all these costumed, stuffed creatures; after creating the invisible orchestra, I would like also to invent the invisible theatre!' (diary entry by Cosima Wagner, quoted in Koss 2010, 249).

With these remarks, Wagner perhaps anticipated some of the later criticism targeted at his *Gesamtkunstwerk* as a realised aesthetic practice. Artistic experiments in modernism, which were heavily indebted to the composer, often celebrated the idea of artistic unification. For instance Oskar Schlemmer, in synch with the Bauhaus school's more general endeavour to resist the isolation of each art form, described his famous *Triadic Ballet* from 1922 as 'symphonic architectonic composition: the fusion of the dance, the costumes and the music' (Schlemmer 1926, 119). The interaction and joining of artistic genres was also at the core of productions by the Ballets Russes, although their attempts to realise the *Gesamtkunstwerk* met with some reservations. Critics of their productions such as André Levinson, for example, admonished the subordination of one medium (choreography) to another (the visual, which was seen as too dominant), and complained that stage sets, which were supposed to help integrate the artistic genres into an aesthetic whole, were actually distracting (see Garafola 1989, 45–46).

Other earlier twentieth-century commentators also had qualms. In 1933, the author Thomas Mann criticised what he saw as mere 'dilettantism' (1999, 96) in Wagner's attempt to engage (superficially) with numerous art forms at the same time – in essence accusing him of being a 'jack of all trades, master of none'. Theodor Adorno (1991, 111) disapproved of his failure to adopt a truly collaborative working approach, suggesting that his claim to have created a 'collective' type of artwork was bogus. Further uncertainty around the concept was voiced by Bertolt Brecht, whose critical stance set the scene for later developments in dance:

> So long as the expression 'Gesamtkunstwerk' (or 'integrated work of art') means that the integration is a muddle, so long as the arts are supposed to be 'fused' together, the various elements will all be equally degraded, and each will act as a mere 'feed' to the rest. The process of fusion extends to the spectator who gets thrown into the melting pot too and becomes a passive (suffering) part of the total work of art. Witch-craft of this sort must of course be fought against. [...] *Words, music, and setting must become more independent of one another.*
>
> (Brecht, 1964, 37–38; emphasis in original)

Brecht's stance might seem antithetical to the entire concept of *Gesamtkunstwerk*. However, as theatre scholar Matthew Smith (2007, in particular 72–78) has convincingly argued, Brecht – who wrote the libretti for several operas, including *Rise and Fall of the City of Mahagonny* (1930) – did not reject the total work of art entirely. He rather envisaged its reformulation: away from the ideal of creating an aesthetic fusion that produced a unified whole (which waters down individual contributions through the need to agree on a common denominator), in favour of an 'uninterrupted collaboration' between various artists who remain independent, so that '[t]he integrated work of art (or 'Gesamtkunstwerk') appeared before the spectator as a bundle of separate elements' (Brecht 1964, 134).

This move towards a new form of *Gesamtkunstwerk* which proclaimed the independence of elements while adhering to the idea of aesthetic unity was motivated not only on artistic grounds but also political ones. Brecht gestures to the dangers of the usurpation of the spectator in the Wagnerian opera, and as various subsequent commentators – among them Henry Sayre (1989), Roger Copeland (2004), and Henk Oosterling (2009) – have argued, the *Gesamtkunstwerk* taken to its logical aesthetico-political extreme could be seen as an instrument of totalitarian fascism. Far from leading to democracy, Copeland notes how critics of Wagner, including Brecht, described fascist spectacles such as the Nuremberg rallies with explicit reference to the composer: 'one great Wagnerian opera: the masses mesmerized, the Fuhrer unified with his followers' (Copeland 2004, 129). Undeniably, Wagner's actual works were (ab)used by the Nazi regime to starkly undemocratic ends: their collectivist and unifying nature being twisted to serve the purposes of the dictatorship. Hence, while Wagner had called for the public to be aroused to 'real emotional [not critical] understanding' (Wagner 1911, 343; my translation), many twentieth-century authors writing in the light of 1930s events understood this as effecting 'a transformation of all spectators into a unified mass' (see Ewen 1969, 218). (Brecht's alienation technique, by contrast, explicitly sought to do the exact opposite: to preclude audience empathy, thereby prizing emotional detachment.)

That said, the extent of passivity and emotional absorption of Wagner's audiences is a subject of contention. In his early writings he seemed to devise a model of active spectatorship, and his visions were partially realised in the architecture of his 1876 Bayreuth Festival House, whose recessed orchestra pit and egalitarian amphitheatrical seating arrangement allowed audiences to concentrate fully on the stage without obstruction. It might also be argued that his intentions were misconstrued by later commentators who, as Juliet Koss suggests, conflated 'the active model of communal spectatorship that the composer demanded in 1849 and the passive spectatorship required of a mass audience under German fascism' (2010, 260). Moreover, at least in Wagner's early work, the individual – and the acting out of their desires and drives – was at the core of his political philosophy; to the point that he demanded a 'Sinking of the State (*Untergang des Staates*)' (Wagner 2012, 24; also 108) which is clearly the antithesis of fascist-style subjugation. Indeed, in the free artistic community Wagner envisaged, particular importance is granted to individuality as only a free individual is able to initiate decision-making processes with others – and thus collaborate in pursuit of a greater good.

In dance, the Cunningham-Cage-Rauschenberg collaboration of the 1950s pointed the way to postmodernist developments. While Wagner's holistic synthesis of the arts was a move against artificial over-specialisation, with one artist retaining control of all the individual elements of the mise-en-scène, here we see the opposite: a close collaboration of contributing artists, but one that emphasises the independent co-existence of the arts in line with Brecht's demands:

> In most conventional dances, there is a central idea to which everything adheres. The dance has been made to the piece of music, the music supports the dance, and the décor frames it. The central idea is emphasised by each of the several arts. What we have done in our work is to bring together three separate elements in time and space, the music, the dance and the décor, allowing each one to remain independent. The three arts don't come from a single idea which the dance demonstrates, the music supports and the décor illustrates, but rather they are three separate elements each central to itself.
>
> (Cunningham 1991, 137)

Merce Cunningham's collaborative pieces gesture to a loosening of authorial control over the work, facilitated by his choreographic method of establishing the sequence or length of dance sections through chance processes which lead to indeterminate structures. Pieces such as *Story* (1963) deliberately transferred 'choice from the choreographer to the dancer' (Banes 1994, 102), for instance by allowing dancers to improvise and invent their own movements in certain sections of the work, while the audience was required to take a more active role as the action often occurred in two or more places simultaneously, or at any point within the space.

## American postmodern dance

A number of postmodern artists in the late 1960s and 1970s set out to disassociate themselves from the intoxicating effects of the Wagnerian *Gesamtkunstwerk* in their collaborative practices. They were influenced,

I believe, on one hand by the experience of ultra-nationalism and the uncanny alliance of aesthetics and politics under the Third Reich, and on the other by Cunningham's experiments. Shedding Wagner's holistic aspirations, they sought what Henry Sayre (1989, 101) has termed a *new Gesamtkunstwerk*: one in which, akin to Brecht's and Cunningham's formulations, the different art forms are not fused in their totality. Rather, the emphasis of collaboration began to shift from the integration of art forms to the relationships between creators, performers and audiences. However, artists still clung to the utopian dimension of artistic collaboration as reflecting a more democratic society and resistance to capitalism.

Various movements and groups in the 1960s, including the guerrilla theatre, were committed to revolutionary socio-political change – targeting for instance the Vietnam War or the capitalist system in general. They also experimented with participatory theatre practice, implanting in those involved an acute sense of the social significance of artistic forms of togetherness. These novel practices reflected the political exigencies of the time. Democratic parliamentarianism, which for Wagner was still a remote dream, had already been established in many Western countries and aristocratic hegemony was a distant memory. The new revolutionaries of the 1960s no longer worried about the 'if' of a democratic state, but the 'how'; their politics aimed at the promotion of equality among sexes and races, human rights, and pacifism. As was the case with Wagner, however, theatre and performance remained important tools in anti-establishment activism.

In American postmodern dance, political overtones could more often be observed in the 'form' than the content of works, although pieces such as Steve Paxton's anti-Vietnam war *Collaboration with Wintersoldier* (1971) attest to the fact that explicit political discourse, while uncommon, did exist. Postmodern artists favoured a more egalitarian society (as had Wagner) and experimented with group decision-making, networking, and centreless structures: offering equivalents, in the artistic realm, of the flat hierarchies and inclusive decision-making processes which dominated the agenda of political progressives of this era. Yvonne Rainer is an interesting case in point. The artist declared in a taped reading during a presentation of *Performance Demonstration* in 1968:

> I want my dancing to be the superstar and refuse to share the limelight with any form of collaboration or co-existence [...]. I simply don't want someone else's high art anywhere near mine. As I said

before, I don't collaborate. Furthermore, I am all for one medium at a time.

(Rainer 1964, 111–12)

Yet collaborate she did. As various commentators (for instance Banes 1994, 317) have pointed out, this statement was somewhat ironic given that *Performance Demonstration* made use of both music and film. But it still contained a kernel of truth, as there clearly *was* an increased interest in movement for its own sake in late 1960s postmodern dance. Rainer's remarks signal her shift in focus from interdisciplinary collaboration towards collaboration with her dancers and even occasionally with untrained performers, troubling the boundaries between choreographer, performer, spectator and artwork rather than those between artistic genres to the point of abandoning the idea of a collaboration of art forms altogether.

One year later, in *Continuous Project – Altered Daily* (1969), Rainer continued her experiments by easing, or eschewing altogether, directorial authority. She allowed performers' 'expressions and responses and opinions to affect one's [Rainer's] own creative process' (Rainer 1974, 128), and encouraged the audience to move between different performance areas during the work. This too had political connotations: Rainer explicitly suggested that there was 'a moral imperative to form a democratic social structure' (Rainer 1974, 128) among the artists, who produced the piece almost wholly through improvisation. As in Cunningham's works which drew on chance procedures, the order of dance sections could vary, though in Rainer's case this depended on the performers' decisions. And while by her own admission, her 1970 variant of this practice was not yet quite 'the result of group decision-making as a whole' (Rainer 1974, 129), this was certainly the direction in which such ventures were headed.

Open devising processes like these were quite in keeping with the political tenets of 1960s American counterculture. The New Left rejected the bureaucratic power of state institutions and demanded *participatory* as opposed to merely *representative* democracy: a clarion call to which some scholars[3] reacted by drawing critical analogies between the largely passive electorate in existing democracies, and the traditional proscenium theatre with its 'passive' mode of spectatorship. Steve Paxton, reflecting retrospectively on the period's concerns and his own artistic response to them, emphasised his frustration at the imperviousness of political leaders to the views of their electors: 'In administrations where spin and lies come to spoil the communication between the populace and their elected representatives, people don't know what to think' (Paxton in Kolb 2006, 20). This disillusionment led to stronger calls for more participation in politics.

In the twenty-first century, as support for far-leftist politics has retreated somewhat to the margins in both Europe and North America, the collaborative experiments of the 1960s and 1970s – in particular those associated with artistic collectives – have been harshly criticised, for instance by Martina Ruhsam (2011, 63–64; and in Greil and Ruhsam 2012) and Rudi Laermans (2012, 94). These collectives, it is argued, demanded a uniformity of purpose in which people merged their interests in solidarity to achieve a common goal projected into the future, thereby failing to acknowledge the heterogeneity of participants and likely conflicts of opinion between them. Instead, compromises had to be reached to enforce harmony, and to merge participants into an organic unity with identifiable aims and interests.

I have no doubt that some collectives such as the Living Theatre, or those formed against the backdrop of actual communist regimes such as former Yugoslavia's Neue Slowenische Kunst (NSK), are fair objects of such criticism. However, it is less clear whether Rainer and her improvisatory Grand Union should be mentioned in the same breath as for example the Living Theatre (as Ruhsam does, 2011, 63, also 64–65). Instead, I would argue that alongside contemporaries such as Deborah Hay, Rainer paved the way for much current collaborative practice which emphasises the negotiation of personal differences between collaborators and the importance of process over product – rather than the subordination under a collective identity in the name of harmony.

This is especially the case in *Continuous Project – Altered Daily*, which was central to the Grand Union's development. Sally Banes' minutious description of this work recognises that some participants, such as David Gordon, were acutely aware of differences and 'conflicts in style, roles and aims' (Banes 1978, 45) during the project's evolution, and it was acknowledged that collaborators were, at least potentially, competitors.[4] Rather than promoting uniformity centered around one body or interest, Banes' description shows that the Grand Union had 'no goals, no expectations' (Banes 1978, 47). The group highlighted instead 'the impossibility of achieving a single, fixed way of looking at facts and behaviour' (Banes 1978, 48); and Rainer – in a spirit of non-hierarchy – underscored her desire not to be credited as the work's choreographer, calling for it to be acknowledged as genuinely multi-authored (Banes 1978, 45).

## Pina Bausch's postmodern practices

In Germany, the 'birthplace' of *Gesamtkunstwerk*, Pina Bausch's Tanztheater can be seen to align itself more directly with Wagnerian principles. It did so by blurring the boundaries between different artistic disciplines (encapsulated in the name of the genre itself), a technique of repetition akin to Wagner's *leitmotif*, and by a revaluation and integration of previously under-explored elements such as stage set and scenery, which became an integral part of the on-stage action. It is thus unsurprising that commentators such as the journalist and writer Suzanne Walther (1984) have repeatedly applied the term *Gesamtkunstwerk* to her works.

In the mid-1970s, Bausch introduced her inquisitive question-and-answer technique: a collaborative devising process which arguably promoted a genuine mode of social interaction in that the authenticity of life – snapshots drawn from the dancers' own biographies – conveyed and transcended real-life experiences on stage. On one hand, this takes Wagner's idea of a 'democratic' expression of people's consciousness to another level (as American postmodernism had done). On the other, I suggest that there are significant parallels (ideological if not explicit) with Guy Debord's theory – advanced in the epoch-making *The Society of the Spectacle* – which encapsulated the desire within the 1960s counterculture to reclaim 'authentic' social life as a remedy for subjugation under the capitalist yoke. 'Directly lived' experiences, Debord lamented, had been superseded by representation in an image-centred society (Debord 1994 [1967], thesis 1). Genuine activity and community spirit were called upon to counteract the 'passive identification with the spectacle' (Debord 1994, thesis 4).

Norbert Servos, one of Bausch's main scholarly commentators, uses remarkably similar vocabulary when talking about her works. Servos speaks of a theatre of 'authentic, subjective experience' (Servos 1998, 39) in which reality is 'tangible as physical reality' (Servos 1998, 37) and passivity in the audience is impossible. The viewer, he writes, 'is no longer the consumer of inconsequential pleasures [...]. He is included in a total experience that allows the experience of reality in a state of sensual excitement' (Servos 1998, 39). Like other commentators, he also applauds the biographical investment in her works as a strategy to empower the dancers:

> An ensemble knows more than a single choreographer can ever know. This method uses the knowledge preserved in each human

> body and brings it to the light of day. It provides every dancer with the freedom to find and present his or her individual experience of the world. It testifies to a deep respect for every individual, each having the right to exist in uniqueness and distinctiveness.
>
> (Servos 2008, 220)

But in contrast with Servos's positive appraisal, journalist Barbara Bogaev problematises the 'authenticity' that Bausch's method achieved:

> The Bausch Process required dancers to live together in the small town of Wuppertal and subject themselves week after week to Bausch's interrogations and commands—to copy someone else's tic, or do something they were ashamed of, or write their worst humiliations in movement. (One ballet superstar once explained why she would never collaborate with her by saying, 'I think it's like joining a cult.' [This was Sylvie Guillem, A. Kolb.]) But can you achieve transcendence without fanaticism? That question bores into your brain during every Bausch performance.
>
> (Bogaev, 2011)

I suggest that rather than speaking of a 'cult', it might be more fruitful to compare Bausch's choreographic approach with the principles of communes, which were much in vogue in 1960s and '70s Germany. Communes sought to reinvent interpersonal life, projecting a sociopolitical model of liberated society after capitalism that was both libertarian and based on grass-roots participatory democracy in involving every individual directly. 'Communal life', as Sam Binkley writes, 'thematised a narrative of self-transformation through learned capacity to release oneself into the authenticity of real relationships embodied by collective ways of living' (Binkley 2007, 184). The well-known German Kommune I in West Berlin, for instance, which was founded in 1967, counted some high-ranking artists among its benefactors and had links with the Situationist International, of which Debord was the *de facto* leader (Holmig 2005).

The communes' ethics of sharing, openness towards one another, anti-conventionalism and social cohesion, were also integral to Bausch's (and other contemporary performance makers') collaborative devising techniques. The centrality of talk and conversation, which took on a ritual character in commune life and crucially included sharing one's biographical identity with other communards, became a key component of Bausch's associative style. Yet there was a notable friction between the communes' benevolent motives and their practised realities. In hindsight, some members of Kommune I cast shadows of doubt at both the collective lifestyle and allegedly liberatory dimensions of the project. They criticised perceived peer pressure, tyranny of the majority, and the lack of any private space; the ritualised discussions even being described as 'psychoterror sessions' (Przytulla 2002: 206).

While I do not mean to equate Bausch – especially in her political views – with the extreme ideology of communes, there are clear points of comparison in some of the criticisms levelled at her practice. I recall one of Bausch's former dancers (who urged me not to disclose her name) revealing some years ago that she felt highly uncomfortable about the constant revelation of her private secrets and emotions, and left the company after a short spell. This casts a shadow of doubt over the democratic thrust of Bausch's works, and suggests that dancers might have experienced peer pressure when faced with rehearsal techniques which drew on the sharing of personal details. One could imagine situations where this could potentially be damaging to individuals, for instance when traumatic events such as sexual abuse or death come to the fore (especially considering that dancers are typically untrained in theatrical techniques such as method acting, which require reaching into and reliving their personal memories).

The 'experience of reality' (Servos 1998, 39) and authenticity, which the 1960s generation upheld as an antidote to a media- and image-dominated society, have become key motifs in late twentieth- and early twenty-first-century collaborative dance, and even in Bausch's later pieces which increasingly accentuated audience engagement. Direct interaction with audiences had always been a component of Bausch's work, with performers talking to spectators, inviting them to stand up and participate in little games, or offering them refreshments. But this aspect of her work became more pronounced when Bausch chose to work with non-professionals. For instance, *Kontakthof*, a piece originally created in 1978, was restaged in versions casting amateur performers from the local community: in one case aged 65 and above (in 2000), and in another teenagers (in 2008).

During a 2014 roundtable discussion on participatory dance at King's College London,[5] participants highlighted authenticity and the audience's social agency and empowerment as the primary motives for audience engagement. Tanztheater Wuppertal dancer Julie Anne Stanzak remarked on the identificatory function of choreographies where a direct link is made between performers and audiences by way of empathy, claiming that 'there is a oneness that happens' (Body Politics 2014). This suggests that by fostering relationships with (professional and amateur) performers and audiences, Bausch's collaborative techniques sought to reflect – in aesthetic form – ordinary people's realities, consciousness and concerns. Indeed, by blurring the boundaries between public performance and private life, she arguably avoided the co-option by elites that Wagner had so bitterly complained of, to an extent that even he could never have imagined.

In summary, Bausch's relation to the *Gesamtkunstwerk* is a complex one. Few dance artists have been as proactive in combining multiple genres within the same piece – film, dance, theatre, soundtracks and text. Yet Bausch's works present mere assemblages of various media and resist the creation of an organic whole in which every individual element contributes to a single coherent idea. Rather, montage and the discontinuity of plot and psychology of character introduce an element of alienation or subversion which – as it prevents a full 'totality' of the artwork – can be seen as somewhat anti-Wagnerian. Instead, the holistic aspects of her pieces can be observed in the 'total experience' (Servos) and the 'oneness' (Stanzak) her pieces offer, created through the collaboration of various participants – performers and audiences alike – in making the piece, rather than the seamless integration of the arts that Wagner had envisaged.

## Outlook on turn-of-the-twenty-first-century collaborations

Turning briefly to more recent developments, we can observe a further diversification of the trends that had begun in the 1960s and '70s. On one hand, technological advances have meant that the scope of the *Gesamtkunstwerk* has been broadened by bringing collaborative experiments into cyberspace. In *me and my shadow* (2012) by Joseph Hyde (dramaturgy Ghislaine Boddington), a piece which is both interdisciplinary and interactive, participants from various locations across the globe interacted in a shared online environment featuring projections and soundscapes. In an increasingly multicultural and interconnected world, interdisciplinary collaborations with artists from different provenances have also become commonplace. *Zero degrees* (2005), a collaboration between the two dance artists Sidi Larbi Cherkaoui and Akram Khan, composer Nitin Sawhney and visual artists Antony Gormley, is an apt example, being advertised not just as intercultural but as 'a seamless fusion of dance styles, music and contemporary art' (DVD cover, zero degrees). Cherkaoui explains that the process was about sharing, adding that 'if people were educated in those terms we'd have a real melting pit [sic] not a point of conflict' (DVD booklet).

However, while Cherkauoi emphasises harmony and shared experiences, the ethos underpinning many of today's other collaborative projects – especially those which take an explicitly reflective approach and emphasise an element of research – tend to eschew notions of unity and consensual agreement. This is quite in synch with the distrust of fixed identities and closure, and the embrace of plurality and diversity in much contemporary cultural thought, for instance in François Lyotard's writing on postmodernism. Consequently, much of the discourse on, and practice of, today's 'radical' collaborations emphasise problem-solving and negotiation of individual differences as opposed to seeking a consensus.

Martina Ruhsam's 2011 book, for instance, offers an informative, in-depth discussion of a number of such collaborative projects, which she argues often question their own practices and embrace, rather than deny, the participants' heterogeneity (Ruhsam 2011, 17 and 57). Again, correlations might be observed between such collaborative work and certain manifestations of democracy. However, rather than labelling these, as the choreographer Xavier Le Roy has done, 'a form of *direct* democracy, which is not dominated by one person representing the others and delegating the execution of his own ideas to them' (Le Roy, in Le Roy and Leeker, 2003, 98, my translation and emphasis), I would contend that the recently established model of 'radical democracy' is more pertinent.

Like most democratic models, radical democracy views people's free and equal participation in power as one of its key constituents. However, it differs from other conceptions: first, in emphasising the centrality of antagonism where conflict and the struggle for hegemony are acknowledged as parts of the socio-political fabric (rather than pursuing, say, a deliberative consensus); and secondly by its self-groundedness and self-constitution, meaning that there is no external legitimation and the power structure is open to contestation (from below) at all times – making it impossible to specify and cement democracy's true form. Today's preferred collaborative working mode is often seen to be 'post-consensual' as it allows for interpersonal distance and conflict negotiation while seeking new ways of working together. Like Laclau and Mouffe's model of democracy, it is 'no longer the expression of a totality which transcends it' (Laclau and Mouffe 1985, 191). Rather, it constitutes a contingent space in which conflicts, tensions and incompleteness – often previously seen as threats to freedom and stability – are accepted as the core of the democratic project. Correspondingly, Ruhsam writes that the political dimension of collaborative work may be found 'in the excessive production of differences' and its 'fragile, temporary and flexible' nature (Ruhsam 2011, 72 and 17, my translation from the German original).

Contemporary radical collaborations, the seeds of which were planted in American postmodernism's experiments with group decision-making, have thus moved furthest away from Wagner's idea of unity. The hyper-nationalism of the 1930s and '40s had issued a stark warning of the catastrophic potential of excessive demands for cultural cohesion. In twenty-first-century, Western multicultural societies, Wagner's perspective might be seen as suppressing the voices of dissenting minorities and failing to account for the specific interests of different ethnic, religious or cultural groups. Yet one must recognise that at Wagner's time, the discourse of unity held the promise of uprooting traditional autocratic structures and increasing freedoms, both political and aesthetic. As Laclau and Mouffe have stated, the 'original forms of democratic thought were linked to a positive and unified conception of human nature', and the public political sphere was construed as a space where 'differences were erased through the universal equivalence of citizens' (Laclau and Mouffe 1985, 181).

Yet even twenty-first-century conscious practices cannot escape a major difficulty with collaboration, namely the frequent discrepancy between the idealistic sentiments invested in collaborative approaches and their actual achievements. I have already illustrated this with reference to Wagner who in later life 'disavowed his youthful radicalism' (Koss 2010, 249), aesthetically as his visions of a total artwork proved too utopian to be realisable, and politically due to his disappointment with the German Revolution's failure and wish to return from exile. It was simply not in his interest to harp on about his earlier ideas. As for Bausch, it is worth questioning whether her collaborative set-up really fulfilled the democratic, egalitarian promise that commentators have assigned to it, or whether by contrast the criticism of 'enforced harmony' that has been directed at so-called artistic collectives also applies to some aspects of her work.

There are comparable inconsistencies between the benevolent ambitions and actual practice in some recent collaborations. As a case in point, Martina Ruhsam (2011, 67) cites the work *Collect-if by Collect-if* (2003), which involved eight dancer-choreographers who explicitly made collective working processes the core of their research. Despite their best efforts to adopt an egalitarian framework, Ruhsam remarks, the project's initiators Emil Hravatin and Bojana Cvejić were soon catapulted into a position of discursive power due to their superior communication skills and training, illustrating how difficult it is to avoid the formation of hierarchies in collaborative set-ups. In addition to the difficulties in navigating group dynamics, there are more general concerns about the positioning of collaborations within a neo-liberal climate. As I have argued in a recent article (Kolb 2013), many twenty-first-century collaborative and participatory works, which emphasise authentic experiences over 'passive' spectacle and highlight physicality and the engagement of the senses, in many ways resemble post-industrial conceptions of labour. Enshrined in a global consumer market, they often no longer fulfil the liberatory, politically progressive function that comparable pieces had in the very different econo-political context of the 1960s and '70s. Rather than presenting alternative societal visions, they can at times be seen to align themselves (even if unintentionally) with the establishment.

## Conclusion

The springboard for collaborative practice has frequently been a dissatisfaction with societal or political forms, which has gone hand in hand with a questioning of traditional artistic structures. The generation of new forms of togetherness has often been associated with revolutionary moments: the 1848 Revolution in Wagner's era, and various liberation movements of the 1960s and '70s. The correlation between artistic and political reform has thus remained a constant of collaborative practice since the 19th century, harnessing a politically progressive impetus of art which rejects egoistic aspirations and authoritarian structures in favour of what are seen as more principled production methods.

Artistic collaboration has in part mirrored certain forms of societal or political organisation, while at times projecting, or gesturing towards, more desirable future possibilities. Different models of democracy have been proposed which seem to correspond to distinct forms of collaborative practice. Wagner's main quest, politically, was for the founding of a democratic and united nation state, but his conception of democracy remained diffuse: as Christian Jansen points out, Wagner fused 'communitarian ideas of justice, an ideal of fraternalism which pays homage to a seemingly democratic, primordial Christianity, hatred against sovereigns, Luddite anti-capitalist tendencies, and a diffuse discomfort with modernity' (Jansen 2013, my translation).

Postmodern practices often reflected desires to establish an effective participatory, as opposed to representative, species of democracy. Shared ownership through shared authorship became one preferred avenue to identify alternatives to existing power structures in dance, although the degrees and quality of this ownership differed from project to project, and company to company. Pina Bausch, for instance, retained a clear authoritative voice over the final shape of her works in comparison with the more overtly non-hierarchical mission of *Continuous Project – Altered Daily*.

Despite the differences in collaborative working methods and the anti-Romantic (and indeed anti-Wagnerian) rhetoric evident in much twentieth- and twenty-first-century work, current collaborative practices can be seen to manifest the continuing relevance of Wagner's concept of the *Gesamtkunstwerk*: either positively by adhering to his principles, or negatively through a more or less conscious reaction against them. Over the last 150 years, Wagner's lineage has been established in an almost dialectical fashion: shifting from a proclaimed *unity of the arts* designed to avoid over-specialisation, to collaboration 'at a distance' (Copeland 2004, 246) as with Cunningham and Cage; and from the *unity among collaborating artists* witnessed in some 1960s collectives, to an increasing sense of separation between those who collaborate. This chapter has sought to show how, by reflecting different models of democracy, presenting alternative modes of working together, or narrowing the gap between art and life, many recent works have sustained Richard Wagner's ideological legacy. There is, for the moment at least, no real need to rescue his *Gesamtkunstwerk* from the rubbish bin.

## Notes

1. I would like to thank Peter Fribbins for his advice on an earlier draft of this chapter from a musical and compositional perspective.
2. In the light of later, twentieth-century events in Germany, many might associate the call for national unity with the subsequent historical experience of (extreme) nationalism. The contemporary situation was complex, though, in that the German confederation (1815–66) consisted of 35 monarchical states and four republican (although hardly democratic) cities. The objectives of the working class, who lamented their poor living and employment conditions, fell in line during the months of the Revolution with those in the middle classes who resented such hardships as feudal duties, heavy taxation and political censorship. Their demands included a national German parliament (i.e. an elected institution) which would more fairly and adequately represent the population and provide greater self-determination. This was a significant, albeit ultimately unsuccessful phase in which the building of unified

nation states was seen as a means of introducing democratic rule by liberal and progressive forces in place of subjections to older Empires and feudal aristocracies. The idea of nationalism as a peaceful and egalitarian doctrine was advocated in other countries too, for example by Giuseppe Mazzini prior to Italy's (later) unification (see Mazzini's 1860s essay 'Doveri dell'uomo', English title: 'An essay on the duties of men addressed to workingmen'). However, the German nationalist movement became considerably more militarist and aggressive around the time of Wagner's death.

3. See for instance Norman Brown, 1966, 119–20.
4. Admittedly, Banes writes that these conflicts were 'undercurrents' (1978, 45) and thus not at the forefront or an explicit subject of enquiry.
5. This discussion, which I attended in late October 2014, was entitled 'Body Politics' and presented by the London-based dance festival Dance Umbrella. Two panel members, including Stanzak, spoke via a video link from New York.

## Bibliography


Adorno, Theodor. 1991. *In Search of Wagner*. Translated by Rodney Livingstone. New York: Verso.

Banes, Sally. 1978. Grand Union: The Presentation of Everyday Life as Dance. *Dance Research Journal* 10(2), 43–49.

Banes, Sally. 1994. Sally Banes: *Writing Dancing in the Age of Postmodernism*. Hanover, New Hampshire: Wesleyan University Press.

Binkley, Sam. 2007. *Getting Loose: Lifestyle Consumption in the 1970s*. Duke University Press.

*Body Politics 2014: Politics of Participation*. 2014. Panel discussion as part of the Dance Umbrella festival. Chaired by Daniel Glaser. [Online]. <http://vimeo.com/110389152> (accessed on 2 November 2014).

Bogaev, Barbara. 2011. Pina Bausch. Posted in HiloBrow on 27 July. <http://hilobrow.com/2011/07/27/pina-bausch> (accessed on 2 August 2014).

Brecht, Bertolt. 1964. *Brecht on Theatre*. Translated and edited by John Willett. London: Eyre Methuen.

Brown, Norman. 1966. *Love's Body*. Berkeley, California: University of California Press.

Copeland, Roger. 2004. *Merce Cunningham. The Modernizing of Modern Dance*. New York & London: Routledge.

Cunningham, Merce and Lesschaeve, Jacqueline. 1985. *The Dancer and the Dance: Merce Cunningham in Conversation with Jacqueline Lesschaeve*. New York and London: Marion Boyards.

Debord, Guy. 1994. *The Society of the Spectacle*. New York: Zone Books.

DiGaetani, John Louis. 2014. *Richard Wagner: New Light on a Musical Life*. Jefferson, North Carolina: McFarland.

Ewen, Frederic. 1969. *Bertolt Brecht: His Life, His Art and His Times*. New York: Citadel Press.

Garafola, Lynn. 1989. *Diaghilev's Ballets Russes*. New York; Oxford: Oxford University Press.

Greil, Mariella and Ruhsam, Martina. 2012. 'I want to work with you because I can speak for myself', a conversation between Mariella Greil and Marina

Ruhsam. Videoskype session recorded for the symposium 'On Collaboration' held at Middlesex University on 4 May 2012. <http://dance-tech.tv/videos/oncollaboration> (accessed on 8 August 2014).

Hines, Thomas. 1991. *Collaborative Form: Studies in the Relations of the Arts*. Kent, Ohio: Kent State University Press.

Hobbs, Robert. 1984. Rewriting History: Artistic Collaboration since 1960. In *Artistic Collaboration in the Twentieth Century*. Edited by Cynthia Jaffee McCabe. Exhibition catalogue Hirshhorn Museum. Washington, D.C.: Smithsonian Institution Press.

Holmig, Alexander. 2005. 'Wenn's der Wahrheits(er)findung dient...'. Wirken und Wirkung der Berliner Kommune I (1967–69). *Kulturation. Online-Journal für Kultur, Wissenschaft und Politik*, 28 (3), <http://www.kulturation.de/ki_1_thema.php?id=88> (accessed on 28 October 2014).

Jansen, Christian. 2013. Komponisten-Jubilaeum: Wagner war ganz Politik. Im Dresden der Revolution von 1848/49 wird der Komponist zum Freiheitskämpfer. *Zeit online* 13 March. <http://www.zeit.de/2013/10/Komponist-Richard-Wagner-Freiheitskaempfer-Revolution> (accessed on 27 July 2014).

Kolb, Alexandra. 2006. Dance and Political Conflict: Three Comparative Case Studies, *The International Journal of the Arts in Society* 1(2), 17–21.

Kolb, Alexandra. 2013. Current Trends in Contemporary Choreography: A Political Critique, *Dance Research Journal* 45(3), December issue, 31–52.

Koss, Juliet. 2010. *Modernism after Wagner*. Minneapolis: University of Minnesota Press.

Laclau, Ernesto and Mouffe, Chantal. 1985. *Hegemony and Socialist Strategy: Towards a Radical Democratic Politics*. Translated by Winston Moore and Paul Cammack. London: Verso.

Laermans, Rudi. 2012. 'Being in common': Theorizing artistic collaboration. *Performance Research* 17(6), 94–102.

Le Roy, Xavier and Leeker, Martina. 2003. Xavier Le Roy im Gespräch mit Martina Leeker. Rahmen – Bewegungen – Zwischenräume. In: *Jahrbuch Tanzforschung* 13. Tanz Kommunikation Praxis. Edited by Antje Klinge and Martina Leeker. Münster: LIT Verlag, 91–105.

Lippert, Woldemar. 2012 [1927]. *Richard Wagners Verbannung und Rückkehr 1849–1862*. Hamburg: Severus Verlag.

Mallarmé, Stéphane. 1965. Art as Aristocratic Mystery. In *The Modern Tradition*. Edited by Richard Ellman and Charles Feidelson. Oxford University Press, 206–08.

Mann, Thomas. 1999. Leiden und Grösse Richard Wagners. In *Im Schatten Wagners: Thomas Mann über Richard Wagner; Texte und Zeugnisse, 1895–1955*. Edited by Hans Rudolf Vaget. Frankfurt am Main: Fischer, 150–73.

Mazzini, Joseph. 1898 [1860]. *An Essay on the Duties of Man Addressed to Workingmen*. New York: Funk and Wagnalls.

Millington, Barry. 1992. Gesamtkunstwerk. In *The New Grove Dictionary of Opera*. Edited by Stanley Sadie. London: Macmillan, 397.

Oosterling, Henk. 2009. Living – in between – Cultures. Downscaling Intercultural Aesthetics to Daily Life. In *Intercultural Aesthetics: a Worldview Perspective*. Edited by Anton van den Braembussche, Heinz Kimmerle, Nicole Note. New York: Springer, 19–42.

Przytulla, Dagmar. 2002. Niemand ahnte, dass wir ein ziemlich verklemmter Haufen waren. In *Die 68erinnen. Porträt einer rebellischen Frauengeneration*. Edited by Ute Kätzel. Berlin: Rowohlt, 201–19.

Rainer, Yvonne. 1974. *Work 1961–73*. Halifax (Nova Scotia): Press of the Nova Scotia College of Art and Design; New York: New York University Press.

Ruhsam, Martina. 2011. *Kollaborative Praxis: Choreographie*. Vienna: Turia & Kant.

Sayre, Henry. 1989. *The Object of Performance: The American Avant-Garde since 1970*. University of Chicago.

Schlemmer, Oskar. 1926. The Mathematics of Dance. *Vivos voco* (Leipzig) 5(8–9), August–September.

Servos, Norbert. 1998. Pina Bausch: Dance and Emancipation. In *The Routledge Dance Studies Reader*. Edited by Alexandra Carter. Abingdon, Oxon: Routledge, 36–45.

Servos, Norbert. 2008. *Pina Bausch: Dance Theatre*. Translated by Stephen Morris. Munich: Kieser.

Smith, Matthew. 2007. *The Total Work of Art. From Bayreuth to Cyberspace*. New York & London: Routledge.

Syer, Katherine. 2009. From Page to Stage: Richard Wagner as Regisseur. In *Wagner and his World*. Edited by Thomas Grey. Princeton University Press, 3–26.

Wagner, Richard. 1911. Mitteilung an meine Freunde. In Wagner: *Sämtliche Schriften und Dichtungen*. Volume 4. Leipzig: Breitkopf und Härtel, 343.

Wagner, Richard. 2012. *Richard Wagner's Prose Works vol. 1. The Art-Work of the Future*. Translated by William Ashton-Ellis. Memphis: General Books.

Wagner, Richard. 1893. *Richard Wagner's Prose Works vol. 2. Opera and Drama*. Translated by William Ashton-Ellis. London: Kegan Paul.

Walther, Suzanne. 1984. Expressionism is alive and well. *The Morning Call*. 16 September. [Online.] <http://articles.mcall.com/1984-09-16/features/2427572_1_pina-bausch-choreographers-dance> (accessed on 20 September 2014).

Woods, Lebbeus. 2010. Online entry on Gesamtkunstwerk. 7 September. <http://lebbeuswoods.wordpress.com/2010/09/07/gesamtkunstwerk-2> (accessed on 8 June 2014).

# 3

# I WANT TO WORK WITH YOU BECAUSE I CAN SPEAK FOR MYSELF: The Potential of Postconsensual Collaboration in Choreographic Practice

*Martina Ruhsam*

The title of this chapter is an adaptation of an assertion by the Bolivian activist Maria Galindo and could be understood as a motto for every self-determined collaboration in which the participants constitute more than the operative limbs of a collective body: 'I can work with you because I can speak for myself' (Galindo, 2005). Many contemporary choreographies are developed in collaborative working processes that are not dedicated to the realization of the ideas of one choreographer but rather emerge from the confrontation of the involved artists, the experimentation with their singular propositions and the interweaving of their materials. These practices are certainly not new, but artistic collaborations in the twenty-first century face specific challenges and problems that I attempt to disclose in this article.

Since the 1980s the context of productions of contemporary performances has changed. During the 1980s and 1990s the principle of coproduction for dance- and performance projects became prevalent in Europe, leading to an increase in the presentations of productions there (Freundt, 2005, p. 120). With a great number of festivals and institutions that were at least partly in pursuit of the coproduction model, a network of organizers and artists established itself that superseded the local attachment of an ensemble or artist to a specific institution.[1] The fixed employment of a choreographer or dancer at a given institution gave way for permanent collaborations. In contemporary dance (at least in Europe), the long-lasting and communal way of working in an ensemble primarily for a local audience became the exception. The ensuing multiplication of presentation and production locations seems to have coincided with a multiplication of artistic collaborators. Artistic co-workers perpetually work with/in different groups of people in varying geographical contexts.

In a collaborative process the act of choreographing takes place in the complex and often inscrutable processes of communication and interaction between those involved – processes that increasingly also evolve online and not merely in physical meetings. In the artistic collaborations that I discuss in this text, the question arises whether it is possible to work in a collaborative way that allows for a singularization of the participants. Such a collaboration would refuse both a hierarchical organization of the group and a collective way of working that presupposes the subordination of the members under the common identity of the collective. The former was predominant in modern and postmodern dance companies with one choreographic authority – as, for instance, in the Martha Graham Dance Company or Ultima Vez – and the latter characteristic of the artist collective NSK – Neue Slowenische Kunst.

In his writings about collaboration, filmmaker, writer and curator Florian Schneider argues that: '[w]hat is at stake is the very notion of establishing a new understanding of the term together, within a contemporary dynamic of working together' (Schneider, 2006, p. 572). I attempt to reconceive the notion of 'togetherness' by revisiting four innovative experiments or initiatives in the field of the performing arts: *Collect-if by Collect-if* (initiated by Bojana Cvejić and Emil Hrvatin alias Janez Janša, 2003), the platform *Sweet and Tender Collaborations* (since 2006, ongoing), the *Cooperativa Performativa* (2009–10) and the choreographic method of reformulation developed by Kattrin Deufert and Thomas Plischke (that brought about the performance *Reportable Portraits*, 2007).

The point of departure for my investigation of the specific potential of collaborative working processes in the field of the performing arts since the beginning of the twenty-first century starts from Jean-Luc Nancy's philosophical concept of 'being-with'. Nancy argues that 'being' is always already a constitutively social form of 'being-with' that does not presuppose a commonness of the group but rather exposes itself to the lack of the latter. Hence, 'being-with' is not envisaged as an amalgamation of individuals, but as a persistent sharing of meaning or, put another way, as communication – an approximation and distancing without communion or unification. Nancy emphasizes heterogeneity and separation rather than similarity, conformity and consensus (Nancy, 2003, p. 14–28).

Ensuing from this philosophical redefinition of community as developed by Nancy in proximity of and in response to the writings of

Maurice Blanchot, I will propose a model of post-consensual collaboration that foregrounds a communal way of working while the singular participants simultaneously claim a certain autonomy from within the collaborative configuration.[2] Even if I am starting with Nancy, the artistic methods and interventions are not discussed as examples of Nancy's theory. On the contrary, I attempt to put theory and practice (two fictional categories which are always already entangled) into a dialogue which reveals congruities, divergencies and contradictions. My aim is to elucidate the specificity of four collaborative endeavours that took place in Europe between 2003 and 2014, and the horizon of possibilities that they opened up as a result of the situations they established in which no ideological conformance was regarded to be the prerequisite of a collaborative working process.

In order to distinguish between the notions 'cooperation', 'collectivity', 'collaboration' and 'complicity', I will compare the artist collective Grand Union (an improvisational dance group that was active in New York from 1970 until 1976) with collaborative projects today – such as the research and performance-project *Collect-if by Collect-if* that was dedicated to the investigation of the phenomenon of collectivity as a specific collaborative strategy in political, social and artistic contexts.

Subsequently, I will collate the concept of 'complicity' as developed by the cultural theorist Gesa Ziemer, who since 2006 has been analysing artistic, scientific and economic projects as forms of accompliceship, with some theses on collaboration outlined by Schneider.

I intentionally refrain from thoroughly analysing the performances that were created by the initiatives and collaborative endeavours that I discuss in this chapter and focus instead on the instituting practices and specific methodologies developed by the artists in collaborative processes.

## The ethico-political dimension of being and working together

The Second World War hollowed out the meaning of the term 'community' thoroughly. It misused the notion as one that would connote a community of those who are unified in their subjugation under a common leader and whose affiliation is dependent on common racial attributes and certain criteria of fitness. In the war's aftermath there was an extensive and exciting philosophical discussion in Europe that tried to rethink concepts of 'community' by detaching it from the prerequisite of belonging to certain groups, nations, parties or other formations.

The protagonists of this debate headed by French philosophers were undoubtedly Nancy, Maurice Blanchot and Georges Bataille.

Nancy investigated the ethico-political potential that our being-with-one-another implies and pleaded for a community of people that could say 'we' without expressing any representational concern. The 'we' of such an unrepresentable community would be 'praxis and ethos' (Nancy, 2000, p. 71). He opposed a conception of community in terms of an intentional project of a social formation based on commonalities to be established in the future (a constitutive idea of National Socialism). The responsibility (also understood as an ability to respond) that is coupled with our co-appearance and the singularity of every other with whom we form a 'we' occupies centre stage throughout Nancy's writing.[3] Even if the 'we' that is outlined evades representational ambitions and tends to elude intentional and teleological acts of production (whether social, political or economical), it is at the same time always also instituted by the representative act of naming it such and can therefore never entirely transcend representation. Nancy proposes a 'being-with' that he delineates as a simultaneity of the different (Nancy, 2000, p. 97) and speaks out in favour of a 'with' that is not linked to any subjection under a common identity, ideology or intention. He envisioned a group of people saying 'we' without projecting an allegedly original unity into this personal pronoun. Nancy stressed that the one who speaks, does so in a singular way. With his suggestion to dissociate from all communities in the name of being together, he clearly affirmed Blanchot's understanding of what his friend Bataille wrote about a 'universal community', 'a community of those who do not have a community' (Blanchot, 1988, p.1).[4]

I argue that the artistic collaborations that I discuss in this text can be considered as attempts to investigate the space that I call 'outside-of-self'. If artists dedicate themselves to a process of listening, negotiating, discussing and sharing, they oppose the obsolete idea of the artist as an inspired individual imagined as the original and lone author of an artwork. By committing themselves to the singular encounters that will evolve in the development of the work, artists are rejecting this conception of the artist impelled by romantic individualism. The latter foregrounds the creative (and at that time so-called ingenious) subject with its ideas and capacities while it neglects or understates the role that the social and artistic context (as well as economic and political factors) play in the development of the work.

The ethical dimension of collaborations was emphasized by Krassimira Kruschkova in the preface of my book *Kollaborative Praxis: Choreographie:* 'The thought of the collaborative [...] has a weakness, a weakness *for* the potentiality of the other'[5] (Ruhsam, 2011, p. 13). And this belief or weakness in the sense of a preference is related to a commitment to the 'outside-of-self'.

The community as an 'outside-of-self' is for Nancy never a fusion of individuals but a 'being- with' of singularities. It assembles entities that are not closed and that are not signified by the relation to themselves. According to Nancy the singularity is always already the locus of a *with* and there is nothing prior to this 'being-with' (Nancy, 2000, p. 85). The singularity is in a permanent state of becoming and therefore open, a being that can never really become itself as it is itself already plural. Nancy even called the singularity the 'first person plural' (Nancy, 2000, p. 33).[6] If a group says 'we', we are confronted with an event of plurality that is reinvented in every encounter and articulation. The political dimension of working together therefore does not consist in an ideological (common) message but in the production of differences and in an uncompromising practice of negotiation and communication of singular plural authors.

## Grand Union

If we speak about the performing arts more specifically, it is necessary to differentiate between contemporary collaborative practices and the artist collectives that experienced their golden age in the 1960s and 1970s (as well as in ex-Yugoslavia in the 1980s). Artist collectives such as Grand Union or The Living Theatre were characterized by the long-term commitment of their members and often by a common socio-political utopia. For instance, the members of the New York City based collective Grand Union were in intense social contact over a long period of time. The collective consisted of a group of nine performers and choreographers[7] in personal union that presented improvisation-based performances from 1970 until 1976. Many of the members had known each other for nearly ten years by 1970. They had performed in each other's performances and most of them had studied with Merce Cunningham before they founded Grand Union and performed as a collective for six years (see Banes, 1987, p. 203). This is a long time span in comparison with artists today who work in collaborations that most often last for the duration of a certain project (meaning between one and six months).

Grand Union developed out of the work on *Continuous Project – Altered Daily,* a choreographic project by Yvonne Rainer that continuously changed with every performance. It was in this project that Rainer started to doubt her position as a choreographer leading a group of performers. The desire for a more cooperative way of working arose. She tested the combination of authorial instructions and the opportunity to make individual decisions. The well-known dance historian Sally Banes largely contributed to the historicization of the Grand Union's work in her extensive writings about the Judson Church Dance Theatre group. Banes explains that Rainer intended to experiment with the possibilities of choice on the part of the performers, giving them options to break a prescribed section, to repeat or continue a section, or to 'do their own thing' and to veto, as a group, the choice of an individual. She points out that Rainer claimed they could rarely reach a consensus on vetoes, however, and states that by the time of the Whitney performances, 'doing their own thing' was limited to one chance per person per performance (Banes, 1987, p. 206).

Artist collectives that were active in the 1960s and 1970s such as Grand Union, The Open Theater, The Living Theater, and The San Francisco Mime Troupe were mostly consensus-oriented. They were driven by a common mission based on shared social, political or aesthetic ideas and intentions (that were linked to a certain collective identity to which the individual members subordinated themselves). On the contrary, contemporary collaborative practices allow a plurality of voices and, more than that, strive to make this plurality of voices productive and heard.

A utopian dimension was underlying the aspirations of artistic collectives – the urge for a more communal way of working (and moreover for a more cooperative society) that would at the same time respect individual rights. Douglas Dunn (a member of the Grand Union) depicted it as follows: 'We made great strides developing a theatrical image-model of a possible ideal world, a viable heterogeneous social organism, one accommodating a wide range of individual rights, one knit together by a mutual search for appropriate levels of tacit contractual tolerance' (Banes, 1987, p. 226). However, this 'tacit contractual tolerance' was not without tensions, and problems arose especially when the members realized that they were regarded as representatives of others' work. Dunn described how the collective was torn between a social utopia and the complexity of the concrete working situation:

> To all outward appearances we seemed to be a happily married group [...] when in fact I believe we were continually uncomfortable with the work choices of each other (or some of us were, certainly) and the fact that we all seemed to stand for everything that each of us did. This got worse as time went by
>
> (Dunn in Banes, 1987, p. 227).

Rainer declared that in the Grand Union 'there were never votes, or anything like democratic process' (Banes, 1987, p. 230). But, the mere fact that the members of the group frequently performed together in improvised performances that were not defined by a choreographer certainly required a consensus on the basic rules of their improvisations and appearance. Nevertheless, this consensus seems to not have been ascertained by voting but apparently rather by a lack of objections.

## Collaboration versus Collectivity

The potentials and aporias of collective working processes were highlighted in a research-process under the title *Collect-if by Collect-if* that lasted from March until June 2003. Initiated by Hrvatin (who changed his name in 2007 to Janez Janša) and Cvejić, the project assembled eight dancers/choreographers that had all danced in successful postmodern dance companies with a distinct artistic leading figure (who made the decisions and ultimately assumed responsibility for the artistic product).[8]

In *Collect-if by Collect-if* the artistic responsibility was to be shared and different performers were to lead different phases. The working process and the prevailing questions are aptly documented in the publication entitled *Collect-if by Collect-if* (Cvejić, 2003). This is also the title of a performance that was developed by the participants of the research-process and that premiered in the theatre Hebbel am Ufer in Berlin in 2004. Particularly interesting in regard to my research is that during the process the group clearly distanced itself from being a collective and disavowed the term 'collectivity'. This was connected with the feedback of various performance theoreticians in response to their project proposal. According to Ric Allsopp, editor of the magazine *Performance Research*, for instance, the word 'collectivity' would be highly charged ideologically and could therefore only be discussed as a modus operandi in the twenty-first century. The term 'collaboration' would rather be associated with a potential space for the negotiation of individual differences. And the latter would be more interesting than the assumption of equality and the search for equivalences (Cvejić, 2003, Chapter 2).

Cvejić highlights that today's scepticism in regard to collectivity had also emanated from the aforementioned famous artistic collectives of the 1960s and 1970s. By combining liberal individualism with modes of collective work they, in her opinion, weakened the idea of collectivity:

> The dramaturgy of the ascending ritualist voyage of an individual within a collective, be it in the life of a tribal commune or in stage representation – as the theatre collectives in the 60s pursued –

> dissolved its own project of social and political change, because in the final stage of the process, it narrows it down to the abstract idea of individual freedom
>
> (Cvejić, 2005).

## The politics of collaboration

In post-consensual practices of collaboration what is at stake is not the fulfilment of a romantic desire for a providential being together or for a revolutionary overthrow of society. The main concern is rather the enablement of singular processes that are characterized by the polyphony of all, the access to different networks and the development of a common practice. The main problem in regard to the adoption of the artistic credos from the 1960s that came to the fore in resistant artistic practices and collectives at the time is the fact that these claims are by now perfectly incorporated into organizational management practices in late capitalism. In a radically different socio-political and economic context with new technological possibilities significant for the twenty-first century the challenges for collaborations have changed. In opposition to the rigidly organized and monotonous working processes predominant in Taylorism, the artistic critique in the 1960s and 1970s included demands for a breakup of hierarchical structures, more autonomy and self-responsibility for workers and more flexibility in work structures so that a certain degree of self-realization of the worker would be enabled (see Boltanski/Chiapello, 2005). Furthermore there were demands for more authentic experiences than those made by consumption and a resistance against the alienation resulting from the standardization of goods and work processes as well as from the transformation of everything into a commodity (see Boltanski/Chiapello, 2005, p. 427, p. 439).

In 2014 the perfect manager is expected to be able to work in a self-responsible manner, in flexible structures, to communicate and collaborate with various people and teams, to be creative and so on. New problems such as the total mobilization and exploitation of the self, the transformation of creativity to an economic factor and the hyper-production of communication have emerged. Against this current socio-political backdrop (see Raunig/Ray/Wuggenig, 2011), the question arises whether collaborative modes of working have lost their critical momentum. The discourse that has evolved around inter-subjective relations in favour of connecting people (especially in the wake of Nicolas Bourriaud's famous book *Relational Aesthetics*, which was first published in French in 1998) has by now become institutionalized. This can be seen in the increasing amount of symposiums, lectures, laboratories, publications and events dedicated to the topic. Hence, there is a danger and paradox if the texts and events produced resemble the narrative of creative capitalism in its praise of plasticity, fluidity, networking, collaboration, flexibility and so on. The shift from collaboration or communal work being a resistant strategy in the performing arts from the 1960s onward to that of collaboration being an essential component and requirement for new modes of production in the context of neoliberalism was outlined in a lecture by Boyan Manchev at the conference 'The Commons and the (Under)commons of art, education and labour' that took place in Frankfurt LAB in 2014.[9]

The artistic collectives of the 1960s and 1970s were bound together by the desire of the participants to emancipate themselves from the rather hierarchical ways of working in modern dance companies. Furthermore, there were common social or political agendas such as the resistance against the Vietnam War. Significant was a common belief in the possibility of a revolutionary overthrow of prevailing social and political norms and a shared faith in the importance of the role that art played in these revolutionary urges. Contemporary artistic collaborations in Europe have no such utopian braces, no 'collective' social or political intention which the collaborating artists would (want to) represent. Moreover there is no belief in any revolutionary effect that their work could unleash in a broader socio-political context. This, however, does not mean that contemporary choreographers or performers are apolitical or less political than their predecessors. With reference to Paolo Virno's reflections about the multitude (Virno, 2004), one might rather state that contemporary choreographers are at most depoliticized because their daily working processes already entail excessive politics. Today collaborating artists are not unified by one socio-political vision or the belief in a revolutionary overthrow of the prevailing political status quo and are not patronized by any authority. They are used to the daily negotiations of opinions, roles, modes of communication and rules of co-working that constitute a politics of collaboration. That's how they come into contact with the political dimension of their modes of working day after day in the here and now and have to repeatedly agree anew on the rules of a specific collaborative project.

## Complicity

For Ziemer a contemporary model of community and a subversive form of collaboration can be best expressed with the term 'complicity'.[10] Due to its criminological connotation the notion is often used as a pejorative one. Ziemer therefore tried to turn the behaviour of criminal accomplices into a productive tactic – regardless of whether it is about legal or illegal acts. Ziemer and her research fellows Andrea Notroff, Nina Aemisegger and Barbara Weber define complicities as allies of people who act together and are totally interconnected and intermeshed. Even if they seem to be loners, they never act alone; nonetheless they are not friends because they know each other only vaguely (Ziemer, 2006). The accomplices have primarily one thing in common: one and the same goal and the intention to profit from the complementary competences of the others. 'Complicity is business-oriented, because it creates a benefit for all the involved. In the ideal case the benefit is mutual and not at the cost of one party' (Notroff/Oberhänsli/Ziemer, 2007, p. 46). It is a 'win-win situation' – if I deploy the neoliberal jargon – that is at the heart of such complicities. In an artistic context, that means pragmatic, affective and temporary communities of purpose or cooperations without loyalty that would last longer than for the duration of a certain project. In the description of the research project *Komplizenschaft – Arbeit in Zukunft* [Complicity – Work in the Future] the difference between complicity and collectivity is depicted as follows: 'They [the accomplices] are always faster and that's why they are not interested in the slowness of teamwork or collectivity' (Ziemer, 2007b).

The subversive potential of a complicity can be detected according to Ziemer in the life of a community without any fixed location or any fixed concept of subjectivity (Ziemer, 2007a, p. 7). The slightly problematic aspect of this concept of complicity is its proximity to economic concepts of cooperation: namely the pragmatic formation of teams or alliances in order to accomplish a certain purpose over the shortest possible path. Even if Ziemer's concept does not exclude the possibility of using complicit tactics exactly in order to resist certain economic developments, I argue that in innovative collaborations in the field of the performing arts there is more at stake than criteria such as (economic) efficiency and effectiveness.

One possibility for undermining hierarchies, aptly highlighted by Ziemer, is the permanent alternation of roles in an artistic collaboration – resulting in the opacity of the structure of the group.

## Everyone's work points to someone else's

Florian Schneider, filmmaker, author and initiator of various Internet platforms, conferences and festivals, advocates the use of collaborative methods that are developed – in contradistinction to cooperative models – by people who can hardly be categorized and identified (Schneider, 2006a). In his opinion artistic collaborations have to counter 'what management theory since the 1980s has been promoting as team-work: the act of subjugation of one's own subjectivity under the omnipresent control regime of a group which has conceptually replaced the classical role of the "foreman" as the disciplining force. Rather than by repression, efficiency is increased by the collective identification of small groups of co-workers' (Schneider, 2006b, p. 572).

Collaborations may entail paradoxical or asymmetrical relationships that are not necessarily based on commonalities. They are propelled by the ways in which the contributing singularities affect each other. Emancipated from a merely utilitarian agenda, collaborations are constituted by interconnected singularities and networks that often do not evolve in established organizations or structures. I agree with Schneider that these impenetrable entanglements are not (always) oriented towards (measurable) exchange; they do not cling to an ideal of symmetry in regard to the input of several clearly identifiable (and apparently autonomous) subjects. Rather, they attempt to put into motion a chain of incalculable dynamics, ideas, associations and practices. This rhizomatic proliferation of thoughts and methods is enabled by flows which circumvent any fixed distribution of roles and any clear allocation of identities: 'everyone's work points to someone else's' (see Schneider, 2006a). The dynamics and accesses induced by a collaboration simply lack any transparency in terms of their origins or goals. Schneider notes that collaborations today are often not driven by solidarity but rather constitute ungenerous practices in which the participants are focused on their own interests and agendas while their dependence on each other increases the more they chase their own interests (see Schneider, accessed 2014).

Schneider's theses on collaboration differ from Ziemer's 'complicity' in regard to the value that is assigned to the product. Whilst Schneider concentrates on the process of the collaboration, the intended goal is central for Ziemer. The performance theoretician Bojana Kunst pleads for the emancipation of artists from the constant need for actualization. She argues that we are confronted with an exploitation of human potentiality today that has structured collaboration as a specific temporal mode where collaboration is linked to the permanent demand for actualization connected with an overestimation of the present (Kunst, 2010, p. 23–29). Schneider emphasizes the unpredictable and incalculable aspects of collaboration and refuses a utilitarian purpose. Ziemer, by contrast, stresses the aspect of efficiency and speed that collaboration makes possible. At last Schneider even defends collaborations for their own sake, which raises the question of criteria for the evaluation of collaboration and may collide with the aim of choreographers to present a performance at some point, but it returns a maximum of potentiality to a collaborative process:

> In contrast to cooperation, which always implicates an organic model and some transcendent function, collaboration is a strictly immanent, wild and illegitimate praxis. [....] It has no external goal and cannot be decreed; it is strict intransitivity, it happens, so to say, for its own sake.
>
> (Schneider, 2006, *The Dark Side*)

The precarious fields of artistic work that may also take place outside of institutions and that are often collaborative, have to be constantly self-organized and built up (not least because of their financial instability). They are spaces of possibility and sites of crisis at the same time. After all, permanent collaboration and miscellaneous linkages (and dependencies) are also a result of the permanent struggle for financial survival.

One example for an independent and self-initiated platform of freelance artists is *Sweet and Tender Collaborations (S&T)*.[11] Since its foundation in 2006, numerous meetings, events and collaborative projects have been organized and realized by the members who emphasize that they do not uphold a shared single artistic value or aesthetic. The initiative is based on self-education and self-organization and is actively engaged in developing alternative forms of artistic collaboration and production. It operates on the idea that any individual who can create the conditions for his or her own artistic production and development can also create the space for someone else. A combination of lengthy periods of work as well as temporary intensives with physical meetings have regularly been developed on all continents. Sweet & Tender meetings are all different in their structure, scope and public accessibility.[12] In the last eight years, various members have elaborated and presented performances in specific sub-groups.

## Cooperativa Performativa

Another unconventional way of incepting an artistic collective was the foundation of the *Cooperativa Performativa*. The collective was founded in 2009 when public funds were cut in Romania; hence, less money was available for artistic projects, which led to intensified competition among freelance artists. The Bucharest-based choreographers Maria Baroncea, Florin Flueras, Eduard Gabia, Alexandra Pirici and Iuliana Stoianescu adopted a communist attitude and decided to apply for subventions together and to eventually split the budget of received monies amongst themselves. The circumvention of competitiveness was not the only motivation for the foundation of the *Cooperativa Performativa*. The choreographers also wanted to test new ways of working together.

They decided to all work in one and the same space – with the aim that each of them would develop a solo. Their fusion was primarily pragmatically motivated and the members of the *Cooperativa Performativa* emphasized that the foundation of the collective was not premised on any utopian concept. The choreographers worked 'together' only in so far as they were sharing the financial and spatial resources. These working conditions created a situation in which the artists constantly influenced, disturbed, inspired, criticized, commented, helped and observed each other. 'We do not have any program or any obligations. Everyone does and proposes whatever he or she feels that helps his process. Each of us chooses how to use the interaction with the others and their proposals. This is the same offline and online', Florin Flueras stated in an interview (Flueras, 2010). The only consent that existed was that there would be no consensus in the group. The members of the collective were primarily concerned with the question of how to avoid endless discussions and negotiations in the group that would merely bring about the determination of the lowest common denominator. The premise that everyone should work on his or her own project and pursue his or her own interests and ideas was a way to avoid a common decision-making process. At the same time, the artists explicitly allowed each other to 'steal' fragments, strategies, materials and conceptual approaches from one another. Mutual contamination was not regarded to be dangerous (as is often the case in artistic processes that take place in the secluded atmosphere of a studio), but – on the contrary – to be productive.

One can construe the *Cooperativa Performativa* as a countermovement to the increasing privatization of public spaces and resources. I want to indicate the influence of open-source models for this way of collaboration. But not all the members of the collective would agree about that. In 2009 the five choreographers presented the *Cooperativa Performativa* in a lecture performance in the frame of the programming series 'Die Haut der Bewegung' [The Skin of Movement] in Tanzquartier Wien. When Florin Flueras stressed the affinity to open-source models, one of his colleagues commented: 'It's important that this is Florin's version of the Cooperativa!' Another member of the collective agreed and explained instantly: 'We don't necessarily feel representative for what he is saying – this Internet thing, for example.' In their performance with the title *(Re-)Challenging the Singular* they exposed the heterogeneity of the five choreographers and their dissent by emphasizing that no one represented the opinion of anyone else in the group. By contradicting and interrupting each other, they *staged* the fact that there was no consent about what or who the *Cooperativa Performativa* was and thereby represented a group that distinguished itself not so much by the similarities of those involved and their views but by their differences. By refusing any enactment of unity, they undermined the desire for identification and representation that is characteristic for many affiliations. As the group did not have a *common* goal that would have required a *common* decision-making process, the choreographers cannot be considered as accomplices in the sense of Gesa Ziemer's definition. Each of them tried to use the cooperative for his or her own agendas and to thereby benefit from it in his or her singular way. That the *Cooperativa Performativa* dissolved after the presentation of the five solos (in 2010) does not diminish the radicality and innovativeness of this experiment (but it raises questions in terms of the sustainability of such practices).

## The method of reformulation

Productive collaborative practices recognize mutual dependencies as unavoidable and positive. They distinguish themselves by the heterogeneity of the participants with diverse skills and flaws as well as by the circulation of roles. It is the singularity of all the participants that makes it possible to articulate together (with numerous voices) what cannot be subordinated to an alleged identity of the group or that is not reliant upon it.

In this respect the experiments of choreographers Kattrin Deufert and Thomas Plischke between 2001 and 2007 were especially intriguing and far-reaching. In projects that Deufert and Plischke realized in collaboration with other artists (for instance, the performance *Reportable,* 2007), they developed a method of collective writing and choreographing in which movement sequences and written notes are passed on to the other collaborators in silence in order to be developed further or reformulated by them.[13] This complex verbal and corporeal process of transmissions makes the attribution of the developed material to an author absolutely impossible. Apart from the micropolitical implications of their collaboration as 'artistwin', the choreographic method of reformulating and spinning out movements and thoughts of other participants enables a collaboration of equal partners. Nevertheless the collective aspect of the work is not defined through parameters like common aims (going beyond the project), similar aesthetic preferences, points of view shared by all or the equality of all participants. The commitment of all performers/choreographers to this shared choreographic method of reformulating avoids a hierarchically segmented labelling of the participating artists. It also avoids the ideology of 'anything goes' in which freedom is (mis)understood as an act of self-realization. Reformulations replace discursive processes of finding consensus or compromises, and the search for moments of relation shifts the focus from the performers' self-expression to choreographing a trace of connection lines. In a newsletter that was sent out by the two choreographers[14] they wrote: 'Reformulation allows because of its formal strictness and the silence during the writing as well as through the communication in the community of strangers everyone who is involved to participate and partake in the process that cannot be controlled by those that always [...] speak up first' (Deufert K./Plischke T., unpublished newsletter).

A performance collaboration is subversive if the participants are not the clones of one choreographic authority and do not perform a multiplication of the presence of the latter. Through methods of disidentification (from a *we*, that would strive to become a stable object of representation with a fixed distribution of roles) diverging ways of the enactment of a *with* can be elaborated.

If one succeeds in avoiding that the constitutive heterogeneity of the participants of an artistic collective is repudiated or ignored due to a need for consent, then fragile, unprecedented, unconventional and subversive collaborations may take place. In such a scenario of 'between us' forms of knowledge, abilities, affects and imaginations can be shared and woven into new sensual constructions and practices. These are choreographic challenges that are in the end linked to the question of how collective structures for singular plural articulations can be found or instituted.

## Notes

1. Freundt mentions networks of producers such as the *Junge Hunde*-network, the *Association of Performing Arts Presenters* (APAP), *Dance Roads* and the *Informal European Theatre Meeting* (IETM). Various other networks could be added to this list, for example *IDEE (Initiatives in Dance through European Exchange)* that was initiated by Tanzquartier Vienna and realized from May 2005 until May 2008 in cooperation with seven European dance institutions (see Freundt, 2005).

2. The *Unavowable Community* (Blanchot, 1983, *La Communauté inavouable*) was Blanchot's answer to Nancy's *Inoperative Community* (Nancy, 1983, *La communauté désoeuvrée*). Both thinkers were striving to undermine totalitarian concepts of community driven by whatever ideology – fascist, communist, communitarian or other.
3. Nancy concisely developed the concept of 'being-with' in his books *La communauté désoeuvrée* (The Inoperative Community – first published in 1983), *Ětre singulier pluriel* (Being Singular Plural – first published in 1996) and in the essay *La communité affronteé* (The Confronted Community – first published in 2001).
4. In Bataille's writing Nancy discovered a conception of (an impossible) community as constitutively open, an acephalic intimacy, a radically non-utilitarian undertaking without any leader. For Bataille, a community is not a work produced but rather the decomposition of national, socialist, communist and religious communities, the realm of an outside-of-self (see Botting and Wilson, *Bataille Reader*, 1997, p. 4–7, p. 121, p. 216 and Noys, 2000, p. 46, p. 51, p. 53–56).
5. Translation by the author. Originally: 'Das Denken des Kollaborativen – und dies prägt die Ethik der heutigen Performance-Praxis – hat eine Schwäche, eine Schwäche für die Potentialität des Anderen'.
6. Etymologically the word individual derives from the Latin term 'individuus' (indivisible) which suggests a conception of the individual as the smallest indivisible element of society, a kind of social atom. Hence, every form of individualism is committed to the numerical logic of addition: the sum of the parts (individuals) amounts to the whole society or community.
7. Trisha Brown, Barbara Dilley, Douglas Dunn, David Gordon, Nancy Green, Nancy Lewis, Steve Paxton and Yvonne Rainer belonged to the core group of the collective (see Lansley and Early, 2011, p. 154). Occasionally other artists such as Becky Arnold, Vicky Ruane, Valda Setterfield and Lincoln Scott also rehearsed and performed with the group.
8. Ugo Dehaes and Varinia Canto Vila had danced in the company Damaged Goods (Meg Stuart), Alix Eynaudi had been a dancer in Anna Teresa De Keersmaeker's company Rosas, Rebecca Murgi had danced in En-Knap dance company (Iztok Kovač), Katarina Stegnar had worked with Matjaž Pograjc in the company Betontanc and Borut Cajnko had been a member of the Ana Monró Theatre.
9. The conference took place from 29 May 2014 until 1 June 2014 and was hosted by the MA programme Choreography and Performance of the Institute for Applied Theatre Studies at the Justus-Liebig-University in Gießen. Manchev's lecture will be published in the forthcoming conference proceedings.
10. *Komplizenschaft – Arbeit in Zukunft* [*Complicity – Work in the Future*] was a KTI-research project of the Institut für Theorie (ith) at the Hochschule für Gestaltung und Kunst Zürich (HGKZ) led by Gesa Ziemer, conducted from June 2006 until December 2007.
11. S&T was founded by an international group of artists that were all recipients of the DanceWEB scholarship at the festival Impulstanz in Vienna in 2006. In 2014, it consists of about sixty artists.

12. In 2014 for instance S&T member Jenny Beyer produced 'Treffen Total Lokal' in collaboration with Kampnagel and K3-Zentrum für Choreographie I Tanzplan Hamburg. For one week 25 choreographers from Hamburg were invited to a shared working and learning space in order to train together, discuss ideas, test proposals and start spontaneous collaborations. The format of this laboratory was borrowed from the S&T meeting 'Treffen Total' that took place in Hamburg in 2010 where 30 members of S&T worked and lived together in K3-Zentrum für Choreographie I Tanzplan Hamburg for three weeks. They opened their processes periodically to the public. In 2013 the collective organized 'Sweet and Tender for the End of the World' in cooperation with Dampfzentrale Bern. It included a symposium (with interventions of S&T members) and the presentation of performances of some artists of the collective.
13. A detailed analysis of the method of reformulating and of the performance *REportable* as well as of the paradoxes of dissolution that are implied in projects with collective authorship can be found in my essay 'The Politics of Separation and the Aesthetics of Kinship. The Artistwin Deufert & Plischke and the Method of Reformulation.' in: B. Kunst (ed.) *Work and Collaboration Processes within Contemporary Performing Arts,* joint issue of *MASKA* and *Amfiteater*, Performing Arts Journal 25, 127–30 (Ljubljana: 2010), p. 155–74. Among other sources, my description of the method of reformulating is based on conversations with Deufert and Plischke and on experiences at the herbst academy in the framework of the festival *steirischer herbst 2007* in Graz, Austria. I participated in the workshop 'Kinship and other Monstrosities' held by Deufert and Plischke on the topic of collective writing, and practised the method of reformulating with the other participants.
14. Kattrin Deufert and Thomas Plischke sent out this newsletter in 2007. It has never been published.

## Bibliography:


Banes S. (1987) *Terpsichore in Sneakers. Post-Modern Dance* (Middletown: Wesleyan University Press).

———. (1993) *Democracy's Body, Judson Dance Theatre, 1962–1964* (Durham: Duke University Press).

Beck J. (1986) *The life of the theatre. The relation of the artist to the struggle of the people* (San Francisco: Limelight Edition).

Blanchot M. (1988) *The Unavowable Community* (New York: Pierre Joris and Station Hill Press).

Boltanski L., È. Chiapello, (2005) *The New Spirit of Capitalism* (translated by Gregory Elliott, London/New York: Verso).

Botting F., S. Wilson (ed.) (1997) *The Bataille Reader* (Oxford: Blackwell Publishers).

Bourriaud N. (1998) *L'esthétique relationnelle* (Dijon: Les Presses du réel). English translation *Relational Aesthetics* (2002) by Simon Pleasance and Fronza Woods (Dijon: Les presses du réel).

Cvejić B. (ed.) (2003) *Collect-if by Collect-if* (Ljubljana: Maska Productions).

Cvejić B. (2005) 'Collectivity? You mean Collaboration', Republicart Webjournal, http://republicart.net/, date accessed 13 January 2010.

Deufert K., T. Plischke, (2007) Newsletter (unpublished).

Freundt M. (2005) 'Komplizenschaften. Michael Freundt diskutiert neue Produktionsweisen sowie Netzwerke zwischen Veranstaltern und Künstlern' in J. Odenthal (ed.) (2005), *tanz.de. Zeitgenössischer Tanz in Deutschland – Strukturen im Wandel – eine neue Wissenschaft*, Arbeitsbuch 14 (Berlin: Theater der Zeit).

Galindo M. (2005) 'No matter how much you love me, I do not want to belong to you', *Republicart Webjournal*, <http://republicart.net> (accessed 9 February 2010).

Kunst B. (2010) 'Prognosis on collaboration', joint issue of Le Journal des Laboratoires and TKH Journal for Performing Arts Theory (No. 17), 23–29.

———. (ed.) (2010) *Work and Collaboration Processes within Contemporary Performing Arts*, joint issue of MASKA and Amfiteater, 25, 127–30.

Lansley J., F. Early, (2011) *The Wise Body. Conversations with Experienced Dancers* (Bristol: Intellect).

Nancy J. (1991) *The Inoperative Community* (Minneapolis: University of Minnesota Press).

———. (2000) *Being Singular Plural* (California: Stanford University Press).

———. (2003) 'The Confronted Community' in R. Young (ed.) *Postcolonial Studies*, Vol. 6, No. 1 (Taylor & Francis).

Notroff A., E. Oberhänsli, G. Ziemer, (ed.) 2007 *Komplizenschaft – Andere Arbeitsformen. (K)ein Leitfaden* (Zurich: Institut für Theorie (ith), Zurich University of the Arts).

Noys B. (2000) *Georges Bataille. A Critical Introduction* (London/Sterling, Virginia: Pluto Press).

Raunig G., G. Ray, U. Wuggenig, (ed.) (2011) *Critique of Creativity: Precarity, Subjectivity and Resistance in the 'Creative Industries'* (London: MayFlyBooks)

Ruhsam M. (2011) *Kollaborative Praxis: Choreographie. Die Inszenierung der Zusammenarbeit und ihre Aufführung* (Vienna/Berlin: Turia + Kant).

Schneider F. (2006a) 'Collaboration – 7 notes on new ways of learning and working together', <http://www.kein.org/node/89>, (accessed 7 March 2010).

———. (2006b) 'Collaboration: The Dark Side of the Multitude', in M. Narula, S. Sengupta, R. Sundaram, J. Bagchi, A. Sharan, G. Lovink (ed.) *Sarai Reader 06: Turbulence* (Delhi: Sarai Media Lab), pp. 572–76.

———. 'Collaboration – some thoughts concerning new ways of learning and working together', <http://roundtable.kein.org/node/525>, (accessed 5 July 2014).

Flueras F. (2010) 'Florin Flueras about Cooperativa Performativa' in V. Oberleithner, A. Ryszkiewicz 'Map it', *Corpus – Internet magazine for dance, choreography and performance*, <http://www.corpusweb.net/> (accessed 26 June 2014).

Virno P. (2004) *A Grammar of the Multitude: For an Analysis of Contemporary Forms of Life* (New York: Semiotexte).

Ziemer G. (2006) 'Komplizenschaft' (*Dictionary of war*, in the frame of the festival *steirischer herbst*), <http://dictionaryofwar.org/>, (accessed 15 June 2010).

———. (2007a) 'Komplizenschaft: Eine Taktik und Ästhetik der Kritik?' in J. Huber, P. Stoellger (ed.) *Ästhetik der Kritik. Verdeckte Ermittlung* (Vienna: Springer).

———. (2007b) *Description of the project Komplizenschaft – Arbeit in Zukunft*, <http://www.ith-z.ch/>, (accessed 3 June 2010).

# 4

# Since Each of Us Was Several: Collaboration in the Context of the Differential Self

*Laura Cull Ó Maoilearca*

In this chapter, I will try to develop a concept of collaboration based upon the discussion of two specific collaborative practices: the collaborative philosophy of Deleuze and Guattari, and the collaborative work of the US-based performance company Goat Island (1986–2009). Both of these practices are instances of collaborative-thinking; or better, perhaps, I want to suggest that whilst *all* thinking-practices belong to a process that tends towards collaboration on the one hand and subjectification or individualization on the other, *these particular practices* tend more towards collaboration than others – and not just because they involve more than one person. After all, why collaborate, if – as Deleuze and Guattari put it – *each one is already several* – or if the self, in other words, is already a site of difference and multiplicity? How can collaboration be conceived if 'self' and 'other' are construed as the *by-products*, rather than as the *basis*, for a more fundamental becoming, processuality or we might say, *collaboration* of all things? What specificity, if any, can be left for collaboration if we acknowledge that the solo artist or author was never self-present or self-identical in the first place? This is an issue that Patrice Pavis has also raised, arguing in the late 1990s, that:

> The cause of the current crisis in collective creation is not only a return to the playwright, the text and the establishment after the collective euphoria of 1968. It is also attributable to the fact that the individual artistic subject is never unified and autonomous in any case, but always disperse, in the collective as well as the individual work.
>
> (Pavis 1998: 63)

Here, I will suggest that Deleuze and Guattari are key figures with regard to thinking through the ways in which each of us is several, and offering ideas of what creative collaboration might mean and how it might work in the context of performance. Admittedly, Deleuze and Guattari's collaborative writings belong to what Pavis calls 'the collective euphoria of 1968', but they were by no means a reactive rejection of the notion of the unified self. On the contrary, their second collaborative text, *A Thousand Plateaus*, famously begins by reflecting on their first: 'The two of us wrote *Anti-Oedipus* together. Since each of us was several, there was already quite a crowd' (Deleuze and Guattari 2004: 3). Needless to say the notion of a dispersed self was hardly news by the late 1960s when they began to collaborate (let alone in the late 1990s when Pavis was writing), but more important for us here are the perceived implications of this 'fact' for collective and collaborative creative practices.[1] Does the dispersed nature of the self make collective creation and collaboration redundant as Pavis seems to suggest? In contrast, in this chapter, I want to propose that the differential self – a self preceded and ceaselessly (re-)constituted by its relations – requires us to rethink the concept of collaboration as relating to a spectrum or continuum of activities, which include works produced by individual authors, as well as those by groups. It demands a reconsideration of what we mean when we say collaboration is about 'working with others', in the contexts of both writing and performance-making. In order to undertake this investigation, I will be looking at the various concepts of collaboration explicated by and enacted in the work of Goat Island alongside those in Deleuze's philosophy – both in terms of his 'sole-authored' writings and those produced with Guattari. As I have discussed elsewhere, Goat Island have been explicitly influenced by Deleuze and Guattari's philosophy (amongst many others sources) in their approach to performance,[2] which goes some way to account for the compatibility between the attitudes of company members to collaboration and the resonance between the strategies they have respectively created in the attempt to affirm collaboration as a transformative encounter.

In turn, I want to advance the idea that we differentiate between what some (such as Pavis) have alluded to as the 'fact' of the individual artist's disunity on the one hand, and the persistence of 'the myth of the solitary genius' and the idea of the creative work as an instance of self-expression, on the other. That is, we will see how the (real) myth of individual autonomy is indeed something that both Deleuze and Guattari and Goat Island hope to dismantle through collaborative activity, but that this is not tantamount to a rejection (and therefore also an implicit confirmation) of a natural self-presence. At the same time, we will need to bear in mind the reality of the myth of the autonomous artist and, correlatively, the fictional nature of the differential self – which is to suggest the deep entanglement of natural and cultural processes in processes of individuation. In this sense, writing and performance are not just the products of pre-existing subjects – however unified or dispersed – but productions of subjectivities, plural.

Underlying the chapter are also some possibly unanswerable questions, such as whether – if *all* authorship is collaborative to some degree – there are still certain modes of collaboration (whether in the context of individual or collective works) which provide greater exposure to the unknown or to new thought. Are there ways of creating performance and philosophy in which we listen to our collaborators and 'encounter' their novelty more effectively than others; where we are unable to 'recognize' others according to existing categories of thought and, as such, stimulated to generate new ideas – to genuinely *create*, in other words?[3] Why make work with others if collaboration can occur and new thoughts can be accessed, in sole-authored projects as well – as Pavis, for one, suggests? Do individual and collectively made works both run the risk – equally but differently – of allowing us to keep the unsettling force of difference at arm's length, of capturing its unknowable affects within our existing ways of thinking and acting? How do we engage in collaborations in democratic ways that produce genuinely polyvocal results, rather than those in which one voice dominates or speaks on behalf of another, as Alain Badiou argues is the case in his critique of Deleuze (Badiou 1999)? But before we can begin to broach such topics, I want to start by trying to go into a bit more detail as to what we mean by 'the differential self': how and why is the individual self-differing according to Deleuze and Guattari? As we shall see, this perspective is not about doing away with notions of identity altogether, but of locating individuality in the uniqueness of compositions of relations and of framing these compositions as more or less open to change.

Ultimately, though, I am less interested in 'collaboration' as the name for a form of practice, and more interested in collaborative and individualist *tendencies* that might emerge in any form of performance. Even the most apparently individual or solo practice might in fact contain strong collaborative tendencies. The creator of a performance may not acknowledge the collaboration of the audience, but this does not prevent that collaboration from happening. And likewise, a project calling itself 'a collaboration' may nevertheless express individualistic tendencies; it might constitute a *working with* some, but at the expense of further extended collaborations with others. And who that 'some' is may not even be human – the possibilities of nonhuman or 'interspecies collaboration' (Jevbratt, 2009) with animals or objects being an important area of research as I will suggest at the end of this chapter.

## Deleuze, Guattari and the differential self

Like many other structuralist and poststructuralist accounts of human experience, Deleuze undermines any notion of 'the self', the individual or the 'I' as a self-identical, self-present entity. 'There is no longer a subject, but only individuating affective states of an anonymous force' (Deleuze 1988: 128), he proposes in his work on Spinoza; or again with Guattari, he suggests that 'the self is only a threshold, a door, a becoming between two multiplicities' (Deleuze and Guattari 1988: 249). However, his account of subjectivity differs from those other poststructuralists like Derrida, for whom it is arguably language, above all, which introduces difference into the self. Even in the event of hearing myself speak, Derrida suggests, my 'self' becomes different and delayed, I can never quite possess my 'self', my thought, my meaning (Derrida 1973). For Deleuze, though, language is not the *only* mode of difference. That is, while Derrida and Deleuze agree that difference comes before identities or selves (it is not that there need to be two self-identities that are different from each other), Deleuze wants to extend the analysis of that differential process beyond the domain of discourse or writing. In turn, he suggests that the self is differential because a human body, like any other material body, is a creative, temporal process; the changing product and producer of a life force that is itself self-different. In particular, Deleuze and Guattari suggest that life differs from itself according to two tendencies or two kinds of movement. On the one hand, life has a tendency towards increased levels of difference and variation. Another way to say this is that it has a tendency towards collaboration, towards greater levels of connection to others – a movement that we could also characterize as a tendency towards instability, disorganization, chaos and an openness to change. On the other, life has a tendency towards increased levels of sameness and stasis – a tendency that we might call individualization, but also sedimentation, organization, closedness to change (Deleuze and Guattari 1988).[4]

At times, for instance in *A Thousand Plateaus*, it seems as if life's tendency towards greater levels of openness to others and to change is deemed unreservedly 'good', whilst its tendency towards stasis and a closedness to becoming different is unreservedly 'bad'. But perhaps we might suggest that this was, at least in part, a polemical response to a specific political context, which insisted that:

> You will be organized, you will be an organism, you will articulate your body – otherwise you're just depraved. You will be signifier and signified, interpreter and interpreted – otherwise you're just a deviant. You will be a subject, nailed down as one... otherwise you're just a tramp.
>
> (Deleuze and Guattari 2004: 177)

Just a page later in the same text though, Deleuze and Guattari make clear that the tendency towards stasis is not all bad:

> Staying stratified – organized, signified, subjected – is not the worst that can happen; the worst that can happen is if you throw the strata into demented or suicidal collapse, which brings them back down on us heavier than ever.
>
> (Deleuze and Guattari 2004: 178)

Trying to do away with 'the self' or subjectivity altogether might have worse consequences than the oppressive experiences involved in having a fixed self or identity forced upon you, something we all experience to varying degrees in everyday life. Indeed, Deleuze and Guattari have argued that this tendency towards fixity or 'stratification' is often 'a very important, inevitable phenomenon that is beneficial in many respects' (Deleuze and Guattari 2004: 45). But although they acknowledge the *reality,* not just the practicality of such organizational tendencies, they also allude to their temporariness and to the perpetual susceptibility of organisms and subjects to being disorganized and reorganized once again. The process of getting away from fixity, from being organized as an apparently unified 'I' is never complete, once and for all.

So, if the self is characterized by these two tendencies, then what does that mean for collaboration? In the first instance, we might say that it impacts upon our understanding of the self/other relation that tends to ground approaches to collaborative practices, most commonly defined as those that involve 'working with others'. What is collaboration, in other words, if the self is always already *among* the other?

One way to go about responding to this question is to look at what Deleuze and Guattari have said about their own experience of doing collaborative philosophy. Deleuze and Guattari met in the summer of 1969, by way of a mutual friend, Jean-Pierre Muyard who was a colleague of Guattari's at the experimental psychiatric clinic where he worked – La Borde – and following on from an exchange of letters during the spring of that year. In the summer of 1969, they began working on the writing that would become *Anti-Oedipus*, their first collaborative text published in 1972. But as both Deleuze and Guattari have separately discussed, theirs was a kind of collaboration at a distance, and one based on a respect for their difference from one another, rather than by a goal to achieve cohesion or consensus. As Guattari put it:

> There is a true politics of dissent between us, not a cult but a culture of heterogeneity that makes each of us acknowledge and accept the other's *singularity*. We're doing something together because it works; something greater than ourselves carries us along.
>
> (Guattari in Dosse 2010: 10 – emphasis added)

And this notion of *singularity*, rather than *individuality* seems key; indicating a distinction between the latter as an individual person and the former as a singular, impersonal process that sweeps up individuals within it but is irreducible to them. Or again, another way that Deleuze and Guattari characterize the differential self is as a 'set of nonsubjectified affects' (Deleuze and Guattari 2004: 289), as a body with a situationally limited yet ultimately open set of capacities to act and be acted upon by other bodies in certain ways. As such, I would suggest that questioning the primacy of the individual is not about saying 'every body' is the same, but about thinking what makes them different or singular in terms of what they can do in specific encounters and relationships. When I collaborate with others (who are not separate from me in the first place) I have to acknowledge and accept that what they can do with and to me will differ from what I can do with and to them. What counts as a good way of working for me, may affect another body differently; what feels like an intolerably slow pace of working to me, may still feel too fast for my collaborator. What is singular too, then, is the collaboration, the encounter, the relation which can be more or less successful, more or less productive or empowering for all those involved.

In turn, Deleuze draws from his own experience with Guattari to offer up a concept of collaboration as *intercession* – a term which is usually understood as a kind of intervention or mediation, often with the religious connotation of someone who prays to God on behalf of another. With Deleuze though, intercession is less about the interaction between two distinct kinds of entities – such as God and man, where one transcends the other – but about the mutual interference of two singular, yet immanent ways of thinking and writing. 'Félix Guattari and I, we are intercessors of one another,' Deleuze says (Deleuze and Parnet 1987: 125) 'which is to say that each of us understands notions put forward by the other *in his own way*' (126). Here, Deleuze emphasizes that his experience of collaboration was not defined by transparent understanding or communication; rather, as Ronald Bogue articulates:

> The generative process of their collaboration requires an openness to the other's different understanding of a concept, and a subsequent development of understandings through a mutual undoing of each other's initial understandings. Intercession is a form of positive dissonance, made possible through an openness to interferences that disturb one's regular harmonic vibrations.
>
> (Bogue 2007: 14)

This is the collaborative tendency we introduced earlier – a willingness to have one's own understandings undone, an appreciation for the ways in which another's understandings of our ideas tells us something about the unstable, mobile nature of thought itself. And just as we might find greater degrees of this tendency at work in Deleuze and Guattari's collaboration in relation to other more dogmatic philosophies, I think we can also locate it within Goat Island's collaborative approach to performance. For her part, Sara Jane Bailes describes Goat Island as 'a collective that values the individual' (Bailes 2010: 11). But I would argue that Goat Island is a group that values singularity rather than 'the individual', and, that their approach to collaboration ensures that they are not just a collection of individuals (1+1+1). In a recent essay, Ric Knowles argues that collective creation in theatre constitutes one practical response to Foucault's call to de-individualization, presented as part of the Preface to *Anti-Oedipus*. Summarizing the text as a manual for living the 'non-fascist life', Foucault argues against the equation of political struggle with the pursuit of individual rights. He states:

> The individual is the product of power. What is needed is to 'de-individualize' by means of multiplication and displacement, diverse combinations. The group must not be the organic bond uniting hierarchized individuals, but a constant generator of de-individualization.
>
> (Foucault 2004: xvi)

But being a theatre group or artists' collective is not enough in itself to challenge the domination of individualized models of creativity. There is nothing intrinsically less individualized about a group, what matters is *how* the group (or indeed the solo artist) conceives and assembles its constituent parts. Next, I want to suggest that Goat Island's archive offers us a number of specific techniques for generating de-individualization in performance: performance exercises and methods that seek to develop a more unacquisitive or less proprietorial approach to thinking-practice.

## Constraints, incompleteness

First, we might think of what Goat Island called the 'Impossible Task' exercise – a well-documented and frequently used exercise in the company's annual summer schools. In this exercise, participants begin by writing down an impossible task on a slip of paper which they then pass to another person, whilst they themselves receive a task written by a third.[5] Participants are then invited to create a movement that illustrates the task, but without miming it. Here, as Bailes in fact discusses, Goat Island encourage participants to let go of any attachment or sense of ownership they might have to the instruction they have written themselves 'and instead accommodate an unknown directive' given to them by another participant (Bailes 2011: 110). In addition, the exercise also involves teaching the movement I have developed in response to my given task, to another participant again, and vice-versa, learning the movement that my partner has created in response to their task. Thus, when the time comes for the participants to show back their impossible task 'solo' to the rest of the group, what they actually perform is a movement they have been taught by someone else in response to a third person's response to the idea of an 'impossible task'.

On the one hand, such a performance might feel incredibly liberating. Given that – as many practitioners may have experienced at some point – it can be difficult to value your own ideas, the diminished sense of ownership for the movement material you learn and then perform may allow you to shift your attention away from worrying about the 'why' and to focus on the detail of the 'what'. The partner teaching me the movement does not tell me what impossible task I am doing, she just shows me exactly how to do it. On the other hand, though, one could see that, for others, this exercise might throw up a challenge to commitment. Why should I take care to come up with a 'good' impossible task (however we might value such a thing), if, once written, it is no longer my responsibility? How can I invest in learning and performing a movement if I am not party to the thinking behind it? One way to consider this issue, perhaps is through the notion of constraint – by seeing our collaborators as sources of much-needed 'creative constraints'. As the composer Igor Stravinsky once remarked: 'The more constraints one imposes, the more one frees oneself of the chains that shackle the spirit... the arbitrariness of the constraint only serves to better precision of execution' (Stravinsky 2003: 65). By constraining myself to copying as closely as possible a movement that does not belong to me, I may be freed from the alternative constraints that conscious intention tends to impose upon how I move.

In conducting exercises like this, Goat Island tend to affirm all responses to the task; if asked a question by a participant about how to interpret a certain aspect of the instruction, they tend to say, 'whatever you do will be right'. The difficulty, of course, comes in trying to differentiate between this *affirmation* of all responses, and a disinterested tolerance of any response whatever. Just because there is no way to get the impossible task exercise 'wrong', does not mean that all responses are equally 'good', for instance from the point of view of our own continuum. For example, we might assign less value to the response of a participant who superimposes her own habitual style of moving onto the learnt action, rather than taking the exercise as an opportunity to enter into a collaboration with another way of moving.

Goat Island's own collaborative processes are similarly challenging with respect to this valuing of the unknown. Take, for instance, the company's use of 'directives': starting points for the process of creating performance material, provided to the company members by their director, Lin Hixson (in a similar fashion to the way I am given an impossible task by another member of the group). As Hixson describes:

> Our process could be described as a series of directives and responses... I produce a directive. The members of the group present responses to the directive – acts in return. In response to the responses, I produce more directives.
>
> (Hixson in Goat Island 2006: n.p.)

But whilst instructive, Hixson's directives are nevertheless articulated in a poetic form that leaves them open to multiple forms of response; they are instructions that seem to divert us from doing what we are told because what we are being told to do cannot be pinned down. 'Create a shivering homage,' Hixson instructs (Hixson in Goulish 2000: 10); 'construct a last performance in the form of a heavy foot that weighs 2 tons and remains in good condition' (Goat Island 2009: n.p.). Clearly, to respond to such an instruction is not to execute a director's idea or command, there is no fixed and predetermined concept of what a 'shivering homage' might look like to which the performers' response must correspond.

Furthermore, Hixson also suggests that this mutually informing process of directive and response works best when material is shared at a certain degree of incompleteness or unfinishedness. She says:

> I learned early in Goat Island the danger of bringing completed thoughts and intentions into rehearsal. The attachment and preciousness that comes from perceiving a movement or a text as mine, halted the group process with its inability to let others in and my inability to let things go.
>
> (Hixson in Goat Island 1999: n.p.)

Sharing an idea when it is almost entirely sewn up is barely sharing it at all. Rather, tending towards collaboration involves taking the risk that others will understand 'your' ideas *in their own way*. Goat Island, Hixson says, 'have the objective of making performance works in an agreed atmosphere of trust and support. But the unintentional and intentional sit alongside this desire' (Hixson in Goat Island 1999: n.p.). Here the unintentional creeps into the process in myriad ways; it is not only that 'Cars break down. [And] People get ill' in ways that affect rehearsal processes, but also that 'someone brings in serious material [to rehearsal] but we think it's funny' (Hixson in Goat Island 1999: n.p.). In sharing an idea – some 'serious material', for instance – the supposedly authorial self confronted with its own internal difference, the irreducibility of its creations to its knowledge of, and intentions for it. In such an instance, the self tends more towards collaboration and away from individualization to the extent that it is willing to resist the compulsion to tell collaborators that they are 'wrong', that they have 'misunderstood' the author's creative intentions. And in this way, we can see how this notion of collaboration must also extend to the audience – who may or may not laugh where we expect them to, and whose singularity of response is also affirmed to the extent that the final performance retains that vital degree of incompleteness that Goat Island's works do.

## Conclusions

I am not alone, of course, in calling for an expanded definition of collaboration – beyond the conventional notion of collaboration as 'two or more people or organizations working together on a shared project' (David Henry in Finkelpearl 2013: 106). Already, particularly in literary scholarship, scholars have begun to question how we can maintain the distinction between collaborative authorship and related concepts such as influence and context, if in the end, our concern is with the forces that significantly shape the nature a creative work. Or again, we might suggest that notions of collaboration based on an emphasis on the definitive effect of *relation* on a creative work can no longer exclude individual authorship in the context of a *relational* account of the individual. For instance, Silverberg argues:

> What's most important is that more than one author has a defining role in the shaping of the text, so that the final work always results from some form of dialogue. This conversation may be highly structured and constrained by particular rules... or wholly spontaneous and improvisational, but in either case *the relationship itself has a defining effect on the work.*
>
> (Silverberg 2013: 2 – emphasis added)

In contrast, McMullan asks: 'How does one define collaboration?... As a text with two [or more] authors?... Or must we acknowledge a broader definition, which acknowledges a certain fluidity of boundary, and allows for inclusion of nonauthorial yet nonetheless shaping voices in the hermeneutic of collaboration, including various aspects of influence and environment?' (McMullan 1994: 140). Relation defines individual subjects and the works they create too.

Maintaining a broad concept of collaboration is not without its risks, of course. For instance, it might be that a broadened concept of collaboration leads us to neglect the specificity of differing collaborative activities (for instance, the difference between a process of 'writing together' that culminates in a text in which partial contributions are attributed to individual authors and one where only the final text as a whole is attributed). But this is an infinite specificity. Deleuze and Guattari collaborate differently in each book, Goat Island on each performance; attribution in collaborative writing operates both similarly and differently in Goulish's *39 microlectures* (2000) than in 'A Diluted Manifesto' (2013), co-authored by myself with Goulish and Hixson. Even within a single project, collaborative relations shift and mutate as a creative process unfolds. This is precisely their fascination. And yet, to expand the activities included under the category of 'collaboration', or again, to keep the concept of collaboration as open as possible, avoids reasserting distinctions on unquestioned grounds – in the way that the distinction between 'working alone' and 'working with others' tends to assume that the self is not also a kind of 'other'. The performative act of opening out definitions of terms is not against distinctions per se (on the contrary, it is liable to proliferate new ones), only a challenge to those that serve to fix processes in place for too long.

As Kathryn Syssoyeva has discussed, collaboration is still often 'presumed to equal discussion, debate, and subsequent accord, acquiescence, or synthesis' largely through its lasting association with New Left values of consensus popular during the 1960s (Syssoyeva in Syssoyeva and Proudfit 2013: 5). And as Mark S. Weinberg describes in many theatrical collectives of the 1960s: 'Decisions are made only when agreement is unanimous, and the strenuous objections of even a single member are sufficient to demand the reevaluation of any decision' (Weinberg in Syssoyeva and Proudfit 2013: 3). But although Deleuze and Guattari's collaboration emerged in the context of May '68, and perhaps would not have come about without it, their own approach to collaborative philosophy was by no means driven by a desire to achieve agreement. As Guattari put it: 'This collaboration is not the result of a simple meeting between two people. In addition to the particular circumstances leading up to it, there is also a political context. At the outset, it was less a matter of sharing a common understanding than sharing the sum of our uncertainties and even a certain discomfort and confusion with respect to the way that May 1968 had turned out' (Guattari in Dosse 2010: 34).

## A Non-human Coda

I began this essay with the already familiar insistence that collaboration cannot simply be opposed to solo or individual practice (whether in performance or elsewhere), since the solo artist or author was never self-present or self-identical in the first place. *All* practices are already collaborative from the start; they are already instances of processes 'working with' other processes, on multiple levels, various scales and across differing time periods. But whilst all practices are collaborative, they are not all collaborative to the same degree. Some practices do more than others to express their work as a working *with*, rather than as working alone (or a working *on, about, for*). And in turn, I want to suggest that we might assign greater ethico-aesthetic value to those practices which affirm this collaborative tendency in our current context, in contrast to an individualist tendency. Ethico-aesthetic because, after Deleuze, I construe both ethics and aesthetics as concerned with the composition of ways of living that are empowering rather than oppressive for all the bodies they involve (albeit that we must continue to remember that greater degrees of collaboration, higher levels of desubjectification can go 'bad' as well as do 'good').

As has been noted, the term 'collaboration' is most commonly used in artistic contexts to refer to working with other *people*, and to some extent this has been the focus of this chapter too: Deleuze's collaboration with Guattari, the collaboration between the members of Goat Island. However, I hope my account also implies the possibilities of extending the concept of creative collaboration to include non-human collaborators, in the same way as the notion of the differential self constitutes a critique of the anthropocentric notion of the autonomous person or discrete subject in favour of an idea of the self as the product of an individual event involving human and nonhuman processes. That is, I want to propose that we expand our idea of collaboration beyond any necessary constraint to working with knowing, intentional or rational others and to include our openness to being altered by the other material bodies involved in our processes. Rather than imposing pre-determined criteria for what counts as collaboration onto potential co-authors, we can invent new concepts of collaboration in response to new experiences of working together or 'in-between' those 'whose experiences, sensations, and knowledge is difficult or impossible to understand' (Jevbratt 2009: 2). Now, for some, this might seem to be an extension of the notion of the collaborative that risks dissolving its specificity altogether. Surely, if we extend the concept of collaboration to include individual practice and to include the ways we work with nonhuman others, then collaboration becomes a vacuous term, a placeholder for everything and nothing? And to some extent these doubts are justified, we must work with the singularity of specific collaborative practices in order to understand more about how, why, when, where greater amounts of collaboration occur. But without an expanded concept of collaboration we equally run the risk of failing to notice what the real stakes of working with others might be, and of limiting the powers of what collaboration can do.

## Notes

1. Collaboration and collective creation are closely related. As Syssoyeva suggests, we might define collective creation as 'the practice of collaboratively devising works of performance' (Syssoyeva in Syssoyeva and Proudfit 2013: 2). That said, the two terms are not synonymous and have their own distinct

conceptual lineages and associations. However, I began with Pavis' statement in order to introduce the oppositions of self and other, individual and collective, which I would argue also tend to linger in discussions of collaboration.

2. See Cull, Laura (2012) *Theatres of Immanence: Deleuze and the Ethics of Performance* (Basingstoke, New York: Palgrave Macmillan).
3. Here I am using the terms of Deleuze's well-known distinction between objects of 'recognition' and those of 'encounter' as developed in *Difference and Repetition*. Deleuze writes: 'Something in the world forces us to think. This something is an object not of recognition but of a fundamental *encounter.* What is encountered may be Socrates, a temple or a demon. It may be grasped in a range of affective tones: wonder, love, hatred, suffering. In whichever tone, its primary characteristic is that it can only be sensed. In this sense it is opposed to recognition' (Deleuze 1994: 139, emphasis original).
4. This is the way I choose to read Deleuze and Guattari's famous development of dualisms such as major/minor, molar/molecular, rhizome/tree etc. in *A Thousand Plateaus*. In other words, rather than seeing these as binary oppositions, I follow Mullarkey (2006) in reading them as tendencies.
5. When I first participated in this exercise with the company at a 2006 workshop, I received a piece of paper that read: 'Drill a hole in the floor using your body'.

## Bibliography


Badiou, A. (1999) *Deleuze: The Clamor of Being* (Minneapolis: University of Minnesota Press).

Bailes, S-J. (2010) *Performance Theatre and the Poetics of Failure: Forced Entertainment, Goat Island, Elevator Repair Service* (London, New York: Routledge).

Bogue, R. (2007) *Deleuze's Way: Essays in Transverse Ethics and Aesthetics* (Hampshire, UK and Burlington, USA: Ashgate).

Cull, L. (2012) *Theatres of Immanence: Deleuze and the Ethics of Performance* (Basingstoke, New York: Palgrave Macmillan).

———. M. Goulish, L. Hixson (2013) 'A Diluted Manifesto' in Causey, Matthew and Walsh, Fintan (ed.) *Performance, Identity and the Neo-Political Subject* (London, New York: Routledge), pp. 119–37.

Deleuze, G. (1988) *Spinoza: Practical Philosophy* (San Francisco: City Lights Books).

———. F. Guattari (2004) *A Thousand Plateaus* (London, New York: Continuum).

———. G., C. Parnet (1987) *Dialogues*, trans. Hugh Tomlinson and Barbara Habberjam (New York: Columbia University Press).

Derrida, J. (1973) *Speech and Phenomena: And Other Essays on Husserl's Theory of Signs*, trans. David B. Allison (Evanston, Illinois: Northwestern University Press).

Dosse, F. (2011) *Gilles Deleuze and Félix Guattari: Intersecting Lives* (New York: Columbia University Press).

Finkepearl, T. (2013) *What We Made: Conversations on Art and Social Cooperation* (Durham, North Carolina: Duke University Press).

Foucault, M. (2004) 'Preface' in Deleuze, Gilles and Guattari, Felix, *Anti-Oedipus* (Continuum: New York, London), pp. xiii–xvi.

Goulish, M. (2000) *39 microlectures: In Proximity of Performance* (London, New York: Routledge).

Goat Island (1999) 'Our Simplest Gestures: 6 short lectures by Goat Island', unpublished source, courtesy of the company.

Goat Island (2006) 'Part 1 - Reflections on the Process: Goat Island's When Will the September Roses bloom? Last night was only a comedy', *Frakcija*, no. 32.

Goat Island (2009) 'The Last Performance' website, available at: <http://thelast-performance.org/project_info_public.php> (accessed 1 November 14).

Jevbratt, L. (2009) 'Interspecies Collaboration – Making Art Together with Nonhuman Animals', *Interspecies Collaboration* website, available at: <www.jevbratt.com/writing/jevbratt_interspecies_collaboration.pdf> (accessed 8 June 13).

McMullan, G. (1994) *The Politics of Unease in the Plays of John Fletcher* (University of Massachusetts Press).

Mullarkey, J. (2006) *Post-Continental Philosophy: An Outline* (London: Continuum).

Pavis, P. (1998) *Dictionary of the Theatre: terms, concepts, and analysis* (Toronto: University of Toronto Press), translated by Christine Shantz.

Silverberg, M. (2013) 'Introduction: New York School Collaborations and The Coronation Murder Mystery' in Silverberg, Mark (ed.) *New York School Collaborations: The Color of Vowels* (Basingstoke and New York: Palgrave Macmillan), pp. 1–16.

Stillinger, J. (1991) *Multiple Authorship and the Myth of Solitary Genius* (Oxford: Oxford University Press).

Stravinsky, I. (2003) *Poetics of Music in the Form of Six Lessons* (Cambridge, Massachusetts: Harvard University Press).

Syssoyeva, K., S. Proudfit (2013) (ed.) *A History of Collective Creation* (Basingstoke and New York: Palgrave Macmillan).

# 5
# Collaboration as a Mode of Labour

*Noyale Colin*

In Volume 1 of *Capital* Karl Marx uses three examples of non-material labours: writing, performing, and teaching. Marx demonstrates that while the production of art could follow the law of value, he did not see it as being productive due to its 'microscopic significance' (Marx, 1990: 1044–45). When Marx was developing his theory of value in the second half of the nineteenth century, art could be seen to escape the capitalist logic of labour because of its relatively insignificant impact on the economy. Yet, from a contemporary perspective, the proportion of artistic and cultural labour in relation to overall production is harder to overlook. Indeed, creative labour is often considered to be at the forefront of a contemporary economy of services and knowledge-based industries. This shift, primarily rooted in the development of a post-Fordist capitalist society in the West, is the result of a transformation of labour away from manufacturing and towards an economy in which (non-material) services predominate.

In this chapter, I aim to develop a theory of the notion of collaboration grounded in the examination of the relationship between contemporary modes of labour and the current motivations of artists for working together in performance practice. To this end, I will refer to contemporary European choreographic practices; and in particular to *Six Months One Location* (*6M1L*) – an international project initiated in 2008 by the artist/choreographer Xavier Le Roy and the artist/theorist Bojana Cvejić. This initiative was established with the intention of bringing together a small group of artists committed to working full-time for an uninterrupted period of six months in the same location.[1]

In the 1990s, following the rise of the digital media and associated industries, including the commercial growth of the internet, a new mode of production was theorized by a range of post-Marxist writers. Part of the Italian autonomist movement, the theorist Maurizio

Lazzarato coined the concept of immaterial labour as applied to work mainly associated with the communication, information, service and cultural industries (Lazzarato, 1996). According to Lazzarato, a classical definition of the term immaterial labour originates as a way to grasp a change in the mode of production in which life becomes inseparable from work. Following the logic of immaterial labour, 'a polymorphous self-employed autonomous work' emerges, embodied in 'a kind of "intellectual worker" who is him- or herself an entrepreneur' (Lazzarato, 1996: 139). Alongside other autonomist theorists such as Antonio Negri and Paolo Virno, Lazzarato developed the claim that these new modes of labour are based on co-operative and creative skills. Together they argue that immaterial labour is 'a collective form' existing 'as networks and flows' (Lazzarato, 1996: 145).

In an attempt to theorize the *politics* of collaboration in the performing arts, it is tempting to correlate the autonomist definition of labour with the *promise* of collaboration within the arts. In the context of European contemporary dance, since the latter 1990s, there has been a resurgence of interest in collaborative practices. Influenced by the global spread of digital communication – and its role in opening possibilities for remote collaboration across time and space – there has been a shift, in Susan Foster's terms, towards 'choreography as collaborating' (2008: 25). Foster describes this shift as one that involves the choreographer becoming 'a manager of a career and of projects... [who] now 'leverages different funding opportunities in the same way that s/he facilitates the collaborative interaction among all participants' (2008: 20). The significance of digital communication in this development is evident in the strategies of groups such as the artist-led online network *everybodystoolsbox* which presented itself as an open source database for research and performance (Everybodys, 2009). Similarly, the international performance platform *Sweet and Tender Collaborations* is organized as a structure that is defined to 'exist as a myriad of individually produced projects' which is 'centralized only in virtual space and through a board of facilitators' (Sweet and Tender Collaborations, 2007).

Whereas such hybrid modes of collaboration might be reminiscent of the collective strategies of the Judson Dance Theatre in the 1960s, the contemporary emphasis on collaboration is not based on harmonizing collective improvisations, but rather on developing projects of creative cooperation. As highlighted by Rudi Laermans, such artistic cooperation requires the sharing of a common premise amongst collaborators grounded in the potentiality of the other and otherness (Laermans, 2012: 95). Similarly, this seems to be the core strength of the autonomists' claim that creativity and cooperation are key to depart from the logic of capitalism. As Negri argues, they imply an internal resistance to dominant modes of labour (Negri, 2008, 20).

However, as observed by the editors in the introduction to this volume, whereas processes of collaboration are generally considered to expand artistic fields of possibilities and resources, they can also be seen as a constitutive element of the contemporary global economy. Several theorists have identified the intermingling of a neoliberal agenda and artistic practices, noting the problematics of flexibility as imposed upon cultural professionals.[2] Whereas the pursuit of project-based conditions of artistic work and a freelance lifestyle were once perceived as a strategy against the standardization of artistic production, today these conditions are experienced by artists more as a restraining influence upon (or even as an obligation facing) the artist rather than as an enabling condition of artistic labour (Klein & Kunst, 2012). Such kinds of development invite us to question the extent to which collaborative processes in performance practice can be seen to challenge the 'project-driven' culture of performing arts.

In this chapter, with reference to a range of post-Marxist ideas, I will discuss the debate around the use of the concept of immaterial labour in relation to artistic practices. In particular, I will investigate whether the notion of immaterial labour is helpful for examining collaborations in performance-making, and explore the extent to which immaterial labour might be seen to resist dominant modes of working. In more precise terms, the inquiry will examine the distinctive characteristics of the labour generated by performance practice. Questions of artistic labour can be found at the centre of the critical and artistic concerns of the artists involved in *6M1L*. By focusing on the choreographic methods and techniques employed in the project, I will reflect upon the ways in which the collaborative practices of contemporary choreographers are shaped by the wider conditions under which artists are working and the conditions under which art is made at the beginning of the twenty-first century. In turn, I will argue that certain modes of collaboration, as typified by *6M1L* collaborative processes, can create conditions within which the capacity of artists' labour to transform the material of its production is enhanced.

## A politics of friendship: open-source curatorial approaches

The model chosen by Cvejić and Le Roy to form the group of participants for *6M1L* was influenced by what they describe as a 'politics of friendship' (Le Roy & Cvejić, 2009: 14). They adopted an open-chain structure, whereby they each issued invitations to two artists, and each of these four invited artists suggested one more artist to take part in the project. Cvejić and Le Roy intended that this method would avert potential drawbacks they associated with other strategies in collaborative group work:

> It is important to base the coming together on [an] affinity, curiosity and desire to work together, so an open call for participation isn't an option for it would emphasize the meeting and the mistake of collaboration [employing] the method 'we come and we see what happens'.
>
> (Cvejić & Le Roy, 2009:14)

Cvejić and Le Roy's understanding of the politics of difference points to a system aimed at ensuring the full commitment of the participants from the outset of the project. In *The Politics of Friendship*, Jacques Derrida asks us to reconsider the fraternalist configuration of Aristotle's politics through a philosophical reassessment of the notion of friendship: 'Let us ask ourselves what would then be the politics of such a "beyond the principle of fraternity"? Would this still deserve the name "politics"?' (Derrida, 2005: viii). According to Sandra Lynch, the main issue at stake in these questions is the Aristotelian claim that politics is the business of friends; and that like-minded men 'agree about their interests, adopt the same policy and put their common resolves into effect' (Aristotle in Lynch, 2002: 100). Drawing on Derrida's writing, Lynch highlights the tensions between the self and other in friendship. She argues that, 'the friend in traditional philosophical literature becomes an impossible ideal – a reflection of oneself and perhaps even of one's own narcissism – but never a threat, never a challenge, never a genuine other' (Lynch, 2002: 101). Derrida's politics of friendship, in contrast, challenges this mirror effect through advocating the importance of recognizing the different and separate identities of friends.

Returning to Cvejić and Le Roy's decisions concerning the selection of *6M1L's* participants, it is now clear that the assemblage of the group based 'on affinity, curiosity and [a] desire to work together' could signal a traditional view of friendship approximating Aristotle's 'like-minded men'. However, the strategic use of an open chain structure allows for an immediate broadening out of decision-making processes. This, in turn, is illustrative of Derrida's argument for difference and separate identities in friendship. The curatorial approach characterizes the collaborative formation as more of a networked structure than an open group of artists. Indeed, Cvejić and Le Roy define their curatorial method as 'the ethic of open-source' (Cvejić & Le Roy, 2009: 13).

The *6M1L* website indicates that the project revolved around a range of individual research objectives that participants were seeking to develop during the residency, which reflect a broader set of concerns within the European contemporary dance network. An example of these concerns can be found in Cvejić's earlier writing which problematized a perceived antagonism between theory and practice within the institutions of European dance education (Cvejić, 2007). Cvejić observes a change of attitude amongst dance practitioners in terms of the placement of greater emphasis on processes of learning over processes of production. This shift is further defined, she argues, as a 'learning how to learn in order to make', which is then associated with 'the type of worker in an immaterial economy of services and information, constantly producing outside of the (paid and recognized) labour-time, in a non-calculated productivity' (Cvejić, 2007). Advocating a new choreographic practice, which should stretch beyond critical theory towards a more experimental approach to 'researching conditions, methods and tools' (Cvejić, 2007), Cvejić cites the Danish choreographer Mette Ingvartsen's performance research, *Why We Love Action,* as an initiative which addresses precisely such questions of artistic labour with respect to the learning process. Ingvartsen was subsequently invited to take part in *6M1L*. Here, Cvejić introduces Ingvartsen's work in relation to her 'user-oriented recourse to theory' as a model of research for potential development in the field of performing arts (Cvejić, 2007). Cvejić expresses a form of affinity with Ingvartsen's work, and her proposal for a new approach to choreographic practice in relation to education and research informed the conditions under which *6M1L* developed. Therefore, it is evident that the collaborative open chain organization of *6M1L* – based on artists' 'affinity, curiosity and desire to work together' – itself rehearses the idea of a 'politics of friendship' (Cvejić & Le Roy, 2009). Furthermore, the 'ethic of open-source' adopted by *6M1L* can be linked to a wider interest in the possible application of open source methods to creative processes and products in contemporary choreography.[3]

If open source projects are a significant social and economic phenomenon, one of the major innovations implied in its model is a logic of collective action which, in the terms of organizational science scholars, 'requires that contributors relinquish control of knowledge they have developed for a project and make it a public good by unconditionally supplying it to a "common pool"' (von Hippel & von Krogh, 2003: 213). A number of applications of this ethic of practice can be found in the arts. For example, situated in the field of cultural research, *Network Cultures* is a recent international investigation of collaborative agency in artistic and cultural production which is partly built upon an open source database.[4] In performance, the application of Open Source Software concepts can be found in creative processes and performance products. Developed in parallel with *6M1L*, the internet platform *Everybodys* (2005) aimed at implementing 'open source methodologies' as an artistic strategy in the performing arts. The site provides practical choreographic exercises and games, performance scores, discussions and accounts of projects (including *6M1L*).[5]

These examples illustrate the potential of the open source model for the creation of new resources, promotion of the distribution of information, and the development of cross-disciplinary discourses. However, for theorist Scott deLahunta, contemporary choreography and open source methodologies diverge because 'dancing bodies are extremely complex in informational terms and will resist reified readings' (deLahunta, 2003). DeLahunta demonstrates his argument with reference to choreographer Jérôme Bel's *Last Performance* (1998) – a piece which illustrates that dancing bodies conform uneasily to a copyright entity as a creative ownership of the (bodywork of) the other is problematic. More recent choreographic gestures also explore the complicated dynamics between dance and copyright issues. Frederic Gies' project *Dance* (2006) provides an example of choreographic application of the open source method including the implementation of licensing. The score of the dance is available online to download accompanied by a *creative commons* licence. The users of the score become co-authors of the piece and can sell it or use it for commercial purposes without the agreement of the original author (Gies, 2006). If the use of scores and instructions in choreography can be traced back to dance practices in the 1960s,[6] an analogy can be made between software source codes and rule-based choreographic methods, where material produced by a performer is already 'over-inscribed' by the intervention of the choreographer.

Shifting away from the score as the notation of a dance, the choreographers' use of instruction can be considered as a tool during the creative process of a new piece. Similarly, Gies' *Dance* is not preserved in its open source format. The score is not used to restage the dance;

but is used instead to propose 'an interface between movements and ideas' (Moran, 2010: 17). Similarly, deLahunta frames choreographer William Forsythe's multimedia project, *Improvisation Technologies: A Tool for the Analytical Dance Eye* (2000), as a way to better understand choreographic process. An interactive CD-ROM is constructed around *building blocks* representing Forsythe's choreographic ideas. According to deLahunta, when distributed as an electronic document, the *building blocks* constitute, 'a form of Open Source code not only providing insight for those who wish to understand more about the process of making dances in general, but making the building blocks themselves available for anyone else to use' (deLahunta, 2003). This brief contextualization of the application of Open Source Software in dance shows that the model of collective action at the heart of its method provides a valid strategy for the development of a collective creativity in choreography. It is within this context that Cvejić and Le Roy's logic of open source is to be understood.

## Re-negotiating performance production through collaborative conditions of time and space

In *6M1L*, several techniques were deployed to encourage the artists involved to reflect upon their own projects and to offer feedback on those of others. However, a key element of the project concerned the way in which time and space were shared. A weekly schedule systematized the participants' time into three categories of activities: education, research, and production. Whereas mornings were dedicated to group practice open to the public, afternoons were organized into two separate slots of three hours for individual project rehearsals. An evening slot was allocated for 'sharings', discussion or further rehearsal. Group meetings between the participants and CCNM staff were scheduled at fortnightly intervals. 'Text practising' was another group activity that was prioritized as a way of engaging with theoretical discourse and to consider a text not only as something to be adhered to, but 'as [an object] standing between partners in dialogue' and allowing for 'thinking aloud further, and drifting' (*6M1L*, 2009: 151). The weekly schedule was designed to facilitate exchanges between individual and collective works; and following a logic of self-organization, it was regularly reassessed to ensure adequate space for both individual and collective practices.

For Cvejić and Le Roy, a central aim of *6M1L* was to establish 'special conditions in order to examine what they produce in terms of procedure, working methods, formats, discourse and ways of working together' (6M1L, 2009: 12). Cvejić and Le Roy outlined three of these conditions as follows:

1. Takes place in one location
2. Lasts the duration of six months without interruption
3. Involves a number of people who apply with a project of their own.

(6M1L, 2009: 12)

While the first two constraints refer to particular distributions of space and time (which are key elements in choreographic practice), the name of the project juxtaposed the conditions and thereby functions – performatively – as an instruction or a score to be activated. More importantly, these requirements of space and time signify a level of commitment standing in opposition to the demands of more flexible freelance projects. Indicatively, Cvejić and Le Roy locate their project in the midst of a contemporary debate around the process of interpenetration between economy and cultural system:

> 15 years ago, this fragmented lifestyle and work style was a choice. Nowadays, it's an obligation. *6M1L* is a way to challenge this 'liquid life' that's becoming the norm in contemporary society, constantly urging us to be more mobile, more flexible, to keep on changing and producing new things. These dynamics add to the precariousness caused by the requirement for rapid change, even though we don't have the means of changing the ways of changing.
>
> (Le Roy, 2008: 4)

In their writings on creativity management, Doris Ruth Eikhof and Axel Haunschild have examined working conditions in German creative industries, and trace the development of artists as 'bohemian entrepreneurs' who integrate artistic and self-management activities. Eikohf and Haunschild recognize that for such artists the point at which 'lifestyle meets market' is of significance (Eikhof & Haunschild, 2006).

In contemporary art, the debate around the notion of relational aesthetics developed by Nicolas Bourriaud reveals the ongoing division of views over the value of collaborative strategies in art and, more generally, over the role and purpose of art in wider society. On the one side, supporters of the positive 'openendedness' of visual arts argue for a new emphasis to be placed on 'the realm of human interactions and its social context, rather than the assertion of an independent and *private* symbolic sphere' (Bourriaud, 2009: 14). On the other, critics such as

Claire Bishop (2004) denounce a neoliberal agenda encompassing the appropriation of creative strategies for managerial purposes to the detriment of art.[7]

From the autonomist's perspective, new contemporary modes of labour are based on co-operative and creative skills including 'intellectual skills', 'manual skills', and 'entrepreneurial skills'. Lazzarato's immaterial labour is characterized by its collective and self-organized form (Lazzarato, 1996, 144–45). Under these terms it is difficult not to associate immaterial labour with the type of labour produced during *6M1L*. In addition to the residency arrangements whereby the boundaries between 'living' and 'working' time disappear, the notions of open source, self-organization and the politics of friendship veer toward similar understandings of production processes. The potential for collective creativity associated to the logic of an open source system was articulated by *6M1L* through the involvement and commitment of the artists to collective and individual projects. The collaborative focus within this structure is upon an interdisciplinary practice of choreographic research skills including intellectual and theoretical skills (collective reading of theoretical texts); manual or physical skills (daily practice sessions); and managerial skills (the ability to manage one's own work as well as coordinating the projects of others) – all amounting to what is currently known as knowledge transfer.[8] Similarly, the collaborative system of decision-making in operation during *6M1L* based on the idea of politics of friendship – or on affinity, difference and separate identities – forefronts the cooperative and creative spirit of immaterial labour as described by Lazzarato.

However, in some ways, Lazzarato's description of the *new* dominant forms of labour appears symptomatic of the form of labour that *6M1L* intended to challenge:

> A polymorphous self-employed autonomous work has emerged as the dominant form, a kind of 'intellectual worker' who is him- or herself an entrepreneur, inserted within a market that is constantly shifting and within networks that are changeable in time and space.
> (Lazzarato, 1996: 140)

This account echoes Cvejić and Le Roy's observation of an expanded system of project-based and freelance work as becoming a central mode of production in the performing arts. *6M1L* was defined in response to that situation. Furthermore, qualifying performance work as immaterial might only emphasize a problematic ontological conception of performance as the art of ephemerality and disappearance (Lepecki, 2004), and lead to an undermining of the value of performance as a material artefact and a product of the institution of performing arts. If immaterial labour is signalling a shift in contemporary labour production, to what extent can it be seen to resist dominant modes of exploitation when it has already been absorbed as a dominant practice of labour? How can artistic labour transform its alienated aspect?

For the autonomists, the labour of the contemporary artist is not separate from other productive labour because it has become emblematic of the changes of the post-Fordist labour process. In his article 'Metamorphoses', Negri argues that contemporary society has taken the transformation of labour beyond the postmodern idea of immateriality: 'From being immaterial, cognitive, affective, it is becoming ever more *bios*: it is *biopolitical labour,* an activity that reproduces forms of life' (Negri, 2008: 24).[9]

This shift is based on the assumption that in the post-industrial economy, production of commodities and production of life have merged. Artwork, therefore, claims Negri is – 'like every object of production' – a commodity and an activity (Negri, 2008: 22). In these terms, artistic labour can be associated with what has been identified as the 'affective turn', referring to the ways in which affective labour is bound to the body's capacity of affecting and being affected.[10] Negri's metamorphoses of labour leads to an ontological transfer in artistic production: from the ontological link to 'creation' and 'sublimation' to 'the power of being creative in the world' (Negri, 2008: 22). This transformation, in turn, allows Negri to deduce that 'artistic labour gains the *ontological relevance* possessed by all forms of labour in their creative facet' (Negri, 2008: 22). On the one hand, this thesis appears in continuation with the post-Kantian conception of the artist/worker in opposition to the artist/genius;[11] and on the other hand it foregrounds 'innovation' and 'creativity' in productive labour as 'something beyond measure' – or a 'creative excess' (Negri, 2008: 24). While Negri's specific reference to the ontological relevance of artistic labour within capitalist production is a way to emphasize the creative aspect of contemporary labour, establishing the impossibility of measuring the creativity of labour prompts him to make the claim for a new autonomous labour-power: 'Labour power as a free bird in the forest of life' (Negri, 2008: 22). In Negri's theory of labour, creativity is the key to depart from the logic of capitalism. For Negri, creativity implies an internal resistance to labour which then escapes exploitation. Immaterial labour finds 'an ethical legitimacy' by defining itself 'as forms of life'. However, 'Metamorphoses' – specifically focusing on artistic labour – does not provide any examples of artistic processes which might have illuminated the ways in which artists might create new 'rich forms of life' (Negri, 2008: 25).

In *Multitude*, co-written with Michael Hardt, Negri draws on artificial intelligence and computational methods research to develop an analogy between 'the new network political organisations' and the notion of swarm as observed in some animal behaviour (Hardt & Negri, 2004: 91–93):

> When a distributed network attacks, it swarms its enemy: innumerable independent forces from all direction at a particular point and then disappear into the environment. [...] If one looks inside a network, however, one can see that it is organised, rational and creative. It has swarm intelligence.
>
> (Hardt & Negri, 2004, 91).

Negri's new labour power can be organized in a way to potentially attack 'as something like a swarm of birds or insects in a horror film' (Hardt & Negri, 2004: 91). The 'swarm' refers to a type of contemporary labour based on a 'collective intelligence' emerging from the 'communication' and 'co-operation' of creative workers. Accordingly, Negri's theory of contemporary production – including artistic production – is based on creativity and co-operation and forms through collaborative modes of labour within the distributed and organized network (Hardt & Negri, 2004: 95).

If we return to *6M1L's* productions, can we find that its collaborative process produced something approximating Negri's 'rich forms of life'? It can, at least, be deduced that Negri's modes of labour are reflected in the formation of *6M1L* as a network of artistic affinities – conceived following an open chain structure with two initiators but with no central direction – and in *6M1L's* self-organizing operations for the sharing of space and time during the residency. However, if the process of collaboration of *6M1L* can be considered as in dialogue with some of Negri's theoretical positions, I will argue that it also problematizes the enormous emancipatory potential credited to contemporary labour by the autonomists, including its collaborative and creative feature.

## Re-assessing collaborative artistic labour

John Roberts (2008) emphasizes that artistic labour, and particularly its collaborative process, remains distinct from productive labour.

The post-Adornian labour theory of culture which Roberts offers casts another perspective on how artistic labour might maintain its critical identity and autonomy vis à vis post-capitalist systems of production. Through a discussion of Duchamps, the readymade and the commodity, Roberts posits that the capacity for artistic labour to transform the material of its production allows for artistic commodities to avoid being subjected to the law of value.[12] Drawing on Theodor Adorno's idea of the 'sensuous autonomy' of the artwork, Roberts highlights that the driving force of this process is the capacity of the artist's subjectivity to determine all the moments of production:

> What is purposeful about the labour of art is that it is transformative of its materials in ways that are non-subsumptive and non-heteronomous, thereby allowing the subjectivity of the artist to penetrate the materials of artistic labour *all the way down*.
>
> (Roberts, 2008: 87)

According to Roberts, the transformative process of artistic labour can be articulated by, '*a dialectic of skills, deskilling and reskilling*'. This accounts, he argues, for the misconception in post-conceptual art that deskilling represents an '*absolute* loss of artistic sensuousness' (Roberts, 2008: 3). Roberts suggests that, on the contrary, the presence of the hand in artistic labour 'remains key to the 'aesthetic re-education', and the emancipation of productive and non-productive labour' (Roberts, 2008: 4). This presence is vital because the immaterial production of art generates 'other, non handcraft, hand-to-eye skills' enhancing 'the totipotentiality of the hand'[13] (Roberts, 2008: 95).

If we consider contemporary choreographic practice within the context of post-conceptual dance, a parallel could be drawn between Roberts' idea of deskilling in arts after the readymade and the deconstructive process of 'detraining' associated with postmodern dance (Dempster, 2010: 235). In the 1960s, Duchamps' Readymade was a major influence on choreographic composition. Running, walking, crawling, and talking while dancing were considered as 'found' movements. This led to the use of pedestrian movements, instruction, score-based choreography and the rise of somatic practice associated with dance training.[14] In the context of contemporary dance training, the emergence of a tension between the nature of contemporary dance teaching and the eclecticism of the dancer's training demanded by dance markets has come to be seen as a problematic development. For Boris Charmatz and Isabelle Launay (2011: 95–97), this tension has led to a conflation of the

UNIVERSITY OF WINCHESTER
LIBRARY

knowledge of dance with the accumulation of skills which they describe as 'a collection of techniques'. In response, they develop a concept of 'undertraining' that would promote the physical and academic skills necessary 'to not merely suffer contemporary techniques but instead construct meaning'.

This approach is also characteristic of *6M1L's* collaborative practice. It is evident in the use of somatic practice for training or as a source of choreographic movement; the use of Feldenkrais technique as a group practice; and the use of the Body-Mind Centering® approach to voice training. In their collaborative approach to training, such practices resonate with Roberts' notion of reskilling. As the *6M1L* participant Eleanor Bauer highlights, training sessions were frequently based on the sharing of information brought to the class by each participant. Training was presented 'as an opportunity for any mover with any history of training to access and develop his or her own unique tools' (Bauer, 2009: 34). If the collective sharing of skills is in keeping with a politics of friendship, Bauer also highlights the aim – through collaborative practice – of diffusing 'the authorship within the group' (Bauer, 2004: 34). The claim that collaborative practice challenges the power of authorship is also developed in Roberts' foregrounding of the role of artistic critique of authorship in transforming alienated labours.[15] However, such calls for collaborative authorship should not be mistaken for a naïve attempt to democratize the arts. If, as Alexandra Kolb (2011: 27) argues, collaboration can be seen as a contemporary force of the global market, then the use by artists of what could be perceived here as alienated collaborative modes of labour would result in the deskilling of the artists. For Roberts, the *dialectic of skills, deskilling and reskilling* implies that deskilling in art occurs when artistic techniques are integrated with the general social mode of production. Whereas, in contrast, the process of reskilling develops through the acquisition of new skills, and emerges in relation to general modes of production, reproduction and distribution but cannot be fully appropriated by them (Roberts, 2008: 86–89).

As previously noted, the motivations which shaped *6M1L* are bound to a desire to shift away from dominant modes of performing arts production. This is primarily grounded in a concern with the freelance and project-based modes of working imposed on the choreographers. Similarly, the proposition to avoid hitching the collaboration to a symmetric reciprocity of exchange ('I give – you give') arguably represents a shift away from an egalitarian mode of collaboration (*6M1L*, 2009: 14). Instead, the collaboration focused on developing experimental techniques and skills in order 'to discover potentialities beyond the known competences' of each participant (*6M1L*, 2009: 14) – a process that I have defined as reskilling. The aim of sharing skills was not to find a common technique for the group but rather to develop individual 'unique tools' which could then be used and transformed within individual projects in relation to each artist's personal research questions. Therefore, collaborative authorship as practised by *6M1L* generates the reskilling of the collaborating artists. While this process involves a certain decentralization of the author, it does not eradicate the individual author. Instead, it offers the potential to locate authorship in relational terms – or what Roberts calls 'expanded authorship' (Roberts, 2008: 123). However, when looking back at the final pieces produced after *6M1L* residencies, as these were located within contemporary modes of distribution (i.e. in website and press reviews), the body of work does not illuminate this expanded authorship. The collaborative process is made invisible for the spectator. Each individual work bears the name of a single artist with only rare references made to *6M1L*.

In *Low Pieces* (2009–2011), Le Roy's choreographic research explores human conditions in relation to three binary divisions: object/subject, human/non-human, and nature/culture. *Low Pieces* emerged from *6M1L* and I was fortunate to experience the work at the Royal Festival Hall in London in 2010. The piece is developed in a series of three tableaux presented as a landscape of bodies and groups moving in exploration of the relationship between machine, 'animal' behaviours and the state of contemplation. The juxtaposition of these different worlds – mechanical, animal, vegetal – evokes different modes of being in the world. In his review of the piece, dance critic Maxime Fleuriot (2011) associates the work to Le Roy's previous choreographic theme: 'Xavier Le Roy thus plays on our senses and *once again* [my emphasis] questions in this creation the way we perceive a body.' This observation refers to the recognition by Fleuriot of a signature, which is here associated to the name of Xavier Le Roy.

Susan Melrose (2009), in her inquiry into 'signature', offers important insights into what the nominative aspect of artistic signature might mean and how it might be theorized in the context of expert arts practice. Melrose observes that in 'signature practices', the name does not 'simply' signalize 'notable practices', but it refers to 'the quality of those signature practices through which the name has achieved its professional as well as aesthetic significance for us' (Melrose, 2009). After pointing out that signature refers to the making of a judgement, she highlights that signature is 'relational and not simply immanent to the "work itself"' (Melrose, 2009). Here Melrose suggests another type of relationality for the artistic practice of expanded authorship, in that signature practices are partly constituted in relation to the 'responses of the wider arts communities'.

If Le Roy's signature thus operates as, in Roberts' term, a *necessary* relation with general social practice, Le Roy does not claim the choreography of the piece but only its conception. Indeed, nobody is credited for the choreography which might represent a hidden recognition of its collaborative aspects. In addition, the practice of crediting the conception of an artwork is often found in visual art when a division of labour has occurred. Similarly, the term 'conception' is also frequently used in multi-disciplinary, large-scale performance. Rarely employed in dance presentations, Le Roy's signature, while implicitly implying an expanded authorship, demonstrates the potential of the transformation of artistic labour, *all the way down.*

At the level of reception and presentation, the collaborative aspect of *Low Pieces* has disappeared but its signature points to 'a relational mark', which recurs, in Melrose's terms, 'across a body of work and between that work and its contextualising framework/s' (Melrose, 2007). For example, one cannot ignore Le Roy's academic background in molecular biology when associating his work to questions of the perception of the body. Similarly, his playful investigation of notions of authorship and ownership in his collaboration with Bel, entitled, *Xavier Le Roy: A Performance By Jérôme Bel* (2000) – claimed by Bel as his own but choreographed and conceived by Le Roy – is relevant when assessing Le Roy's choice to sign only the conception of *Low Pieces*. What Melrose's notion of signature of practice helps to illuminate is that it refers to '*a way of working* that is specific to a particular artist' (Melrose, 2009). In the case of Le Roy, this might imply an experimental, conceptual and often collaborative way of working.

This returns us to the issue of subjectivity in artistic labour and how the focus on individual development in collaboration, through its potential of transformation *all the way down*, leads to the emancipation of its mode of labour. We find in Roberts' emphasis on the 'totipotentiality' of the hand that artistic autonomy is assured by the reflective power of the author to make manifest 'world knowledge' – empirical knowledge based in senses and gained 'laboriously' – through the presence of the hand. He identifies this process as 'aesthetic thinking'.[16] In the context of performing arts, aesthetic thinking is a process of ongoing decision-making related to knowledge which is specific to performance practice expertise. This mode of thinking implies a judgement of expertise by performance makers informed by 'world knowledge', which in this instance, includes a heightened sense of proprioceptive, tactile and visceral sensibility (Massumi, 2002: 58–59). It operates often collaboratively and in relation to the economy of production particular to the making of the work which is qualitatively transformed by the artists' '*singular* ways of seeing, doing and knowing' (Melrose, 2009). For example, Le Roy's individual project developed during *6M1L* was concerned with issues of representation specific to the field of performance. Using the analogy of a performance as a zoo, he argues for an inversion of the role of spectators whom, he claims, are too eager to see (Le Roy in Kurdian, 2009). Le Roy stated his interest in the idea of landscape in relation to contemplation, or in doing, 'something which is given to contemplate and not something that is given to follow, to look at' (Le Roy in Kurdian, 2009). Although Le Roy's critique of the avid onlooker points to the notion of the 'male gaze', traditionally articulated as part of a critical-theorist discourse, what is interesting here is how Le Roy makes reference to it from the outset of his choreographic project.[17] In these terms, as is common in the working of creative practitioners, theory does not enter at the point of reflection upon work already made (by others), but rather at a different point as a means to inform and stimulate a singular way of working and, in turn, to inform compositional decisions. This was evident in Le Roy's use of time in the choreography of *Low Pieces*.

As an audience member, I experienced a number of compositional elements, which played with my gazing at the performers. For example, in the first tableau, on the floor, a group of five naked performers wearing headphones move individually in a mechanical way to a rhythm that spectators cannot hear; their precisely performed gestures seem to have been reduced to an automatically executed gesticulation. This section lasts for twenty minutes on a fully lit and bare stage without any space changes. This opening scene (which follows fifteen minutes of black out) initially sets the conditions for a scopophilic gaze. However, over time, and in the absence of scenography and sound, I am forced to watch the performers in terms of the duration and repetitive rhythm of their small gestures. The particular act of watching through time requested from the audience constitutes the basis for time to be considered as a central ontological characteristic of performance, but also foregrounds the theoretical understanding that time – when perceived in its continuity – can induce the nature of the gaze to change. At the same time that the composition puts forward 'the body' as the only thing to see on stage; with time, as Derrida suggested in another context, there is 'nothing to see' (Derrida, 1992: 6).

Such accounts give us an insight into Negri's 'rich forms of life' emerging from creative production, and how the process of complex labour – understood as ongoing decision-making – involved in performance-related artistic productions, and articulated by Melrose (2003) as 'performance mastery', resists the determined alienated type of labour characteristic of productive labour. If this is the result of a process of infiltration by the subjective skills of the performance maker into the material of his/her production, the way in which a new work emerges is often bound to a movement of collective thinking. By which I mean that the process of performance making in its multi-participant aspects emphasizes the relationship between individual and collective thinking. The negotiation of this relationship is constitutive of performance mastery, which here includes collaborative skills. *6M1L's* subscription to a *collaborative process* represents a resistance to determinism: its outcome cannot be individually imagined; it cannot be predetermined, but must be uncovered collectively in the practice. Similarly, *6M1L* points to a collaborative process rather than a collaborative product, or the idea as articulated by Ingvartsen of 'practicing performance without actually making one' (Ingvartsen, 2009: 154).

As sociologist Karin Knorr Cetina points out in another context, performance can be defined by its 'lack of completeness of being'. Its processes of production 'must simultaneously be conceived as unfolding structures of absences' (Knorr Cetina, 2001: 528). What is important to note here is that it is within these gaps that the future work finds its force. Each 'failure' to complete an idea feeds back into the development of the artist's research inquiry which unfolds across his/her body of work. Whereas Roberts argues that artistic autonomy consists in the capacity of the artists' subjectivity to determine the central moments of production, we have seen that the modes of practice specific to performance mastery – grounded in the artist's '*singular* ways of seeing, doing and knowing' the world – are constitutive of an aesthetic thinking which always operates according to a logic of production bound to its 'unfolding ontology' (Knorr Cetina, 2001: 191). It is in these terms that collaborative practice can begin to create the expansion of performance mastery and might subsequently resist alienated modes of labour. However, as previously discussed, collaborative work runs the risk of being subsumed under a dominant logic of production. Therefore, the capacity of the type of labour generated by *6M1L* for resisting the dominant mode of labour – characterized in this instance by alienating experiences of time and place – can only be assessed in relationship to its power of transformation, *all the way down*. In summary, I set out below a number of elements which in this sense appear as central to contemporary collaborative processes of transformation in performance practice:

**1. Reciprocal modulated systems**

Systematic arrangements of time and space in collaborative performance practice allow a renegotiation of the logics of production, which is both modulated by the needs of the artists at the time of the making process, but also modulates the creative process by the enforcement of its specific conditions of production.

**2. Economy of affect**

This post-Marxist approach to collaborative labour in performance practice draws on the skills attributed to affective labour, referred to as the ability to affect and be affected. In current performance practices the influence of the politics of friendship – concerned with artistic affinities – in conjunction with the open logic of sharing information and skills, forefronts the subjectivity of each artist. Through a collective process, it is at the level of individual subjectivity that a transformation is expected.

**3. Reflective authorship**

The underlying dialogue with theoretical ideas in contemporary performance (which was evident in the collaborative process of *6M1L*) contributes towards an individualized theorization, *through practice*, of aesthetic thinking processes. By which I mean that the creative process in operation during *6M1L* allowed for the location of artists' signatures in relational terms, but was bound to the skills of the individual artist to reflectively think through his/her decisions in his/her own terms.

**4. Reskilling performance mastery**

Physical collaborative training in performance practice – when following a dialectics of deskilling, and reskilling of labour – leads to the acquisition of new technical and collaborative skills which can be developed and transformed in relation to the particular making of a piece. This process contributes to the enhancement of performance mastery insofar as it enriches the artists' singular modes of thinking. In turn, the potential for reskilling performance mastery in collective modes of labour offers a viable means to renegotiate the relationship between individuality and collectivity.

## Notes

1. The project eventually involved two residencies held in France. The first phase of the project, lasting six months, was implemented at The Choreographic Centre of Montpellier (CCMN). A second residency was held at the Performing Arts Forum based at St Erme.
2. For example, Boltanski and Chiappelo offer an influential and aggressive critic of artistic complicity with the establishment (Boltanski & Chiappelo, 2007).
3. The notion of open-source originates in the Open Source Software, which is software that is freely distribut(ed/able) with its source code. Users can modify the software or use it for other software in compliance with its original open-source licence.
4. Network Cultures was initiated by Peter Mörtenböck in partnership with Goldsmiths University. For details, see the online platform http://www.networkedcultures.org. [Accessed November 20, 2014].
5. The website was hacked in 2011. It is currently under re-construction however general information can be viewed at the following address: http://www.everybodystoolbox.net. [Accessed November 28, 2014].
6. I am referring here to the work of the Judson Dance Theatre Group's choreographers.
7. For a discussion of the impact on collaborative practice within the visual arts context, see Nikos Papastergiadis (2008).
8. Lazzarato argues that immaterial labour is 'characterized by real managerial functions that consist in (1) a certain ability to manage its social relations and (2) the eliciting of social cooperation within the structures of the basin of immaterial labor.' (Lazzarato, 1996: 138) The term *knowledge transfer* refers to a broader framing of the post-industrial society as a knowledge-based economy in which knowledge and creativity constitute significant driving forces for economic growth. Alan Weber, former editorial director of Harvard Business Review, wrote that 'the revolution in information and communications technologies makes knowledge the competitive resource' (Weber, 1993). In this context, *knowledge transfer* might arguably better reflect the idea of education within a new economy.
9. The term biopolitical in this context draws on Michel Foucault's concept of 'biopower' and refers to the structure of power within modern societies as it is exercized indirectly by disciplining bodies and regulating populations.
10. The increasing interest in 'affective labour' has emerged partly from the reviving of Spinoza's *Ethics* in the writing of Deleuze, Guattari and Massumi; and partly from the work of autonomist theorists such as Negri and Hardt. The relationship between bodily experience and affect has been central to the articulation of the 'affective Turn'. See Brian Massumi (2008).
11. I am referring here to a shift from Kant's notion of genius as outlined in *The Critique of Judgement* – 'The talent which gives the rule to art' – toward a post-Kantian view of the artwork developed in the critical writing of theorists including Walter Benjamin (2008) and Roland Barthes (1977).
12. Roberts explains that Duchamps' readymade transforms the commodity of the work: 'The commodity's metamorphic function is made transparent by the act of artistic transmutation which occurs. By transforming a reproducible non-art object into an unreproducible art object in the form of a

reproducible art object, the logical relations of artistic labour and productive labour are exposed and inverted' (Roberts, 2008: 33).

13. Roberts draws here on the writing of Raymond Tallis who demonstrates that the ability of proprioception and protension of the hand is key to human evolution: 'The hand opens up the body to itself as an instrument, awakens the sense of self and of the (cultural) world to which the self relates' (Tallis 2003, cited in Roberts 2008: 94). Roberts further concludes that, 'we owe our escape from biology, therefore, to what Tallis calls the *totipotentiality* of the hand' (Tallis 2003, cited in Roberts 2008: 94).
14. An obvious example of the relationship between deskilling and reskilling in dance is the trend amongst European choreographers in the 1990s to use stillness and durational devices to slow down movement rhythms as a critique of representation. In this instance the virtuosity of the dancers is not in the execution of movements but rather in the capacity of not doing them (Lepecki, 2004).
15. Recalling Marx's assimilation of cooperative work to the logic of capitalist production, Roberts argues that artistic 'processes of cooperation and collaboration result in forms of complex labour, rather than simple labour, at the level of the collective intellect' (Roberts, 2008: 125).
16. Roberts observes that in the context of 1920s avant-garde – with the new reproductive technologies subjected to capitalist development – the hand became the site of 'aesthetics thinking'. He notes that, 'Retaining the sovereignty of the (totipotentiality of the) hand, in contrast, was a way of retaining the sovereignty of aesthetic thinking as a form of labour qualitatively different to that of heteronomous labour' (Roberts, 2008: 218).
17. I am referring here to the notion of the 'male gaze' as understood by feminist British film theorist Laura Mulvey (1975), who used Freudian and Lacanian psychoanalytical concepts – including scopophilia – in order to theorize the representation of women in film as the object of male desire.

## Bibliography

Barthes, R. (1977), 'The Death of the Author' in Heath, S. ed. *Image – Music – Text,* Hill & Wang.

Benjamin, W. (2008), *The Work of Art in the Age of Mechanical Reproduction,* Penguin Group.

Bishop, C. (2004), 'Antagonism and Relational Aesthetics', in *October* (110), pp. 51–79.

Boltanski, L. & Chiappelo, E. (1999), *The New Spirit of Capitalism,* Verso, 2007.

Bourriaud, N. (2002), *Relational Aesthetics,* Les press du Reel.

Charmatz, C. & Launay, I. (2011), *Undertraining: On A Contemporary Dance,* Les Presses du Réel.

Cvejić, B. (2007), 'Learning by Making'. [Online] Available from: http://summit.kein.org/node/235. [Accessed April, 2012].

DeLahunta, S. (2003), 'Open Source Choreography', Ars Electronic Archive. [Online] Available from: http://90.146.8.18/en/archives/festival_archive/festival_catalogs/festival_artikel.asp?iProjectID=12520#. [Accessed June 20, 2012].

Dempster, E. (2010), 'Women Writing the Body: Let's Watch a Little How She Dances' in Carter, A. & O'Shea, J. *The Routledge Dance Studies Reader*, Routledge, pp. 229–35.
Derrida, J. (1992), *Given Time: 1, Counterfeit Money*, University of Chicago Press.
Eikhof, D. & Haunschild, A. (2006), 'Lifestyle Meets Market: Bohemian Entrepreneurs in Creative Industries', in *Creative and Innovation Management* (5:3), pp. 234–41.
Everybodystoolbox (2006). [Online] available from: http://everybodystoolbox.net/index.php?title=Accueil. [Accessed November 19, 2014].
Fleuriot, M. (2011), Avignon Festival Programme. [Online] available from: http://www.xavierleroy.com/page.php?sp=69caa2510bce2be93732e5c2739db89ba96ccaaf&lg=en. [Accessed June 20, 2012].
Foster, S. (2008), 'Choreographies and Choreographers: Four Definitions of the Terms' in *Modern Dance: Multifaceted Dimension*, edited by S. Bandopadhay, Kolkata, pp. 5–26.
Gies, F. (2006), *Dance*. [Online] available from: http://www.dancepracticable.net. [Accessed June 20, 2012].
Hardt, M. & Negri, A. (2004), *Multitude, War and Democracy in the Age of Empire*, The Penguin Press, New York.
Hippel, E. & Krogh, G. (2003), 'Open Source Software and the "Private-Collective" Innovation Model: Issues for Organization Science', Organization Science, Vol. 14.
Ingvartsen, M. ed. (2009), *6 Months 1 Location: (6M1L)*, everybodys publication.
Knorr Cetina, K. (2001), 'Postsocial Relations: Theorizing Sociality in a Postsocial Environment', in Rizter, G., Smart, B. eds. *Handbook on Social Theory*, pp. 520–38.
Kolb, A. (2011), 'On the politics of Interdisciplinary Collaboration', *Brolga: an Australian Journal about Dance* (35). pp. 26–36.
Kurdian, G. (2009), *Sound Diary*. [Online] available from http://www.gerald-kurdian.fr/index.php?/radio/6-mois-1-lieu-et-le-comportement-de-lensemble/. [Accessed July 3, 2012].
Laermans, R. (2012), 'Being in Common: Theorizing Artistic Collaboration', in *Performance Research Journal* (17:6), pp. 94–102.
Lazzarato, M. (1996), 'Immaterial Labour' in Virno, P. & Hardt, M. eds. *Radical Thought in Italy: A Potential Politics*, University of Minnesota Press, pp. 132–46.
Lepecki, A. (2004), *Of the Presence of the Body: Essays on Dance and Performance Theory*, Wesleyan University Press.
Marx, K. (1990), *Capital*, Volume 1, Penguin Group, UK.
Melrose, S. (2009), 'Rosemary Butcher: Jottings on Signature in the Presence of the Artist', Presented at Bodies of Thought at Siobhan Davies Studio, London. [Online] available from: http://www.sfmelrose.org.uk/jottings/. [Accessed July 27, 2012].
Melrose, S. (2007) 'Confessions of an Uneasy Expert Spectator'. [Online] available from: http://www.sfmelrose.org.uk. [Accessed November 20, 2014].
Moran, J. (2010), in Chauchat, A. & Ingvarsten, M. eds. *Everybodys Performance Scores*, everybodys publications.
Mulvey, L. (1975), 'Visual Pleasure and Narrative', in *Screen* (16.3), pp. 6–8.
Negri, A. (2008), 'Metamorphoses', in *Radical Philosophy* (149), pp. 21–25.

Papastergiadis, N. (2008), 'The Global Need for Collaboration', Collaborative Art, Conversation on Collaborative Arts Practices, [Online]. Available from: http://collabarts.org/?p=201 [accessed June, 2012].

Lynch, S. (2002), 'Aristotle and Derrida on Friendship', Contretemps An Online Journal of Philosophy, 3, pp. 98–106.

Roberts, J. (2008), *The Intangibilities of Forms*, Verso.

Sweet and Tender Collaborations (2007). *Sweet and Tender Collaborations* [Online] available from: http://www.sweet-and-tender.org. [Accessed November 20, 2014]

Six Months One Location (2008). [Online] available from: http://www.mathilde-monnier.com/upload/editor/files/booklet6m1l.pdf. [Accessed November 20, 2014]

Weber, A. (1993), 'What So New About The New Economy' in Harvard Business Review. [Online] available from: http://wiki.douglasbastien.com/images/e/e1/Harvard_Business_Review_71-1-What's_So_New_About_the_New_Economy.pdf. [Accessed July 1, 2012].

# Part II
# Workings – Ways of Practising Collaboration

# 6

# Ten Propositions for Research-Creation

*Erin Manning*

## 1. Create New Forms of Knowledge (Embrace the Non-Linguistic)

- Research-creation generates new forms of experience; it situates what often seem like disparate practices, giving them a conduit for collective expression; it hesitantly acknowledges that normative modes of inquiry and containment often are incapable of assessing its value; it generates forms of knowledge that are extra-linguistic; it creates operative strategies for a mobile positioning that take these new forms of knowledge into account; it proposes concrete assemblages for rethinking the very question of what is at stake in pedagogy, in practice, and in collective experimentation.
- Research-creation proposes new forms of knowledge, many of which are not intelligible within current understandings of what knowledge might look like
- Consider that new processes will likely create new forms of knowledge which may have no means of evaluation within current disciplinary models.

## 2. Practice Thinking (Don't Be Afraid of Philosophy)

- How might a resituating of research-creation as a practice that thinks provide us with the vocabulary to take seriously that 'philosophical theory is itself a practice, just as much as its object. It is no more abstract than its object. It is a practice of concepts, and we must judge it in light of the other practices with which it interferes'? (Deleuze, 1989: 280, *translation modified*).

- This will mean opening thought beyond its articulation in language toward 'the movement of thought,' engaging it at the immanent limit where it is still fully in the act.
- Consider that making is a thinking in its own right, and conceptualization a practice in its own right.
- Think of philosophy not as that which frames an already completed process, but as that which has a history of launching its speculative apparatus in relation to modes of knowing beyond its purview such as artistic practice.

## 3. Make Beyond the Object (Work the Work)

- Take art in its medieval definition as 'the way.' If 'art' is understood as a 'way' it is not yet about an object, about a form, or content.
- Consider that research-creation is less about an object than a mode of activity that is at its most interesting when it is constitutive of new processes. To be constitutive of new processes it is necessary that potential be tapped in advance of the work's alignments with existing disciplinary methods and institutional structures (this includes creative capital).
- Take seriously that generating new forms of knowledge implies generating new forms of experience for which there are no pre-given methodologies, for which there is no pre-determined value. What research-creation can do is propose concrete assemblages for rethinking the very question of what is at stake in pedagogy, in practice, and in collective experimentation.

## 4. Dwell in the Transversal (Keep Moving)

- The unquantifiable within experience can only be taken into account if we begin with a mode of inquiry that refutes initial categorization
- Instead of holding knowledge to what can already be ascertained (and measured), let us, as William James suggests, find ways to account not only for the terms of the analysis, but for all that transversally weaves between them.
- Let us be up to the challenge of radical empiricism as that which begins in the midst, in the mess of relations not yet organized into terms such as 'subject' and 'object.' James calls this field of relations 'pure experience,' pure understood not in the sense of 'purity' but in the sense of immanent to actual relations. Pure experience is on the cusp of the virtual and the actual: in the experiential register of the not-quite-yet. It is *of* experience in the sense that it affectively

contributes to how experience settles into what James calls 'knower-known' relations.

- Note that to reorient the real to include that which can be experienced (rather than known as such) is to profoundly challenge the notion that knowledge is based on quantification. [Return to Proposition 1]
- This is the force of radical empiricism, that it gives us a technique to work with the in-act at the heart of experience, providing subtle ways of composing with the shifting relations between the knower and the known, keeping in mind, of course, that the knower is not the human subject, but the way relations open themselves toward systems of subjectification.

## 5. Be Speculatively Pragmatic (Enjoy the Process)

- Speculative pragmatism is key to this process.
- Speculative pragmatism is an approach that is interested in the pragmatic force of the conditions of the here and now, while simultaneously remaining oriented to the as-yet-unknown.
- A speculative pragmatism takes as its starting point a rigour of experimentation. It is interested in the anarchy at the heart of all process, and is engaged with the techniques that tune the anarchical into new modes of knowledge. It is also interested in what escapes the order, and especially in what this excess can do. It implicitly recognizes that knowledge is invented in the escape, in the excess.
- Keep in mind that a speculatively pragmatic approach never begins with a pre-formed subject.
- A speculatively pragmatic approach takes the event, not the subject, as its point of departure. Its pragmatism is that it remains interested and engaged with all that the event can do, which includes how it positions itself in the field of relation. Whitehead's notion of the 'superject,' the subject of the event, is useful here. The superject emphasizes that the occasion of experience is itself what proposes knower-known relations, resulting in a subject that is the subject of the experience rather than a subject external to the experience. Experience, it reminds us, is not constituted first and foremost of human relations.

## 6. Invent Beyond Technique (Activate the More-Than)

- An account of method is inextricably linked to a belief in reason. In this account, reason functions as an apparatus of capture – it diagnoses, situates, organizes, and ultimately it surveys, judges and understands. Though methods are always open to change, their task is to reasonably safeguard against the ineffable - that which cannot be categorized cannot be made to account for itself, and so falls by the wayside. Conscious knowledge is privileged over the prelinguistic and the preconscious; writing is privileged over speech and certainly over all other kinds of making. Method, however open it may seem in a given context, serves to define knowledge to its core, disciplining the very question of what constitutes knowledge.

- Whitehead seeks to go beyond a Kantian definition of reason toward what he calls 'the function of reason.' Whitehead sees reason not as a content to be allied to a method, but as a cut that reorients the field of experience. Reason, he suggests, is the process's appetition for difference. It is what pushes occasions of experience to distinguish themselves from the welter of activity; it is the 'counteragency which saves the world' from mere life. This cut is not an endpoint, not the capture of a process. Reason here no longer belongs to Kant – it has appetite. The cut is operative, it activates potential and sets things in motion. Method, on the other hand, works as a stilling, as an endpoint. 'The birth of methodology,' Whitehead writes, 'is in its essence the discovery of a dodge to live' (1929: 18).
- What we need are not methods for curating life-lived, but techniques for life-living.
- Consider technique as propositional, where method is positioning.
- Define technique as what tunes the field of resonance of a system in the making. Think technique as the act-in-repetition that hones the system, bringing rigor to it.
- A technique has to be invented for each process, and as the process changes, so does the technique. Technique builds repetition and difference into the act, opening a process to its potential to differentiate itself as this or that.
- Technique is necessary to the art of thought – to thought in the act – but it is not art in itself.
- The key is to go to the heart of technique – close reading, engaged exploration of material, repeated daily practice – and then to go further still.
- Techniques become methods if they are not outdone. Technicity is the outdoing of technique. It is the modality for creating out of a system of techniques the more-than of system, the experience of the work's opening itself to its excess, to what cannot be captured by repetition.

- Technique and technicity coexist. Where technique engages the repetitive practices that form a composing body – be it organic or inorganic – technicity is a set of enabling conditions that exact from technique the potential for co-composition. Think technicity as the process that stretches out from technique, creating brief interludes of the more-than of technique, gathering from the implicit the force of form.
- This quality of the more-than that is technicity is ineffable – it can be felt, but is difficult to articulate in language. [Return to Proposition 1]
- What research-creation can do is make technicity palpable across registers. It can work, as radical empiricism does, in the complex field of conjunctions opened up by the transitions in experience, transitions which attune to the more-than. [Return to Proposition 4]

## 7. Metamodel (Make It An Event)

- What the conjunction between research and creation does is make apparent how modes of knowledge are always at cross-currents with one another, actively reorienting themselves in transversal operations of difference, emphasizing the deflection at the heart of each conjunction. The conjunction is at work, actively adjusting the always immanent coupling of research and creation, asking how the thinking in the act can be articulated, and what kind of analogous experience it can be coupled with, asking how a making is a thinking in its own right, asking what that thinking might be able *to do*. [Return to Propositions 1, 2, 4 and 5]
- A reorienting of thought as a practice in its own right is part of the creation and evaluation (or, better said, valuing) of new forms of knowledge.
- In the final pages of his account on the function of reason, Whitehead writes: 'the quality of an act of experience is largely determined by the factor of the thinking which it contains' (1929: 80). Challenging the habit of situating facts above thinking – 'the basis of all authority is the supremacy of fact over thought' – Whitehead inquires into the tendency to place thought outside experience. This, he suggests, is what is wrong with method. How might the fact of this occasion – what it does, how it feels, where it moves - be separated out by its thinking when thought itself 'is a factor in the fact of experience' (80).
- Thinking in the event suggests that the machinations of appetition are at work, and that they have thoroughgoing effects.

- The transversal activation of the relational fields of thinking and doing is what I am calling research-creation.
- Research-creation does not need new methods. What it needs are techniques that enable modes of valuing the process, techniques that enable the tuning to technicity of a practice.
- If nonlinguistic practices are forms of knowledge in their own right, as research-creation makes apparent, and if knowledge has the habit of being valued according to the standards of language, how might research-creation assert its value, valued not for what it leaves behind but for its appetite to always begin anew.
- Guattari's concept of metamodelling may be a place to start.
- Metamodelling makes felt lines of formation, starting not from one model in particular, but actively taking into account the plurality of models vying for fulfillment. Metamodelling is against method, active in its refutation of pre-existing modes of existence, meta in the sense of mapping abstract formative conjunctions, in continuing variation, across varying deflections.
- Metamodelling shouldn't be thought as that which frames a process. It is radical empiricism in action. It is a technique for activating the lived abstractions in the event, for making felt the thinking at the heart of the doing.
- As Guattari writes: 'metamodeling de-links modeling with both its representational foundation and its mimetic reproduction. It softens signification by admitting a-signifying forces into a model's territory... What was hitherto inaccessible is given room to manifest and project itself into new and creative ways and combinations. Metamodelling is in these respects much more precarious than modeling, less and less attached to homogeneity, standard constraints, and the blinkers of apprehension' (2008, n.p).

## 8. Render Formative Forces (Create a Platform for Relation)

- An event by definition activates the field of relation. An event is how an ecology comes to be known as such. There is nothing outside the event.
- An event's relational force cannot be reproduced. It remains, always, a singular movement. It has a velocity, uniquely played out from the initial conditions at hand. It is potentializing, and renders potential. It follows the arc of a tendency working itself out. [Return to Proposition 6]

- Tendencies are as singular as an event's generative force. They can be iteratively reactivated, to variable effect. But each event will activate its own tendency. [Return to Proposition 5]
- If you follow the technicity of singular tendings, you will be eventfully setting into motion a metamodelling of emergence. [Return to Proposition 7]
- A tendency, metamodeled, is an incipient assemblage (a platform for relation).
- Consider that meta-modellings of generative process are deterritorializing. They move tendentially across institutionalizations, and morph them. An event of metamodelling must be self-expiring. It must creatively find ways to affirm its generative power in its passing.
- Invent techniques that assist in allowing the event to move toward and beyond its formative forces. Follow them to see what they can do. [Return to Proposition 4]

## 9. Create Altereconomies of Value (Value Emergence)

- We remain held by existing methods because we remain incapable (or unwilling) to evaluate knowledge on its own incipient terms, or better, to engage productively with new concepts of valuation. [Return to Proposition 1 and 7]
- In a formal economy, valuation is quantitative, and is derived using conventional measures.
- Monetary economy can mean only one thing: the capitalist economy. The capitalist economy taps into all other formal and informal economies in a continuously varied attempt to annex them to itself, which is to say, to its particular forms of formal valuation and indexing. The capitalist economy is not only a universal process of subsuming all forms of value to monetary valuation. It also formally builds into its definition of value an imperative to quantitative value-adding. Capital is by definition money that grows more money. The capitalist economy is formally dedicated to quantitative growth, over and above all other values. Capitalist techniques of relation are without exception mechanisms of accumulation.
- There are also informal economies. These revolve around assessments of value that are directly qualitative in nature, and therefore vaguer and less easily indexed. This kind of valuation is often called prestige-value. A formal economy also generates its own prestige-value as a spin-off of its quantitive valuations, or it captures prestige-value, a

value produced by informal economies the formal economy taps into and annexes to itself.

- All of this matters for the experimental practice of research-creation because the universal subsumption of all other economies, formal and informal, under the capitalist economy amounts to a capture of every species of event – including their respective fields of emergent expressibility, the heterogeneity of their co-composing polyrhythms, their improvisational power to repeat singularly with variation, their tendential arcs, their cresting expression on social surfaces of recording that constitute evolving genres of co-activity.
- When the capitalist economy subsumes all other economies, it is not just capturing monetary value. It is capturing processes of individuation. It is capturing entire fields of emergent relation. It is capturing powers of becoming. Capitalism endeavors nothing less than the universal capture of *forms of life*. It subsumes them, sometimes gently, more often brutally, to techniques of relation dedicated to quantitative value-adding and accumulation.

## 10. Activate New Forms of Life (Invent at the Interstices)

- It is important not to mistake this capture for a homogenization. The forms of life captured by the capitalist process produce value by distinguishing themselves from each other. Capitalism is as *singularizing* as it is subsuming. The issue is that the singularization is subject to competition in a way that foregrounds quantitative measures of success over the richness of qualitative diversity. The heterogeneity of forms of life are important only to the extent that they add capital value. Although the capitalist process creates the conditions for the singular emergence of forms of life, and feeds off their heterogeneity, it ultimately attributes no value to them as such. It is supremely indifferent to the qualitative richness that animates its field.
- If capitalism is a universal process of capture, there is no simple way out. All activities are at some point, in some way, taken up in it. But if capitalism is also singularly inventive of new forms of relation, then despite this complicity there are emergent forms of life always on the make which might come to assert greater autonomy. The result can be leakage in the system – lines of flight toward a non-capitalist future.
- An altereconomics of research-creation, understood as a practice of the event, is informal. It is unquantifiable. Its valuations directly concern qualities of life. But the affirmation of qualities of experience

refuses to settle around prestige-value. Its process is autonomous in the sense that it is self-propagating. What propagates is an evolving form-of-life that partners thinking and making at the emergent level where they already come co-causally together. This is a polyrhythmic economy of germinal forms attuning – of *forces of life* finding new collective expression not for what it leaves behind but for its appetite to always begin anew.[1]

- Emergent life, lived less as value-adding than *as a* value in itself.
- Research-creation: the value produced is the process itself, is its very qualitative autonomy.

## Note

1. Propositions 9 and 10 are taken almost verbatim from 'Thought in the Act' in Erin Manning and Brian Massumi *Thought in the Act: Passages in the Ecology of Experience* (Minnesota University Press, 2014).

## Bibliography

Deleuze, G. (1989) *Cinema 2: The Time Image* (Minneapolis: Minnesota University Press).

Guattari, F. in Genosko, Gary and Murphie, Andrew "Metamodels" in *Fibreculture Journal*, 12, (2008). www.fibreculture.org

Manning, E. and M., Brian (2014) *Thought in the Act: Passages in the Ecology of Experience* (Minneapolis: Minnesota University Press).

Whitehead, A.N. (1929) *The Function of Reason* (New York: Free Press).

# 7

# Rowing to Hilversum: Double Vision in Performance and Architecture

*Ewan Forster and Christopher Heighes*

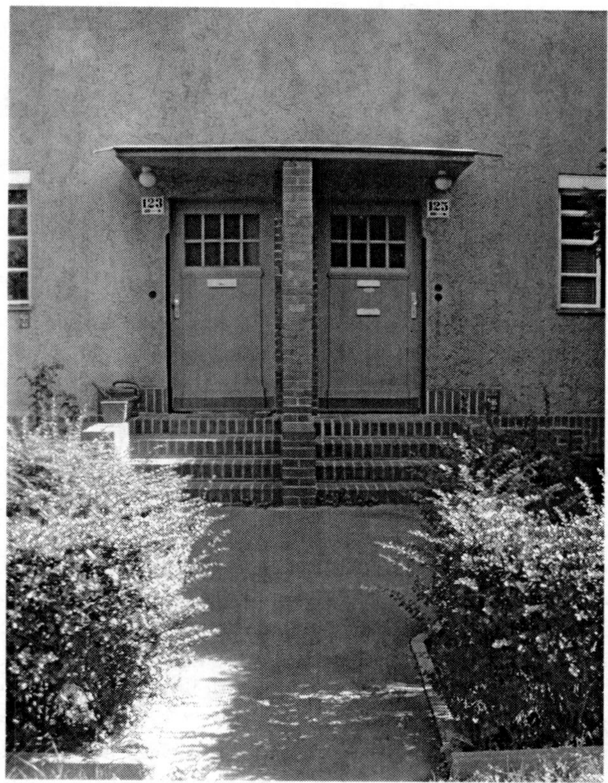

*Fig. 1* Doors on the Hufeisensiedlung, Berlin, *Die Erde eine gute Wohnung*, 2007, Forster & Heighes, Photograph by Christopher Heighes

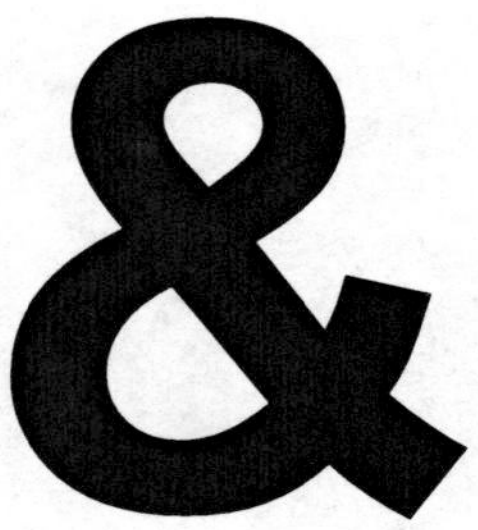

We've not got long to speak, so we've decided to be honest, graphic in fact, about the conjunction of Ewan Forster with Christopher Heighes. We would like to discuss what it is exactly that we keep between ourselves, both on the page and stage.

The word 'and' seems a crude grammatical staple with which to join our names, thoughts and actions, so instead long ago we settled on the wild stitching of the 'ampersand': Forster & Heighes. Its cursive form seems to properly articulate the meandering and fluid dynamics of our joint enterprise. Two loops, two intersections and ambiguous points of exit and entry that might suggest the beginning of a strong knot or a dismal tangle, something self-contained yet open, a rhetorical flourish or a senseless ramble, an exhilarating gyratory or a pensive doodle – for us it is a visual reminder of the cognitive spasm necessary for working in partnership.

We might talk about how the embroidery of the ampersand represents for us a peculiar contract of endeavour. How it illustrates a relationship, but not a fixed bond. How it is a mark of rapport, liaison, collision, and misunderstanding; strong but flexible, knowing and unknowing, one line in search of many possibilities. Then again, we might not agree on that. We may go another way.

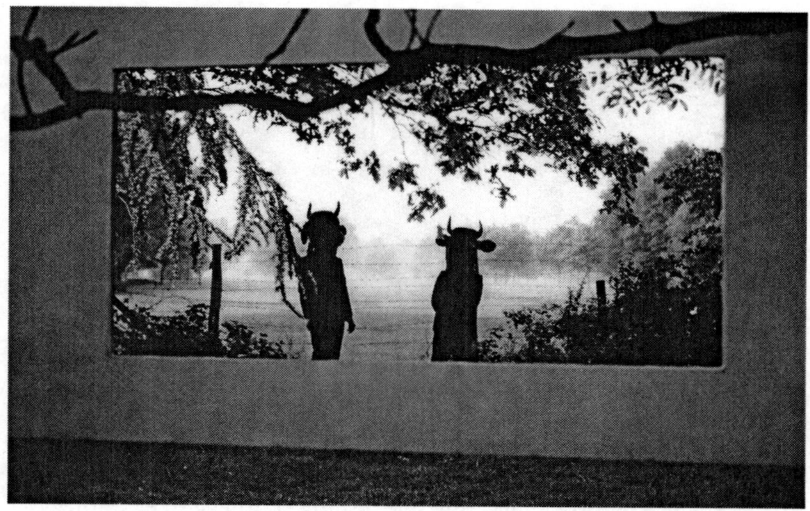

*Fig. 2* Viewing station, *The Curriculum,* 1999, Forster & Heighes, Photograph by Chris Forster

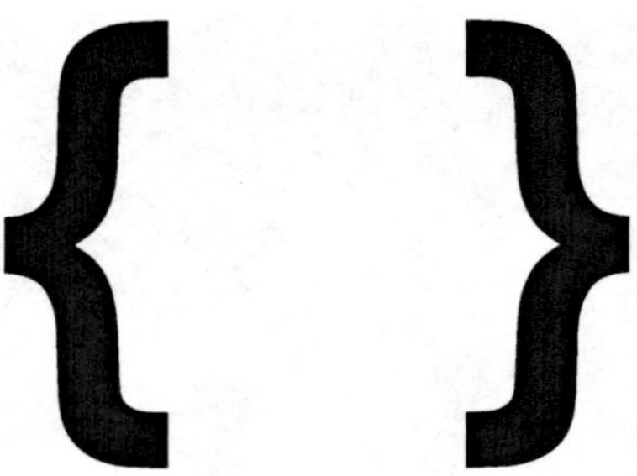

The 'brace' is a very particular form of parenthesis. It denotes not the setting apart of text as does the more common 'bracket' but the deliberate binding of text together. Its origins are musical, tethering the treble line to the bass in the printed score.

In 1977 I began a course of orthodontic treatment to encourage a pair of wayward lateral incisors back into a more uniform arrangement in my upper jaw. My brace was an elegant stainless steel framework set in an acrylic cast of the roof of my mouth. At the age of eleven I was impatient for progress and would regularly adjust it with pliers to increase the pressure and speed the results. Eventually my dentist intervened. I remember being sat down and told that you can't force a tooth to move. That if you push it will resist. The trick is to create a looser framework, an imperceptible pressure that will in time encourage the tooth to change its position.

People often ask how Chris and I come to our compositional decisions and are a little bemused when they discover that we very rarely stop each other from doing anything, preferring to accommodate disparate and often only partially connected ideas within the same composition:

> *"Why do you need the icing sugar so badly Chris?"*
> *"I'm making a birthday cake for the Einheit child in the shape of Bruno Taut's Crystal House for the final scene."*
>
> *"Ewan, are we just going to sit at the back during Patrick and Sarah's newly-weds scene in the Duomo?"*
> *"Well I know it's a little late in the day but I've been working on a 12 verse mediaeval pageant that I thought we might perform in the background."*

The partnership survives through the looseness of its framework and although a brace of performance artists has an inherent strength – a doubling of resolve in the face of opposition – we are all too aware that strength derived from rigidity often leads to fracture.

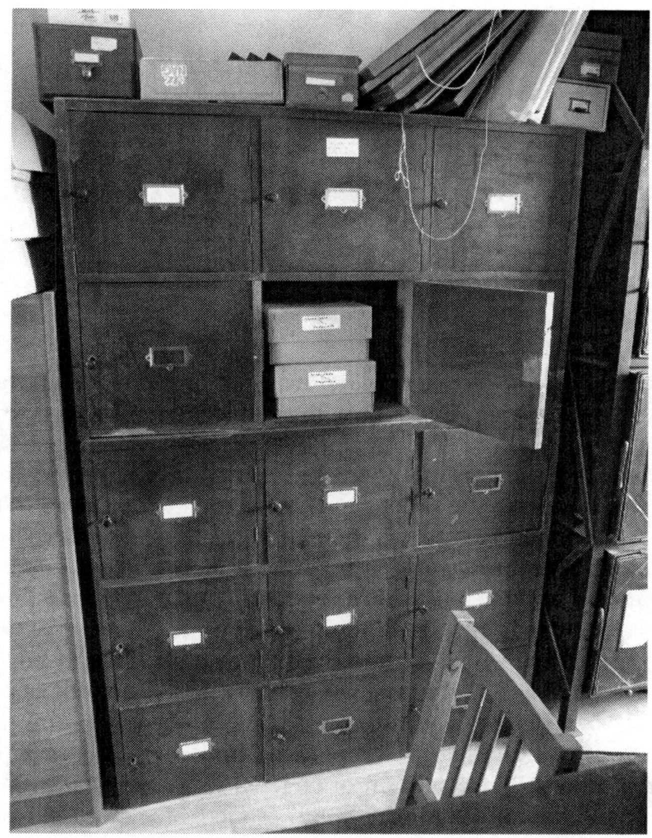

*Fig. 3* Herbarium cabinet, South London Botanical Society, *Plant Science*, 2013, Forster & Heighes, Photograph by Christopher Heighes

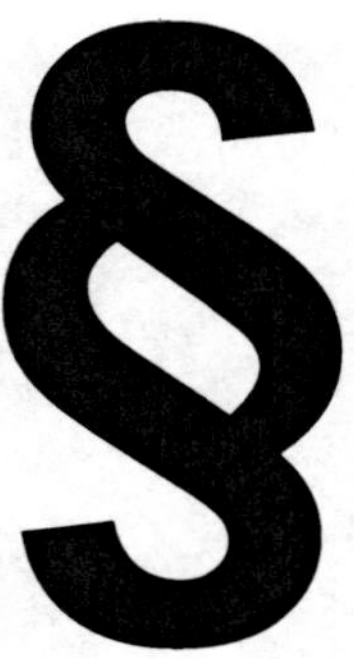

Those of you who are active mountaineers will be familiar with the term 'belaying', a technique climbers use to exert friction on a rope so that a falling climber doesn't fall far. A climbing partner creates a resistance at the other end of the rope whenever the other climber is not moving, and removes it whenever the other needs more rope to continue. Whether from a snow-bound base camp, the rehearsal studio, or university committee room, places where the air is always thin, the 'paired', metaphorically 'tethered' approach has much to recommend it. It helps if one party remains observing from a fixed point, just behind, below, or to the side, because the partner who steps into the unknown often has to stop thinking, and as often as not, starts behaving badly (in a good way, of course).

Like a belay device, a well-directed look, a silence, prompt act of verbal reconfiguration, or a compliment from the observing partner can act as a good 'hold', a point of targeted resistance that makes, say, an act of trespass into a private building successful or a bold concept palatable to others. Artful decompression, that allows space for connection. A good partnership can play with holding points, exchanging responsibilities, nimbly sectioning through a situation to create a plane of understanding.

I like the word accomplice, from the Latin 'com' meaning together and 'plicare' to fold. Two persons folded together by circumstance and ideas, a layered enterprise, laminated – stronger and tougher. Sometimes my accomplice identity may shrink to be that of a valet or builder's mate; there is a lot of preparing, cleaning and carrying in our performance work – but at other times I'm the get-away driver, a bad ass Ryan Gosling sort of figure, some punk who's gotten in too deep, and there's no turning back. Running away on your own is no fun. Making a break for it together, tyres burning, is a creative adventure.

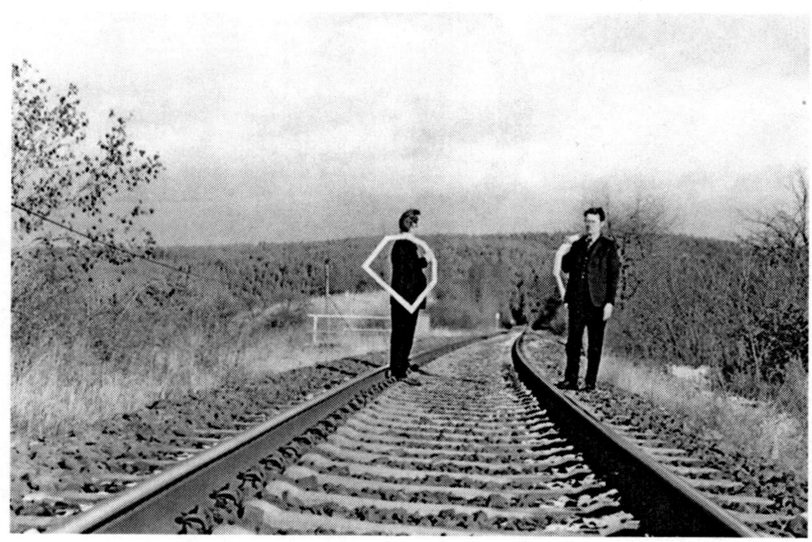

*Fig. 4* 'Curriculum' frames, Bad Blankenburg, Germany, *The Curriculum, 1999*, Forster & Heighes, Photograph by Chris Forster

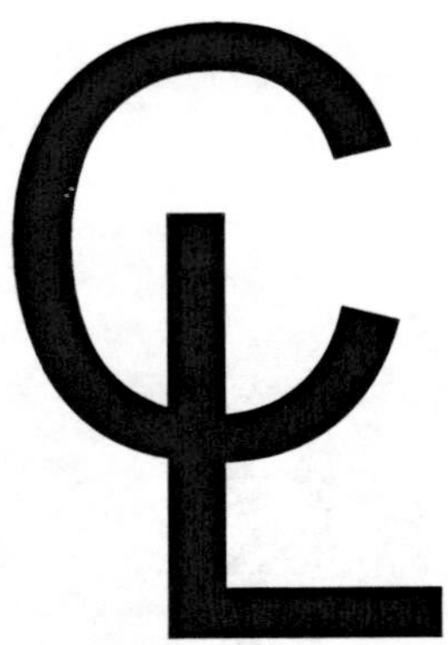

In the architect Sidney Kaye's beautiful hand-drawn plans for his modernist office block at 22 Kingsway – the 1960 curtain walled building which is currently preoccupying Chris and I – the centerline symbol that denotes the principal axis by which one can make sense of various elevations in an architectural plan, has a signature flourish that its Unicode equivalent doesn't quite capture.

For those of us studying at Dartington College of Arts in the 1980s the idea of a centre line has an additional resonance, as many hours were spent in the dance school trying to locate it under the watchful eyes of choreographers such as Mary Fulkerson and Steve Paxton. The imaginary axis that extended from the top of the head and about which your skeleton, its musculature and all the image memories therein contained arrange themselves, was the starting point for all experiments in physical image-making at Dartington.

Although both of us are a little hunched and asymmetrical in our approach to projects these days, our hope is that, with a little axial realignment of this kind – a little *'in through the nose and out through the mouth'* – 22 Kingsway might be encouraged to shake off its Reichian body armour and start to reveal itself to us over the coming months.

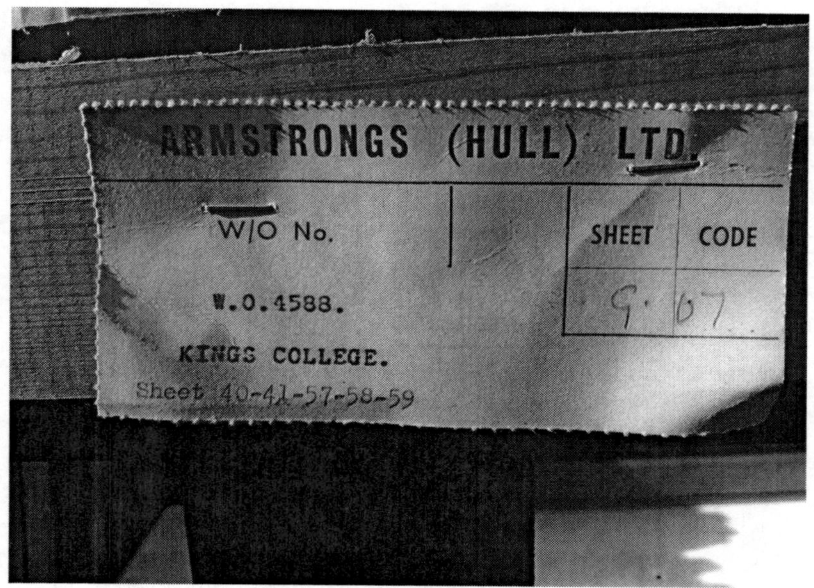


*Fig. 5* Laboratory bench label, *Plant Science,* 2013, Forster & Heighes, Photograph by Christopher Heighes

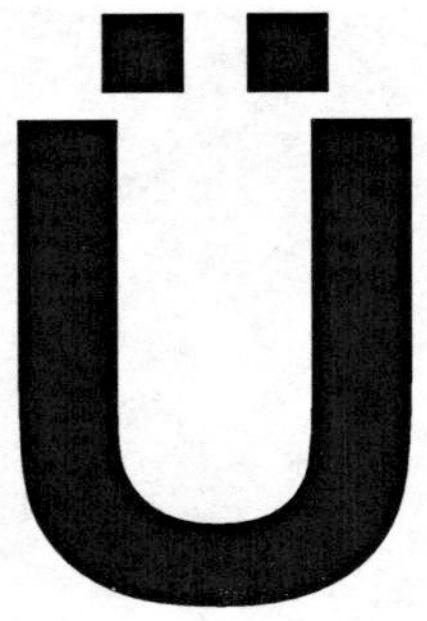

We have always had a deep, though perhaps over-cursive, embroidered affection for North European countries. Places such as Holland and Denmark, seemingly non-ideological and proudly domestic places. Great countries of things observed with love and no particular heroism. Canals, Medieval guildhalls, earthenware; lime washed church interiors, a still life with dead hare, pine forests fringed with dunes; you know the thing.

We have a fondness too for the Umlaut – 'Laut' in German means sound, 'um' means around – an around/other way sound. An accentuation, a change in tone, a shift in stress signified here by two dots on a white field. A counterpoint that hooks the ear and a positioning that beguiles the eye.

When and how do those dots arrive? From where have they journeyed? What is between them? What do they make us think? Are we them?

Anyone can form a company of two, it requires no qualifications, it really is your own business, your own intimate academy, you set the rules – but ironically partnership is all about qualification, arguing the point, making things less absolute, working by degree, inhabiting the increment, marking but not fixing, detailing together, setting one thing against another, the subtle mechanics of persuasion and detonation.

Imagine two offset people, placed separately to the left and right eye of the viewer. Do then these two-dimensional 'ampersand' men combine in the brain to give the perception of depth. I wonder, I wish, what's your gloss on it?

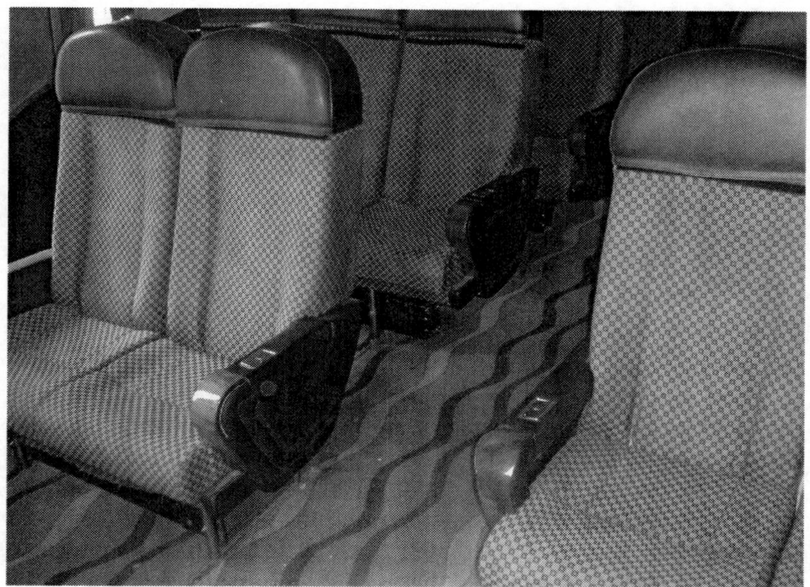

*Fig. 6* Passenger seats, SRN4 hovercraft, *Hovernaut*, 2012, Forster & Heighes, Photograph by Christopher Heighes

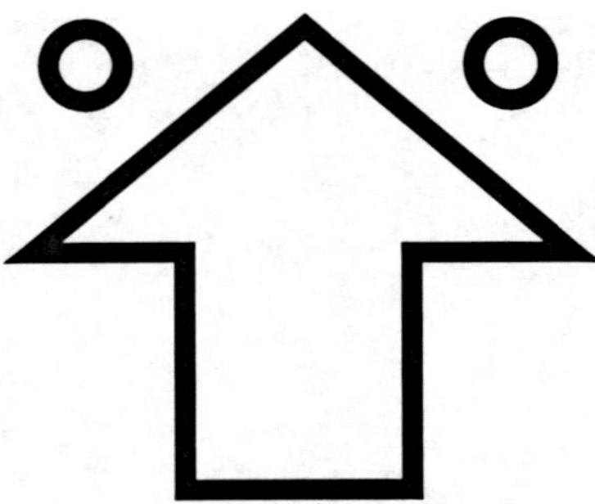

The International Association of Lighthouse Authorities (IALA) system of visual aids to navigation is based on the principle of reds to the right and greens to the left when travelling downstream and vice versa when travelling upstream. The direction of buoyage symbol which we adopted for our installation *Trans Mittere* in 2004 and thereafter became the navigation icon of our over-laden website, clarifies the direction of buoyage where it is not immediately obvious on the chart. Of course to navigate by one set of coloured marks alone is to endanger your vessel, the red 'can' and the green 'cone' mark the extremes of a channel with the safe water flowing somewhere in between.

Chris and I develop most of our projects through meetings with third parties. These are often set up as fairly standard pre-production meetings to establish a collaborative framework for example. The experience of meeting with Forster & Heighes – we've been told – can often be a rather disorienting experience as two often wildly divergent positions are laid out in a rather discourteous rapid-fire manner. It quickly becomes apparent to third parties that we are not actually having a meeting with them but rather are using the opportunity to have a meeting with each other, to test out ideas that we haven't previously discussed and to get some insight into each other's thinking on a project. Over time the disparities in our two visions of the work become less apparent allowing a general course to be plotted and a passage plan prepared.

This method of preparation for journeying offshore is characteristic of the way we are working at present. With no real consistency of form and no perceptible trajectory to the projects, we find ourselves embarking in metaphysical vessels towards phantom waypoints in uncharted waters.

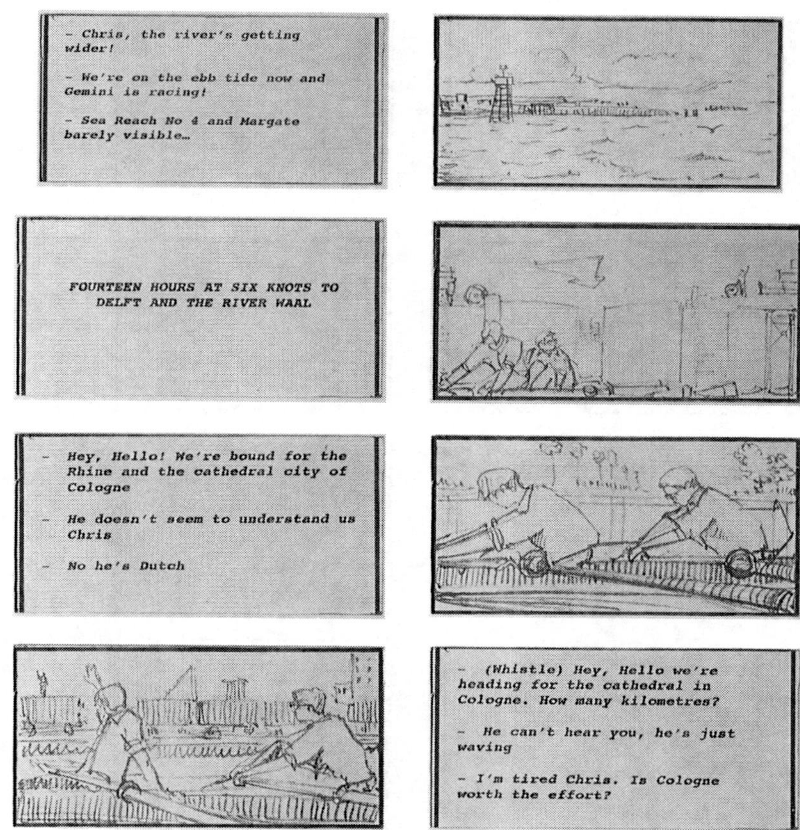


*Fig. 7* 'Rowing to Hilversum' storyboard, *Middle English,* 2003, Forster & Heighes, Artist Chris Forster

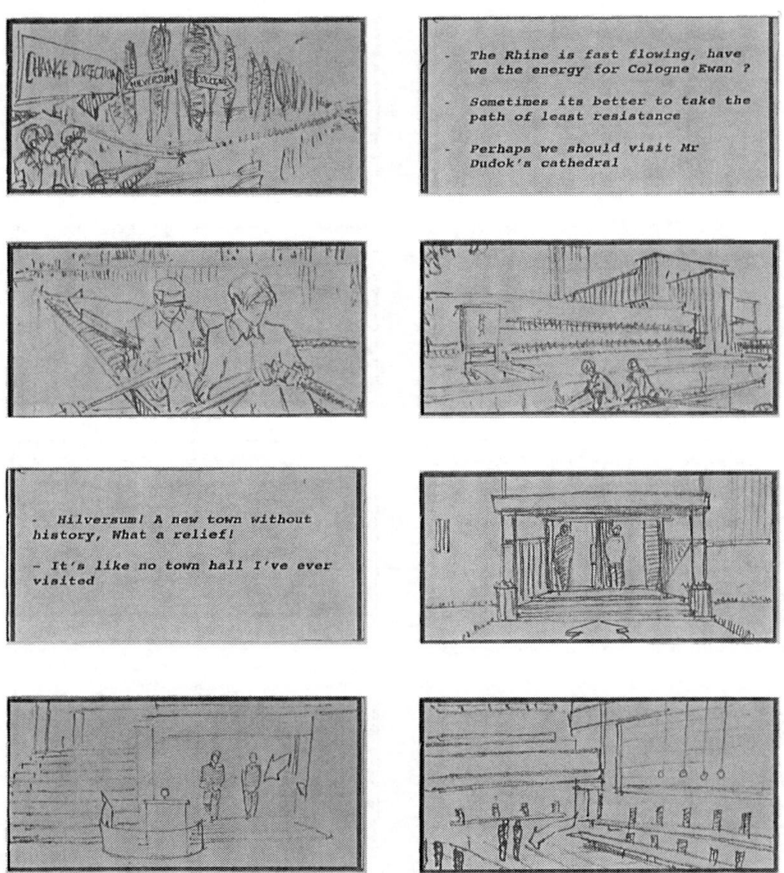


*Fig. 8* 'Rowing to Hilversum' storyboard, *Middle English,* 2003, Forster & Heighes, Artist Chris Forster

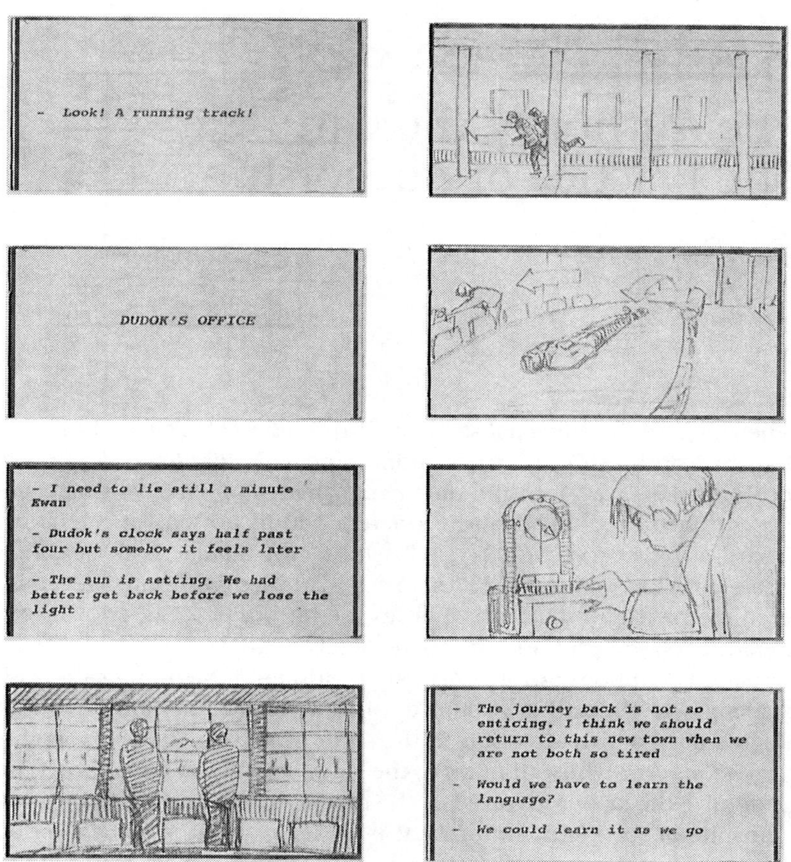


*Fig. 9* 'Rowing to Hilversum' storyboard, *Middle English,* 2003, Forster & Heighes, Artist Chris Forster

# 8
# The Author of the Gift: The Practice of Authorship

*Tim Jeeves*

When Roland Barthes published *The Death of the Author* in 1967, he described authorship as 'the epitome and culmination of capitalist ideology' (1977: 142). In the time since, the sociologist Eve Chiapello has critiqued the individualism inherent within notions of the 'artist genius' as 'aristocratic' (2004: 588) whilst, in a similar vein, Foucault writes in 'What is an Author?' that such identities constitute the 'privileged moment of individualization in the history of ideas, knowledge, literature, philosophy, and the sciences' (2008: 281).

These descriptions are, as Chiapello continues, rooted in a variety of challenges to the author's status as an individual. As she notes, sociologists have drawn attention to the social structures that support the creative process, whilst thinkers in the Marxist tradition have chosen to emphasize the labour involved in the production of art (2004).

In spite of such criticism of what is, in its essential prioritization of the individual, the capitalist identity par excellence, most forms of art practice continue to operate systems of attribution and recognition that identify discrete units of authorship in such a way, either by ascribing the role to a sole artist or a clearly defined collective.

Within theatre practice, collaborative modes of devising have been conceptualized as engaging with the questions of authorial status that *The Death of the Author* explores (cf. Govan, Nicholson and Normington, 2007). Nevertheless, as demonstrated by the history of devising that Govan, Nicholson and Normington presents, the emphasis of such practice can be seen to shift from a critique of the authority of the playwright and director in the 1970s to the contemporary economic and creative practicality of skill-sharing and division of responsibilities. With much acknowledged and well-recognized artistic directors heading up world-renowned devising companies such as Forced Entertainment and The Wooster Group that were formed in the late 1970s and 1980s,[1] it is apparent that whilst modes of developing work may rely less on a single authorial voice in the creative process, systems of individualist attribution remain, to a marked degree, intact.

More recent interrogations that challenge the idea of a distinct authorial identity include Jerome Bel's 2000 dance work, *Xavier Le Roy*, in which Bel asked the eponymous artist to make a work 'for' him that was then presented under Bel's own name, as well as the example of the three artists who all renamed themselves Janez Janša after a Slovenian right-wing politician in 2007 (Wilmer, 2011).

Continuing the trajectory of these interventions into the practice of authorship, throughout the summer of 2012 I developed six new interventions and performances which, upon their performance, had their authorship gifted to six other artists. Through this act of gifting, all future rights of presentation and adaptation of the work were transferred to the artist, meaning that, if they wanted, they could re-present the piece in its entirety (as two of the artists went on to do), or reuse elements of it in other work they might make.

Gifting the authorship also meant that each work was presented in the name of the recipient artist as a part 2012's *Giving in to Gift* festival in Liverpool, under the collective title of *The Horse's Teeth* (with one work, 'a belated gift', performed at the end of January 2013).[2]

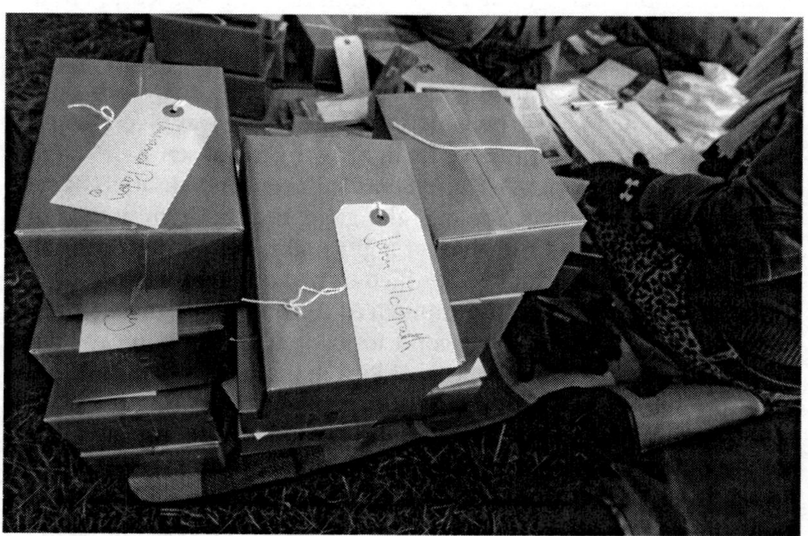

*Fig. 10* Britt Jurgensen: *Gifts to the Dead* (Photo: Mark Loudon)

The six recipient artists were all people that I had, to differing degrees, either a professional or personal relationship with, all worked in performance and all were artists whose work I was interested in and had engaged with previously in a variety of ways, either through workshops, as audience, by giving peer feedback, or as collaborator. Whilst I did not make work 'as the artist' – this was not an exercise in impersonation – I did look to make work that sat appropriately within their artistic practice. In other words, I did not look to introduce a radically different aesthetic, site or political sensibility in the work gifted than was to be found within their previous work. Therefore, whilst not a collaboration in the sense that our combined efforts consciously came together to form a new work, a collaborative process can nevertheless be identified in the way that the pre-existing practice of each artist explicitly informed and guided the work I made for them. The resulting works were presented both within performance spaces (such as Mamoru Iriguchi's *Hand Wash with Similar,* a performative clothes swap party that explored the utopian potential of such events), and the public spaces of Liverpool (as was the case with Britt Jurgensen's *Gifts to the Dead,* a work that drew attention to a largely forgotten cemetery – now a park – by leaving 80 gifts addressed to those buried there that shared a surname with Jurgensen's Facebook friends).

Throughout this writing, *The Horse's Teeth* – and the specific mode of collaboration that is to be found within it – will be used to critique notions of a discrete authorial identity, in particular the tendency such identification has towards capitalist accumulation. Whilst specific works are referred to at points, the emphasis of this analysis is on the project itself, the manner by which the authorship was given, and the qualities associated with these gifts in a more general sense.

I use the anthropologist's Pierre Bourdieu's conceptualisation of symbolic capital to highlight some of the gains that both an author of a performance work and the giver of a gift make, before suggesting that the authorial identity can be identified in two different ways.

One of these identities, the capitalized Author, holds these stores of symbolic capital, whilst the second form, that of the non-capitalized author, is presented, using aspects of Rosi Braidotti's work on subjectivity, as the subject in which the lived experience of creating the work is to be found. With an awareness that this second identity includes, but is not limited to, emotional experience, one of the works presented in *The Horse's Teeth,* Rachel Gomme's *Bodies in Space,* is then used to analyze more closely this affective dimension. I use Sara Ahmed's thinking on emotion here, in particular the quality of 'stickiness' she identifies as a way of understanding its operation.

Taking such a metaphor as a tool for understanding both gift and collaboration more broadly, I conclude by arguing that such an understanding of gift generates insights into ways in which the collaborative process can operate and how discrete formations of identity can be problematic, whilst also making clear the disparity between lower case authorship and capitalized notions of the Author.

Throughout, there is an awareness of the intersection between gift and collaboration. By this I mean the way in which gift can be seen within collaboration (the manner in which those involved in a collaboration 'give' something to the communal process), and also the collaborative processes inherent to gift; the way in which both the giver and the givee need to work together in order for the gift to be given (explicitly, for the gift to be such, the giver needs to give and the givee accept it).

Writing on community-based collaborative art practice, Claire Bishop argues that authorial renunciation is a form of self-sacrifice rooted in 'a tacit analogy between anticapitalism and the Christian "good soul"' (2006: 182). Whilst the work produced in *The Horse's Teeth* is not readily positioned in the socially engaged sphere that Bishop addresses, she nevertheless does, in the instance of this work, still prompt reflection upon possible motivations for authorial distortion. In the context of *The Horse's Teeth* however, I argue that, far from being based in naïve assumptions about the nobility of self-renunciation, the root of this intervention into authorship is an attempt to draw attention to the presentational methods by which ownership of the creative process are typically attributed, to investigate the boundaries of where authorial identity might lie, to make a gift to the participating artists (with the possibilities of emotional investment/return and development of interpersonal bonds that often accompany the giving of gifts) and, to a degree, make gains for myself by producing the project. This last is worth noting for, aside from any acknowledgement that the work itself may have received from the performance community, attention should also be drawn to the fact that there are gains in symbolic capital to be had from writing about the work in a scholarly context.

## Accumulation and symbolic capitalism

Reflecting on thirty years of writing practice, Pierre Bourdieu notes that a significant theme throughout his work is a consideration of the manner by which symbolic capital operates as a conduit for power within any given field (be that the 'capital' manifest in those objects that have a particular symbolic status, the people an individual has relationships with, or even the manner by which an individual presents themselves physically). He writes that:

> [...] struggles for recognition are a fundamental dimension of social life and that what is at stake in them is the accumulation of a particular form of capital, honour in the sense of reputation and prestige, and that there is, therefore, a specific logic behind the accumulation of symbolic capital.
>
> (1994: 22)

By accruing symbolic capital in a variety of ways – for example, presenting in certain locations, being associated with key institutions and people, being written about in particular publications – access to power is gained within the field of performance. In what is often its idealized form, an arts career is a feedback loop in which, by repeatedly making gains in symbolic capital, the chances of making further gains grows more likely.

Writers on generosity also draw attention to the non-financial gains made by the giver of gifts. Lewis Hyde observes that, '[i]n communities drawn together by gift exchange, "status," "prestige," or "esteem," take the place of cash remuneration' (2007: 80). As Bourdieu points out, recognition of these gains is typically taboo, but nevertheless, gift, typically presented as being outside the realm of capitalist gain, is seen to risk reintegration when the movements of symbolic capital are considered.

Unlike examining a monetary trail, there is a difficulty in defining the movements of symbolic value due to its inherently unquantifiable nature. This is not to say that it does not move in recognizable ways, nor that it is impossible to identify an individual with a greater or lesser store of capital in a given situation. Instead, it is that it is near impossible to describe the transactions made within this non-quantitative economy in terms more specific than a generalised sense of the movements of the 'social energy' that Bourdieu describes (1986: 54). Although he develops this notion to talk about how 'labour in the broadest sense' generates capital (labour that would include the work of previous generations, and the development of a particular network of contacts), there are still qualitative elements that radically transform the value of even this broadened definition that are ultimately down to chance, rather than 'hard work'.

A striking similarity between the different forms of capital is the potential they have to be used for capitalist gain.[3] In the analysis presented by Marx, the capitalist is the person who invests money in the production and sale of commodities in order to generate more money. He presents this in the formulation M-C-M, an equation used to represent 'the transformation of money into commodities, and the re-conversion of commodities into money: buying in order to sell' (1990: 248). As Marx and those who have followed him have articulated however, one of the problems with such a system of accumulation is that those with substantial capital are able to pay others to work for them in the production and sale of commodities (the M-C part), but are under no obligation to equitably distribute the gains made from the latter part of the equation (C-M). As the worker's labour is treated as a commodity like any other, they only partially reap the benefit of their labour through the wage that they are paid; there is additional value, on top of this, that the capitalist takes even though they have not performed the labour that created this value. This, the difference in value between the first and last 'M' in the equation – that which we typically understand to be profit – Marx identifies as 'surplus value'.

Whilst all forms of capital can be utilized for capitalist gain, not just the monetary form of which Marx writes, it is important to reiterate that there remain significant differences between the symbolic and financial forms. To understand how the forms differ, an analysis of *Work Fair*,[4] the performance Taylan Halici presented as part of *The Horse's Teeth*, proves useful.

In this piece, a day was spent seeking work by distributing flyers and approaching potential employers. Whilst doing this, it was explained that a condition of the work was that usual wage relations would be reversed and the employee (that is, myself, as performer in Halici's work) would pay the employer for the work undertaken. Although there was inevitably a degree of confusion, and sometimes suspicion, when the offers were made, work that was paid for in the two iterations of the piece (for Halici also presented the work as a part of Camden People Theatre's *Sprint* festival in 2013) included setting up a bar for a celebrity Christmas party, working on a market stall, distributing flyers and 'locating a space to chill' by the river Mersey.

By giving the fruits of labour freely to another, the piece ostensibly shares some characteristics with the donation of authorship in *The*

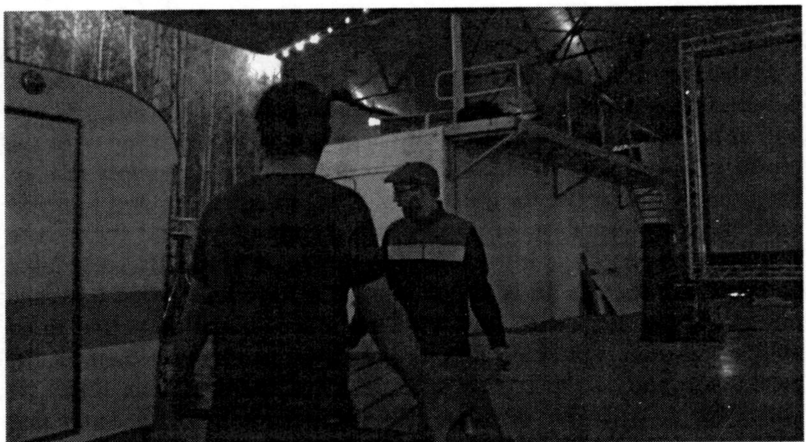

*Fig. 11* Taylan Halici: *Work Fair* (video still)

*Horse's Teeth*. A key difference however is that whilst the labour in *Work Fair* is explicitly concerned with wage relations and the financial economy, *The Horse's Teeth* explores relations of symbolic capital.

To use Marx's terms, in *Work Fair*, notions of surplus value are taken to an extreme: the employer receives all the value gained from the labour. On top of this however, the employer also makes financial gains in excess of the labour's value; the rate of £6.19/hour (the national minimum wage as of November 2012) was paid to them. This monetary value was brought into the employer/employee transaction by labour performed elsewhere (in this instance, through the work that had gone into funding the project).

In the instance of *The Horse's Teeth*, the recipient artists make symbolic gains from my labour even though they are not my employer. Such gains are made as soon as the piece is attributed to them, meaning that I, as in conventional Marxist analysis, am – as worker – only making a proportion of the symbolic gains generated by my labour. Since this is symbolic surplus value however, unlike monetary value, the gains made by the recipient artists are not at the cost of my own.

To explain this, it needs to be understood that the unusual relationship we have in *The Horse's Teeth*, the fact that the work is presented by a different authorial identity than the person who developed it, actually acts to increase the symbolic return over the gains that would have been made had the pieces been created and presented by a single artist.

By diminishing my share of the total symbolic gains, the piece is made more interesting (a marker in the valuation of an artwork), and the total gains are thus increased.

In *The Horse's Teeth,* symbolic capital from labour performed previously is also brought in to the project,[5] although this capital is not, as is the case with the money in *Work Fair,* transferred from one individual to another in a simple transaction. Whilst it is possible for symbolic capital to move from one individual to another – by writing a reference or a letter of introduction for instance – in these instances, unlike with transferrals of finance, the stores of capital of the person making the recommendation are, again, not necessarily reduced.

Although it is important to note the significance of the difference between the operation of the symbolic and financial forms, namely that the movement of symbolic capital does not necessarily reduce the original store, the potential for capitalist accumulation of symbolic value remains. Whilst I do not want to single out individual examples (the practice is too prevalent for this to seem fair), it does not take a prolonged examination of the various e-mail lists on which positions for artists are advertised to come across opportunities to work with a high-profile artist or institution for little more than the opportunity to 'gain experience' and list such associations on a CV. Whilst some benefits to the volunteer artist may be identifiable, in these situations the majority of symbolic (and financial) capital accumulated will go to the lead artist or institution.

In *The Horse's Teeth,* as well as financial payments, the recipient artists received a portion of symbolic capital by being presented as author of the work, whilst I, as donating artist, also made gains: both through my 'generosity' as donor, and also whenever my role as originating artist is acknowledged.

In Derrida's exploration of the gift in *Given Time,* he argues that to make gains from a gift invalidates it since this reabsorbs it into economy. As recognizing the giver's generosity leads to their store of symbolic capital being increased, and thus gains being made, he suggests a paradox as potential solution: '*At the limit, the gift as gift* ought *not appear as gift: either to the donee or the donor*' (original emphasis, 1992: 14).

However, to bring this contradiction into the specific situation of *The Horse's Teeth,* if identification of my position as donor of authorship is made too obliquely then the gift would not actually be made; there would only be a deceit in attribution, and the essential question of where to locate the authorship that arises once it has been given would never be asked.

An alternative solution to the Derridean enigma is proposed by the contemporary French philosopher and theologian Jean-Luc Marion. Marion presents a phenomenology of givenness in which all phenomena 'give' themselves to the witness: 'nothing appears except by giving itself to and in the conscious I' (2002: 16). Whilst he is careful throughout his theory to avoid any suggestion of a transcendent other, stating instead that 'the origin of givenness remains the 'self' of the phenomenon, with no other principle or origin besides itself' (2002: 20), Marion identifies a particular form of excessive 'givenness' that he labels the 'saturated phenomenon'.

Inverting Husserl's identification that '[i]ntuition is (almost) always (partially) lacking to intention, as fulfilment is lacking to signification' (2002: 191), saturated phenomena are to be found when what is received from any given phenomenon (in Husserl's terms, as 'intuition') is in excess of what was understood to be given (or what 'intention' anticipated); they are phenomena 'in which givenness not only entirely invests manifestation but, surpassing it, modifies its common characteristics' (2002: 225).

Reminiscent of Derrida's observation that '[a]s soon as it delimits itself, a gift is prey to calculation and measure' (1992: 91), such excess means that what is received cannot be calculated, even whilst there may still be a recognizable intention. As Marion continues, the fundamental quality of these phenomena 'lies in the fact that intuition sets forth a surplus that the concept cannot organise, therefore that the intention cannot foresee' (2002: 225).

To contextualize this in the instance of *The Horse's Teeth*, it is possible that those encountering the project perceive that what is received, i.e. the authorship of the performance works and any accompanying affective response, is in excess of the gains that I make (be they symbolic or financial), even whilst the substance of those gains are acknowledged. Should that be the case then the gift successfully maintains its status as gift. If, on the other hand, the gains I make as giver are understood to be the chief motivation, then the gift 'fails' and will not be seen as a gift but, instead, as a manipulative act of generosity.

Whether the gifts given in *The Horse's Teeth* are intuited in excess of what I intended is something that will be determined on an individual basis by the various recipients and the witnesses of the gifted performance works. Noting that it is not just the perception of the donor and donee that have the power to determine this quality of saturation within the gift, but is instead an assessment made by all who encounter the project, breaks the binarism of giver and givee and suggests that the gifts I made were not just to each recipient, but were, in some way, 'given' to all who encounter them.

Throughout *The Horse's Teeth,* the donation of the authorship was only obliquely acknowledged in the project publicity in an attempt to avoid such reduction of the gift and to maintain a focus on what was given rather than on the gains made. There was no mention of my involvement on the project flyer, whilst in the publicity emails my role as the originating artist for the work presented was mentioned only in a footnote. On the project website, subsidiary to the main page presenting the artists' work an additional page explained the role I had (Giving in to Gift, 2012).[6]

## The disguises of the author

Arguably, instead of acknowledging that the authorship of the works in *The Horse's Teeth* had been gifted at all, a more direct challenge could have been mounted on the tendency towards the accumulation of capital that lies within normative practices of authorship had my identity been completely hidden. Yet this may not have been the most efficacious tactic. Those encountering the work would still be approaching it from within those normative modes, and have certain expectations on how authorship should be encountered. In other words, either the recipient artists would be assumed to be the author in the conventional sense if my contribution was completely concealed but they were still named, or – if the work was presented completely anonymously – to know that an author exists (by merit of an encounter with the work), but not know whom they are most likely acts to stimulate curiosity, which could then become the dominant response to the work. Returning to Foucault's analysis:

> [...] if a text should be discovered in a state of anonymity... the game becomes one of rediscovering the author. Since literary anonymity is not tolerable, we can accept it only in the guise of an enigma.'
>
> (2008: 287)

By gifting the authorship to the six other artists, a more oblique challenge is made on the dominant modes of production by encouraging analysis of how systems of authorship operate. By 'giving away' these behaviours, attention is drawn to the manner by which the role of the author is not fixed, but is actively performed. In much the same way that Shannon Jackson notes that Brechtian actors 'attempt to de-autonomize individuated acting styles that produced individuated heroes… [when they are asked] to perform the context of one's character' (2011: 121), here the recipient of the gifted authorship performs the conventions of individuated authorship whilst not fully inhabiting that role. Gifting the authorship enables distance to be gained on the phenomenon, creating an alienation device in the Brechtian sense that allows it to be labelled 'as something striking, something that calls for explanation, [and] is not to be taken for granted, not just natural' (Brecht in Counsell and Wolf, 2001: 47). In this way a challenge is mounted on 'the holders of capital [who] have an ever greater interest in resorting to reproduction strategies capable of ensuring better-disguised transmission' (Bourdieu, 1986: 55).

Even when a work is presented anonymously there will always have been an interplay and focussing of forces that led to the work's formation. This more fluid conception of identity (or number of identities) challenges the notion of the 'Author' (with a capital 'A' to signify it as the identity that holds the stores of capital) as a vast simplification of these effects. Fluid, permeable and dynamic, this more nuanced understanding of authorship (with a lower-case 'a') can be understood as the self(s) that create the work.

The feminist writer and philosopher Rosi Braidotti identifies the subject as 'a radically immanent, intensive body, that is, an assemblage of forces or flows, intensities, and passions that solidify in space and consolidate in time, within the singular configuration commonly known as an "individual" self' (2006: 238). Although any number of subjects might converge to author a text, to deny a place for the intersection of these forces in a porous subjectivity (a denial that the notion of individuated Authorship demands) is to also simplify what the writing subject is.

To avoid setting up a too easy opposition between the two forms of authorship, it is worth also noting their mutuality and interdependence; the fact that, whilst it is conceptually convenient to highlight their differences, they are not two separate entities. Capitalized Authorship has real consequences in the lived experiences of an author; it is a significant determinant in how an individual feels, acts and is received: it is one of the flows of which Braidotti writes. Meanwhile non-capitalized authorship both influences and is the manifestation of the capital held by the Author, any capital raised only accumulates because of the actions, impulses and temperament of the non-capitalized self.

In *The Horse's Teeth*, I attempted to give away the Authorship of the work, the Authorial identity in which symbolic capital is accumulated, whilst arguably, lower case authorship, the lived subjectivity of creating the work that I am using Braidotti's 'assemblage of forces and flows' to conceptualize, could only be partially given (although an attempt at this was made by sharing blog posts that I used to document the creative process). In attempting to separate these modes of authorship, even if such a task could only ever be partially complete, it becomes possible to analyse them, including the flows of affective energy that are to be found within the latter conception of the subject.

Speaking informally with the participating artists after the production of the work it became apparent that, even though the emotional experience of creating the work could not be given to them, they nevertheless experienced a range of affective responses on seeing their name used to promote work that they had not actually made. Some did not feel bothered at all; they felt pride to be associated with the project, whilst others talked about it in terms of distancing and even moderate discomfort.

In *What is an Author?* Foucault suggests (without providing examples) that modern notions of authorship arose as a result of the potential for discourses to be transgressive, a consequence of the need for authors to be 'subject to punishment' (2008: 286). Although such retribution remains a very real threat for some, in the context of *The Horse's Teeth,* where possible legal or physical retribution was very unlikely, any discomfort felt by the artists can perhaps be explained instead because the structure of their identity was challenged and the symbolic capital associated with their name was put in the hands of another.

The title of the project is a reference to the adage 'Don't look a gift horse in the mouth' which, in turn, refers to the way in which the health of a horse can be assessed by examining the state of its mouth. Although the saying tells us that it is inappropriate to perform such examinations – that one should be pleased with any gift that is given (even if it is a diseased horse) – when an artist finds themselves publically responsible for a work over which they have had no control of the making, and may end up disliking, a degree of discomfort becomes understandable.

Nevertheless, perspectives on the significance of this risk varies. Gill and Pratt, commenting in their analysis of 'precarious' cultural work, suggest that a pervasive mentality amongst such workers is that '"you are only as good as your last job", and your whole life and sense of self is bound up with your work' (2013: 34). On the hand, art activist John Jordan presents a very different take on risk-taking in the art world:

> There's a big difference between taking risks in the world of art and in the world outside. In the art world when you provoke, disobey the rules, push the boundaries, question the cannons [sic] you get discovered, rewarded, acclaimed. In the real world when you push the social boundaries you are marginalized, surveilled, beaten and imprisoned. (2006: 5)

Alongside a potential feeling of risk that comes with this manipulation of Authorship, there is a sense that something quite fundamental is changed when Authorship is transferred. Performance works are read from within an identifiable discourse, which includes the past works, symbolic capital, attitudes, and physical attributes of the artist presenting them. By locating a work in relation to a particular Author's identity (and by extension, the stores of capital within that identity) how it is read is affected (as an example, consider how *The Horse's Teeth* would have been received if all six pieces had been presented in my name, rather than the six artists who were involved). It is, as Susan Melrose notes about the choreographer Rosemary Butcher, that 'in invoking the name of a choreographer, it is likely that I and those I speak with are using her name to invoke her past works, through which many of us... probably know the artist. In other words, we utter the proper name as a shorthand for the work itself – or rather... for our experience of it' (2009).

Whilst Barthes asserts the primacy of the text and places the Author outside it so that he can assert the Author's death, this is a fallacy. Although he is right that 'there is one place where this multiplicity [of writings] is focused and that place is the reader, not, as was hitherto said, the author' (1977: 148), the author nevertheless still affects the way in which the text is focussed onto the reader. They, and their stores of capital, are an integral part of the text that the reader activates.

## Economies with emotion

As noted, the lived subjectivity of the non-capitalized author includes the emotional affect that accompanies the encounters, acts and thoughts that make up the creative process. When the capitalized Author is emphasized, this emotional aspect is often passed over, in much the same way that the emotions that accompany the giving of gifts will often be ignored in critical analysis of the phenomenon (for typically, going back to Mauss' foundational anthropological analysis of generosity, *The Gift: The Form and Reason for Exchange in Archaic Societies* (2000) it is the implicit exchange that remains the focus).

Neither is the propensity towards devaluing emotional content to be found solely in these places. Indeed, as Sara Ahmed suggests, it can be seen in critical thought more generally. She notes that the common assumption is that '[t]o be emotional is to have one's judgement affected: it is to be reactive rather than active, dependent rather than autonomous' (2004: 2).

To gain insight into the operation of affect in gift exchange and as collaboration, a reading of *Bodies in* Space, Rachel Gomme's work from *The Horse's Teeth,* proves useful.

A one-to-one piece in a large, half-lit performance space, *Bodies in Space* quietly places the audience and performer in a series of different proxemic and spatial arrangements. On entering the space for the first time, the singular audience member sits for five minutes opposite an empty chair on the far side of the performance space. Once this time has passed, an assistant takes them out of the space and, on re-entering, I, as performer, am now occupying the facing chair. After another few minutes, they again leave and, on returning again, the chairs are much closer together and positioned next to a vase filled with water placed on a table. After another few minutes of sitting together, at the conclusion of the piece, the performer and audience member touch hands and submerge them in a vase of water. The water displaced by this action is captured in a small tray, poured into a jar and, once the lid is sealed, given to the audience member as a gift.

Teresa Brennan observes that whenever two or more people meet, the 'parties bring their affective histories into relationship' (2004: 43). With a substantial part of the performance involving both audience and performer sitting silently, with little stimulation other than the quiet and half-lit presence of the other, a space was created that was particularly conducive to noting such an intersection of emotions. How I, as performer, felt interacted with the emotional state of the audience and determined the specific mood within each repetition of the work.

Sometimes the audience would look interestedly about the room, sometimes they would laugh, some would appear discomforted, one cried, and others would remain quiet and still. As performer, there were times when I would feel comfortable with the structure of the work and my place within it, at others I would experience feelings of clear connection with the person opposite, and sometimes boredom or anxiety would suggest themselves. My emotional state would also depend on what I witnessed in the person opposite me, just as the audience would react to the emotions they sensed in my presence. Sometimes these reactions would act to mirror the other's emotion: if they smiled, I would smile back. At other points however, the affect would be transformed; when they looked disinterested, I would be concerned at the reception of the performance. The emotional character of the space was negotiated between us in a manner identifiably collaborative; by bringing our affective histories in to the encounter something new was

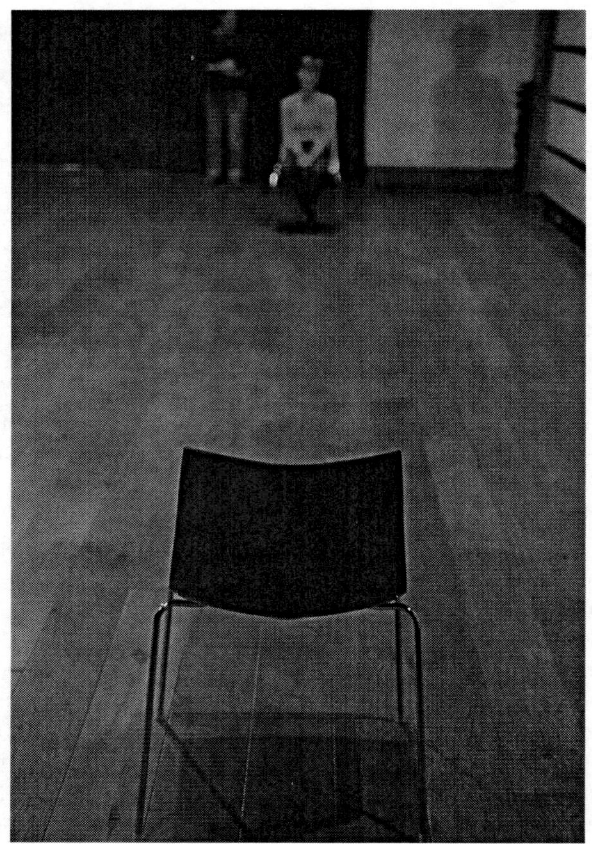

*Fig. 12* Rachel Gomme: *Bodies in Space* (Photo: Mark Loudon)

created. The ambience within the space was unique to and created by the particular configuration of subjectivities.

The conflation of these complex, changing and reactive states determined how the time of the performance was perceived by each of us and this perception was then invested into the jar of water given at the end, acting as a physical reminder of our experience of the time we spent together. The jar acted as document of the 'collaboration' between performer and audience.

As a method of understanding the manner of this investment, Ahmed's theory around the stickiness of signs, objects and emotions can be used. As would be expected, her ideas around stickiness relate

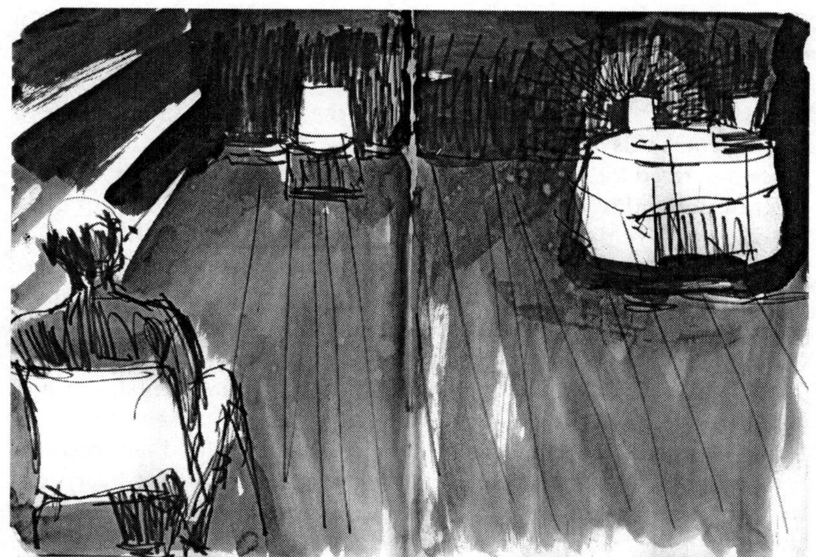

*Fig. 13* Rachel Gomme: *Bodies in Space* (Drawing: Emma Gregory)

to the conceptual surfaces of these phenomena, and how they interact with other surfaces. She writes:

> [...] a sticky surface is one that will incorporate other elements into the surface such that the surface of a sticky object is in a dynamic process of re-surfacing. The incorporation can lead of course to surfaces becoming less sticky. But the stickiness of that surface *still tells us a history of the object that is not dependent on the endurance of the quality of stickiness:* what sticks 'shows us' where the object has travelled through.
>
> (original emphasis. 2004: 91)

In the instance of *Bodies in Space*, the jar of water would have remained a jar of water void of particular memory or affective attachment, but the experiences of the performance 'stick' to the object and are, when the recipient re-encounters the gift at a later date, reconstituted according to the demands of that later context.

A gift's surface is not inherently sticky; a jar of water could be given without any particular weight or significance attached to it, but instead the stickiness is '*an effect of the histories of contact between bodies, objects, and signs...*' (original emphasis. Ahmed, 2004: 90).

Amongst all these different histories of contact, the giver of the gift is one such body that impresses on the surface of the gift object, and through this remains stuck to the gift; both in the metaphorical sense described by Ahmed, and literally in the case of the jar of water where my hand left a faint mark on its surface. Often, the gift-giver (or collaborative partner who 'gives' their contribution to the creative process) remains ensconced with what is given, reappearing each time the gift is encountered and thus, like the other attachments Ahmed references, 'call[s] into question its [the gift's] integrity as an object' (2004: 91).

In *The Horse's Teeth*, the capitalized Author's (formal, legal, attributable) ownership of the work was given to the six presenting artists. However, as was observed previously, the non-capitalized authorship – the thoughts, labour and emotional experiences that went in to constructing the work – was not, and cannot be, transferred simply by changing who presents the work. For, not only does lived experience resist such renaming but, as will be explained, in the instance of *The Horse's Teeth*, the other could already be located within the non-capitalized author.

Returning to Braidotti's definition of the subject, the boundary that structures the identity of the creating author is permeable and what is found within is the result of the 'forces and flows' that originate externally and are potentially externalized again (likely after some form of transformation when passing through the self).

When the identification of the subject as a bounded and self-contained individual is questionable in this way, it becomes similarly uncertain how to definitively identify what is included in 'my' creative process in *The Horse's Teeth*. By drawing on the past works of the recipient artists when generating the work that would be later gifted to them, their artistic identity was blurred with my own, and the work made was something that was situated somewhere between our practices. As Xavier Le Roy said of the work he made for Jerome Bel:

> I thought I was doing what you would do. But in actual fact we realise that it's impossible. Yet, what's interesting in all of this is that I would never have done this performance. From the beginning I would never have done it.
>
> (ctlgrsnn, 2009)

The work made was collaborative in the sense that it existed between my own practice and the recipient's although never settled into either completely.

This is illustrated by *Fěn Hóng Sè*, the work that Richard Layzell presented in *The Horse's Teeth*. In this performance, an afternoon was spent spray-painting the litter in Liverpool's China Town pink (the title is the Mandarin word for this colour). Although I developed the work as a reflection on the forced expulsion of the hundreds of Chinese men in Liverpool who had their UK residency revoked in the period after the Second World War, the work was equally influenced by Layzell's previous work *White on White* (which saw him painting small areas of white walls with white paint in the Greek village of Skyros), the lessons in Mandarin that Layzell was having at the time and the fact that an earlier gift exchange as part of the project had seen him give me a small pot of pink paint. This conflation of influences that could be attributable to either myself or Layzell make clear the impossibility of settling on a singular identity for accrediting the work.

Translating the motion of the 'forces and flows' in the Braidottian self into Ahmed's model, both a subject's and an artwork's identity is determined in terms of all that 'sticks' when the energetic encounters that Braidotti identifies pass through.

Not all encounters 'stick' to the same degree though, a reason for this being, as Ahmed notes, that repeated encounters are more likely to determine identity: 'signs become sticky through repetition; if a word is used in a certain way, again and again, then that "use" *becomes* intrinsic' (2004: 91). Ahmed paraphrases Judith Butler's ideas of performativity to note 'the way in which a signifier, rather than simply naming something that already exists, works to generate that which it apparently names' (2004: 92), and so draws attention to the significance of a specific temporality in determining the power of the performed repetition in determining stickiness. It 'depends upon the sedimentation of the past; it reiterates what has already been said, and its power and authority depend upon how it recalls that which has already been brought into existence' (2004: 92).

It is not just simple acts of repetition that determine identity and meaning though; not all repetitions have the same force; those with a higher store of financial or symbolic capital – be they an institution or individual – in any given field will often carry more weight in determining what 'sticks' to an identity within that sphere. As Bourdieu writes, power and capital 'amount... to the same thing' (1986: p.47); those with capital have more power in determining meaning and identity through the repetitions they influence and implement.

Returning to the feelings of discomfort that some of the artists felt on seeing their name attached to something that was not 'of them' when a work they had not made was presented in their name, I would argue that – since a name is one of the signs repeated most consistently, and therefore sticks most strongly to the self-identification of the individuated subject – it is one of the most key elements of an individual's identity. When the stickiness of the sign is challenged and, as was the case in *The Horse's Teeth*, attached to that outside the borders of the determined self, so the perceived integrity of that identity is destabilised, and potentially ruptured.

Writing in an essay on the blurred identity identifiable in conjoined twins, Margrit Shildrick notes that 'the conventional understanding of the only proper form of subjectivity requires a clarity of boundaries between self and other, an affective and effective autonomy that is fully realised only by singular embodiment sealed by the skin' (2001: 67). The bridging of identities facilitated by both collaboration and the gift provides another example of how such normative understandings of the self are flawed, which, as Shildrick writes elsewhere, has ethical implications that 'demand an openness to the encounter with the unmarked other, the other that is neither the same nor different' (1997: 213). When the distinction between selfhoods is identified as porous, otherness becomes integral to the self, making the possibility of locating the other fully outside the boundaries of selfhood impossible.

To return to the understanding of collaboration as a process of gifting, what is given by each collaborator is inevitably a result of their subjective history and, although this history cannot be fully comprehended by those that receive what they give (be they the collaborative partners or audiences of the work), an intuited sense of that donating subjectivity nevertheless accompanies the act of giving.

This history, when filtered through the medium of a gift that is accepted and 'sticks' to the recipients, leads to the gift acting as a bridge between the parties concerned, and maintains a sense by which ownership is attributable to all those that are stuck to the gift, including the giver. Once given, despite attempts of the law to fix its location, and attribute capital to a discrete, individuated and capitalized Author, *the gift, the capital it signifies, and the emotional response, is a part of, belongs to and affects – in other words, is stuck to – both giver and (all the) recipient(s).* It is for this reason that it feels ethically suspect to dispose of a gift as soon as it has been received; it is not entirely the donee's to do with as they please.[7]

## Notes

1. The artistic directors being Tim Etchells and Elizabeth LeCompte respectively.
2. Video, drawn and photographic documentation of each performance (as selected by the authoring artist) can be viewed on the project website at www.givingintogift.org.
3. Bourdieu (1994) creates a taxonomy of capital that includes the economic, social, and three forms of cultural capital (embodied, objectified and institutionalised). Since he groups all forms of non-economic capital under the label of symbolic, this is the term I am using.
4. The name is a homonym of workfare, a reference to the modifications to the welfare state implemented by the coalition government that forced the mid- to long-term unemployed to work for free at employers such as Poundland, Tesco and Greggs the Bakers in order to continue receiving their benefit (Boycott Workfare, 2013).
5. All the artists involved were, to differing degrees, 'known' artists within the field of performance – they all have presented work both throughout the UK and internationally, some have produced publications about their work, and, taken together, they have decades of experience in making performance artworks.
6. It is worth noting that this writing, and the attention it draws to my role, affects the likelihood that the reader will perceive the gifted works as 'gifts' in the sense described by Marion. There is a chance that the perception of generosity will be reduced by the awareness of the increased gains I make by publishing this text. On the other hand, the hope is that this risk is offset by the value a reader might find within the analysis.
7. Which is not to say that the object cannot be transformed, gifts purchased on holiday by well-meaning friends and family often end up in the charity shop. Arjun Appudurai writes 'today's gift is tomorrow's commodity. Yesterday's commodity is tomorrow's found art object. Today's art object is tomorrow's junk. And yesterday's junk is tomorrow's heirloom' (2006: p. 15). Stickiness does not mean that a permanent bond is forged.

## Bibliography

Ahmed, S. (2004) *The Cultural Politics of Emotion*. (Great Britain: The Cromwell Press).

Appudurai, A. (2006) The Thing Itself. In *Public Culture*, 18:1. 15–22.

Barthes, R. (1977/1967) 'The Death of the Author' In *Image, Music, Text* Translated from French by Stephen Heath (London: Fotana).

Bishop, C. (2006) 'The Social Turn: Collaboration and its Discontents', *Artforum* 44:6. 178–83.

Bourdieu, P. (1986) 'The Forms of Capital' In J. G. Richardson (ed.) *Handbook of Theory of Research for the Sociology of Education*. Translated from French by Richard Nice. (New York: Greenwood Press)

———. (1994) *In Other Words: Essays towards a Reflexive Society*. Translated from French by Matthew Adamson. (Cambridge: Polity Press).

———. and Haake, H. (1995) *Free Exchange*. (Cambridge: Polity Press).

Braidotti, R. (2006) Affirmation versus Vulnerability: On Contemporary Ethical Debates. In *Symposium: Canadian Journal of Continental Philosophy* 10:1. 235–54.

Brecht, B. (2001/1938) The Street Scene. In Counsell , C and Wolf, L, eds. *Performance Analysis: An Introductory Coursebook*. (London: Routledge).

Brennan, T. (2004) *The Transmission of* Affect. (New York: Cornell University Press).

Chiapello, E. (2004) 'Evolution and co-optation', *Third Text* 18:6, 585–94.

ctlgrsnn, (2009) *about 'Xavier le Roy'(2000) 3*. [video online] Available at: https://www.youtube.com/watch?v=OJWMLHGu6Xs [Accessed 10th September 2013].

Derrida, J. (1992) *Given Time 1. Counterfeit Money*. Translated from French by Peggy Kamuf. (Chicago: University of Chicago Press).

Foucault, M. (2008/1969) 'What is an Author?' In David Lodge and Nigel Wood (eds.) *Modern Criticism and Theory: A Reader* (Harlow: Pearson Education).

Gill, R and Pratt, A. (2013) 'Precarity and Cultural Work In the Social Factory? Immaterial Labour, Precariousness and Cultural Work' In *ONCurating.org* 16 [online] Available at: <http://www.on-curating.org/issue_16.php> [Accessed 6 Feb 2013].

Giving in to Gift (2012) *The Horse's Teeth* [website] Available at: <http://givingintogift.org/the-horses-teeth> [Accessed 13 July 2014].

Govan, E., Nicholson, H. & Normington, K. (2007) *Making a performance: devising histories and contemporary practices*. (Abingdon, Routledge).

Hyde, L. (2007) *The Gift: How the Creative Spirit Transforms the World*. (Edinburgh: Canongate Books).

Jackson, S. (2011) *Social Works: Performing Art, Supporting Publics*. (Oxon: Routledge).

Jordan, J. (2006) *In the Footnotes of Library Angels: A Bi(bli)ography of Insurrectionary Imagination*. [online] Available at: <http://www.thisisliveart.co.uk/resources/Study_Room/guides/SRoom_Guides.html> [Accessed 25th February 2013]

Marion, J. (2002) *Being Given: Towards a Phenomenology of Givenness*. Translated from French by Jeffrey L. Kosky. (Stanford: Stanford University Press).

Marx, K. (1990/1867) *Capital Volume 1*. (London: Penguin).

Mauss, M. (2000/1924) *The Gift: The Form and Reason for Exchange in Archaic Societies*. (New York: Routledge).

Melrose, S. (2009) *Rosemary Butcher: Jottings on Signature in the Presence of the Artist*. [Online] Available at: <http://www.sfmelrose.org.uk/jottings> [Accessed 20 September 2013].

Shildrick, M. (1997) *Leaky Bodies and Boundaries*. London: Routledge

———. (2001) Reconfiguring relational economies. In: Ahmed, S. and Stacey, J.eds. (2001) *Thinking through the Skin*. London: Routledge.

Wacquant, L. (1989) 'Towards a Reflexive Sociology: A Workshop with Pierre Bourdieu', *Sociological Theory*, 7:1, 26–63.

Wilmer S.E. (2011) 'Renaming and Performative Reconstructions: The Uncanny Multiplication of Janesz Janša', *Theatre Research International*, 36: 1, 47–63.

# 9
# Asking 'What is Collaboration?' on Behalf of Jerzy Grotowski

*Kris Salata*

## A word of justification

The recent revival of interest in Grotowski's legacy, (as evidenced by a spate of new publications, as well as by UNESCO's 2009 'Year of Grotowski'), comes, in my opinion, as a result of our unsatisfied interest in the autonomous practical investigation of human potentiality – which the modernist avant-garde moved from the realm of utopia to the realm of practical research on the craft of the actor. By 'autonomous practice' I mean long-term laboratory research on the obscure properties of performance: *encounter, presence, aliveness,* and *event* – notions scholarly discourse cannot fully own, and a form of labor typically unaffordable in the academic or professional setting. Our interest in this domain has not been fully satisfied by happenings, performance art, or improvisational theatre, where performance celebrates its unrepeatability. There, the presence, aliveness and encounter that emerge in the mode of the event can be deeply experienced, but not rigorously studied. It seems that such studies can be undertaken only if the form is precisely set and repeatable – in an acting studio in the Stanislavski tradition, of which Grotowski's lab has been one of exceptional examples in contemporary theatre.

Defined as such, Grotowski's autonomous practice faces the incompatibility between the mode of *being* and the mode of *thinking,* directing most its effort to the former, while never losing interest in the latter. Theatre scholarship, on the other hand, finding this incompatibility one of its greatest challenges, overcompensates by thinking about thinking. If phenomenology promises better results by chasing after being, it also leaves many thinkers puzzled. Heidegger, struggling to capture 'being' in his analysis of Heraclitus, notes that the pre-Socratic thinker was called 'The Dark One' or 'The Obscure', precisely because he was attempting to enlighten us about the nature of light in the language of thought.[1] As performance scholars, finding ourselves in Heraclitus' sandals every writing day, we tend to write on the side of clarity, and yearn after the obscure wisdom contained in and through the theatrical event – yearn after the knowing that comes in the kind of practical research that Stanislavski began and Grotowski continued.

Not surprisingly then, despite the increasing output of books and articles on Grotowski-related themes, his work remains relatively obscure. Similarly not surprisingly, the scholarship on Grotowski thrives in a large but closed circle of practitioners and artist-scholars, only rarely engaging 'pure academics,' who are not historians. Consistently, advanced work focused on the craft of the performer falls outside of mainstream contemporary scholarship. Current leading questions in theatre tend to come from broad theoretical perspectives and narratives that vividly engage scholars across disciplines, but seldom originate from the quarries of practical work in the studio.

Therefore I will treat Grotowski as a prolifically present but still rather unfamiliar agency in postmodern theatre, and begin with the introduction of major phases of his artistic research. Each of these periods seems to represent a different mode and perhaps even a next step in his approach to collaboration. Yet rather than claiming evolution and progress, I will treat the shifting meaning of collaboration as a response to naturally occurring turns and changing (refining, narrowing) focus in the artistic work of a ripening, maturing, and then aging director. What follows is a brief narrative of these shifts and their focus.

## Grotowski's phases of artistic research[2]

### Theatre of Productions (1959–1969)

Grotowski directs performances in the Laboratory Theatre, the work for which he is still most recognized. He collaborates with:

- the theatre critic and dramaturg Ludwik Flaszen on the vision for their company as a laboratory, and eventually as an institute;
- the architect Jerzy Gurawski on new concepts of theatrical space;
- his actors, notably with Ryszard Cieślak who played the legendary role of the Prince in *The Constant Prince* and became Grotowski's assistant in the company's last production, *Apocalypsis cum Figuris*. During the rehearsal period of *Apocalypsis cum Figuris*, Grotowski worked increasingly in the mode of collective creation and called the

piece the least his own yet the most rewarding of his productions: 'What was my role in it? The whole paradox is that, for me, it was the most personal performance.'[3]

### Paratheatre / Active Culture (1969–1978)

Grotowski resigns from directing new works for the stage and focuses on active participation.[4] Also referred to as Active Culture, the new work was divided into several separate projects prepared by the company members and led by designated leaders – all overseen by Grotowski.

His main collaborators during this phase were project leaders, each of whom conducted work best suited to his or her interest: Ryszard Cieślak, Zygmunt Molik, Jacek Zmysłowski, Zbigniew Spychalski, Ludwik Flaszen (who from the company's dramaturg shifted to a performance practitioner and project leader), and Włodzimierz Staniewski (later the founder of Gardzienice).

### Theatre of Sources (1976–1982)

Grotowski refocuses on the craft of the performer, works with different traditional cultures around the world. His collaborators become master-practitioners from India, Haiti, Mexico, Nigeria, and other countries.[5] While the momentum for Theatre of Sources was still on the rise, the project was interrupted by political events in Poland and the imposition of martial law. At that point, Grotowski left Poland and received asylum in the U.S.

### Objective Drama (1982–1986)

Grotowski holds professorship at the University of California, Irvine, and continues to work on selected themes from Theatre of Sources.[6] He also meets his future 'essential collaborator' and artistic heir, Thomas Richards.

### Art as Vehicle (1986–)

This marks Grotowski's last phase of work, conducted at the Workcenter of Jerzy Grotowski, his new home base in Tuscany. Partially drawing from the research in Theatre of Sources and Objective Drama, this phase of work centered on the craft of the performer, particularly on the subtle inner work that accompanies a deep process (Grotowski called it 'verticality'). Peter Brook, Grotowski's friend and supporter, eventually titled this last phase 'Art as vehicle', referring to what Grotowski meant by using Stanislavski's phrase, 'the actor's work on himself.' However, besides the study on verticality, Grotowski also focused on what for him was the final interest: the process of transmission of knowledge and research between the master and his chosen disciple. Grotowski considered his ultimate legacy not his texts, but his laboratory work, which he conducted throughout his entire life. He left the publishing rights to all his texts to Thomas Richards and Mario Biagini, two key practitioners at the Workcenter. The special collaboration that took place between him and Thomas Richards as his artistic heir was Grotowski's lasting gesture on behalf of his legacy.

## Which Grotowski? Which collaboration?

In theatre history textbooks, Grotowski's legacy has been mainly associated with some terms coined by him, e.g., 'poor theatre,' 'holy actor,' as well as the few emblematic performances, e.g., *Akropolis, The Constant Prince*, and *Apocalypsis cum Figuris*. There is certainly 'that Grotowski', the avant-garde director of 1960s, and the author of *Towards a Poor Theatre* (in print since 1969). The fortune of theatrical legacies, like the fate of theatricality, depends heavily on writing – the irony of this fact never escapes those who seek theatre's autonomy from the dramatic text. What survives as historical legacies tends to be discourse-friendly; what prevails speaks through a haunting phrase and refers to ideas. However, there is yet 'another Grotowski', only briefly referred to in the dictionaries, and there is yet another legacy, not written in a book, but left behind in the experiences of those who met him through work in all its phases, those who were inspired by his work, and those who have worked and continue working with Richards and Biagini. And as much as I acknowledge that the topic of this chapter is not a theatrical legacy but collaboration, I see these two notions as tightly related in Grotowski's case. Collaboration is part of his legacy as it is simultaneously its means. To put it more directly, I will quote from Grotowski's first collaborator, Ludwik Flaszen:

> Grotowski's project, to some degree – as much as his life, as much as theatre in general – is a group project. How much is his personal biography, his artistic biography, connected with the biographies of other people? It had been after all a never-stopping exchange of energy, imagination, ideas. [...] Is there such a thing as Grotowski without a company? Grotowski without a company – who would it have been?[7]

This insight, true for many other theatre artists, yet not necessarily universally applicable (the likes of Tadeusz Kantor or Richard Foreman seem to be notable exceptions, or entirely different phenomena, despite their insistent use of the same actors), prompts us to a careful analysis of Grotowski's relationships with those with whom he worked, or rather, with whom he "truly met" through work. During the Theatre of Productions period, that 'true meeting' would take place in the shared labor of the actor and the director:

> Each of us is to some extent a mystery. Something creative may happen in theatre – between the director and the actor – exactly when a contact between two mysteries takes place. By coming to know the mystery of another, one comes to know his own. And vice-versa: by coming to know one's own, one comes to know the mystery of another. It is not possible with everyone. Speaking in this way, I don't intend to make a pronouncement on the worth of other people. Simply, life made us in such a way that we can meet: you and I. We can meet for life and death – carry out a deed together. Create as if it were the last time, as if one was to die immediately after.[8]

This concept of work characterized by fervent labor towards unveiling oneself through meeting another human, but also by the singularity and exclusivity of such an encounter, Grotowski took as foundational for his theatre, as it was, for him, foundational in human experience. For him, it would always be a meeting between two individuals, even in a group situation.[9] In other words, he was not interested in some universal social models of collaboration, but rather in what uniquely can happen between two people. Certainly, collaboration based on such unique events must also be inimitable.

## Meetings with the devil's advocate

Ludwik Flaszen was Grotowski's first major collaborator and a key figure during the entire Theatre of Production period, including the paratheatrical activities in 1970s. Thus he was perhaps the most important collaborator of Grotowski in the traditional sense – as a literary director/dramaturg of the company, but also as a co-manager taking care of administrative issues, co-strategist securing the company's survival, and co-dreamer about the artistic mission and aspirations. It was Flaszen who invited Grotowski to co-direct the Theatre of 13 Rows in a small remote town of Opole in 1959. Only twenty-nine years old, but already an accomplished theatre critic and a man of certain influence, Flaszen received a proposition to take over a small provincial theatre. He agreed and persuaded a charismatic directing rookie (three years his junior) to leave Kraków, Poland's theatrical mecca, and join him in the cultural desert of the country's remote southwestern region. The company's subsequent placement in the hall of fame of twentieth-century world theatre must be owed to the unique quality of Flaszen's and Grotowski's collaboration.[10]

Their relationship is often compared to that of Konstantin Stanislavski and Vladimir Nemirovich-Danchenko in the Moscow Art Theatre, and Juliusz Osterwa and Mieczysław Limanowski in the Polish interwar Teatr Reduta. These two research theatres, both governed by collaborating leaders, developed the model the Laboratory Theatre could take after – the model based on creative critical dialogue, mutual inspiration, and conscious development of the work. In a letter to his biographer, Grotowski cautions against drawing too much from the analogies and emphasizes differences rather than similarities in the modus operandi of these collaborations.[11] Here again, Grotowski insists on the uniqueness of each relationship, while silently accepting the collaborative leadership model. The similarities between these 'theatrical couples,' however, show that an affirmative agreement to create and maintain the institutional basis for the collaborative project comes despite vivid distinctions between individual attitudes. Or rather, the decision to work together involves the acceptance of those distinctions as productive. To put it in other terms, collaboration involves the play of affirmation and difference, and the affirmation of difference.

Two radically dissimilar directors, the actor-oriented and studio-bound Stanislavski and the dramaturgy-oriented Nemirovich-Danchenko, greatly differed in their artistic ideas and approaches to craft, and constantly fought with each other both professionally and privately. Nevertheless, at a critical moment for the company, Danchenko 'recognized Stanislavski's "mania" (his System) as the key matter of the entire enterprise.'[12] Similarly, Limanowski had written negative reviews of Osterwa's work, only to later provide an institutional home for Reduta, where he joined Osterwa as his key collaborator. Their subsequent deep friendship never compromised their sharp evaluation of each other's work.

Similarly in the Laboratory Theatre case, Flaszen, who invited Grotowski to take over a provincial theatre: 'You will be the manager and the director, and I will be your main collaborator,'[13] did so despite having written highly critical reviews of Grotowski's previous work. While the two became close friends, they constantly engaged in polemics, or, 'the games of polemics.' To further emphasize the 'play' aspect of their debates, Grotowski jokingly compared himself and his colleague to the famous pair of circus clowns, Koko and August.[14] In his recent book, *Grotowski and Company*, Flaszen describes these debates, often held late at night at the only-open restaurant at the train station, as wordsmithing sessions: 'During our first years working together, but also later, I was Grotowski's advisor and a kind of sparring partner in the art of producing words.'[15] It was during these sessions that 'poor theatre,' 'holy actor,' and other key terms had been rehearsed, and then coined. Having been a fearless theatre critic, radical thinker, original writer, and erudite, Flaszen proved himself to be an ideal partner and 'advocatus diaboli', as Grotowski refers to him, to a young director trying to reinvent theatre for the twentieth-century spectator. Therefore Flaszen's modest statement (contained in the same book): 'I have been to Grotowski like Johann Peter Eckermann was to his friend Goethe: just a humble recorder, meticulously writing down the master's words for the benefit of the next generations,'[16] must be disregarded as indeed too humble. He was certainly more than a recorder of Grotowski's words.

Flaszen held his advisory and literary post throughout Theatre of Productions, but later, during the expansion of collaborative work in paratheatre, he expanded his role to a practitioner leading sessions of his own creation, Meditations Aloud. In them, Flaszen sought alternative modes of conversation that transcended debates held in public: 'Debating is a sickness of our times: the uncertainty whether we exist or not. And the end of a debate is often an acknowledgment of authority, a bowing the head in front of power, any power.'[17] What Flaszen looked for in these sessions paralleled what other paratheatrical projects sought as well: concrete ways of liberating individuals from social mechanisms, ways of unlocking individual potential, and new possibilities of ritual play with nature and through nature with others.

What seems particularly interesting to me, is that after a decade of playing 'the devil's advocate' and advisor to Grotowski, Flaszen joined the rest of the company in practical research, becoming an active 'doer' and scholar-practitioner: 'As a man of letters, a theorist, I sensed a chance to satisfy my hunger. I entered the path of acting, not really realizing where it might lead me.'[18] In the context of the 'theatrical couples' of the Moscow Art Theatre and Teatr Reduta, Flaszen's transformation seems to be significant, and despite Grotowski's cautioning, I would like to draw some conclusions from the similarities between those collaborating pairs.

Nemirovich-Danchenko was a man of the letter, even though he staged plays. His alliance with Stanislavski brought him close to studio practice. His decision to support Stanislavski's insistent pursuit of the system of training and preparing the actor should probably be seen as his recognition of the practice-based research. Limanowski was a scientist (an accomplished geologist), who embraced a famous actor in a pursuit of "liturgical theatre," and new pedagogy. He too recognized studio work and theatre-institute as foundational for the future of theatre. When theoretically-minded Flaszen provided Grotowski with the opportunity to do research in the studio and then develop an institute, he also embraced the performance-as-research model and found in it his own way to practice. All three enterprises acknowledged the primacy of practice-based research, and in all three cases the institutional basis came secured by literary men who recognized the agency of intuitive visionary practitioners and provided them with constructive criticism (even if this criticism varied in form in each case). In my attempt to summarize these cases of collaboration in a modern theatre laboratory, I merely wish to emphasize the role of the theorist as catalytic rather than programmatic, supportive rather than leading, and facilitating rather than formulatory.

Within that model, however, other vital collaborations took place, involving the director and the actor. During the production years, Grotowski managed to keep his relationship with Flaszen quite separate from his creative work on performances, using Flaszen's critical view at the point when some key components of the new work had been already established. In that way, Flaszen could provide a more objective analysis and references on behalf of the work that developed organically from the direct confrontation with the actor's material. Such work bases itself on the text embodied by the personal response of the actor and becomes shaped in the direction of that deeply subjective response rather than fashioned by dramaturgical (or even directorial) ideas. Slowly developed rather than programmatically imposed, such an approach became Grotowski's fully-elucidated modus operandi in his two last productions, *The Constant Prince* and *Apocalypsis cum Figuris*. The latter production completely abandoned the original text of the play the group took on and moved along the actors-created material to finally 'acquire' texts from various sources – poems, scriptures, and fragments of prose the actors proposed by themselves. The former production involved a slow incubatory rehearsal process with a single actor and stands today as a great example of the collaborative work that Grotowski branded as directing, and which he also called, 'ideal spectatorship.' It is that process that I wish to comment upon next.

## Meeting the holy actor

The labor of theatre begins for Grotowski as an individual confrontation with source material. In this primarily introspective but reciprocal process (the actor 'reads' the material, and the material 'reads' the actor), the actor should be able to 'meet himself.' This foundational encounter in the theatrical event, however, does not take place in solitude:

> Actors and I confront the text. We cannot express that which is objective in the text, and frankly, only really weak texts yield barely one interpretation. All great texts are like an abyss. (...) My encounter with the text resembles my encounter with the actor and his with me. And for the director and the actor, the text serves as a scalpel enabling us to open ourselves and transcend ourselves, to discover what is hidden in us, and to fulfill the deed of encountering others.[19]

Thus the essentially subjective primary process of 'meeting oneself' depends on the intersubjective and objective processes in which others take part. All three of these modes of relating, and ways of knowing – the Davidsonian 'tripod of knowledge'[20] – exist in all encounters in the creative process in theatre. All three modes take part in what we might call 'collaboration.' Grotowski's working encounter with Ryszard Cieślak in *The Constant Prince* serves as a great instance of the function of the 'tripod.'

Based on Calderon's play adapted by the Polish Romantic poet, Juliusz Słowacki, the Laboratory Theatre's *The Constant Prince* is often mentioned as an exemplary performance of Grotowski's 'holy actor.' In his 1990 speech commemorating Cieślak's lifework, Grotowski reflected on his work with the actor in that performance as an extraordinary encounter seldom possible between the actor and the director:

> It happens very rarely that the symbiosis between the so-called actor and so-called director transcends all boundaries of technique, philosophy, or convention. Here this symbiosis reached such depth that it was hard to determine whether there were two human beings working together or one human being working in two persons.[21]

Grotowski started to work with Cieślak alone, without witnesses, in 1963, several months before he slowly introduced the rest of the cast to what was shaping. He then continued his individual sessions with Cieślak in addition to the whole cast rehearsals until the opening night in 1965, and then beyond. As it had been the case at the Laboratory Theatre, the work on the performance continued until the closing night, which in this particular case would mean 1971. The rehearsals always involved the creative process that would further refine or alter the performance score, and for as long as there was something left to explore and discover for the actor (and consequently for the director), the work would be shown to the audiences. A performance that would no longer be in a discovery phase, or in other words, a performance that had reached perfection, would no longer be shown. For Grotowski, the end of exploration marks the end of the encounter and thus the end of the performance's life. The creative progression that propels the life of the performance is one in which the actor confronts himself in a process that is 'ultimate, sincere, ordered, precise, and total – not only with one's thoughts, but rather a confrontation that engages one's whole being from the instincts and the unconsciousness all the way to the clarity of the mind.'[22] And consequently, the cease of self-revelation for the actor simultaneously means the end of the run of the show.

What took place in the rehearsals with Cieślak will remain a secret. Grotowski revealed only some aspects of their work, and only those that Cieślak himself talked about with some of his own students. The delicate sphere of recalling his first physical intimacy with a lover (on which the actor based his performance score) demanded isolation, time, and an uninhibited enduring witness. Grotowski compared Cieślak's process to that of a shy animal in the wild, easily alerted or frightened, taking a long time to fully open up. However, when he would reach that sphere of openness, he could remain there for several months, working patiently and methodically on the smallest details of the acting score, to the level of impulses that initiate the subtlest physical actions. Yet the actor's work did not aim at the reenactment of the past experience, but rather, at 'that seemingly impossible prayer.'[23] It was in the territory of the prayer that the actor's process of associations and recollection met the character of the martyr in the play – the textual man and God, and the lover and the beloved brought in by the actor in collaboration with the director. The final directorial montage of the mise-en-scène involved the rest of the cast as the chorus applauding the sacrifice of the prince. Their costumes referred to the military prosecutors of 1950s Poland, while Cieślak wore a Christ-like lion cloth. The design of space put the audience in the position of the peeping tom looking down at the stage from behind a palisade. Grotowski weaved it all into the momentous connection between the carnal prayer of the lover and the martyr.

## Meeting in collective creation

The final Laboratory Theatre production, *Apocalypsis cum Figuris*, began from an attempt to stage a play by a Polish Romantic poet Juliusz Słowacki, but after an extended development process it ended as a devised piece that at one point disposed of the play to later introduce to the developed work new texts brought in by the actors and the director. The premise of the final version of the work was a bold and even blasphemous confrontation with myths that underpin contemporary society. Working in the spirit of an ultimate resolve (according to Grotowski's motto: work as if this was to be your last deed), the actors built theatrical circumstances for their personal confession. Not only was *Apocalypsis* a site for each actor's confrontation with him/herself, but also a confrontation of the ensemble with performance creation. In an illuminating commentary on the shaping of what ended up as the most celebrated and last theatrical work of the Polish Theatre Laboratory, Grotowski makes several key points on the nature of collaboration during this transitional phase from theatre into a larger, participatory cultural experiment. It is there that Grotowski married artistic and human interest and thus creative work and a meeting through work: 'If such interest – human interest – is not there, I don't think one can be a director in the deep sense. At most, one can be the one who mounts a play.'[24] Grotowski's 'director in a deep sense' is a person who meets the actor not within the socially formed and performed behavioral patterns (personality), but through resignation from such responses. More pragmatically, Grotowski meant resignation from pretending, or from falling into one's own stereotypes – evenly applicable to one's life and art.[25] On the other side of that negation, Grotowski sets the highest goal: to be a fully revealed human being: 'That's why I was able to discover that the actor should seek what I called – with Theophilus of Antioch – "his Man [*Człowiek*]": "Show me your Man and I will show you my God."'[26]

Grotowski consequently realized that, in order to make the performance, the director has to resign from his own creation, because there is someone more important than him.'[27] This statement must be read in conjunction with the ending sentence in the same text: 'The whole paradox is that, for me, it was the most personal performance.'[28] Yet if he says that through resignation from one's self-expression on behalf of the manifestation of another's self-revelation (not self-expression!), paradoxically, one becomes realized, he claims it for both the actor as well as the director. Self-revelation means resignation from self-expression.

UNIVERSITY OF WINCHESTER
LIBRARY

What operates here as a formula is hardly a method, but rather a general observation that points to a unique problem-solving for each unique creative process. There is no 'Grotowski method.'

*Apocalypsis* turned out to be an exhaustive creative process and complete act that asked actors as people and as actors to resign from the veil of habit, routine, compromise, trick of craft, social behavior, automatic response, and even the safety of the text. It was Grotowski's and his company's culmination of growth in the acting craft, collective creation, and questioning of theatre. It was theatre and at the same time, a real deed done as secular ritual. On the other hand, the performance was scored in the smallest detail and never improvised. The work leading to its creation (which one can historically see as the path from the beginning of the Laboratory Theatre) had to also be singular and thus final: 'Not only I, but no other member of our group could repeat that process.'[29] Even though he would return to the very challenges that he encountered in "that process" – secular ritual, aliveness, self-revelation through the process of creation, the inner aspect of the acting craft – *Apocalypsis* meant for him the end of directing productions and the movement forward with research on the encounter via completely irreproducible participatory events that were open to the public.

Thus the naturally emerged collective collaboration manifested itself as a transformative and transitory phenomenon – one that is unrepeatable but also one that inflicts a non-returnable shift to other challenges.

## Meeting through craft

Since the company performed (and continued rehearsing) *Apocalypsis* throughout the entire paratheatrical period (and through most of Theatre of Sources), many of its audience members would naturally want to engage with Grotowski and his company in a project where they could become active participants and perhaps experience some of the process they witnessed in the actors. Simultaneously, the company was eager to meet new people under new circumstances, testing new grounds for theatre. This, of course, brought in many new challenges, the biggest of which was the absence of the skills Grotowski's actors developed over the years of training. I do not mean the objective skills of the performer, such as vocal, physical, or improvisational, but rather, the ability to resign from pretending.

Therefore the company gradually opened up to include first a small group of outsiders, and then increasing the numbers, and dealing with the consequences of moving in the direction:

> [T]here exists some particular mystery of work among people; it is not a mystery in the sense that it is unclear, but rather that it is something very hard to disseminate broadly. When one begins to disseminate it, one must immediately fight against the loss of the mystery in each individual – this is the risk that one has to take if one doesn't want to become entirely closed off. On the other hand, [working] entirely closed off is also dangerous, because then we become like a lake that is drying out [...]. Work with a limited number of people makes sense in the laboratory phase, but then we have an obligation to come out and face other people. [...] Opening of the work revealed individual tendencies in my colleagues, varied possibilities and needs, while in the beginning mainly my needs were deciding, because I worked with small groups. So then all sorts of different directions took off in the work, and [...] we reached the phenomenon of 'dzieło-rzeka' [work-river].[30]

Paratheatre depended on two different modes of collaboration: that of the members of the company, who would work together in small groups preparing and leading different projects, and that of the participants who would join in for a single event and co-create it in active relation with others. Thinking about this situation, one must wonder about sustainability of the creative momentum for the leaders who must face the fact that the participants, for whom the experience will not pass the level of initiation – how long can this kind of encounter be rewarding for the company? It seems that the 'drying lake' syndrome threatens both closed and open work. Noticing this limitation prompted Grotowski to leave paratheatrical projects and focus on work in smaller groups with master-performers, where new levels of the performance-based encounter would become available through craft, and where work could be closed for periods of time and open to meet other performers.

In Theatre of Sources Grotowski reached out to many masters of performance craft in different countries, beginning a broad intercultural collaboration researching sources of performance techniques that belong to the craft but precede the cultural distinction. This short-lived but extremely productive period also marks Grotowski's return to the questions of the craft, on which he would spend the rest of his days, first in Poland as a home-base, from where he would make research trips to India, Haiti, and other parts of the world, then in his new home base in the United States, during his tenure at the University California, Irvine in the Objective Drama, and finally in Italy, at his Workcenter.

## An exceptional encounter: Transmission

Grotowski chose an actor, not a director, or scholar-practitioner, to take over his Workcenter in Pontedera, reclaiming the most profound kind of the theatrical encounter he had undertaken. We should note, however, that Grotowski was first educated in a theatre conservatory as an actor, and only later did he take on directing. Such had been a natural path in the conservatory system in Poland at that time: directing was only offered as a post-graduate degree, and typically was pursued by actors with some experience in the field. Untested on professional stages, Grotowski enrolled in the directing course straight after graduating from the acting program.[31] Did he seek in the process of others what he intuitively yearned for as an unrealized actor? Certainly his understanding of the role of the director as an ideal mentor and spectator for the actor confirms his belief in the actor's creative act as the most essential work in theatre, and in the encounter with the actor as most meaningful to him. Profound and fruitful during the Laboratory Theatre period, his collaborations with dramaturgs, designers, and scholars, did not extend into the post-commercial research phase.

In his essentialist stripping of theatre from dramatic literature, scenography, production conventions, and then the production itself, he spent his final years in a remote barn in Tuscany, surrounded by a group of actors. They would live nearby and work intensely for years without a plan to perform for the audience. The research evolved around the questions of the inner work of the actor and related notions such as aliveness and verticality. Yet simultaneously, Grotowski pursued his final collaboration that involved transmission of knowledge to Richards and therefore a conscious effort to counter the written documentation of his lifework with an ongoing practical research.

Richards started as Grotowski's student in the workshop in Irvine, then assistant-apprentice in Pontedera, to become a leader of one of two groups there. With the other group dropped due to funding issues (a group led my Maud Robarts), Richards became Grotowski's main assistant, soon referred to as his 'essential collaborator.' Grotowski invested most of his dissipating energy in the individual work sessions with Richards, focusing on the acting propositions based on songs from the Afro-Caribbean tradition. He would also prepare the young American to lead and shape the work of others. Soon it was Richards who conducted all creative work and all individual training at the Workcenter. Grotowski gradually withdrew from active participation in the group work, to take a role of Richards' advisor. If on the one hand their collaboration had undergone several distinct stages, on the other, it developed organically as traditional transmission between the master artisan and his apprentice. Richards talks about his work with Grotowski and about his nascent research at the Workcenter in two books, *At Work with Grotowski on Physical Actions*, and *Heart of Practice: Within the Workcenter of Jerzy Grotowski and Thomas Richards*.[32] In my interviews with him, I never asked about the meaning of the term 'essential collaborator,' to avoid engaging in territorial disputes that surround Grotowski's legacy. Culturally 'other' as American, but also young and relatively inexperienced when he first met Grotowski, Richards remains unacknowledged as Grotowski's artistic heir by many of those who had been close to the Polish director in the earlier phases of his work.

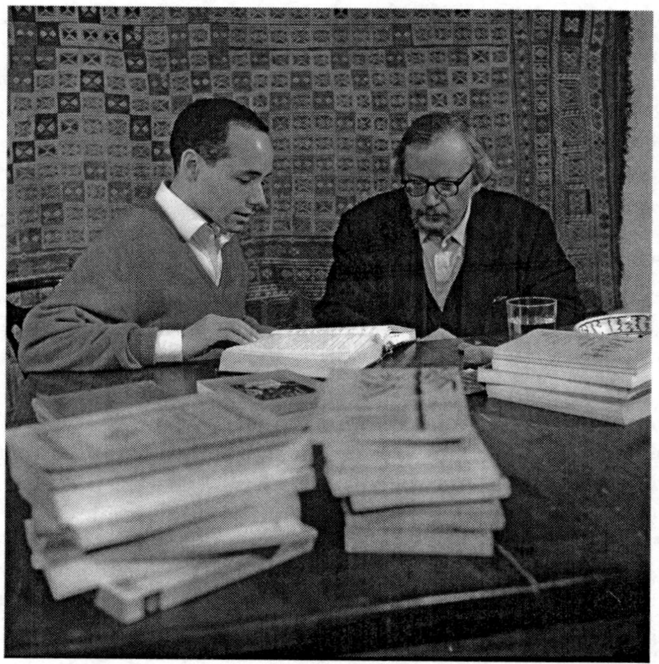

*Fig. 14* Jerzy Grotowski with Thomas Richards in the early 1990s. Photograph by Piergorgio Castellani

Yet any conversation with Richards brings in the echo of Grotowski's presence, whether it comes as a particular reference to his teaching, or as a radical question about something that is uncritically assumed about the nature of theatre, the actor's work, the role of the spectator, or 'methods' that lead to creativity. It seems that in Richards one gets Grotowski's philosophy applied and modified in today's reality. Yet it is also genuinely Richards' philosophy, one he had grown into during his thirteen-year-long apprenticeship, one he had helped shape through his research with Grotowski, and finally one that he had developed since Grotowski's passing. But in addition to credit and burden that Richards received as a bearer of Grotowski's legacy, I also see in him the bearer of the weight of the human meeting that took place between the dying master and his artistic son and caretaker.

## In conclusion

Grotowski died in his modest apartment near the Workcenter studio on January 14, 1999, at the age of 66. His last act of collaboration was a decisive effort on behalf of the intersubjective and subjective modes of the encounter, and on behalf of practical work in performance as the primary mode of documentation/depository.

As a thinker as well as a practitioner, Grotowski kept re-asking the oldest questions in our field: What is an actor? What is a director? What is a spectator? What is a theatrical event? Far from searching for pedantic definitions and ultimate methods, he sought instead clarity of purpose and boldness of action. In his uncompromised pursuit of the answers, he was able to meet others in a profound way. It seems that for him, theatre – or rather, his questioning of theatre – was a means of the human encounter.

Deep thinker, yet declared non-theorist, Grotowski deserves two separate critical approaches, one on the written, and another on all the unwritten work. His last will gives agency to the latter. It is also in the latter where the full understanding of collaboration resides.

## Notes

1. Martin Heidegger, *Early Greek Thinking*, (San Francisco: HarperCollins, 1984), 103.
2. Simply because of the limited scope here, and a large number of quite distinctive long-term collaborations and friendships that would require special studies, I will not be able to discuss several key figures in Grotowski's life, such as: Richard Schechner, Eugenio Barba, Peter Brook, Andre and Mercedes

Gregory, Michelle Kokosowski, Zbigniew Osiński, Leszek Kolankiewicz, Magda Złotowska, Maud Robart, Roberto Bacci, Carla Pollastrelli, Lisa Wolford, and many, many others. Several of them have published their own extensive accounts of meetings with Grotowski. Some others have already been accounted for in the extensive literature on Grotowski. Hopefully more is yet to come. My humble goal in this chapter is to begin asking about the nature of collaboration in Grotowski's work and hopefully sketch the directions for a larger study to follow.

3. Jerzy Grotowski, 'On the Genesis of *Apocalypsis*,' trans. Kris Salata, *TDR: The Drama Review*, 52, no. 2 (2008): 51.
4. The Laboratory Theatre still performed *The Constant Prince* until 1971, and *Apocalypsis cum Figuris* until 1980, both in Poland and internationally. Zbigniew Osiński, 'Występy gościnne Teatru Laboratorium 1959–1984. Kronika działalności 1978–1984,' *Pamiętnik Teatralny*, 49, no. 1–4 (2000): 627–90.
5. Jairo Questa, a Columbian actor, was one of the first to engage with Grotowski in what later became Theatre of Sources. He remained Grotowski's important collaborator throughout this period.
6. In Irvine, Grotowski collaborates with a young director, James Slowiak, who becomes his main assistant there.
7. Ludwik Flaszen in: Agata Chałupnik, Zofia Dworakowska, Malgorzata Terlecka-Reksnis, and Joanna Woźniacka, eds., *Grotowski – Narratives* (Wrocław-Warszawa: Instytut Grotowskiego, 2013), 134. Transl. by the author.
8. Jerzy Grotowski, 'On the Genesis of *Apocalypsis*,' 41.
9. For example, Grotowski did not like the term 'audience,' and preferred 'spectators,' in which individuals are not generalized as a group.
10. Zbigniew Osiński, *Grotowski i jego Laboratorium* (Warszawa: PIW, 1980), 62.
11. Zbigniew Osiński, 'Grotowski o "parach teatralnych"' [Grotowski on 'Theatrical Couples'], *Pamiętnik Teatralny*, vol.1–2, 2001, 5–13. Translated by the author.
12. Osiński, 'Grotowski ...,' 13.
13. Osiński, 'Grotowski ...,' 13.
14. Osiński, 'Grotowski ...,' 13.
15. Ludwik Flaszen, *Grotowski and Company*, (Holstebro: Icarus, 2010), 55.
16. Flaszen, *Grotowski*, 277.
17. Flaszen, *Grotowski*, 139–40.
18. Flaszen, *Grotowski*, 136.
19. Jerzy Grotowski, 'Teatr jest spotkaniem' [Theatre is an Encounter], in: Jerzy Grotowski, *Teksty zebrane* [Collected texts], (Warszawa and Wrocław: Instytut im. Jerzego Grotowskiego, Instytut Teatralny im. Zbigniewa Raszewskiego, Wydawnictwo Krytyki Politycznej, 2012), 325. The quoted fragment has been translated by the author from Polish, from the recently released collection of Grotowski's texts. 'Theatre is an Encounter' was first published in English in: Jerzy Grotowski, *Towards a Poor Theatre* (Holstebro: Odin Teatrets, 1968) in Robert Dewsnap (with Grotowski) translation. The original text came from a 1967 interview with Naim Kattan, conducted in French in Montreal, Canada, during an international theatre symposium. Because the original English translation is old and problematic, I opted not to cite from

*Towards a Poor Theatre*, and instead, to rely on the Polish version of the text, which consulted the French as well as the English versions, and which is now considered 'final' in Polish, and which I translated.

20. Donald Davidson, *Subjective, Intersubjective, Objective*, (Oxford: Clarendon Press, 2001).
21. Jerzy Grotowski, 'Książę Niezłomny Ryszarda Cieślaka' [Ryszard Cieślak's The Constant Prince], *Notatnik Teatralny*, no. 10, Spring-Summer, 1995, 21–28. Translated by the author.
22. Grotowski, *Teksty zebrane*, 325.
23. Grotowski, 'Książę Niezłomny Ryszarda Cieślaka,' 24.
24. Grotowski, 'On the Genesis of *Apocalypsis*,' 41.
25. Grotowski, 'On the Genesis of *Apocalypsis*,' 42.
26. Grotowski, 'On the Genesis of *Apocalypsis*,' 41.
27. Grotowski, 'On the Genesis of *Apocalypsis*,' 42.
28. Grotowski, 'On the Genesis of *Apocalypsis*,' 51.
29. Grotowski, 'On the Genesis of *Apocalypsis*,' 41.
30. Grotowski, *Teksty Zebrane*, 696.
31. Grotowski studied his first year in Moscow, and then transferred to Kraków, back to his alma mater, where he finished his degree. Zbigniew Osiński, *Grotowski i jego Laboratorium* (Warszawa: PIW, 1980), 24.
32. Thomas Richards, *At Work with Grotowski on Physical Actions* (New York: Routledge, 1995), *Heart of Practice: Within the Workcenter of Jerzy Grotowski and Thomas Richards* (New York: Routledge, 2008).

## Bibliography

Chałupnik, Agata, Zofia Dworakowska, Malgorzata Terlecka-Reksnis, and Joanna Woźniacka, eds., *Grotowski – Narratives*. Wrocław-Warszawa: Instytut Grotowskiego, 2013.

Davidson, Donald. *Subjective, Intersubjective, Objective*. Oxford: Clarendon Press, 2001.

Flaszen, Ludwik. *Grotowski and Company*. Holstebro: Icarus, 2010.

Grotowski, Jerzy. *Teksty zebrane* [Collected texts]. Warszawa and Wrocław: Instytut im. Jerzego Grotowskiego, Instytut Teatralny im. Zbigniewa Raszewskiego, Wydawnictwo Krytyki Politycznej, 2012.

———. 'On the Genesis of *Apocalypsis*.' Translated by Kris Salata. *TDR: The Drama Review* 52, no. 2 (2008): 40–51.

———. 'Książę Niezłomny Ryszarda Cieślaka' [Ryszard Cieślak's The Constant Prince], *Notatnik Teatralny*, no. 10, Spring-Summer, 1995, 21–28.

Heidegger, Martin. *Early Greek Thinking: The Dawn of Western Philosophy*. Translated by David Farrell and Frank A. Capuzzi. New York: Harper & Row, 1984.

Osiński, Zbigniew. 'Występy gościnne Teatru Laboratorium 1959–1984. Kronika działalności 1978-1984,' *Pamiętnik Teatralny*, 49, no. 1–4 (2000): 627–90.

———. *Grotowski i jego Laboratorium*. Warszawa: PIW, 1980.

Richards, Thomas. *Heart of Practice: Within the Workcenter of Jerzy Grotowski and Thomas Richards*. New York: Routledge, 2008.

———. *At Work with Grotowski on Physical Actions*. New York: Routledge, 1995.

# 10

# *Te Kore* and the Encounter of Performance

*Carol Brown and Moana Nepia*

> *E kore au e ngaro; te kākano, i ruia mai i Rangiātea.*
> *I will never be lost. The seed that was sown from Rangiātea.*
> (*Ancient Māori Proverb*)

> Walking together means: when you walk into the hole I cannot walk alongside, I must walk-with. This walking-with is more than taking a step with you; it is creating a movement with you.
> (Manning, 2009, 107)

How can dancing an indigenous concept open a collaborative space of uncertainty through which the future can be imagined differently to a colonized or imperial past and neocolonial globalized present?

In this joint writing, we share insights into our research exploring collaboration as a choreographic encounter through the body – sharing connections to place, histories and personal experience *kanohi ki te kanohi* (face-to-face). Our conversation is voiced not through the dominant western paradigm of theatre, but from a space of physical and cultural proximity in which the layering of cultural interpretations and contemporary insights draws upon indigenous Māori and settler influences. The challenge of this approach towards a new theatre of cultural alignment is to articulate individual vocations as physical calls and listening in pursuit of knowledge. These are investigative performances where doubt, uncertainty, and creative instability are perceived as positive moments to be reconciled as part of an ethical process.

We position our collaborative work as a performative and spatial conceptualization of *Te Kore*, the Māori concept of void, absence and nothingness also understood as a space or time of potentiality. Extending threads of Moana's positioning of *Te Kore* as a realm of theatrical, choreographic and social possibility within his practice-led PhD thesis, our writing stems partly from choreographic investigations devised as part of this investigation (Nepia, 2013). In this chapter we also reflect upon collaborative work led by Carol where we have touched upon and sensed connections to other bodies and traditions of thought. Carol previously wrote about this experience as an encountering of limits, 'confronting that which is outside our experience, something unknown, different and potentially uncomfortable' (Brown, 2003). This openness to exploring new possibilities, her previous experience working with Charles Koroneho, and advocacy of academic enquiry through choreographic and performance research was what attracted Moana to her as a potential collaborator.

## History of Our Collaboration

As dancers and scholars, our bodies incorporate movement in ways that are familiar yet different. Carol trained in dance in New Zealand and the UK and Moana trained in New Zealand and Australia. We had parallel careers in Europe before returning to Aotearoa New Zealand in the 2000s where we eventually met. Our coming together through shared interests and backstories from the European performance environment is also marked by our differences, as we cross gender, sexuality and cultural identities. Carol is *pākeha,* of European, predominantly Irish ancestry. Moana is of Irish, English and Māori ancestry from the Ngāti Porou, Rongowhakaata, Te Aitanga a Hauiti and Ruawaipu tribes on the East Coast of the North Island of New Zealand. Through conversation we established an additional important connection – Carol's family had settled and established a family farm on the East Coast, in Tolaga Bay, where Moana's father was born. We sense commonality as grounded rapport, shared histories, memories and connections to place. Our collaboration makes space for us to work with each other, aligning histories, memories and words that place us together.

Context is further embedded in what we make and how we relate. We have moved from physically intimate partnering through dancing together in real-time, to a remote collaboration calibrated by Wi-Fi connectivity and the erratic rhythm of emails, Skype conversations and words shared between two different time zones. Moana writes from Honolulu in Hawai'i while Carol is in Auckland, New Zealand. Screens now form the interface for collaboration. Keys nuance touch and kinesthetic exchanges. Our challenge is to maintain the sense of each other's bodies – their weight, orientation and speed – as well as the feeling of what happened in our dancing together, as we write out of these experiences and into a new typographic space of potentiality.

This tracking between spaces that are physically real, virtually distant and palpably present to each other demands of us an elastic perception of time and space. Affective traces of our dancing propel this writing as a catalyzing force. We recoil from other commitments to make space to write and question:

> How might our dance, as kinesthetic enquiry, mediate digital platforms and modes of discourse?
>
> How can writing open spaces of indeterminacy and affective charge, in excess of enclosure and exclusivity?

The concept of *Te Kore* offers spacialities of thought that are open to possibilities of uncertainty:

> *Te Kore te Whiwhia – the void in which nothing is entwined or bound together.*
>
> *Te Kore te Rawea – the void where nothing is suitably resolved.*

*Te Kore* is interpreted as a realm of nothingness and potentiality from which everything else emerged in most Māori tribal cosmogenic narratives. *Te Kore* also features as a phase to move through periodically in Polynesian lunar calendars. *Korekore* phases of the moon, are not complete absences, or voids, but part of a cycle that determines tidal patterns, which in turn help to regulate and balance patterns of social activity.[1]

In addition to these shared understandings between Māori and other Polynesian cultures, Moana's thesis highlighted specific teachings and interpretations of *Te Kore* by a nineteenth century Māori *tohunga*, philosopher and scholar, Mohi Ruatapu, to whom he is connected through tribal genealogy.[2] In Ruatapu's cosmogenic narratives *Te Kore* is personified and given ancestral presence within a sexual procreative narrative that also describes the origins of sensory perception. This provided a focus for his investigations through video, creative writing, choreography, performance and installation, including the work he invited Carol to be part of.[3] We address some of these ideas in relation to specific choreographic projects later in this chapter.

## Choreographing Contemporary Indigeneity

As artists exploring global possibilities for the development of ideas, indigenous scholarship provides a broader context for positioning our work. In the first instance, however, our coming together to investigate *Te Kore* through choreography and performance arose out of personal circumstances, experiences and an invitation. This investigation was rooted in a contemporary indigenous Māori paradigm of thought and evolved through establishing specific relationships to environment, place and historical context in Aotearoa New Zealand. Māori concepts and customary practices provided cultural precedents and sources of generative potential for this choreographic encounter, together with those offered through our training, research and professional experience. Deliberately privileging Māori perspectives in this context constitutes a decolonized approach to choreography, and contemporary theatre.

Alignment through the Māori concept of *whakapapa* (to ground, make, or place into layers) provided us with a genealogical paradigm to connect and establish a working relationship. *Whakapapa* connect people to histories, land, concepts and ideas, people to one another and traditions of thought and creative practice. In our case, Uawa (Tolaga Bay), the home of one of the *iwi* (tribes) to which Moana belongs, and site of the famous Rawheoro *whare wānanga*, house of higher learning where Mohi Ruatapu taught, was also a place of connection for Carol. Our shared experiences and professional histories of working in London provide another layer of connection that can also be understood in terms of *whakapapa*. This does not mean that Moana could *whakapapa* to the body of feminist theory that Carol's work has engaged with in the same way, or that Carol could *whakapapa* to Ruatapu and Rawheoro's creative traditions in the same way that Moana could. *Whakapapa* connect and also differentiate. Central to Māori perceptions of the world in customary contexts, this relational way of knowing also helps to confer senses of order and relevance in contemporary Māori society.

Our choreographic *kaupapa* (platform and agenda) is both grounded and fluid. As Moana notes, Māori view themselves as *kanohi ora*, the living faces of their ancestors (Nepia, 2013, 100). Positioned in this way, through knowledge of *whakapapa*, the *kau* (ancestor, swim) comes into view and we move or swim on from there.[4] For Carol, similar understandings of the performer as a vessel or conduit through which ideas might flow, permeate her writing about performance and embodiment that responds to writers such as Donna Haraway (2004), Elizabeth Grosz (2011) and Erin Manning (2009).

Our collaboration moved beyond acknowledging different genealogies, histories and affiliations. After sharing stories about *whānau* (family) histories, and connections to places within and outside New Zealand, we pondered, what if Moana's father, born in Uawa (Tolaga Bay) had met Carol's mother, raised on a farm up the road? Carol was invited to generate gestural movement in response to experiences Moana had written about featuring an absent lover. Carol layered some of this movement with additional material responding to moments from her own past. In the studio we took turns to lead and follow each other, curious as to what might emerge from a movement conversation attuned to parallel, but quite distinct relationships to place and histories of colonial encounter. We recognize that 'the descendants of the colonizers [may] have different decolonization tasks from the descendants of the colonized' (Nairn, 2002, 210), but our collaboration was not motivated by a single decolonizing 'agenda'. The choreographic nature of our enquiry gathered momentum through privileging different perspectives and forces at different times.

The French-Carribean author Édouard Glissant describes a 'Poetics of Relation' that is rhizomatic, nomadic, and in contrast to a settled way of life. Each and every identity is extended by a relationship with the other (Glissant in Bishop, 2006, 71). Anthropologist Ann Salmond particularizes this relation for us in her invoking of the spaces 'between worlds' opened by the co-existence of Māori and European world views. Aotearoa New Zealand is a place where an 'order of relations', rather than 'things', reverberates with the generative force of memories, affects, sensations, ideas and dreams. Māori see the cosmos in terms of dynamic networks of relations, generated by complementary pairings (rather than binary oppositions) between different elements, each necessary for survival. *Pākeha* New Zealanders as well migrants from other parts of the world encounter and adapt to indigenous forms of sociality and expressions of culture within an environment that, after the Treaty of Waitangi, requires listening, reciprocity and acknowledgement as well as resolution of the abuses of the colonial era.[5] Salmond describes this process as a visceral practice in dialogue with Māori partly as philosophy (Witchel, 2013). For contemporary New Zealand artists attuned to this possibility, the process can be exhilarating and transformational.

Charles Royal asked: What might an indigeneity of the future rather than an indigeneity of the past look like (Royal, n.d.)? Against the backdrop of growth for Pacific artists, whose work is increasingly in demand on the global stage, we devise questions to lead us across the threshold of the unknown, peering into a creative abyss of uncertainty.

Our future is potentiated through what we bring to this space of *Te Kore*, and through trust.

## Contemporary Pacific and Māori Spatial Thought in Performance

Our collaboration is also situated within the regional context of contemporary performing arts production in Aotearoa and the Pacific Islands. In what follows, we explore two examples of contemporary performance artists from New Zealand and the South Pacific whose work embodies contemporary indigenous and Pacific cosmological thinking in their practice.

Lemi Ponifasio, Samoan director of the New Zealand theatre company Mau, who regularly feature in the most prestigious international arts festivals – writes of the importance of genealogy in opening a relational space in his work as a contemporary Pacific artist. He refers to this work not as theatre or dance but as *karanga*, 'a genealogical prayer, a ceremony, a poetic space' in which the audience, by virtue of their presence, participates: 'I try to activate the space,' he says, 'to create a sort of *cosmological space* where we can somehow realize that we are part of the whole process of earth.' To him, these works are 'not dance, not theatre: those are Western ideas,' they are an embodiment of a cosmological order founded in Pacific thought through the notion of *va* (Ponifasio in Hill 2013). This concept is understood in Samoan as a relational space that weaves and binds the body with the world.

> To negotiate this exchange in life, Samoan parents tell their children the most important motto: to teu le va – to tender the space, to reverence the space, to be the space, to beautify the space, to embellish the space, [...] this is relational space, consciousness, a cosmological relationship with all existence. We call this 'va'.
>
> (Ponifasio, 2012)

*Va* is a dimension where all are inseparably intertwined; a permeable network. The work of MAU, in being premised on activating the *va*, allows for a process of constant change, a never-ending vibration of unrest.

A further example of indigenous thought in action can be found in the work of Māori choreographer Charles Koroneho, a collaborator with Ponifasio through MAU, and previously with Carol in *Aarero Stone: Two solos in a performance landscape* (2006). His performance and pedagogical practice proposes a philosophical space for dance based on the Māori concepts of *tūāhu (sacred space for ritual practices).* As a founding member of New Zealand's first Māori contemporary dance company *Te Kanikani o te Rangatahi,* Koroneho was part of a Māori performance movement, later known as Marae Theatre. The *marae* (tribal gathering place) and customary rituals have provided contexts and sources of inspiration for many Māori writers and performing artists seeking to promote indigenous perspectives and experiences through literature, film and theater. The TŪĀHU Choreographic Research Project builds upon this earlier history but utilizes a multi-layered approach; with workshop, collaborative and performance outcomes taking place under the same conceptual framework. The intention is to share an approach to an evolved method of Marae Theatre practices, emphasizing aspects of *pōwhiri* (welcome ceremony), *noho marae* (living, immersed in the place), *take* (topic, issue, concern) and *utu* (reciprocity).

Koroneho's solo, *PURE* (2013), is an instance of work emerging through this concept of *tūāhu.*[6] In Māori language, *pure* is a ritual and action which consists of 'loosening' from dangerous elements and 'binding' to beneficent ones. Set in a place of thresholds, Koroneho's performance moves through a series of ritual enactments where the body vibrates at a limit between realms; the physical and the spiritual, the present and the past, the material and the virtual. As Charles explains, these performance 'tests' of endurance and concentrated energy seek to alter the past to bring about change (Koroneho, 2013). In this context, the theatre becomes a *marae,* a tribal meeting place that is sacred – accenting and embellishing the role of the theatre as a place where we meet with our ancestors.

For *Pure,* Koroneho began his collaboration in Montreal with Brad Gledhill (performance design, lighting, production) and Alejandro Ronceria (dramaturgy, choreography, direction). In this work, a performance landscape of stone, wood, stars, earth and light is activated with an extended *karakia* or incantation that rebinds Charles to his ancestors. At the Tempo Dance Festival event – where Carol was present – chains of words spilled over the audience in a torrent that seemed to fold back into Charles' body, thickening his speech until he was visibly choking in an outpouring cry. A rift in his core was opened until a point of release. At the post-performance forum Charles related his story of attending his father's *tangi* (a Māori funeral) and the requirement for him, as his father's oldest son, to perform certain obligations. Charles explained that his solo was a way to connect with his ancestors, in particular his recently departed father.

Both Koroneho and Ponifasio align indigenous Pacific communal practices, where actions of the sacred and profane, the everyday, ritual and ceremony inform contemporary art and theatre. Both see questions of space in performance as central to the reconfiguring of the Western stage if it is to adapt and be responsive to non-European understandings of the body, environment and relationships. Space and genealogy are inextricably connected in these 'worldings' of the stage, as it is through relationships that one is located.

This view of the stage aligns with Rudi Laermans' understanding of collaboration as dependent upon the pre-existence of a social commonality. This sense of 'being in common', he argues, following Jean-Luc Nancy, simultaneously activates and deconstructs the performer's subjectivity.

> The participants in a collaborative dance project create and sustain an always particular commonality through repeated acts of communication, thinking, feeling or moving that both transform and exceed their subjectivities.
>
> (Laermans, 2012, 98)

Surfacing ancestral presence in Charles' performance of *Pure* moves towards a state of becoming beyond subjectivity. This state is not essentialist however, as it recognizes the creative common that is shared with the past through genealogical connections to place and affiliations with ancestors.

Through their work with *va* and *tūāhu* respectively, Ponifasio and Koroneho express contemporary manifestations of Pacific and indigenous thought in action. As contemporary expressions of space that go beyond Western and European understandings, their work opens the stage to perceptual thresholds and liminal spaces that speak to long memories of place, choreographing relations between the past and the present, and imagining a different kind of future. Although neither artist specifically references *Te Kore*, we find in their work a common interest in creating performance spaces that operate as liminal thresholds for accessing dimensions of experience hidden from view within daily life.

## Collaborative Atmospheres

Carol felt that her work as a non-indigenous artist in collaboration with Moana required a deep listening and learning, rather than a different approach to making. For Moana the experience of listening and learning about Carol, through oral and movement conversations was similarly important. Their shared histories of working in Western theatre dance and training as performance artists provided a layer of understanding that included exposure to improvization, which they both utilized to devise work with each other. Working with Moana and being introduced to an indigenous way of perceiving the world, required Carol to establish a work place that came from an understanding of her own relation to land, history and genealogy. Internalising ideas and taking breath to initiate movement together felt like being part of, and also creating an atmosphere that was imbued with our subjective interpretations of pre-colonial, colonial and post-colonial memories. *Te Kore* provided an initial philosophical focus for our investigation, and also a way for us to conceptualize how this collaborative space might be potentiated. *Te Kore* within the creative process of choreographic exploration articulates a space and movement between absence and presence, specters of the known and unknown, connections and differences, unsettling assumptions about what performance could be and how it operates.

## Practices of Unsettling

Through asserting commitment to the page and acts of writing as a choreographic sensibility, we seek to unsettle a presumption that words necessarily perform a facile distinction to actions. Separations of up and down, comfort and unease, directions, encryptions and questions of particularity, multiple directions, tensions and lexicographic contiguities, are choreographic grist for the mill. Words like gestures are ripe for reinterpretation, to be unsettled and destablized, as part of a process of testing through the body. For us, the dancer's *plié* is also a squat gathering force, a movement in several directions that simultaneously stretches and relaxes...

Settle down
Settle up
Settle with
Settle into
Settle her
Settle for[7]

To unsettle is to disturb, to unnerve, to agitate and to discompose. In this writing we explore the potentials of collaboration as a practice that unsettles, both metaphorically and physically. Writing alongside and together from our situated perspectives as Māori and Pakehā New

Zealanders, we question assumptions about the cooperative labor of collaboration that denies differences and difficult conversations of coming together. Our irreducible differences must necessarily acknowledge the impossibility of standing in each other's places, that where we stand and how we stand are different and that we must negotiate these differences across and through our different histories and genealogies.

Donna Haraway claims that to know *with* one another what we cannot know on our own, to 'walk-with', requires engaging in 'otherworldly conversations,' conversations with others and their worlds that cannot, *must not*, resolve, but are ongoing (Haraway, 1991, 193). This knowing is always partial, located, and finite, always in process and never finished. Such partiality allows us to join with another, complementing and contradicting one another, being together in 'without claiming to be another,' knowing together what we cannot know on our own (Haraway, ibid). How does this apply in a context where specific cultural knowledge forms the core material for exploration and the ability to know is rooted in *whakapapa* (genealogy)?

For Carol 'working-with' Moana, it was only possible to have a partial insight into *Te Kore*, the Māori concept under investigation. Without a *whakapapa* or genealogy that stitches her into the weave of a Māori cosmology, it felt difficult for her to access deep layers of meaning and interpretation of this concept for it is part of a different worldview. At the center of our collaborative practice, there endures a fundamental unknowability, a maintenance of the 'other' as only ever partially knowable.

For Moana, a sense of the unknowable is part of the creative process, part of what is involved with materializing and giving form to ideas. His investigation into *Te Kore* arose out of a quest to understand this process. For Moana, a sense of the unknowable is also present when attempting to understand some of the more esoteric features and cryptic allusion prominent within ancestral tribal narratives, including those pertaining to *Te Kore*. While attempting to understand what others have offered, our findings are limited by our own experiences.

*Te Kore* perceived as a collaborative space is informed partly by what we offered each other. Through our dance together we explored a series of provocations without knowing where they might lead us. By moving-*with* we learned to align our respective movement histories, vocabularies and spatialities of thought. This jointness as collaborative practice demanded an engagement in 'otherworldly conversations' – conversations with each other and encounters with each other's worlds. We sustained an ongoing, creative relationship through questioning each other and orienting thoughts towards a future of other possibilities. Through performance, ideas about *Te Kore* were layered as propositions and materialized through the body.

Individual gestures were progressively prolonged and slowed down in rehearsals to explore subtle shifts of balance and breath in order to potentiate movement with increasing nuance and control. This is not an entirely innovative strategy for athletes, dancers or musicians in training. In the context of our exploration of *Te Kore* however, this physical strategy was adopted as a way to highlight and explore creative motivation, heighten spatial and sensory awareness, and locate potential to move as an individual while remaining sensitive to motivations from others. *Te Kore* in this context is not found in the fulfillment of movement, but in its preparation and awareness of the possibility for the body to move.

In the collaborative context this involved sensing weight, momentum, distance or separation between bodies, and while in close contact with one another. Layering motivations arising out of narrative texts, we tested multiple possibilities for shifts of energy or changes of direction arising out of this shared focus. *Te Kore*, here, provided us with a way to articulate a phase of latent emotion, physical potential and energy between bodies, heightened through the preparatory focus on conversation and shared experience.

In performance, *Te Kore* can be perceived as a generative space where performers, designers and directors gather and layer ideas. The performance space is further potentiated by the sensory responses, questions, and projections of meaning generated and embodied through relationship with audience.

## Lexicon of Concepts

We offer a lexicon of concepts that inform the way we have worked together based upon interpretations of Māori concepts Moana offered in his thesis as part of his methodology. These concepts shaped our modes of encounter with each other, and provided ways for us to situate our ideas and experiences in relation to broader contemporary fields of knowledge, theory and creative practice.

This lexicon is also a bridge between performative actions, and serves as a tool for naming our language of collaboration. Holding principles of dancing together lightly, the lexicon touches the ground of our 'walking-with', its flows, commons and sinks. It coordinates measures of identity, and positions memories in row upon row of gestures entangled in sweat. While the shifting vectors of our relationship oscillate to and fro in a gymnastic lexico-disequilibrium, this is also a corporeal lexicon of labor.

*Aratika* - The appropriate pathway or approach (from *ara* – approach, line or path and *tika* – appropriate), positions our collaboration in a culturally prescribed ethical and environmental context. Appropriateness was partly determined through *whakapapa*, histories of connection and shared understanding.

*Tikanga – Māori* ethical concerns, values and concepts informed what we determined to be *tika*, appropriate or correct

*Akoako* – the Māori concept for both learning and teaching, helps to describe the sense of reciprocity we maintained within our collaborative investigation – at different times we asked questions, followed, lead and learned from each other

*Kōrero* – speech or speaking, was the term we also used to describe physical conversations, sharing information, and speaking between narrative texts and personal experience

*Whakaaro* – idea, thinking or thought, can also be used to describe making sense of ideas through the body, through heightened states of sensory perception, through attunement of performers to one another and their environment

*Hurihuritanga* – turning, a metaphor used in place of reflection, is much more than an optical experience – it describes turning to perceive ideas from multiple positions, turning ideas over in the mind, within the body and between performers while moving

*Whakapapa* – is a genealogical paradigm of thought. Translated as genealogy, to make or place in layers. *Whakapapa* position people and ideas through tracing and also making connections. *Whakapapa* are referred to in Moana's thesis as a form of making and analysis.[8]

*Whai Whakaaro* – to follow the thought, was used to describe the processes of extended investigation and theorizing.

As Māori lawyer and Indigenous Rights Advocate Moana Jackson (one of Moana's uncles) points out; *Whai Whakaaro* is the name of a rock where new students arriving on Waikawa Island to attend the *whare wānanga* (ancient house of learning) would anchor their canoes. From there they journeyed, following signs in the land and paths others have followed, to the opposite side of the island, to a place called *Te Timatanga* – the beginning. The process of investigation, journeying to the source of an idea, was understood as a situated and embodied physical and intellectual process. *Whai whakaaro* in this context sustain *whakapapa*.

## *Te Kore* and Ethical Co-existence

To consider orientations to the world as ways of approaching, modes of engaging, and styles of moving across our differences without reducing or eliminating them, is the shared condition of precarity – a vulnerable life. As Haraway has asserted, we are bound 'to seek perspectives from those points of view, which can never be known in advance, which promise something quite extraordinary, that is, knowledge potent for constructing worlds less organized by axes of domination' (Haraway, 1991, 192).

Our dance, exploring these ideas through the body, comes from shared positions of strength, knowing who we are and where we come from as individuals. It also comes from places and experiences of uncertainty and insecurity. This paradox aligns with the liquid ground of collaboration articulated through *kaupapa* earlier in this article, and with Gilles Deleuze, who explained how, while on land, movement involves moving from point to point and is always between two points, and in water 'the point is always between two movements' (Deleuze, 2005, 81). Collaboration in this context explores possibilities for the future while investigating the past, turning and returning to consider ideas from new positions and perspectives. While making these creative propositions, we are also striking a balance between giving and taking place.

Turning to position ourselves *kanohi ki te kanohi,* face-to-face, we established common ground through layering associations, sharing ideas, personal histories, and narratives weighted with breath. This turning is relational, a re-positioning both of us undertook in order to physically and conceptually face each other, confronting partial and incomplete ways of knowing, we responded differently to projects initiated by each of us in turn.

## *Te Kore* and *WHERO*

As part of his inter-disciplinary research into *Te Kore* (the concept of void, nothingness or potentiality), Moana undertook a series of inter-disciplinary explorations that included a choreographic and videographic residency with dancers on his family's ancestral land in Tokomaru Bay. In 2012, Carol performed in one of the works that evolved out of material generated at this wananga titled *WHERO*, which was an hour-long performance and video installation devised in a large warehouse space in West Auckland with nine other performers, a Harley Davidson motorcycle and one dog. *Te Kore* was explored in making this work through creative writing featuring themes of absence and loss found in personal, family and tribal narratives, and through video and choreographic material that explored absence and presence of imagery and recognizable form. In the empty shell of an industrial warehouse, sound, light, projections and movement evoked foreshore, patterns of taking away and return.

Individual solos, including movement for Carol, were developed in response to selected poetic texts using gestural drawing exercises connecting bodies, landscapes in the texts, and architectural features of the rehearsal space. Carol's solo drew upon shared experiences and narratives of loss, while envisaging an historical scenario and imagined physical setting for an historical event – a cry for help and no reply. Spatial restrictions reinforced the emotional dynamics of the narrative and helped to direct and develop movement material for this solo.

This material was expanded and given spatial direction through layering supplementary material from additional segments of text. The opening scene was conceived as *whai whakaaro* (following a thought), in which a procession of dancers in silhouette entered through motorbike headlights, and as *powhiri* (ritual welcome) drawing past and present together. Duets and group material spaced throughout the performance space drew the audience deeper into the dimly lit warehouse.

The soundscore, devised in collaboration with composer Paddy Free, featured a seascape of crashing waves, wind, screeching gulls, and *ruru* (New Zealand owl) calling through the night, dissolving into echoes of amplified breath, a horse, layers of soprano voice and electronic orchestration. *Te Kore* as auditory space within breath and waves helped to punctuate the physical reverberation of surround-sound with rhythm, moments of suspense and accent.

Spotlights and video projected onto fabric as well as tent-like structures helped to establish specific zones within the darkened, cavernous, industrial space for dancers to move through. The audience was free to move around the perimeter of the performance space encountering the work from multiple positions.

*Te Kore* was explored as the appearance and disappearance of imagery in projections, as the absence and presence of light, as silhouettes, reflections and shadows moving across different surfaces – illuminating and traversing pathways, following the edges of spot-lit zones. Between dancers and between movements, *Te Kore* was also explored as an intimate space of moving together.

## *1000 Lovers*

In 2013 Carol invited Moana to perform as part of *1000 Lovers*, a performance event staged on Auckland's foreshore as part of the Auckland Arts Festival White Night programme. In *1000 Lovers* Moana, referencing the pan-Pacific story of Hine and Tuna, crossed a strip of reclaimed harbor land (now Wynyard Quarter) as an eel-man. On this journey he met and interacted with other characters, including a colonial bride, a mourner, and a group of young women representing elvers (young eels).

Having invited Moana to perform in this work, Carol was interested in how his movement history as a dancer and swimmer might inform exploration of a liquid pathway between sea and land that crossed a reclaimed strip of industrial harbourland undergoing gentrification as a civic recreational zone. Themes of recovery, emergence, submergence and connection informed development of movement vocabulary for his performance. After emerging on steps leading up from the sea while carrying a rope and stick, Moana negotiated a series of reed beds and bridges to cross from one side of the harbor to the other. Carol (as a veiled 'widow') intersected his linear path by gliding across the bridges in a serpentine pattern, gesturing to the distant chorus of dancers on an elevated gantry ahead of his approach. A figurative and visceral connection was affected through the choreography of intersecting pathways, the sense of two distant but related stories crossing, and movement towards a distant chorus leading the audience through Wynyard Quarter.

This work acknowledged the specificities of a particular history of colonialism, and how we have become entangled in the enduring legacies of ecological imperialism that have radically altered the foreshore of Waitematā (Auckland harbour). It also attempted to negotiate the reverberations of this history through a re-telling of multiple stories that have emerged from this place. These stories included the pan-Pacific story of Hine and Tuna, stories of colonial women (the blind bride and the widow), and the indigenous long-finned eel. During the process of making the work, the appropriation of stories as dramaturgical material was questioned by Moana: 'Where does that story come from? Who does this story belong to?'

A performance that considers how the past reverberates in the present, and what this means for the future, requires a careful and ongoing negotiation of its traces. Working in collaboration with Moana to create this 'crossing', Carol was challenged to consider whose stories were being told and what their sources were. Moana's questioning was

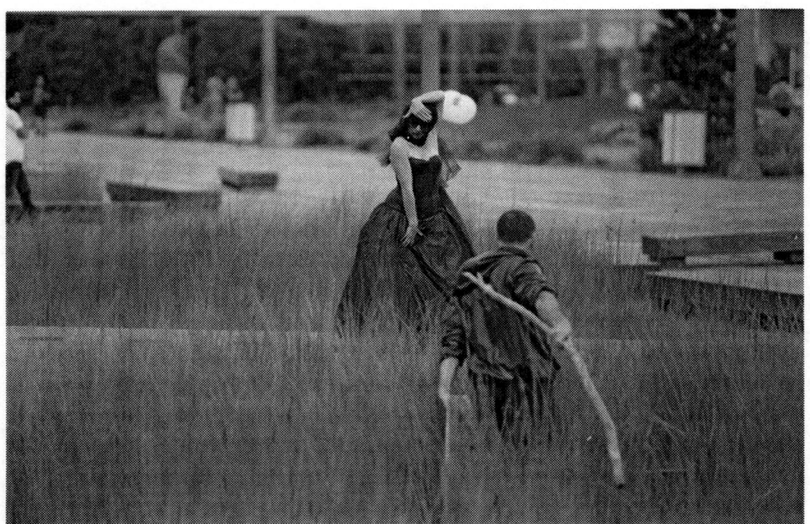

*Fig. 15 1000 Lovers,* Photograph by Dean Carruthers

provoked by a need to establish *whakapapa*, understand origins, and establish connections to the historical context and narrative content of the work as it evolved.

As the living faces of our ancestors we were both evoking ancestral encounters and embodied ways of knowing to recover a sense of place, and to inform the way we might move together. In this way, our cultural exchange as collaborators can be considered an ethics of encounter experienced first through the body.

In *1000 Lovers,* moments of encounter are experienced within a shifting landscape as the performers negotiate cultural differences and physical challenges – weather, reed beds, boat moorings, harbor walkways, pedestrians, harbor workers and the sea. These differences relate to the layers of history within the site as a pre-colonial place of passage and source of *kaimoana* (seafood) for Māori, as a colonial frontier for early settler culture, an industrial silo, contaminated harbor, contemporary civic playground, and gentrified waterfront zone. Through movement, costumes and sound, this historical landscape was further mapped by moments of entanglement where the different histories symbolically coincide, collide and intersect. As eel-man, Moana confronted the 'bride' at the start of the North Harbour. Dressed in a grubby wedding gown, Converse trainers and sunglasses, she performed a series of krumping moves on a bench before jumping onto the ground to meet Moana in a *wero*, challenge, or ritual encounter.

As Emmanuel Levinas suggests: 'To count as an ethical partner one must be a potential interlocutor,' (Levinas in Connor, 1999, 233) as if the face-to-face were, from the beginning, an ethical concreteness. A performance ethics that takes account of indigenous ways of being in the world might in this sense be said to begin 'before the exteriority of the other [...] before the face of the other, which engages my responsibility by its human expression' (Levinas, 1993, 35).

In our collaboration together, we sometimes confronted each other with physical *wero* that were unspoken, expressed and felt through movement – back to back, or side by side. In these instances we were often forced to sense internal energies, intervals and motivations, before engaging or responding to external appearances or expressions. Through writing we face similar challenges to develop an ethical responsibility towards one another that is based upon mutual respect.

## The Interval in Being-With

Erin Manning (2009) describes how moving relationally is to create an interval – 'the more we connect to this becoming-movement, the more palpable the interval becomes' (Manning, 108). The interval is a palpable presencing, a texture that our bodies fold around. For both Carol and Moana, these moments of sensation are culturally weighted and situated places. *Te Kore* is perceived as potential, pause, and an in-between space that propels our dancing together. Our bodies in relation to ground and cosmology form a triangular force field with this interval between us.

We began work on Carol's solo for *WHERO* through reading some of Moana's writing that explores themes of love, absence and loss within landscapes and family narratives. Carol related these stories to some of her own experiences. The poem *Crawl*[9] in which a small boy crawls onto the lap of his dead mother chimed with Carol's own experiences of recent loss. Moana gave Carol the task of working with a sense of *Te Kore* within the body, where it may be perceived as pleura – mediating pressure to inhale; as diastole – relaxation phase within heartbeat; as womb; space within joints; and as the potential to move.

This solo was later developed into a duet with Moana for the opening of the Tempo Dance Festival in October 2012. From a solo devised partly in relation to themes of loss and absence of a male figure, the duet took as its motive the desire to fill this absence with the possibility of return. Described as one of the highlights of the year in the Dance Aotearoa New Zealand Critics Survey (DANZ, 2012, 22) and as 'a highly symbolic duet of shifting relationships' in the NZ Herald (Whyte, 2012), it also attracted comment from Māori critic Tru Paraha as a 'dance of fractured absences [that] becomes satiated by delayed moments of exquisite collision. An overlapping of image, movement and partnering curves the edges of dark/light, *Te Ao* and *Te Pō*' (Paraha, 2012).

## Performance as an Ethical Encounter Between Worlds

> Choreography is a trace-work of feeling in time. Choreography is that which connects the animate to the inanimate, the air to the ground, the living to the dead.
>
> (Heathfield, 2013)

*WHERO* imparted *Te Kore* with movement, force, volume and direction – collisions between bodies potentiating partnerships of male and female elements within space, collisions between realms of darkness or night (*Te Pō*) and enlightenment (*Te Ao Mārama*) shaping and morphing space. Turn-taking (*hurihuritanga*), to listen, read and sense each other, allowed the spatio-temporal, emotional and ethical possibilities for *Te Kore* to be negotiated within the movement – in the push and pull of alternating leads, embrace, counter-balance and separations, in moments of anticipation, hesitation, sharing weight and breath.

This physical emphasis augments Emmanuel Levinas' ethics of meeting 'face to face' with experience that is weighted, rhythmic and culturally positioned. For Levinas, it is the reciprocity of encounter that sustains us: 'all real [*wirklich*] life is meeting' (Levinas, 1993, 36). For *Māori,* sharing breath in *hongi* (the ritual greeting and pressing of noses) potentiates the ethics of meeting *kanohi ki te kanohi* (face to face) with added physical intimacy. As a choreographic ethics of encounter, *kanohi ki te kanohi* facilitates trust, effective communication, mutually beneficial and successful outcomes in tandem with principles outlined by *Kaupapa Māori* researchers such as Linda Tuhiwai Smith (2012) and Graham Hingangaaroa Smith (1997). Embracing technology as an extension of the body (as a conduit and vessel for contemporary convergences, sensory articulations and iterations) takes on new and extended meaning when faced with this proposition.

For the final iteration of *WHERO,* the duet *Extract* took on a new form within a series of solos for three additional dancers – Eric Baltran,

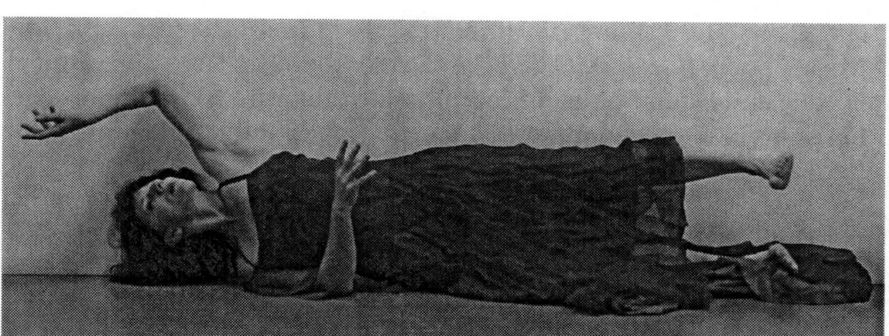

*Fig. 16* Carol Brown, *WHERO 2* development. Photograph by Moana Nepia

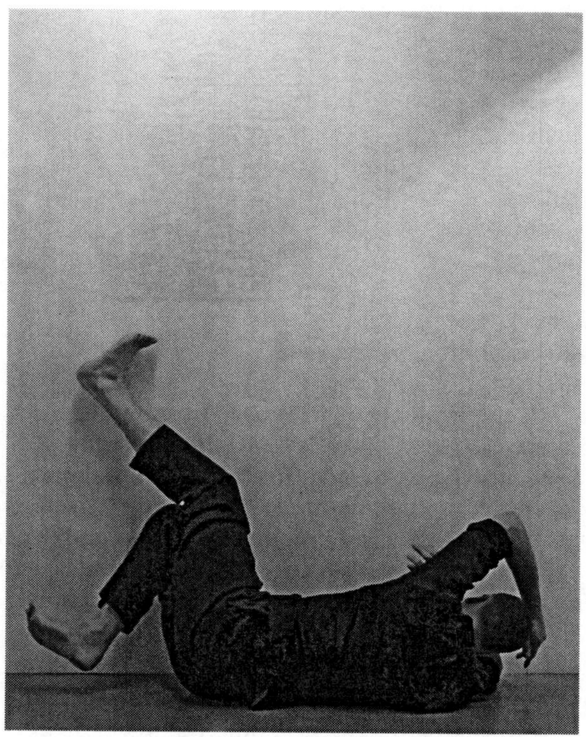

*Fig. 17* Moana Nepia, *WHERO 2* development. Photograph by Carol Brown

Tia Reihana and Pauline Hiroti. Responding to selected segments from Moana's poem *Breath and hand,*[10] movement phrases were teased out to replicate and extend moments of initiation and indecision on the edges of possibility and resolution, as a journey along walls and through the interior of a stark white gallery space.

## Breath and Hand

Stand tall,
Gaze fixed on horizon's ocean air.

Breathe in to under arm space,
Rise and fall with waves.

Empty lung steady stance
With palms and fingers curled

Extend knuckles
Wind between arms,
Heavy, light,

Elbows soften
Lead forearm side.
Ripple body out.

Lie head along one palm.
To press where lilting breakers curl.[11]

This pared-back, minimalist work without video or set elements, resonated with echoes of earlier versions of *WHERO* in its layering of voices, decisions to allow the audience to move freely through the space, and crisply defined pools of light reverberating to the sound of speakers mounted into the wall. Our duet provided a moment of climax and dynamic counterpoint to the predominant slow pace of this performance, including a slow motion exit and procession up a long flight of stairs.

## Returns

An important aspect of indigenous cultural politics in New Zealand is a reworking of our understandings of the impact of imperialism and colonialism on the contemporary present. Linda Tuhiwai Smith (2012) describes how within this process there are two major strands: The first looks to a time before colonization when indigenous people lived in a world that was of their own making, cosmologically, spiritually and socially; and the second, demands an analysis of *how* indigenous people were colonized and what this has meant for the past as well as for the present and future (Smith, 2012, 25). We are not decolonizing ourselves in this collaboration, but moving instead beyond this theoretical preoccupation to find a collaborative methodology that is also a physical one – working with a Māori sense of space-time through *Te Kore*, while testing the relevance of Western European concepts in dialogical relation. We ask how the Māori sense of *Te Kore* might co-exist, complement and be in dialogue, with Levinas' theories of meeting face to face through encounters of performance that cross Māori, European and Pacific cosmologies.

For Linda Tuhiwai Smith the future, in one sense, is now. It is not an abstract, theoretical or even visionary picture of what the world may be like in fifty years or a hundred years. It is, rather, the potential we hold now in the present moment (Smith, 2013, 228).

Within the push and pull of our writing and dancing together, moments of uncertainty, fluid and grounded energies offer a source of potentiality... and at this threshold there is resolution in *Te Kore* within and between bodies.

An extract from Moana's writing expresses the cumulative and sensory nature of our creative investigation:

*Ara, course of action,*
*evolves un-scripted,*
*revealing form*
*awakening thought...*
*between what has already been there,*
*travelled, placed,*
*whispered,*
*sung, touched,*
*shouted and danced...*
*before.*

Through *Te Kore* we experience differences as situated relationalities, catalyzing thoughts, places and perceptions at the edge of the unknown.

*Anei... te kōrero o te tīnana kia whakatītahatatha, kia matāra, kia matapopore.*

*Here... the language of the body tilts, alert and braced for challenges ahead.*[11]

## Notes

1. Maori Marsden, a Tai Tokerau elder and Anglican minister, described *Te Korekore* (a variant of *Te Kore*) as 'the realm between non-being and being: that is the realm of potential being' (original source) Although this interpretation highlights the notion of potentiality, it also privileges the concept of 'being', a concept for which there is no equivalent verb 'to be' in Māori or any other Polynesian language.
2. Performance works we have collaborated on include: *WHERO* (a full length work directed by Moana as part of his PhD at the Corban Estate Arts Centre 2012); *Extract* (a duet that evolved from *WHERO* for Tuakana, Tempo Dance Festival 2012); *1000 Lovers* (choreographed by Carol for Auckland Arts Festival White Night 2013); and *WHERO 2* (a performance at St Paul Street Gallery that was the culmination of Moana's Phd); and a co-authored conference paper, *Te Kore and the Encounter of Performance* for the conference, In the Balance: Indigeneity, Performance and Globalization (October 2013).
3. Nepia, Moana (2013). *Te Kore – Exploring the Māori Concept of Void.* [Unpublished PhD Thesis]. *Auckland, Aotearoa New Zealand: AUT University.*
4. Te Tiriti o Waitangi (The Treaty of Waitangi), signed between Māori chiefs and representatives of Queen Victoria of England, is the founding document of New Zealand. The Waitangi Tribunal, established in 1975, investigates grievances arising from breaches of the Treaty, including confiscation of Māori land, the loss of the Māori language and other *taonga* (treasures) such as forests, seas and fisheries supposedly protected for them under the terms of the Treaty.
5. *Pure* was performed at Public Energy, Ontario, May 2013; Tempo Dance Festival, Auckland, October 2013; and MAI Montreal, Canada.
6. Old English *setlan* 'to seat, place', from settle. Oxford English Dictionary.
7. Nepia, 2013, 3: 120, 125, 129.
8. Nepia, 2013, 1: 37.
9. Nepia, 2013, 1: 31.
10. Nepia 2013, 1: 31.
11. Muru, Selwyn. (2013). Personal Communication. This *whakatauki* (proverb) was offered by Selwyn Muru (Ngāti Kuri), a senior Māori orator, artist and pioneer broadcaster, after Moana discussed our choreographic ideas and collaborative process with him.

## Bibliography

Brown, C. (2003). *How we are Here: Afterthoughts on Te Pou Rahui.* http://www.carolbrowndances.com/writings_pubs.php (date accessed 20 November 2014).

Connor, S. (1999) 'The Ethics of the Voice', in Rainsford, D., & Woods, T. (eds.) *Critical ethics: text, theory, and responsibility* (Basingstoke, Hampshire: Macmillan Press; New York: St. Martin's Press).

DANZ Quarterly: New Zealand Dance (2012) 'Highlight of the year critics survey, Carol Brown and Moana Nepia in Extract' No. 30, Dec, pp. 22–23 (date accessed November 2014).

Deleuze, G. (2005), *Cinema I*, (London: Continuum).

Douglas, T. (2013) 'Choreographer Lemi Ponifasio explores flight and shade with Mau Dance Group. The Australian 20 April.

———. (2013) 'Choreographer Lemi Ponifasio explores flight and shade with MAU dance group' *the Australian* http://www.theaustralian.com.au/arts/review/choreographer-lemi -explores-flight-and-shade-with-mau-dance-group/story-fn9n8gph-1226623401200 (date accessed 17 Oct 2014). http://www.oxforddictionaries.com/definition/english/unsettle (date accessed 25 September 2014).

Glissant, É. (2006) 'Poetics of Relation' in Bishop, C. (ed) *Participation*. London: Massachusetts Institute of Technology, pp. 71–78.

Grosz, E. (2011) *Becoming Undone: Darwinian Reflections on Life, Politics and Art*. Durham: Duke University.

Haraway, D, J. (1991) *Simians, Cyborgs, and Women: The Reinvention of Nature* (New York: Routledge).

———. (2004) 'Otherwordly Conversations; Terrain Topics; Local Terms' in *The Haraway Reader* (New York: Routledge).

———. (2008) *When Species Meet*, (Minneapolis: University of Minnesota Press).

Heathfield, A. Choreography Is: A short statement on choreography (Answers 22–28). *What is Choreography?* http://www.corpusweb.net/answers-2228-2.html (date accessed 15 November 2013).

Koroneho, C. (2013) http://tuahu.tetokiharuru.com/tuahu-korero.html (date accessed 16 November 2013).

Laermans, R. (2012) 'Being in common' Theorizing artistic collaboration' *Performance Research: A Journal of the Performing Arts* 17:6, 94–102.

Levinas, E. (1993) *Outside the Subject*. Translated by Michael B. Smith (Stanford, California: Stanford University Press).

Manning, E. (2009) 'The Elasticity of the Almost' in Lepecki, André and Joy, Jenn (eds.) *Planes of Composition* (London, New York & Calcutta: Seagull), pp. 107–122.

Nairn, M. (2002) 'Decolonisation for Pākehā' in J. Margaret (ed.) *Pakeha Treaty Work: Unpublished Material*, (Auckland: Manakau Institute of Technology Treaty Unit).

Nepia, M. (2013) *Te Kore – Exploring the Māori Concept of Void*. [Unpublished PhD Thesis] (Auckland, Aotearoa New Zealand: Auckland University of Technology).

Paraha, T. (2012) 'Privileged Encounters' in *Theatreview*, 10 October. http://www.theatreview.org.nz/reviews/review.php?id=5237 (date accessed 24 October 2014).

Ponifasio, L. (2012) 'Mau spreads its wings at home' *NZ Herald* 18 February, http://www.nzherald.co.nz/entertainment/news/article.cfm?c_id=1501119&objectid=10786383 (date accessed 17 Oct 2014).

Royal, Te Ahukaramū, C. (n.d.) 'New expressions of indigeneity through whare tapere' (p.2) www.orotokare.org.nz (date accessed 21 October 2013).

———. 'Te Ao Mārama (2012) 'the natural world, the world of light and darkness', *Te Ara – the Encyclopedia of New Zealand*, updated 22-Sep-12 http://www.TeAra.govt.nz/en/te-ao-marama-the-natural-world/page-3 (date accessed 24 September 2014).

Salmond, A. (2012) 'Shifting New Zealand's Mindset' *The New Zealand Herald*, 18 August http://www.nzherald.co.nz/nz/news/article.cfm?c_id=1&objectid=10827658 (date accessed 1 December 2012).

Smith, G. H. (1997). *The Development of Kaupapa Māori: Theory and Praxis*. [PhD Thesis]. (Auckland: University of Auckland).

Smith, L. T. (2012) *Decolonizing Methodologies* second edition (London & New York: Zed Books).

———. (2013) 'The future is now' in Rashbrooke, M. (ed.) *Inequality: a New Zealand crisis* (Wellington: Bridget Williams Books, pp. 228–35).

Tarnas, R. (1991) *The Passion of the Western Mind: Understanding the ideas that have shaped our world view*. London: Pimlico.

Walker, R. (1989) in 'Māori Identity', in Novitz, David, and Wilmott, William (eds, *Culture and Identity in New Zealand* 21–34. Wellington: GP Books, pp. 35-52).

Whyte, R. (2012) *The NZ Herald*, 11th October http://www.nzherald.co.nz/entertainment/news/article.cfm?c_id=1501119&objectid=10839787 (date accessed 15 Nov 2014).

Witchel, D. (2013) 'An Interview with Ann Salmond' *The New Zealand Listener* http://www.listener.co.nz/current-affairs/dame-anne-salmond-interview/ (date accessed 21 November 2014).

# 11
# 'Nothing About Us Without Us': Collaborations between Disabled and Non-Disabled Practitioners

*Pedro de Senna, with Caroline Bowditch and David Bower*

## About this chapter

This chapter stems from a conversation between David Bower, Caroline Bowditch and me, which took place within the context of a symposium on the politics of collaboration at Middlesex University on 18 May 2013. The conversation was followed, months later, by a brief email exchange, in which further questions were asked, ideas developed and positions clarified. As such, it is itself a collaborative effort – my part being, in a sense, curatorial, trying to collate and provide an academic framework within which the observations of these practitioners can be seen. Born in Australia, but now Glasgow-based, performance artist and choreographer Caroline Bowditch describes herself as a performer, maker, teacher, speaker and a mosquito, buzzing in the ears of the arts industry in the UK and further afield. David Bower is a Deaf performer and Artistic Director of SignDance Collective (SDC), where he works alongside Dance Director Isolte Avila, who created the art form of 'signdance theatre'.[1] His philosophy pertaining to Deaf and disability identity holds that action speaks louder than words; his determination to pursue a career in the arts was driven, among other things, as an act of defiance against discrimination. Each of them has a long history not only of collaboration, but also leadership in the arts.

Here, two important disclosures are necessary: first, that I am not disabled. I cannot claim to know what it is like to live and perform with a disability; but I work regularly with SDC (second disclosure), and have experienced with, and learned from them some of the difficulties and pleasures of engaging in collaborative efforts across (dis)ability. My writing and thinking therefore come from the perspective of a non-disabled collaborator. What follows, then, is an attempt to organize what was a lively and free-flowing conversation under a certain structure, and inevitably something is lost in this process. What is gained, I hope, is a more systematic approach to the various topics covered, couched in a theoretical understanding of disability performance and politics.

The chapter begins with a brief examination of disability politics, identity and agency within the context of collaborations; this is followed by a discussion surrounding the visibility of disability arts (and indeed of people with disabilities). The issue of visibility is closely associated with that of an aesthetics which pertains to disability arts and culture; the recognition of such an aesthetics, I argue, is one of the important contributions that disability studies has made to the field of cultural studies in general. Finally, the chapter looks at some practical aspects of collaboration, engaging with notions of leadership and the need for openness and dialogue in the creative process. Formally, the chapter will intersperse theoretical propositions and observations with direct transcripts from the conversation (the latter in *italics*); the email questions and their answers are included as a post-script. Moreover, it will try to advance an argument for the tactical use of collaborations by disabled artists.

## About politics

Having cleared the ground with regard to my position and the origins of this chapter, I would like to turn my attention to its title. The disability rights slogan, 'Nothing about us without us', has been used by activists at least since the 1980s, and has been appropriated a number of times, most notably in the title of James Charlton's seminal text on disability oppression and empowerment (Charlton, 2000). It acquires particular vehemence when applied to the performing arts, where questions such as 'what is this piece about?' are never distant (for better or worse) from audiences' minds. The physical presence of the disabled performer's body determines much of this 'about-ness', and complicates the relations between signifier, signified and referent. Cohesive meaning-making is undermined, and along with it the idea of a coherent 'author'.

What are the implications of this, then, for collaborations between disabled and non-disabled practitioners? Collaborative processes inherently disperse authorship, but they also dilute authority. Because of this, such collaborations are inherently political, in that they place disabled and non-disabled people on an equal footing. Charlton posits that '[b]eliefs and attitudes about disability are individually experienced but socially constituted', and that this constitution involves a default positioning according to which disabled people are seen as either helpless or heroic – a positioning that is fundamentally oppressive, because it is paternalistic (Charlton, 2000: 51). It is not enough, however, that the collaborators are on an equal footing: it is important that collaborators are *seen to be* on equal footing. Audiences coming into contact with disability arts often bring their prejudices with them. Of course, audiences are themselves diverse (the many problems about accessibility notwithstanding), and disability performance attracts a higher than usual proportion of disabled audience members. Inter-corporeal relations between dancers, performers and spectators therefore are complex and multifaceted by definition, and by extension can only be possible across difference. Bowditch and Bower explored some of these ideas in our discussion.

*Pedro de Senna: What are your thoughts on and experiences of creating work together – between disabled and non-disabled performers – also bearing in mind the diversity of the audiences, who are collaborators as well, creating work through understanding?*

*Caroline Bowditch: Any time you put a disabled body near, or on a stage, you're making a political statement, whether you want it or not. It is hard to differentiate the Body as object or subject. I don't think making art about disability is interesting.*

*PdS: Audience members are collaborators in the meaning-making process – do audiences assume a show is about disability?*

*David Bower: Our responsibility in SDC is to investigate and explore the relationship between Sign Language, dance and theatre, but we don't take responsibility for audience perception of the work, though we do consider it. Politics has to do with how we do things together – doing and being. We have things that define us: I'm a man, born in the north, I have political beliefs, and one of the things that defines me is my Deafness – that defines me, so I try to allow that to be of its own and not allow that to separate me from the 'other'. Our focus is on the process: on Sign – Dance – Theatre, and that is our main objective.*

*CB: It brings up the question of how we talk about and market the work and what we're labelled as. We're also reliant on visible disability. When I'm on stage I make a statement. We worked with people with invisible disabilities, so were it not for some use of Sign [Language], people passing through would not know it was made by a disabled choreographer. If I'm not physically going to be in a piece I'm interested in putting dancers in places where I could physically never get to.*

## About visibility

The notion of visibility is crucial in the politics of collaboration with disabled artists. Ju Gosling traces the origins of contemporary British (and, more broadly, Western) society's discomfort with disability – and indeed any bodies that do not conform with a presumed norm, a condition she calls body dysphoria – back to the ideals of beauty espoused by the Ancient Greeks. In that society, physical fitness and athleticism were 'inextricably linked to good citizenship [...] not least because they trained the body for war' (Gosling, 2011: 19). Of course, 'the reverse was also true, and people with bodies that were obviously "imperfect" were regarded as being bad citizens' (Gosling, 2011: 23).[2] In the visual arts, this perfect body was codified by sculptor Polykleitos in his *Kanon*, and the notion was later taken over by the Roman architect Vitruvius, who mathematically established the ideal proportions of the human body (famously later represented by Leonardo da Vinci's 'Vitruvian Man'). Moreover, Gosling claims that this disregard for 'imperfection' has origins in the Judeo-Christian tradition, too, citing a number of biblical passages referring to disabilities as a sign of impurity or impiety, and even divine punishment. In addition, Christian doctrine dictates that we help those in need. As Charlton points out, '[p]aternalism is often subtle in that it casts the oppressor as benign, as protector' (Charlton, 2000: 53). Our culture, product of the fusion of Greco-Roman and Judeo-Christian traditions, has inherited these prejudices and attitudes.

With a long history of representations of disability (from Tiresias to Richard III and beyond), theatre and performance have long been fascinated by the problematics of 'abnormal' bodies – even if these bodies were generally not allowed to perform themselves. While the disability arts movement has done much to redress this imbalance, disability performance is still perceived as a niche/ghetto practice.[3] Disabled characters are still regularly played by non-disabled actors (for instance, the latest Richard III on the London stage was Martin Freeman, and before him, Kevin Spacey); and when no reference to disability is made in a script, it is even rarer to see a disabled performer in a role. It is fairly common practice in mainstream theatre for a black man, or a white woman (though not a black woman) to play the role of Hamlet, for instance. But a disabled prince? Nabil Shaban's 1988 rendition with the Cleveland Theatre Company (Stockton-on-Tees) is a notable exception.[4] Along with casting, mainstream theatre and performance programming is still very ableist and exclusionary.

*PdS: A provocative question: is the fact that a lot of disability arts happen in the streets simply a choice to reach out to audiences, or is it also a result of the fact that disability arts are not programmed enough, so you need to go to the streets because no venue will have you?*

*CB: I think it's a bit of both. I received the Unlimited commission to create my most ambitious piece ever.*[5] *So I made a list of things I hadn't done, and outside work was one of them, and that was part of what my commission was about.*

*PdS: SDC often work on the streets. Can you, David, talk about that?*

*DB: Yes, it affects the creative process. It's also about reaching an audience that might not go to a rarefied atmosphere in a theatre, to reach an audience which theatre seems to have lost. We've been working with Ana Desetnica [street theatre festival] in Slovenia, and there is a large following in the festival; and artists meet and work together, and this also spawns collaborations. It's a cycle of energy, and from that cycle we start to generate some kind of an income. We perceive that income as being energy, so we send that out again to try to activate a dynamic of activity. It is an alternative way of looking at the economic processes of working as a company, as well as trying to source funding from organizations such as the Arts Council etc.*

*CB: I love David's idea that it's the art that brings about the collaborations, the fact that you're all street performers together, and that brings you to the point of saying: what are the potential collaborations now, what are the exchanges that could go on? This, rather than someone saying: I really want to work with a disabled performer so I can have a new experience, or tick a box or whatever – which I think has the potential to happen. But in that other scenario, you ask: what are the things that you have in your energy as a company, in your being, in your way of practising that we want a part of, which we want to exchange with you on? I think that's a lovely thought.*

*PdS: Questions of funding, marketing arise – but is there something, besides that, about the aesthetic of the work itself that comes through in disability arts?*

*CB: Disabled performers are constantly struggling with the question of what is the aesthetic of that work? Are we interested in a mainstream aesthetic or generating our own? If you're working with non-traditional dance bodies, then you instantly are challenging that aesthetic anyway. The attraction of doing stuff in the streets is that you don't have to sell tickets, because often you don't get programmed into spaces, because programmers think there's not a public for this work. But last year 6000 people saw my work, just because they were walking past. I don't know if I believe that – I think we haven't really tested those boundaries, whether that aesthetic is attractive or not, we just know it's different.*

## About cultures

The notion of a disability aesthetics is one that has existed and been discussed for some time within the disability arts movement.[6] In the last few years, however, it has acquired a new, broader significance. The idea, espoused by Tobin Siebers, that disability is to be regarded as an aesthetic value 'important to future conceptions of what art is' (Siebers, 2010: 20) has been gaining traction. I have suggested elsewhere that this notion is akin to Barthes' interest in the grain, that which makes a text rough, interesting, writerly, and that the idea can usefully be applied, for instance, to an understanding of translation (de Senna, 2013). Here, I would like to propose that the writerly positioning that a disability aesthetics imposes on viewers – one that, in Barthes' terms, 'makes historical, cultural, psychological assumptions of the reader, and the consistency of his tastes, values and memories vacillate' (Barthes, 1973: 25–26, my translation) – is also a productive paradigm for discussing collaboration.

In other words, an aesthetic which challenges our assumptions puts us in a position of instability, and forces movement, towards or away from the Other. The direction of this movement, naturally, depends on a number of circumstances, but no collaboration can occur in stasis. This stasis is epitomized by the image of the non-disabled dancer pirouetting around a wheelchair user; this type of 'collaboration' is often tokenistic, and based on a mainstream aesthetic, which attempts to 'raise' the disabled body to a level of pseudo-equality. These attitudes and challenges can only be surmounted, I argue, by a disability aesthetics, and the inclusive working processes that are its corollary. Discussing process as a corollary to aesthetics may seem counter-intuitive, as the latter normally depends on the former; but accepting an aesthetics that is 'grainy' (to borrow again from Barthes) reorders working processes and hierarchies – and thus disability becomes a democratizing force. In fact, this positioning is essential in any collaboration, which, by definition, requires a process of approximation. This, of course, is not always easy. Within the disability arts movement itself, there is a debate regarding the nature of disability culture: a tension between the need to establish and maintain an identity which is distinct, and the danger of reinforcing ghettoizing attitudes. Petra Kuppers explains that:

> there is a fine line here, between exclusionary essentialism on the one hand, and, on the other, the desire to mark the differences that disability-focused environments (which can include both non-disabled and disabled people) offer to mainstream ways of acknowledging bodies and their needs. I do not think that disability culture is something that comes 'naturally' to people identified or identifying as disabled. And I do not think that disability culture is closed to

> non-disabled allies, or allies who do not wish to identify as either disabled or not. To me, disability culture is not a thing, but a process. (Kuppers, 2011: 4)

The word 'allies' is key here. Quite apart from the issues of authorship and ownership that any collaboration might give rise to, collaborative processes between disabled and non-disabled practitioners offer the opportunity for 'alliances'. The notion is borrowed from feminist discourse;[7] it has also been appropriated in Deaf Studies: Joan Ostrove and Gina Oliva define it as 'an effective, mutually respectful relationship across (at least one) difference of identity that acknowledges oppression, privilege, and the complicated nature of identity' (Ostrove and Oliva 2010: 106). Indeed, such discussions take place with regard to Deaf culture and nationalism. This is compounded by the fact that Deaf communities are also linguistic minorities in their respective countries, with cultural identities often shaped by the use of sign languages and indeed by struggles to achieve recognition of such languages, with different degrees of success in different parts of the world. Moreover, within Deaf communities there is also an internationalist movement, with the organic development of International Sign Language, creating a transnational community, which has a complex set of linguistic negotiations to navigate. If communication and a movement towards the Other is essential in any collaborative process, then Deaf practitioners are particularly well-versed in such practices: by definition, they exercise communication across difference on a daily basis.

There is a complicated relationship between Deaf Studies and Disability Studies (and movements). Nonetheless, Deaf and disabled practitioners have found allies in each other, and often work together in collaboration: the constitution of SDC itself, where Bower is Deaf and Avila is disabled, is a good example – but also organizations such as DaDa and Graeae. These partnerships may extend to hearing, non-disabled agents. The purpose of the collaboration may vary, but it is always centred around process, and has a strong 'meta-processual' element, focusing on finding ways to work together across difference. This means such collaborations are political alliances by their very nature.

*DB: I think what is important when you work collaboratively, or just before making the decision to collaborate, is that what you have when you work is not just a vision, but that you share a process, a working methodology, the development of the art form; so that you have something to take to the collaboration, and that your partners also do have something – and that we've already had that discussion about what happens when you interface. In our case of SDC we've been exploring this for 25 years. For example, we collaborated with a company that explored behavioural archaeology, and they were interested in our work, because we are talking about the body as a historical document, both by watching form and physicality – and what that can say about the past and contemporary dance now – and how that interfaces with Sign Language, for example.*[8] *The history of Deaf people is not very well known (only for the past 200 years or so it has come to the surface) – but it's possible to find within the dynamics of Sign Language – to infer some of its historical origins. And examinations of questions like this yield creative possibilities, and we both go away having evolved our working processes and taking our methodologies to a new chapter as a result.*

*CB: When I look for people to collaborate with, I'm looking for people with skills I don't have. I don't think this is unique to me as a disabled artist, I think that's what we all do, effectively; I look for people who can expand my thinking about the piece or the way I'm practising as an artist; I'm also looking to establish the conditions so that when I come into that situation, I do it with strength, that I feel I am contributing equally to the process. This brings me to the question of leadership. This is something that disabled people – or at least I – struggle with: the awareness that we do have skills that come to the table to make effective collaborations.*

## About leadership

It is indeed rare for disabled people to be seen in positions of leadership. As a trope of human disqualification, disability is extremely powerful, and has served as a springboard for other forms of oppression and dehumanization, be it towards women, gay people or people of colour; all deemed to be, in one way or another, physically or mentally inferior, abnormal, sick (Siebers, 2010: 24). Underlying this is an idea of normalcy that holds a strong ableist bias. What Grayson Perry recently described as the tribe of 'Default Man' (2014) still occupies the collective imagination as the standard to be aspired. No wonder, then, some disabled people are often themselves diffident about their leadership skills and capabilities, when we have all been interpellated to the contrary. Harlan Lane in *The Mask of Benevolence*, another key text for Deaf and Disability Studies, has noted that 'paternalistic authority is likely to give a very different description of its charges than the one they would give of themselves – provided they have not internalized the stereotype promulgated by the authority' (Lane, 2000: 41). So again the question of visibility becomes key. More examples, and crucially more visible examples of disabled people in positions of leadership are needed.

How, though, can this desire for leadership be reconciled with the idea of collaboration within the arts? There is perhaps a paradox here, which, I believe, still needs to be resolved in terms of promoting an inclusive agenda. Perhaps it is the role of the arts to point towards models of behaviour, organizational structures and hierarchies that go beyond the binary of leadership/subordination. In this sense, the meta-processual focus discussed above might open new avenues for work. Even so, there is a certain pragmatism that needs to be maintained. In late-capitalist societies, very much in thrall of the individual, leaders (or at least spokespeople) are still in demand. No matter how collaborative the processes of Complicite may be, for example, the company is still very much associated with Simon McBurney's name.[9] It is important, then, that, even as disabled and non-disabled artists are collaborating on an equal, democratic footing, the disabled artist(s) is (are) seen to be at the forefront of the endeavour. To a certain extent, the 'grainy', radical aesthetics of disability arts, sometimes called the last avant-garde, should ensure this. Ultimately, process, product and the makers themselves cooperate to bring about a change of perception and attitudes.

*PdS: Is the notion of leadership contradictory to the notion of collaboration? Are they mutually exclusive?*

*CB: I think they're not. Leadership is about a way of being in a particular scenario. Any good leader comes with openness – they're not closed.*

*PdS: In what ways is the image of the disabled artist as leader important?*

*DB: I think when dealing within the dynamics of power it's important to find a way to make sure the integrity of the work is safeguarded and protected, and that the process follows this objective – a positive leadership, where a leader yields and allows democratic discussion to exist within the process. Then again, you get leaders who absolutely dominate and can also have extraordinary results. But I think in our situation we have Deaf and hearing people working together, so we're still investigating how that dynamic works, how we work together. So sometimes people who are further in the field have to yield so that others can catch up and we can work together in a democratic way; otherwise it becomes just about one person, and we're very much about the group, and the art-form is informed by what different people bring to the work: Deaf people, dancers, theatre people... Sometimes we've had very strong types of leaders in SDC and we've had to discuss and figure out how to convey each of our meanings. Not everybody understands what Disability Arts is, for example. Some people have a block as to what that is – they think it's a kind of political activist group. But one of the definitions of Disability Arts is asking: what are the creative possibilities that our disabilities suggest, and how can we contribute to the sum-total of the human story?*

## About dialogue

The idea proposed by Bower of artists contributing chapters to the human story brings us back to the notion of authorship. The beauty of the concept lies in that it is universal without being homogenizing. The story being told is not that of a group, but that of our species, in all its variety – and the authors of this story are all of us. If one of the fundamental questions of art in general is what is it that makes us human, then certainly the story to be told is one that is full of diversity and complexity. It is a story that is polyphonic, dialogic. The politics of collaboration between disabled and non-disabled practitioners hinges upon the acceptance of this multivocality. Charlton points out that the power of the slogan 'nothing about us without us' stems from 'its location of the source of many types of (disability) oppression and its simultaneous opposition to such oppression in the context of control and voice' (Charlton, 2000: 3). Dialogic relations can be critical, and this is perceived as positive. The various voices that make up the work of collaboration often are contradictory, and rub against each other, and force a reconsideration of assumed positions. This is fundamental for artistic growth, and the work of the collaborator as critic is highlighted. This seems to be more productive when collaborations are long-term, or when companies/practitioners keep returning to one another in different projects across time.

*Audience member 1: This notion of intersubjective communication is always predicated on inequality, because there are differences of capacity and this is intertwined with that idea: Collaboration needs difference. How do you ensure the mutuality in the process?*

*DB: You need to establish a dialogue that comes from a principled place. Instead of a constructed 'pyramid' structure, when you have dialogue, natural leadership emerges and the group is allowed to flourish as a result.*

*CB: For me there is always a fascination about this issue, because people think that equality is treating everybody the same, and I think it's about treating everybody differently. So I try to build this environment where I assume nothing about anyone. I absolutely agree with David in terms of having a dialogue about what do people need in order to excel in that environment, and what can I do to make that happen. Troubleshooting, lateral thinking, openness: common sense for me, but things which do become tripping points for some people.*

*Audience member 2: Some of these things take time. My worry is that there is not time for these things to flourish, for these intercorporeal relations to happen, because they don't just happen like that.*

*PdS: I think we can all agree that collaboration is time-consuming. In some sense you need to quite literally learn each others' language to be able to communicate. There's the communication that happens offstage, discussing ideas in the process, but also on stage, with your fellow players. Performance-making not only from a rehearsing point-of-view, but performance-making there and then, as you're working, which is itself a collaborative process.*

*CB: This idea about time fascinates me. These things do take time, yes. But as an artist I feel privileged that these things are part of my process, so I make that time. It's part of what I do because it's important. We don't often do it because we don't necessarily see it as important – it's like reflection after a project. You need to take time for that. That self-assessment is important for your development as an artist. When you're out there, there's no one, perhaps critics who will talk about and evaluate your work, making you think about what happened; but collaborations are brilliant for that because they can make you think about the lessons you learnt and how you move forward. So we need to make time for those relationships to develop.*

*PdS: I think it's a great notion to finish on: the collaborator as a critic, who not only helps you in a project, but helps you develop as an artist for your next one. I know from working with SDC, they keep bringing back things that they've learnt from past collaborations.*

*DB: Yes, when we worked with Betontanc*[10] *of Slovenia, Primož Bezjak could look at us objectively and say what signdance theatre is, and the work he did as a choreographer was extraordinary. He had no background in disability arts or working with Deaf people, had no Sign Language skills – he was just watching from an artistic point-of-view, and the work that he brought to us is just extraordinary – this dialogue between a hearing artist and us, exploring signdance theatre; and also the fact that he was coming from Slovenia, and us from the UK, Cuba (we're an international company based here, with people from different places); that cultural interface actually changed one another's working processes. So, cultural objectivity is essential as part of that dialogue, without which our work would not progress. As a result of it our work has become more open, become more oxygenated.*

It is clear that in the case of these two practitioners collaborative processes across dis/ability have been formative. If such collaborations are to be successful at all, dialogue and a will to explore working practices together are fundamental. The internal politics of such endeavours becomes just as important as, and implicated with, the political nature of the act itself. Tactically, such collaborations may ensure the visibility and dissemination of aesthetic practices that all too often are ghettoized.

***

What follows is a post-script, with questions that were sent to the Bower and Bowditch via email, and their respective answers. These additional questions address the roles these artists have played in collaborations, and discuss problems they have encountered. This extended conversation offers further insights into the topics addressed in the live conversation, and presents a clear picture of these artists' thinking about collaborative practices. Furthermore, it allows for their distinctive individual voices to come through in the writing.

*PdS: Are there different types of collaboration for you – or different 'roles' you take when collaborating? What are they, and how does this affect the work produced?*

*DB: All collaborations differ from artist to artist, or group to group. The working methodology of the collaborator with whom we collaborate informs the nature of the process. With Carovana S.M.I.*[11] *for instance, the process is firmly grounded within the context of contemporary dance-theatre and behavioural archaeology, and the body as a medium of expression, and its particular manifestation through signdance theatre. The overall spatiality and placement within an architectural, cultural and historical context is also taken into consideration when approaching the expressive, the dramaturgical and the internal/external dialogic terrain of the performer/performance/audience; this is particularly apparent in site-specific productions, but no less applicable in studio work.*

*The fusion of modern contemporary art processes and behavioural archaeology yields fresh insight that impacts on our performance practice. My role in this kind of collaboration is primarily as a performer that informs through practice the nature of Deaf theatre, and by being present, I therefore function as one; a working member of the ensemble and at the same time as a cultural agent of a specific working methodology. So therefore my function extends to both roles: as a teacher and student.*

*Collaboration is in our case very much a reciprocal process in that when we come away from a successful collaboration, we gain an extended experiential performance vocabulary and in turn have been able to, among other things, broaden the overall map of enlightened performance practice in disability art terms.*

*CB: The most recent projects I've worked on I've been in a role as Artistic Director, so many of the final decisions have sat with me. My collaborators tend to be other artists that I hand-pick for the specific skills they bring into the process, and which I don't have. I have incredible respect for the skills that they bring and very much value what they are able to offer me. In 2013, I worked as a choreographer on a project; this was different process, as I was commissioned to make the movement, and the artistic team for this was chosen by someone else – and I was just one part of it.*

*This collaboration worked differently from the way I usually work. The process felt somehow more disconnected, and it felt harder to have an overview of the whole project. It was also challenging, as I had never worked with any of the other artists involved before and not a lot of time had been built in to the making process to allow us to 'get to know' each other.*

*PdS: What is/are the main pitfall(s) or difficulty(ies) you have encountered in working collaboratively? Was disability ever an issue?*

*DB: Ongoing problems in effectively communicating disability art as a genre do occur. Sometimes there is a desire to collaborate from all sides for positive artistic reasons. But then sometimes there is failure to convey disability art as a genre. Sometimes there is a misconception as to the use of Sign Language within a theatrical context: for example, when it is mistakenly perceived as an interpretative tool, as opposed to an aesthetic and embedded feature of our working methodology. Anti-intellectual sentiments can also at times stymie discourse and lead to confusion. It is also not always so easy to break through the deep-seated cultural tendency to perceive an individual in terms of the supposed [non-disabled] ideal.*

*On a personal level, I can in some ways sympathize with a certain healthy scepticism about overly intellectualizing a process to the point of saturation, particularly when the intellectual process is lacking grounding within actual experience. Recent research pertaining to the site of consciousness has suggested consciousness as being seated within the entire physicality and not necessarily just located within the regions of the hypothalamus or the prefrontal cortex and so-on. In dance-theatre, for instance, we often work in the opposite direction from, say, theatre processes. We start from deep within the physical core to create movement and then arrive finally at the last stage, a script. This is effective when working with groups who don't necessarily have language at their disposal, for example in the case of deep autism or dyspraxia etc, or if the group don't share a language in common – i.e. that we all speak different languages.*

*This methodology holds a particular point of interest for the SignDance Collective and forms one of the core guiding principles of our working methodology, we believe that it is a functional artistic process in its own right and has much merit as an applicable universal methodology which holds particular ground-breaking possibility in terms of realizing potentially new artistic avenues. One of the main pitfalls that I have experienced is a failure to communicate the principles of working practices such as these. When anti-intellectualism becomes an excuse not to learn and of course vice-versa when the intellectual fails to put into practice, theory. It is often considered that disability is relative – in that when a Deaf and a hearing person attempt to communicate and fail. From the paternalistic perspective which favours a supposed ideal, it is often said, that they can't communicate because he or she is Deaf. But from a relative perspective it would be perceived from all angles – i.e. the failure happens between people.*

*CB: Physical distance between collaborators can prove to be difficult. I work best when everyone is 'in the room' so having collaborators (e.g. composers) at a distance can be really difficult. I was really fortunate in the making of* Falling in love with Frida, *in that the set and costume designer was with me in the studio for much of the making time. I think this really enhanced the end product. I am very specific in the collaborators and performers that I work with. I tend to work primarily with women, as I find there is less ego to deal with, and I avoid working with anyone with 'diva-like' behaviours.*

*I think roles and responsibilities need to be really clear at the outset of any project, and a transparency and openness about the budget for a project. Paying people well also really helps along with valuing the artistic contributions that everyone in the project team makes.*

*I also commit to supporting people's access and family requirements, and disability has never been an issue because I state what I need up front, as facts, rather than as anything that needs to be negotiated.*

## Notes

1. See https://sites.google.com/site/signdancecollective/
2. Lord Freud's recent comments about the economic value of disabled workers come to mind. See http://www.theguardian.com/politics/2014/oct/15/welfare-reform-minister-disabled-not-worth-minimum-wage [date accessed 29/10/2014]
3. For more information on the Disability Arts movement, see http://www.disabilityartsonline.org.uk/
4. *Hamlet 88*, which toured the north of England and was also performed in London's Half-Moon Theatre (Stepney), was directed by Alasdair Ramsay. It was set in a futurist techno police-state country, where Rosenkrantz and Guildenstern were represented by CCTV cameras.
5. Unlimited is a funding scheme of the Arts Council, celebrating and supporting the work of Deaf and disabled artists. For specific information on Bowditch's project, *Leaving Limbo Landing*, see http:/leavinglimbolanding.tumblr.com/.
6. See for example Kuppers, 2000.
7. See, for example, Burns, L. (ed.) (2006) *Feminist Alliances* (Amsterdam and New York: Rodopi).
8. The company Bower is referring to is Sardinia-based dance-theatre company Carovana S.M.I., led by Ornella D'Agostino and Alessandro Mellis. http://www.carovana.org/
9. See, for example, Alexander (2010) or Knapper (2010).
10. http://www.bunker.si/eng/production/betontanc
11. See note 8.

## Bibliography

Alexander, C. (2010) 'Complicite – *The Elephant Vanishes* (2003/4) – "The elephant and keeper have vanished completely... They will never be coming back"' in Harvie, J. and Lavender, A. (eds) *Making Contemporary Theatre: International Rehearsal Processes.* (Manchester: University Press), p. 59–80.

Barthes, R. (1973) *Le Plaisir du Texte.* (Paris: Éditions du Seuil).

Burns, L. (ed.) (2006) *Feminist Alliances* (Amsterdam and New York: Rodopi).

Charlton, J. I. (2000) *Nothing About Us Without Us: Disability Oppression and Empowerment* (Berkley, Los Angeles and London: University of California Press).

de Senna, P. (2013) 'When Creation, Translation and Adaptation Meet: SignDance Collective's *New Gold*' in Krebs, K. (ed) *Translation and Adaptation in Theatre and Film.* (New York and London: Routledge), p. 196–215.

Gosling, J. (2011) *Abnormal* (London: Bettany Press).

Knapper, S. (2010) 'Simon McBurney: Shifting Under/Soaring Over the Boundaries of Europe' in Delgado, M. and Rebellato, D. (eds) Contemporary European Theatre Directors. (London and New York: Routledge), p. 233–48.

Kuppers, P. (2000) 'Accessible Education: Aesthetics, Bodies and Disability', *Research in Dance Education*, 1: 2, p. 119–31.

Kuppers, P. (2011) *Disability Culture and Community Performance: Find a Strange and Twisted Shape* (Basignstoke: Palgrave Macmillan).

Lane, H. L. (2000) *The Mask of Benevolence: Disabling the Deaf Community* (San Diego: Dawn Sign Press).

Ostrove, J. and Oliva, G. (2010) 'Identifying Allies: Explorations of Deaf-hearing Relationships' in Burch, S. and Kafer, A. (eds) *Deaf and Disability Studies: Interdisciplinary Perspectives* (Washington, DC: Gallaudet University Press), p. 105–19.

Perry, G. (2014) 'They Walk Among Us' in *New Statesman*, 10-16 October, p. 24–31.

Siebers, T. (2010) *Disability Aesthetics* (USA: The University of Michigan Press).

Watt, N. and Wintour, P. (2014) 'Welfare Reform Minister: Some Disabled People 'Not Worth' Minimum Wage'. *The Guardian*, 15 October 2014. Available from http://www.theguardian.com/politics/2014/oct/15/welfare-reform-minister-disabled-not-worth-minimum-wage [date accessed 29/10/2014]

# Part III
# Failures – Compromising and Negotiating the Collaborative Self

# 12

# Positive Negatives: Or the Subtle Arts of Compromise

*Susan Melrose*

> Compromise: Middle English, mutual promise to abide by an arbiter's decision, from Anglo-French *compromisse,* from Latin *compromissum,* from neuter of *compromissus,* past participle of *compromittere* to promise mutually, from *com-* + *promittere* to promise... First Known Use: 15th century
>
> intransitive verb
>
> 1 *a*: to come to agreement by mutual concession
> *b*: to find or follow a way between extremes
>
> 1400–50; late Middle English < Anglo-French *compromisse,* Middle French
>
> *compromis* < Latin *comprōmissum* joint agreement < comprōmittere to
>
> enter into an agreement[1]

How slippery a term 'collaboration' is. Definitions aplenty tend to return to the notion of 'working together' (or 'co-working'), and on this sort of basis we should be able to conclude that all performance-making collaborations are vital because performance tends to involve the input of a wide range of practitioners, working together. Amongst these practitioners we can list stage, sound and lighting designers, stage managers and many others who work alongside both performers and – in general terms – a lead decision-maker. Does this model fit widespread understandings of the meaning of the terms collaboration or 'Collaborative Theatre'?[2] The lead decision-maker might be the stage director or choreographer, familiar to many performance-making traditions, or might equally be one key member of a performance collective – as is the case of the long-established and internationally-renowned UK company Forced Entertainment and key decision-maker Tim Etchells, and, in theory at least, the Théâtre du Soleil, Paris, and the central decision-making role of Ariane Mnouchkine. However, few of the chapters included in this collection seem to be concerned with collaborations viewed from this default perspective. Instead, collaborative performance-making in many of these chapters seems to assume the status of a particular genre or mode of performance-making, that brings with it – inseparable from it – its own celebrated histories; and uses of the term, in certain circles at least, seem tto carry with them a number of abstractions – a certain aura, a particular ethos, a set of popular discourses, and even a warming sense of *commitment*. Central amongst those circles of use is Performing Arts or Performance Studies in the British university, where collaborative making in an undergraduate or postgraduate module might seem to achieve a useful degree of empirical fit with popular discourses concerned with political action and agency. In the undergraduate and postgraduate Performance Studies module – in my experience – collaborators set out, curiously enough, from the premise of equality of potential: that is, each student is understood at the outset to have as much to offer the project as each other – however much it turns out to be the case, eventually, that those with skill, experience and persuasive personalities take the lead in decision-making.

Amongst these positivities, however, I want to speak the word 'collaboration' again in order to sound a contrary note. Although many colleagues in the university might argue, and indeed some do argue in these pages, that there are no failures in collaborative performance-making in the university context – since all such practices offer participants a learning experience – I am more concerned, in this chapter, with large or little failures in collaborative working practices that take place in the expert or professional performance-making sphere. I am interested, in this case, in both collaborative practices between expert practitioners, and in how things *work* in the performance collective, which seems to me equally to involve the 'working together' with which I began, but to do so with fewer or different claims to parity between diverse practitioners. I am arguing here that failure in the collaborative process in expert or professional performance-making is likely to put both or all practitioners involved at professional risk, and this is particularly but not exclusively so, where public funding and public reputation are involved. Professional co-working, in such circumstances, is likely to set out from a sense of artistic affinity, and professional falling out, as a consequence, tends to be particularly bitter, even if public failure is often avoided – because it must be – by one or the other participant stepping in to reassert her or his ('signature') control. In even the best of cases, however, collaborations in *expert* performance-making tend to proceed through, and to end in compromise. By compromise, here, I understand 'to come to [a professional creative] agreement by mutual concession'.

The issue of little or larger failures in expert or professional performance-making, and the matter of compromises, similarly minor or major, brings not only reputation but *affect* to the fore in the collaborative equation – where, in fact, it has always been, even if it has, until relatively recently, been largely omitted from the dominant discourses of theoretical writing in Performance Studies. *Practitioner* affect in the making processes is undoubtedly hard for most researchers – let alone practitioners themselves – to capture, and harder still to write about, yet practitioner affect – sensing or feeling *something* – is likely to be key to her or his experience in the making.[3] I have already used the words 'at risk' and 'bitter', above, suggesting, as I do so, that more is at stake, in collaborative practice between established practitioners, than the performance outcome. A practitioner's name, and her signature (practices) are relatively fragile, as far as cultural capital is concerned, but so too are her or his feelings (professional as well as personal). In the always fraught world of arts funding, reputation tends to be a key token of exchange, hard won and easily lost. A professional choreographer working 'collaboratively' with a major theatre director may find that her or his input is subsumed under the signature of that director, late in the decision-making process, when the project is about to reach its audience.

In such circumstances might the choreographer's input not be, properly speaking, *compromised*, or unable to function optimally? The highly reputed signature practitioner's name so easily takes the place allotted to it by those who fund, write about and market professional performance in the wider arts communities. Hence the work will always be that of Ariane Mnouchkine, Robert Wilson or Tim Etchells, regardless of the importance of the input from choreographer, dancer, or expert performer (for example, Catherine Schaub, Lucinda Childs and Cathy Naden, amongst others). Plainly other artists understand the importance of the latters' collaborative input – as they do themselves – yet it would be foolish, on that basis, to make any claim as to parity of esteem for their input with the 'signature' practices and effects of the three theatre directors. Is the input of these other expert practitioners compromised, or 'unable to function optimally', as a consequence?

If my argument is valid here, then not simply do collaborations proceed through and end in compromise – even in the very best of cases – but they do so precisely because an established artist working collaboratively does so, explicitly or not, in order to open her work to difference, to give way to difference, to the end (or at least to the possibility) of what Brian Massumi has called 'qualitative transformation':[4] in this case, what is entailed is a transformation in the practitioner's experience of self under the gaze of the (respected) other. That other looks back – and this is vital – at the established artist, and 'sees her', and her or himself, differently. The relationship, as I have already indicated, is affectively charged, as well as professional. She sees the other seeing her, and it is on the basis of shared artistic affinity, as well as professional respect, that professional or expert collaborative practices engage with and *work through* this affective charge. This complex scenario may perhaps signal why the failure of a collaborative undertaking is likely either to be so damaging, or to force one practitioner to assume a fragile control in difficult circumstances. It is not necessary to have read a great deal of the work of French psychoanalyst, Jacques Lacan,[5] to recognize that the gaze of the (respected) other exposes the self, and is likely to interrogate her as well as reassure her. On these sorts of bases, I propose to identify such collaborative undertakings as *experimental in process* (if not necessarily in outcome); as such they are likely to be characterized by a particular intensity of *experience*, as each practitioner involved attempts to negotiate with her or his other – and, effectively, with her or his self – with a deadline in view and a reputation at stake. What follows, in time, is the further development of *expertise*.

The scenario I have outlined above may however also hint at the reasons for undertaking these sorts of highly charged collaborative experiments: the expert practitioner learns through *the experience of* expert practice, whether it is judged by others to be successful or less successful. Her *expertise* is not simply developed or elaborated 'through practice',[6] but rather more importantly through the *experience of practices* (in the plural). She learns – and this is key – through difference, and she learns, as I suggest below, retrospectively, when some of the intensity of the collaborative or collective experience has lessened. Collaborative practices potentially enhance by energizing other, more established single-practitioner modes of practice, by bringing expert otherness into the making processes: on these bases the quality of the experience is likely to be intense, and that intensity may well not be lived as entirely positive in the short-term. Time, time present and time passing, in other words, is key to the development of experience and expertise.

I have suggested that expert collaborations tend to be experimental in process; that they are likely to involve a certain intensity of experience, and that it is this sort of intensity of experience, however difficult at the time, that is likely to develop expertise in a practitioner who might be more accustomed to make work alone (or in her or his own name). Although there has been much written about experimentation in performance in the twentieth century, neither 'experience' nor 'expertise', for different reasons, has been widely theorized in the major discourses of Performance Studies in the university – as distinct, undoubtedly, from the disciplinary fields of Psychology, Sociology or Education, or the more recently emerged and interdisciplinary 'practice theory'[7]. Few have suggested however that all expert or professional collaborations are *experimental* in process – for the practitioners involved (this has little to do with what has been called 'experimental theatre' in the 20thC), and it is their contribution to *expert* practitioners in terms of *experience* that is vital. Certainly such collaborations bring uncertainty into the equation, starting from the fact of artistic affinity: where expertise has been bound up with the ability to exercise a certain control upon process and outcome, collaborations require, as I indicate above, a certain agreement to loosen that control, and to admit difference into play. By compromise, in this case, I refer to a joint agreement and 'mutual concession' between practitioners, each of whom, in the event of collaboration, is likely to contribute differently to an end or ends unlikely to be discernible in advance of the fact of working together. Surely this is the challenge of such an undertaking? Mutual concession seems to me to suppose a degree of letting go, indeed of loss, in both or all participants, in order to gain something more and other, but it also seems to me that there are few guarantees, in such a framework, that the collaborating practitioners will experience loss to the same degree and/or extent.

The notion of a 'promise to abide by an arbiter's decision' (above) is a delicate one, in the collaborative framework or the framework of collective creation, but it is one that I return to below with reference to both the (emergent) decisive role of one practitioner within the collaborative undertaking, and the role in creative invention played by disciplinary codes. Rather than a belief in a seemingly non-hierarchical mode of creative decision-making – which is undoubtedly useful in the undergraduate context where group devising is a widely adopted model of pedagogy – I have already identified *affinity* between artists, who are likely to work, in many instances of performance-making, in quite different artistic disciplines, as a basis for and means to working collaboratively. Artistic affinity is a curiously under-discussed notion, as far as academic writing about performance is concerned, yet it is a vital factor within the arts.

UNIVERSITY OF WINCHESTER
LIBRARY

> affinity c.1300, "relation by marriage" (as opposed to consanguinity), from O.Fr. lit. "bordering on," from ad- "to" (see ad-) + finis "a b order, an end" (see finish). Used figuratively since c.1600 of structural relationships in chemistry, philology, etc. Meaning "natural attraction"[8]

Affinity can operate productively in the professional or expert sphere without the need for a pre-existing personal affinity. Mutual respect *for the other's work*, similarly under-theorized in academic writing[9], is likely to be a vital factor in expert collaborations. Working together, in the case of what I have called 'signature practitioners' – publicly recognized, named practitioners whose work and name are one – is particularly challenging because of the degree of 'mutual concession' to be negotiated.

Where expert performance-makers choose to collaborate, or to create collectively, in other words, they do so on the basis of some kind of perception of *professional or expert affinity and respect*, but in the light of an equally-strong perception of difference or heterogeneity viewed as likely to be productive. Such perceptions are often rapidly made, and there does tend to be a sense of recognition involved, likely to appear to be holistic rather than analytical, although it is also my sense that analysis of potential is likely already to have occurred elsewhere – hence Shobana Jeyasingh's decision to collaborate with Michael Nyman, in making dance works that will bear her signature as choreographer,[10] is likely to have been informed by a pre-existing and very complex exercise, by Jeyasingh, of judgement of his compositions. In these instances, besides, Jeyasingh generally commissions Nyman's collaboration, with very clear implications as regard to signature and/or 'ownership' of what is made. I am supposing that from the outset, however, Jeyasingh recognizes a possibility of working productively with the composer, without knowing perhaps at that point in time how the composer himself works – his working in isolation, for example, whereas she works with others; the rhythm of his working, for example, in contrast with her own dance rehearsals with a group of highly-skilled dancers, develops over what is sometimes an extended period of time. What this suggests, succinctly enough, is making-processes significantly at odds with each other. What seems to me to be important to note about this sort of collaboration is that it brings together disciplinary difference – at least two complex knowledge sets, with their attendant and relative hierarchies – as well as different ways of seeing, knowing and working – and that it is likely that each participant will at certain key moments struggle to keep a sense that these two knowledge sets and ways of working, as well as the aesthetic preferences of each, will at some point – because they are both professionals – achieve a sense, however fragile and momentary, of empirical fit, the one with the other to the advantage of both.

My own sense nonetheless is that collaboration triggers a stronger rather than weaker sense of ownership in each participant, a stronger sense of disciplinary mastery, a stronger rather than a weaker sense of the rightness of a way of working. It can also trigger, as far as I have been able to discern, frustration, anger, anxiety, anticipation, despair, irritation, all of which seem to me to be normally a part of this sort of collaboration, and all of which seem to me to be 'containable', in the experience of it, only on the basis of a pre-existing and *expert* exercise of judgement as to the credibility of the other professional artist involved.

I want to direct your attention now to one particular instance of the history of collaborative or collective performance-making, as some of us experienced it in the 1960s and 1970s, and to draw on it in order to come back to one or two of the issues I have already identified. Rather than a collaborative company, the Théâtre du Soleil identified itself in terms of a *'sociéte coopérative ouvrière de production'* – a cooperative workers' production group or corporation or collective. I have written 'so-called' because of a curiosity of English language reporting practised by the esteemed David Williams, whose *Théâtre du Soleil Sourcebook,* noted above, is entitled *Collaborative Theatre,* even though the term 'collaboration' figures twice only in his book's Index. The term preferred throughout by the practitioners themselves was and is 'collective'. This raises again the notion of the impact on the exercise of judgement of heterogeneous models of intelligibility. One of the two references to the collaborative, in William's book of that name, dates from 1975, when Mnouchkine declared that

> Remember that the [theatre] director has already achieved the greatest degree of power he has ever had in history. And our aim is to move beyond that situation by creating a form of theatre where it will be possible for everyone to collaborate without there being directors, technicians, and so on, in the old sense.[11]

Ironically, perhaps, Mnouchkine was already, in her own words in 1971, a director within the Théâtre du Soleil as collective, but her understanding of her role contrasts with her knowledge of the *metteur en scène* in the French tradition, that she qualified as 'in the old sense'. In 1971 – that is three years after the cultural revolution of 1968 – the theatre director to whom Mnouchkine alluded advisedly as 'he', had constructed himself as 'l'auteur de la scène'('the author of the stage') whereas David William's way of seeing theatre directors, in 1999 from the UK, was not informed by the lived experience of that French peculiarity. William's genuine concern with collaborative practices, which I would argue he has retrospectively projected onto the Théâtre du Soleil's work for an English-language audience, needs to be positioned in the context of the British university's recourse, from the 1980s onwards, to group-devised performance-making as a highly economical way of undergraduate and postgraduate teaching and assessment, following upon the growth of performance as a very popular discipline in the university.

The French did have good reason in the 1960s and 1970s not to like the term 'collaboration', because of the still-ongoing accusation that many French had collaborated with occupying Germans during WII. For me, however, the term 'collective' is interestingly different in implication from 'collaboration'. It can suppose that parts of the making might occur separately, or elsewhere, and be brought together, possibly with catalytic impact on the rest, possibly not – especially if the staging is identified as 'carnivalesque' – without nonetheless emerging from a collaborative 'working together'. What Williams has called collaborative, in the early significant work of the Théâtre du Soleil, was, in the making, cooperative and collective, as far as I have been able to discern, in that *1789*, at least, grew out of already-established practices of the group mastered for *Les Clowns*: these consisted of the perfecting of 'each person's individual creation', but in *1789* the co-creation was informed by each participant's shared knowledge of French myth – for example, the French revolution and its frustrated aspiration to liberty, equality and fraternity. (Mnouchkine refused in interview in 1970[12] with Emile Copfermann to call preparation for *Les Clowns* 'collective creation', precisely because of its emphasis on collecting together individually-created and evaluated performance units.)

Preparatory work for *1789* was explicitly 'group work', but it made no claims, as far as I could see, to a dissolve of hierarchies in the exercise of judgement in creative decision-making. Mnouchkine, tellingly, did not perform in the work that has progressively associated itself with her signature and, as tellingly, when we see some of the images from the making[13] in the case of her *Tartuffe* (1995), the very fact that everyone else in the shots is in costume, while she is not, signals this division and this decision-making hierarchy: she is, as I have suggested above, in the rehearsal room and in this scene at least, the signature practitioner, the 'arbiter' to whom I refer, above, with whose decision-making all others present agree (*com- + promittere* – to promise mutually) to abide. Is this 'collaborative performance-making'? Certainly it is a 'working together' – *collectively* – and it assumes, I would argue, as expert or professional collaborations in the arts communities tend to, that final creative decisions are likely to be taken by the (possibly emergent) decision-maker *within that group* – from which comes the notion that something is *com*-promised, by the collective, to the end of the work's emerging in a timely manner. That decision-maker, in a collective, may well not be the same single individual in each instance, since the work of the collective makes different demands in different times and places, but what seems to me to be clear is that detailed decision-making, before the work is made public, cannot be practised by the collective. The weight of judgement is openly assumed by a spokesperson/signature-maker, who may well be taken to represent the group of practitioners, but cannot usually represent the individual choices of all present. Whence compromise, that most delicate art.[14]

In the case of the work of the Théâtre du Soleil there was clear evidence from its establishment in the 1960s of a political persuasion and that sense of commitment referred to above, coupled with an open distaste for certain established institutions, but I can find no evidence of a collaborative ('equalising') ethos as others might identify it. The choice of carnival was explicit and principled: they chose to operate to multiple viewpoints, dispersed in the spaces and times of performance; yet even in the photographic evidence, there are moments of sharp performance delineation, of what I would characterize as an 'older' judgement of a theatricality *that works*, that one might argue is necessitated precisely because of the performance-making expertise of each member of the collective, plus the aspiration, of each, to the multiple, to difference and dispersal within the one. Yet even in the 1960s, Mnouchkine's role as director within the collective is clear and acknowledged. I noted, above, that one understanding of 'compromise' from the Middle English, the notion of a 'mutual promise to abide by an arbiter's decision', might nonetheless refer less to a person, as arbiter, than to the discipline, to theatrical codes and conventions themselves. In the work of Théâtre du Soleil, I would argue that it is her understanding of theatricality itself that drives Mnouchkine's interventions. In the instance of Théâtre du Soleil, it is plainly also a theatricality that bears her signature, and it draws performers from around the world who want to work with her theatre collective. The compromise to which all eventually bend in the name of a particularly dazzling notion of theatricality – in the case of difficult rehearsal work for *Tartuffe*, to which we turn below[15] – can be

***mis***understood as something that Mnouchkine imposes, leaving the performer's own invention compromised.

In the collective's preparations for Molière's T*artuffe,* a French cultural classic, the director's aesthetic signature remained absolutely clear and – I would argue – unrepentant. It is consistently Mnouchkine's signature – it can be identified in what I call her *signature practices,* which tend to work on every performance detail contributed/mediated by a performer arrived at within the work of the collective, that determines the detail as well as the larger lines of the performance aesthetic (and how the work is likely to be interpreted), and reinforces my hypothesis that this is an aesthetic/political practice that has developed consistently over thirty years, taking long-established members of the collective with it. In rehearsals for *Tartuffe,* as we see in the film *Au Soleil même la nuit,* by 'Éric Darmon et Catherine Vilpoux[16] my hypothesis is that the intensity of individual experience for one particular member of the collective, developed painfully over time within the event of creative performance-making, demonstrably involves a powerful experience of the self as other. According to Milet's interpretation of Heidegger, to which I return below, that experience, importantly, is likely to be grasped, retrospectively, as transformative, however painful it is in the throes of the intense experience itself.

In *Au Soleil même la nuit,* a filmed account of the preparations for the production of *Tartuffe,*[17] what we can see, in one particular segment, is an exercise of judgement that is individually voiced but collectively performed; it seems to be visited upon a single male actor by the collective, of which he is a privileged member. I would argue that his experience is overtly *transformative,* in the immediate circumstances, *for that performer* in terms of his ability to engage with the work of the group as a whole – indeed the production itself depended upon that development. In the longer term, it is likely that what was at stake was the development of his own expertise and artistry, and his ability to work productively with the other. What is staged in this extract from the film is a clash between the exercise of judgement of the director and the collective and the judgement of one performer, cast in one of the key performance roles (Valère) on the basis of his performance experience and growing expertise. In this short clip we see Mnouchkine in a state of what I take to be some distress,[18] before the assembled collective, because of rehearsal delays caused by the apparent inability of the actor concerned to work collectively (*'tout est pour l'autre'* – everything is done for the other), rather than individually, on the basis of his reflections of the night before. The film offers a privileged insight firstly into the drama of the development of expertise in the performer-to-collective relationship, and secondly into what some of the few twentieth-century writers on experience have called the 'technicity of experience'.[19]

The notion of the technicity of experience derives from a particular understanding of the self that supposes that the self is both plastic rather than fixed, and that it is performed by each of us. It follows that theatrical performance, drawing on the self of the actor in that context, might be grasped as a set of techniques that serve, symptomatically,[20] to seem to expose that self either in the name of character or in the name of the performer concerned. In 'Experience as Technique of the Self', Jean-Philippe Milet argues 'that the very heterogeneity of experience is to be found in its technical dimension; that is, that there can be no experience without transformation, above all, without transformation of the self, and that there can be no transformation without technics'.[21] The techniques of the self tend to be sharply exposed in performance-making contexts, not least where a performer – as in the case of *Tartuffe* – is cast to play a pre-established dramatic character. The technicity of characterization in performance involves the actor's explicit access to and choices made from sets of physical symptoms, identifiable as such, that the expert performer her or himself can thematize: that is, he or she is able to work explicitly with a set of physical options, trying them out, testing and discussing, with those involved, what works and what works less well, and why. These physical choices, plainly, can equally be understood as symptoms of or pointers to notions of the interiority of self (of dramatic character, as well as the actor's self[22]). The work of the collective that is Théâtre du Soleil is highly technical, explicitly choreographed, and *Tartuffe* emerged in the context of what in the UK was called – curiously enough – 'physical theatre', highly choreographed and physically demanding, where performer choices demonstrate considerable physical plasticity and control. Actors working in the so-called 'physical theatre' are likely to be clear as to the sort of systems of options available, as well as their anticipated effect and affective potential.

In my experience over the years, some viewers of this particular clip tend to see the individuals involved – as though these *were individuals* and personalities experiencing difficulties – rather than the productive *work-based* clash between different ways of making performance, where that performance, finally, will be identifiable in terms of the signature of a master performance-maker and the collective within which she works. The individualization of players in the collective tends to distract the onlooker from what are both heterogeneous work practices, for the individuals concerned, and collective practices specific to the company concerned. Working technically *for the other ('tout est pour l'autre')* in terms of Mnouchkine's expertise, is a matter, in the instance cited and in the dramatic context concerned, of minutely detailed gestuality and movement, dependent always on responses to tiny triggers emitted by the other performer.

Many of us speak about qualitative transformation in performance-making, but we tend to be reticent as to the practices themselves that are capable of bringing creative transformation about, as a stage in the acquisition of expertise. Plainly a key difficulty for writers is that transformation in performance-making expertise can only be *practised* in a relational framework – that is, in the active presence of an other, who brings difference, as I point out above, into the equation. Within that relational framework, as the video clip makes fully clear, the actor concerned appears to be unable to grasp the need to work technically, in the first instance, *with the other*, that is, in live interaction with the finely articulated performance techniques of the long-established company member (Juliana Carneiro da Cunha, seen below, standing) that seem to be alien to him. The approach of Martial Jacques (seen below in rehearsal, fig.19) was intellectualizing, and he argued that he worked out what to do in the course of thinking it through the previous evening.

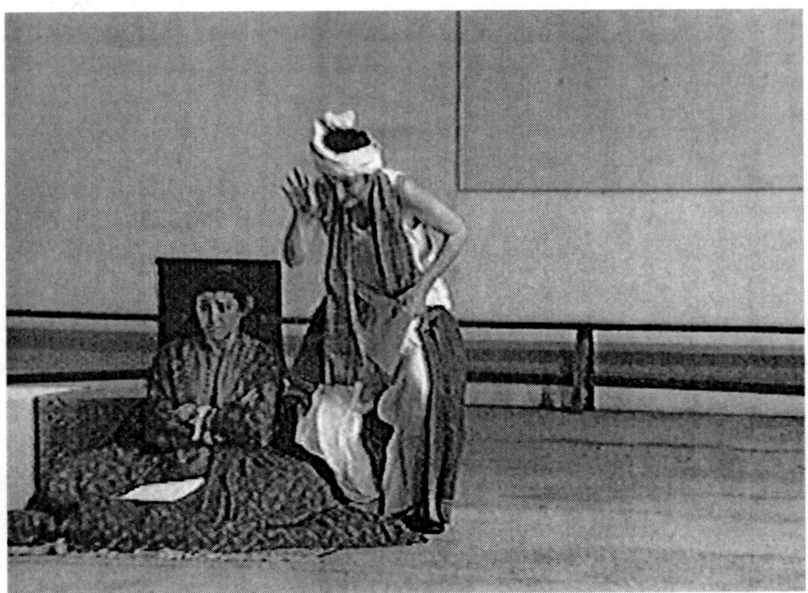

*Fig. 18* Juliana Carneiro da Cunha. *Au Soleil même la nuit* (1997), Film d'Éric Darmon et Catherine Vilpoux en harmonie avec Ariane Mnouchkine

Milet paraphrases from Heidegger's writing on technicity, arguing that transformation of the self is arrived at *retrospectively* through a 'becoming other' of the self.[23] When we transpose Milet's heideggerian observations to this example of a quasi-public event presented to the gaze of the largely sympathetic other (the theatre collective assembled as audience – see figs 20 and 21), what needs to be understood is that the theatre worker concerned must *endure that experience*. In Milet's terms, he receives it as it strikes him, and he submits to it, with some very evident difficulty, not because the director in the collective imposes it upon him – this is to give way to myths of the tyrannical director – but because the collective judgement is engaged, and because he has committed to that collective. Is his own inventive work compromised, or 'unable to function optimally', as we saw above?

I prefer to argue, instead, that what can eventually be seen in this clip is one aspect of the evidently painful experience that will lead, progressively, to a qualitative transformation, following intensive interactive and detailed work with the highly expert, long-time member of the collective. He will become other to his (former sense of) self and therefore differently himself, through close confrontation with difference. We

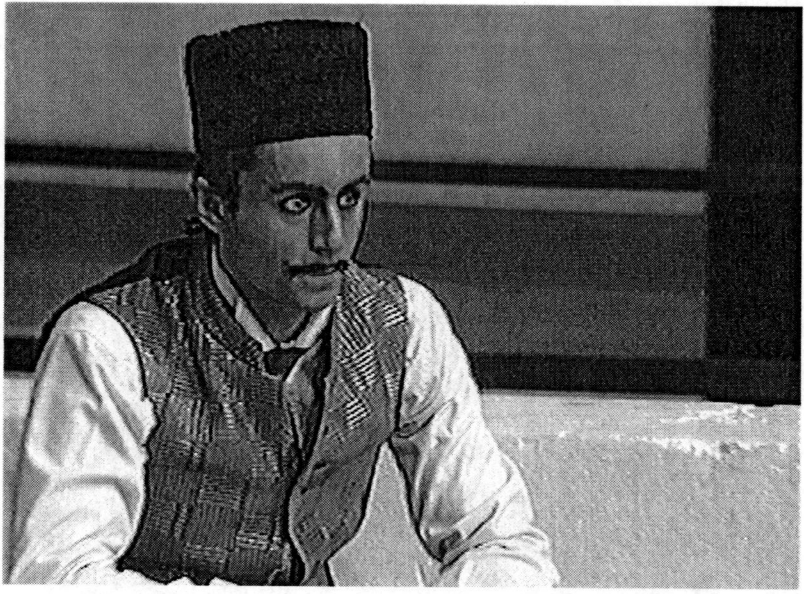

*Fig. 19* Martial Jacques. *Au Soleil même la nuit* (1997), Film d'Éric Darmon et Catherine Vilpoux en harmonie avec Ariane Mnouchkine

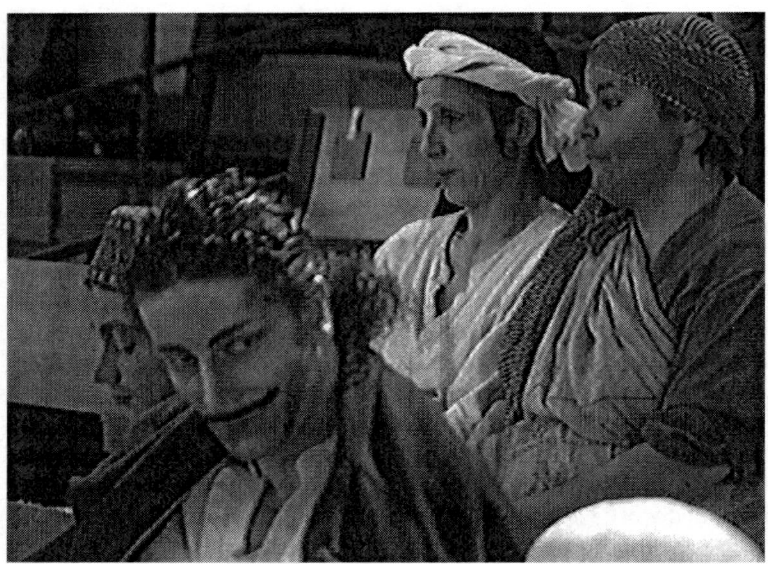

*Fig. 20* Cast members of the collective serving as audience. *Au Soleil même la nuit* (1997), Film d'Éric Darmon et Catherine Vilpoux en harmonie avec Ariane Mnouchkine

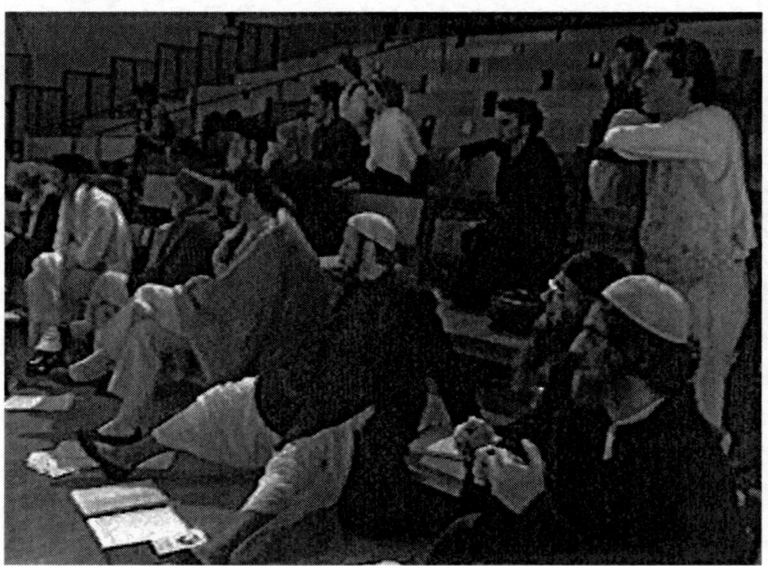

*Fig. 21* Members of the collective serving as audience at rehearsals. *Au Soleil même la nuit* (1997), Film d'Éric Darmon et Catherine Vilpoux en harmonie avec Ariane Mnouchkine

might argue the same, in the case of Mnouchkine, who – and this is rare enough – is later interviewed, alone in the shot, on the difficulties that beset her here, and the actions she felt obliged to take. It is plainly never too late, in the case of a major creative practitioner, to undergo a challenge to and a readjustment of the self.

'Constitutive of identity', Milet adds, 'this alteration is not [immediately] absorbed within identity', as we might expect of a short-term learning experience. Instead, alteration, experienced in – for example – productive collaborations, 'opens [the identity of the self] up in a double sense'. Alterity or difference, in these instances, 'both articulates and directs [identity], and [it] divides and splits it.' As I suggested above, this is precisely, to my mind, why expert practitioners agree and – in some cases – go on agreeing to collaborate.

Thus any significant development in expertise and hence in practitioner identity as a working member of Théâtre du Soleil 'is attained . . . as [an] event, [a] singularity', and 'it is always [acquired] retrospectively'. Collective creation, and/or collaboration, in this sense – and I realize that this view may not be popular – can do something of a

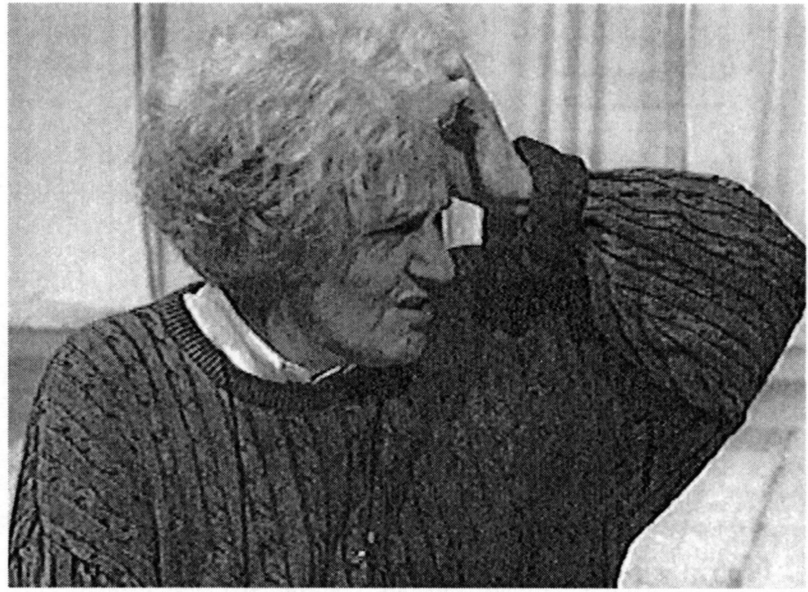

*Fig. 22* Ariane Mnouchkine addresses the question of rehearsal delays and her intervention. *Au Soleil même la nuit* (1997), Film d'Éric Darmon et Catherine Vilpoux en harmonie avec Ariane Mnouchkine

violence to the self who commits ('compromisse'; 'comprōmittere'; 'to find or follow a way between extremes') to it: the expert practitioner, open to develop through qualitative transformation and keen to work collaboratively, agrees in advance to this, endures it, before grasping its significance retrospectively.

Now, transformative experience of the self, within the collective (or social group, or group of collaborators) might well – curiously enough – be seen as straightforwardly positive and quickly perceived by the performer concerned. Curiously, because an individual's sense of self, ways of thinking, seeing, saying and doing, attitude and sense of the possible, tend, as far as I have been able to discern, to be impressed gradually over time, internalized, as well as externalized in actions taken, and many of us tend, as far as I can tell, to suppose that our own 'sense of self'- entailing techniques of the self, modes of action in the everyday, that we consistently practise – is more or less stabilized and embedded. The ways we understand self in the everyday could be argued to constitute a major model of intelligibility, a way of understanding self and world that actually also contributes to both self and world. In this sort of understanding, a 'learning experience' might seem to be readily assumed, a positivity, that is effectively added to that already stabilized, carefully constituted self. The self expands. Yet, the sort of qualitative transformation I have identified here, that is hard won, likely to disrupt and even to rupture the established sense of self and others, is likely, in Milet's reading of Heidegger, to be perceived retrospectively. It is likely to be experienced, in the acutely intense events of collective making that we see in *Au Soleil même la nuit*, as publicly wounding; yet I am arguing that it is precisely through this intense engagement with the other that the practitioner acquires some of the ingredients of an expertise that he or she does not necessarily recognise at the time. In performance-making, as it develops in the individual practitioner, through one or another instance of collaboration, it is experienced at best, in the event of it, as experimentation – 'gained by repeated trials', 'tested', 'felt and undergone'.[24]

A withdrawal from a collaboration which 'is not working', at any point in the proceedings, might entail, for one or more party to the project in hand, 'an endangering of reputation', an 'exposure to danger or suspicion', both of which are likely to have ongoing implications for the way each performance-maker involved views her or his own situation. One tends in the first instance to say 'That woman/man/individual is impossible!', rather than, quietly to oneself, 'Am I impossible?' Such an exposure or endangering rankles, and goes on rankling, and my suggestion in this chapter is that one of the reasons for elation, when a collaboration finally *'works'*, is precisely because of a sense of relief coupled with a sense of expansion: expert collaborations tend to work, for one and another practitioner, by fracturing the established sense of self, to admit an otherness that challenges, for those artists for whom a challenge is desired. The elation seems to me to be relatively short-lived, and it is retrospectively, at some length, that the collaborator grasps the changes to the self that constitute an acquiring of expertise.

I have suggested above that working together (or collaboration), even between expert or professional practitioners tends, where those practitioners operate within a similar discipline – such as theatre-making and performance – to be characterized by differences in skill, experience and potential, necessitating ongoing negotiation and what might be merely an interim arrival at compromise. Performer expertise is both a curious phenomenon and an undertheorized field in the UK context. Training institutions differ in approach and the working individual tends to acquire expertise progressively through the shared experience of expert practices. For the less skilled with less experience of 'working together', whether in a formal collaboration or in collective performance-making, a 'successful outcome' will almost certainly constitute a training through practice, an elaboration of her or his own potential, yet I have also argued above that that experience of enhancement is likely to be painful *in the event*, if it is to be transformative after it. I am interested in how we might theorize that kind of learning through experience which is both bruising and potentially transformative of the self of the practitioner.

Does the dominant engagement of the one mean that her other is necessarily dominated, within collective or collaborative practices? I am supposing that the matter is less straightforward than such an oppositional model would suggest, and that 'the same' complex, collective or collaborative undertaking is likely to be differently experienced by each practitioner, both at the time and after it. What ensues is likely to be experienced as 'not [wholly] of our own making'. To undergo it would 'mean [in part to...] submit to it'. What *can go wrong* in expert collaborative practices with a first night in view is likely to go wrong, and on this basis many of our ensuing actions will constitute *ways of coping*. These ways of coping are characteristic, in my view, of a mastery in collaborative or collective performance-making whose implications are likely to be grasped at length, as I suggest above, rather than 'in the moment'.

Experience gained in collaborative or collective practice, from this perspective, 'transforms in the sense that it acquires form at the end of a crossing, of a trial of endurance, *après coup*'.[25] For the 'co-labouring' practitioner, then, *becoming other* – a stage involved, I would argue, in acquiring mastery – 'is to become self'. 'One can only become [oneself, as an expert practitioner], through becoming other (*en s'altérant*), through alteration'. This fracturing of the self, that I am arguing is constitutive of the elaboration of (expert) identity in the collaborative practitioner, is not immediately absorbed but opens identity up, in both articulating and directing it, dividing it and splitting it. To return to the definitions of compromise, then, with which I began, compromise in expert collaborative or collective making practices can entail a settlement of differences by mutual adjustment or modification of opposing claims, principles, demands; an agreement by mutual concession; but also – as we see in the film of the making of *Tartuffe* – a potential endangering, especially of reputation; an exposure to danger or suspicion, when what the performer undertakes is viewed critically, in the instant, by all other members of the collective.

## Notes

1. I quote here and in 8 below from a number of online etymological dictionaries, including www.oed.com; www.etymonline.com/index.php; www.merriam-webster.com/dictionary.
2. The title of David Williams' *Théâtre du Soleil Sourcebook*, London & New York: Routledge, 1999.
3. Brian Massumi writes explicitly about affect, in his *Parables for the Virtual: Movement, Affect, Sensation* (2002), where he notes, in spinozan terms, that affect 'is synesthetic, implying a participation of the senses in each other: the measure of a living thing's potential interactions is its ability to transform the effects of one sensory mode into those of another' (p.35). See also M. Gregg and G. Seigworth's *The Affect Theory Reader*, Durham: Duke University Press Books, 2010.

   The play of affect is complex and shifting; it is likely to be experienced, by the practitioner, as singular.
4. Brian Massumi, *Parables for the Virtual: Movement, Affect, Sensation*, Durham & London: Duke University Press, 2002.
5. Jacques Lacan, *The Four Fundamental Concepts of Psycho-analysis,* trans. A. Sheridan, 1977, London: Vintage, 1998.
6. Charles Spinosa, 'Derridian dispersion and Heideggerian articulation: General tendencies in the practices that govern intelligibility', in Schatzki, Knorr Cetina and Von Savigny (eds), *The Practice Turn in Contemporary Theory,* London; Routledge, 2001.
7. See, indicatively, K. A Ericsson, N.Charness, P. J. Feltovich, R. Hoffman (eds), *The Cambridge Handbook of Expertise and Expert Performance,* Cambridge: Cambridge University Press, 2006. On 'practice theory', see T. Schatzki, K. Knorr Cetina and E. Von Savigny (eds), *The Practice Turn in Contemporary Theory*, London: Routledge, 2001.
8. See note 1, above.

9. Michel de Certeau, in his 'What we Do When we Believe', in M. Blonsky (ed), *On Signs,* Baltimore: Johns Hopkins University Press, 1985, seems to me to approach such questions but to–date few published writers in Performance Studies have done so.
10. The two collaborated on – amongst other pieces – Configurations, 1988 and 2012; Strange Blooms, 2013.
11. Ariane Mnouchkine, L'Age d'Or: the long journey from 1793 to 1975, *Theatre Quarterly* 5: 18, 1975.
12. Emile Copfermann, 'Entretiens avec Ariane Mnouchkine', *Travail théâtral,* 1976.
13. Film *Au Soleil même la nuit,* AGAT Films & Cie, le Théâtre du Soleil, La Sept Arte.
14. S. Bryant Bertail, in her 'Gender, Empire and Body Politic as Mise en Scène: Mnouchkine's "Les Atrides"', *Theatre Journal*, Vol. 46, No. 1 (Mar., 1994), pp. 1–30 takes up this sort of issue. Relatively few English language texts approach the Mnouchkine phenomenon. Notable is A. Kiernander's *Ariane Mnouchkine and the Theatre du Soleil,* Cambridge: Cambridge University Press, 1993. In contrast, French language publications and articles abound, and many are included on the website http://www.theatre-du-soleil.fr.
15. I first visited this rehearsal in "'Constitutive Ambiguities': Writing Professional or Expert Performance Practices, and the Théâtre du Soleil, Paris", in J. Kelleher & N. Ridout (eds), Contemporary Theatres in Europe, London and New York: Routledge 2006. The 'difficulties' revealed by the filmed sequence have been variously interpreted, but not otherwise as a clash relating to expertise.
16. © Agats Film & Cie, Théâtre du Soleil, La Sept ARTE – 1997.
17. A clip is available online at: http://www.theatre-du-soleil.fr/thsol/notre-librairie/le-tartuffe,300/le-film-au-soleil-meme-la-nuit,800?lang=fr
18. I have written 'what I take to be...' because interpreting facial and vocal options, along with other bodywork options/actions, tends to entail recourse to what I have called 'major models of intelligibility'. These, in turn, relate to positioning, perspectives and points of view (eg practitioner perspectives and/versus spectator perspectives). Most of us use these interpretive models on a daily basis, to seem 'to read' others' facial and other modes of expression, in terms – generally – of what cannot be seen but must be sensed or intuited on the base of what can be seen or heard. What is at work here in semiotic terms is called symptomatics.
19. The term 'technicity' comes initially from Foucault's notion of what translators have called 'technologies of the self' (*'technique de soi'*), where the focus is quite particular to his enquiry into power (1992). The notion of 'technicity' relates more specifically to the ways technology operates in the human everyday ('arts of existence'), and in this sense, I would also identify a technicity specific to 'acting' or to 'dance 'in the European and English traditions. More particularly in the terms of this chapter, a technicity of the self supposes ways of being and doing that tend to be patterned, consistent, and to a certain extent culturally shared. That they are shared, rather than singular, seems to me to be apparent in the ways we *can* interpret and indeed critique our own and others' ways of being and doing in the world.
20. Symptomatically, because the self, in many senses an abstraction, cannot be directly represented; instead, a performer materially articulates what she or he (and onlookers, if the work is effective) take to be indices of self. In this

sense 'self' is a model of intelligibility, that informs certain sorts of interpretation of material 'signs'. Interpretation of symptoms applies equally to performer and onlooker; sometimes there is disagreement.

21. J-P Milet 'Experience as Technique of the Self' in *Tekhnema 2 /Technics and Finitude/* Spring 1995, online at http://tekhnema.free.fr/2Milet.htm, consulted April 2013); see also M. Heidegger, 'The Nature of Language' in *On the Way to Language*, trans. P.D. Hertz, Harper Collins, 1982.
22. Various models of intelligibility apply here, and are exercised whenever we attribute imagination, thought and emotion – mainstream ways of interpreting material actions – to either character or to performer self.
23. Milet ibid.
24. Milet ibid.
25. Milet ibid.

## Bibliography

Bryant Bertail, S. 'Gender, Empire and Body Politic as Mise en Scène: Mnouchkine's "Les Atrides"', *Theatre Journal*, Vol. 46, No. 1 (March, 1994).

Birringer, J. 'This is the Theatre that was to be Expected and Foreseen' *Performance Research* Volume 1 Issue 1.

de Certeau, M. 'What we Do When we Believe', in M. Blonsky (ed), *On Signs*, Baltimore: Johns Hopkins University Press, 1985.

Copfermann, E. 'Entretiens avec Ariane Mnouchkine', *Travail théâtral*, 1976.

Foucault, M. *The Use of Pleasure. The History of Sexuality: Volume Two*. T.R. Hurley. Harmondsworth, Middlesex: Penguin, 1992.

Gregg M. and Seigworth G. (eds) *The Affect Theory Reader*, Durham: Duke University Press Books, 2010.

Heidegger, M., 'The Nature of Language' in *On the Way to Language*, trans. P.D. Hertz, New York: Harper Collins, 1982.

Kiernander, A. *Ariane Mnouchkine and the Theatre du Soleil*, Cambridge: Cambridge University Press, 1993.

Lacan, J. *The Four Fundamental Concepts of Psycho-analysis*, trans. A. Sheridan, 1977, London: Vintage, 1998.

Massumi, B. *Parables for the Virtual: Movement, Affect, Sensation*, Durham & London: Duke University Press, 2002.

Melrose, S. 'Rehearsing Reconciliations: Mnouchkine's Molière at the Théâtre du Soleil' *Performance Research*, Volume 2, Issue 2 .

Melrose, S. 'Constitutive ambiguities: writing professional or expert performance practices, and the Theatre du Soleil, Paris'. In Kelleher, J. & N. Ridout (eds), *Contemporary Theatres in Europe*, London: Routledge, 2006.

Milet, J-P.'Experience as Technique of the Self' in *Tekhnema 2 /Technics and Finitude/* Spring 1995, online at http://tekhnema.free.fr/2Milet.htm.

Mnouchkine, A. 'L'Age d'Or: the long journey from 1793 to 1975', *Theatre Quarterly* 5: 18, 1975.

Schatzki, T., Knorr Cetina K., and Von Savigny (eds), *The Practice Turn in Contemporary Theory*, London: Routledge, 2001.

Spinosa, C. 'Derridian dispersion and Heideggerian articulation: General tendencies in the practices that govern intelligibility', in Schatzki, Knorr Cetina and Von Savigny (eds), *The Practice Turn in Contemporary Theory*, London; Routledge, 2001.

# 13
# Messy Bits

*Emilyn Claid*

Failing – I know what that feels like. I knew failure as artistic director of Extemporary Dance Theatre (Extemporary) in the 1980s.[1] Extemporary was a repertory dance company, nurtured by Thatcherism that encouraged a culture of individualism and neo-liberal consumer empowerment. The company was expected to be innovative and at the forefront of contemporary ideas as long as innovation fed a market economy and maintained a hierarchical management structure. Fulfilling the expectations to be experimental *and* marketable, Extemporary's products were judged through a success/failure binary where I experienced a sense of shame for each product that failed the meet the demand.

I know failure differently now: living life queerly and relationally; embracing failing in artistic process as a letting go of fixed things; where uncertainty, un-knowing, between-ness and here-and-now process breathe different energy into performance making. So I live a kind of then-and-now paradox of failure – as a shame-based paradigm *and* an inspirational creative source for change.

To highlight this notion of paradoxical failure I am looking back to my experiences as artistic director of Extemporary, with my knowledge now as choreographer, academic and Gestalt relational therapist. I am revisiting the unquiet grave of *Grace & Glitter* (*G&G*), a dance theatre production created for the company in 1987. The work illustrates Extemporary's compromised position. It was innovative in being a collaboratively devised performance created and performed by women and sparked by a passionate engagement with feminism, racial and postmodern politics. Simultaneously, the work had to be packaged and sold for audiences on a UK touring circuit.[2]

The writing begins with a description of *G&G*, remembering its content and its feminist and racial context. Drawing on a critical post-performance review of *G&G* I plunge back into an experience of failure as artistic director of Extemporary to describe how, following initial performances of *G&G*, directorial decisions were made to cut fragments of material from the performance. One of these lost fragments, which now I name as 'Dawn's moment', has remained with me ever since as a contentious memory of *G&G* and in this writing I want to understand why it was cut and how it continues to engage me.

To pursue this enquiry, I come forward in time and outline my current understanding of creative failure as an effect of relational, intersubjective uncertainty, drawing on the collaborative event *What_Now 2014*, which I attended as an artistic researcher. I then return to *G&G* to unravel Dawn's moment, which emerges as a central pivot for this writing on paradoxical failure, seesawing between a shame-based paradigm *and* an example of failure as an inevitable and necessary source of creativity for collaboratively devised performance making. Along the way, I draw on Tim Etchells' writings about *Forced Entertainment* (1999)[3] to support key points of analysis from a performance perspective, together with Jack/Judith Halberstam's inspirational writing on the queer art of failure (2011).

## Grace & Glitter

*G&G* was co-directed by Maggie Semple and myself, alongside writer Tash Fairbanks, set designer Jacqueline Gunn, musician composers Sylvia Hallett and Lucy Wilson, process writer Christy Adair[4] and an educational team headed by Sue Davies.[5] The piece was devised with performers Saoirse Barron, Fin Walker, Chantal Donaldson, Dawn Donaldson, Lindsey Butcher and Kaye Brown.

The performers improvised with scores and ideas that were initiated by directors and developed through group discussion. The material devised was then shaped by the directors into a product for proscenium arch small- and middle-scale theatre venues in the UK. Structured as a collage of fragments, images were placed for dynamic interest rather than ongoing narrative. Although not obvious, a loose theme of loss of innocence threaded the work, represented in Tash Fairbanks' text, spoken by Maggie Semple's mother as part of the sound score:

> [...] Girls becoming women. With their bright new secret. Their secret passed to the women in the street. To the women who shift babies from arm to arm, who read beauty tips and forget them, who lie in bed and watch partners' sleep, who take tablets with their tea.

> To the women who sit hours in doctors' surgeries, who have photographs of daughters far away, who wipe away saliva, who fumble in a drawer for faded ribbons, who try to remember to smile when necessary and think [...] of a slow fuse burning. The girl passes on her secret and the women nod and smile.
>
> [...] The old woman watches the women pass and thinks of water massing, moving vast and irresistible. The sway and swell of women down the years. Laughing they spilled through gaps and crevices, finding secret ways of their own. Angry, they burst banks, barriers, boundaries, flowing outwards into forbidden places. A rising tide, a laughing, angry tide, a rush and roar of breaking through. A tidal flood of women down the years.
>
> (Fairbanks, 1987)[6]

Performance material was drawn from a wide range of provocative themes, that were relevant to our lives: friendship, body image, sexism, envy, rape, clothing, anorexia, anger, loss, ageing, poverty, white appropriation of black culture, sex industry, marriage, hair, mothers, grandmothers, daughters and sisters, tomboys and femmes. Issues bubbled up between us in discussion and were worked through with laughter, improvisation, theatrical image, one-to-one and group processes. We brashly employed stereotypical images and humor to highlight differences between black and white cultures. For instance the performers characterized their mothers and grandmothers through clothing, stylized walks, gestures of greeting, exaggerated body pose and conversation. These scenes were cheeky and irreverent. Influential readings were Audre Lorde's *Uses of the Erotic: The Erotic as Power* (1984) and Maya Angelou's autobiographical novels.[7] Black dancers Chantal and Dawn performed a duet in white tutus, accentuating the issue of black dancers' absence from classical dance. White appropriation of black was represented through a hair scene: three black women – doing each other's hair and verbally sharing stories of their lives – are interrupted by a white woman singing a Bob Marley song and showing off an afro wig, provocatively parading in close proximity to the black women. Adair commented on this hair scene:

> From a history of hot combs which burnt the scalp, grease which left pools on the dance floor and straightening processes, many black women now choose to wear their hair in ways which feel best to them. Plaiting is something black women have grown up with, it is a special time shared. Black women are expressing a rejection of dominant

> culture and insisting on their right to dress, think and act Black, finding a form of self-knowledge which transcends the stereotypes.
>
> (Adair, 1987)[8]

To reference her use of the term 'Black', Adair called on the writing of Bryan, Dadzie and Scafe, whose book *Heart of the Race* (1985) influenced our politics at that time.

> When we use the term 'Black' we use it as a political term. It doesn't describe skin color, it defines our situation here in Britain. We're here as a result of British imperialism, and our continued oppression in Britain is the result of British racism.
>
> (Bryan, Dadzie and Scafe, 1985: p. 236)

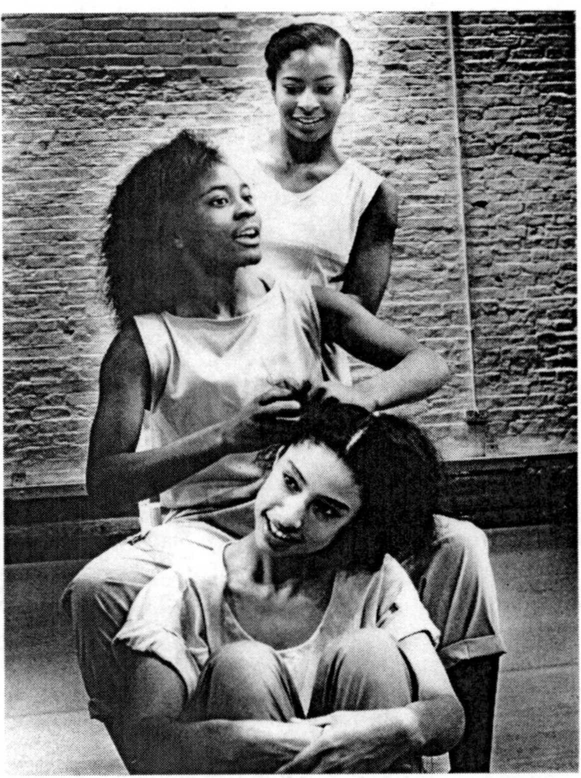

*Fig. 23* Chantal, Dawn & Kaye, Photograph Sheila Burnett. Held at National Resource Centre for Dance (NRCD)

Theatrical scenes were linked and separated by choreographed movement sections offering a range of qualities, from athletic power to minimal lyricism. For these dances, politically correct new dance uniforms – baggy t-shirts and cotton trousers so familiar at that time as a feminist costume that rejected spectacle – alternated with tightly fitting black shorts, cropped tops and Reebok boots revealing plenty of glistening flesh, as a statement of power and subversion.

The musical score was a melee of found music by Alice Coltrane, Hildegard von Bingen and Marjorie Hellyer together with newly composed songs by collaborators Sylvia Hallett and Lucy Wilson. The sound score included a wicked track of revving traffic and slamming car doors for a scene where performers in raincoats and high heels slowly make their way downstage through a series of distorted, aggressively exaggerated sexual poses. Skittering around the performers' legs are remotely controlled toy cars. The first sound to be heard in *G&G* is Maggie's mother speaking Fairbank's text and the last sound to be heard, long after the lights fade, is a high-pitched energized war cry from the dancers, wearing their black shorts and boots and standing strong.

## Feminist Frames

*G&G*, as a women's collaborative venture, bridged two eras of feminist politics, reflecting my experiences of working with the X6 Collective (1975–81). Fiona Williams, who writes from the perspective of social politics, reminds me how 1970s 'feminism emerged as part of and out of the Enlightenment' and focused on:

> [...] the struggle for women to be equal to men – to be allowed into the public world of social, political and economic progress, to be seen as reasoning and powerful subjects, to play more than a bit-part in the grand scheme.
>
> (Williams, 1996: p.63)

Both Adair and Fairbanks' writing for *G&G* demonstrates where we were in terms of this feminist thinking. Striving for equality took priority, which meant resisting patriarchy in order to establish matriarchal lineage, a sense of female subjectivity 'that passes through the mother, not the father' (Halberstam, 2011: p.125).

Yet *G&G* was also a consequence of 1980s feminism influenced by postmodernist and poststructuralist acknowledgement of difference, an understanding of multiple truths rather than meta-narratives about feminism and shifting towards recognition of differences between women (and men) across class, sexuality and race.

*G&G*, like X6 before, was honoring issues of oppression but also being parodic, applying postmodern performance strategies to install and subvert fixed ideologies. We played between the 'clankingly mechanical concepts' of 1970s feminism and 'feline ironists and revelers in relativism, dancing light-heartedly upon the waters of difference' of 1980s postmodernism (Soper, 1991: p.9 cited in Williams, 1996: p.62). We pursued equality, while acknowledging that, between us, there was no universal meaning for that term.

Discussions with co-director Maggie Semple and black performers revealed how our feminist views on issues such as sex industry, family and representation in dance were not necessarily the same. Liberation strategies for black women could not be subsumed into white heterosexual women's goals for equality, challenging universal assumptions of feminist sisterhood (Williams, 1996).

Feminism had different consequences for black and white women in contemporary dance. For instance, white feminist urgencies to claim equality and subjectivity by resisting roles as objects of desire certainly

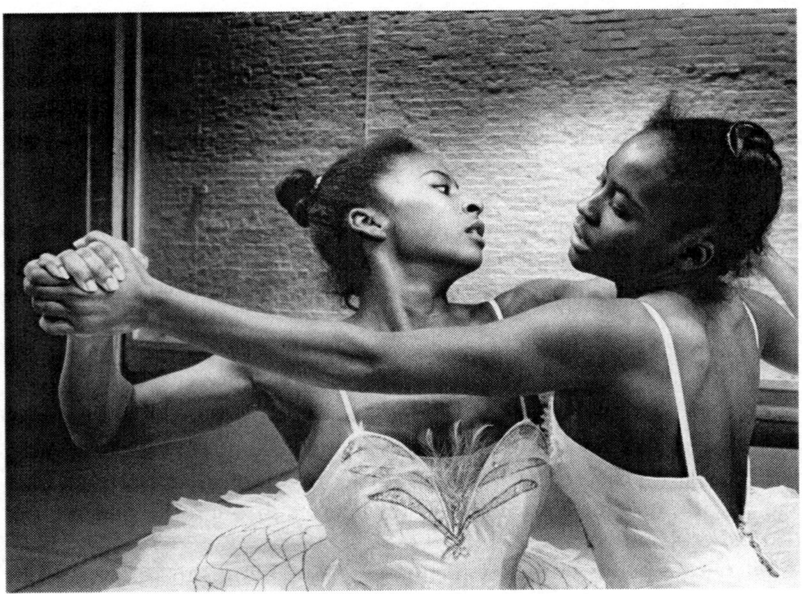

*Fig. 24* Chantal & Dawn, Photograph Sheila Burnett (NRCD)

proved successful. Yet, in giving up that dazzling spectacle we also became invisible within the performance market. As I have stated elsewhere (Claid, 2006), embracing invisibility in this way can be read as a white privilege and was not necessarily on the agenda for black women.[9]

## Shame-based Failure

During the collaborative process of making *G&G* we sat about laughing and talking, making, discarding, often discovering images through accidental and spontaneous interactions, that confounded each day's good intentions and resulting in a burgeoning of multiple images, stories and personas, through interaction with each other. We created a mixed bag of unfixed fragments that Etchells welcomes as artistic messiness associated with collaboratively devised process. Etchells invigorates a quote from The Place director John Ashford, who:

> [...] once called experimental theatre 'a compromised art... a mucky, mutable, dirty, competitive collaborative business', and we always like the quote recognizing in it the great mess of our own process but also appreciating the fine word compromise – no clean single visions in our work, no minimalist control freak authorial line – since by collaboration – impro, collage, the bringing together of diverse creativities – one gets an altogether messier world – of competing actions, approaches and intentions.
>
> (Etchells, 1996: p.55)

As an artist, I embraced messiness in *G&G's* process, yet I was dis-eased in my external facing role as artistic director of Extemporary whereby I took responsibility for the company's artistic decisions. Here I was confronted on a daily basis with product-based judgments of success and failure that conflicted with our excitement about co-created material of collaborative process.[10]

There was positive audience feedback including statements such as:

> Fabulous show, there must have been plenty of confronting/exploring.
>
> I loved it – its youthfulness, sensitivity, inventiveness, breadth of emotion portrayed, its intensity, subtlety, confrontation, challenge and power. The best, most inspiring thing I've seen for ages in any artistic medium.

> Thought the performance was excellent, especially the tension between the four dancers in the lesbian scene. Thought the prostitute part was superbly choreographed – the little car going round them ingenious.[11]

However, national reviews were mixed and London critics in particular tore the piece apart for its failure to uphold Extemporary's reputation as an Arts Council-funded, British, repertory dance company. The fact that national newspapers were reviewing *G&G* at all demonstrates the company's marketing and publicity strategy that attempted to package innovation into conventional boxes. *G&G* required audiences to be intimate with the action, accept spontaneity and uncertainty between performers, engage in a range of modes of performance from pedestrian action to theatrical image. We needed witnesses, not spectators. I refer to 'witness' similarly to Etchells, writing about *Forced Entertainment*: 'to witness an event is to be present at it in some fundamentally ethical way, to feel the weight of things and one's own place in them' (Etchells, 1999: p.17).

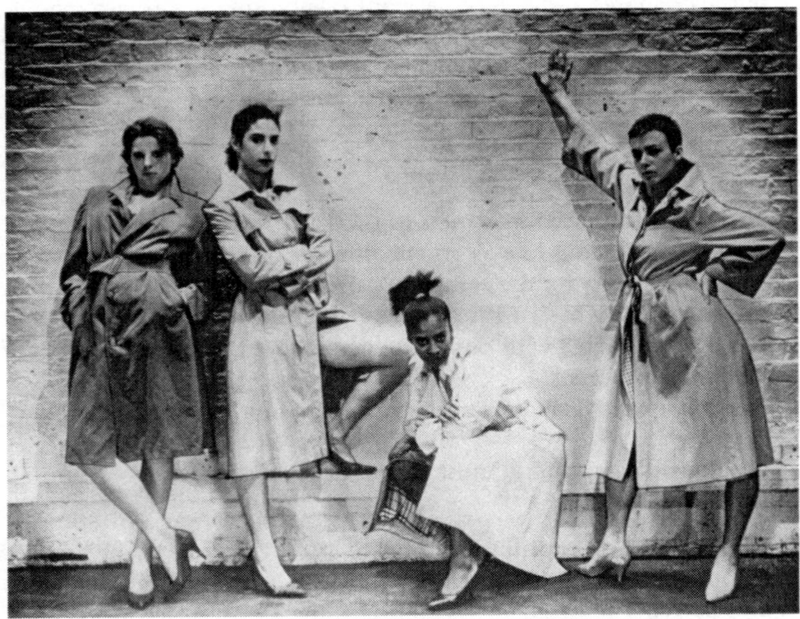

*Fig. 25* Saoirse, Kaye, Chantal & Lindsey, Photograph Sheila Burnett (NRCD)

Here is Thorpe's review from *The London Evening Standard*:

> I have not been able to enthuse over the work of Extemporary Dance Theatre. With their latest production, Grace & Glitter, they would seem to have reached an absolute nadir – or, perhaps, I should employ the vernacular and say "the pits". [...] Most women I imagine, would wish to dissociate themselves from this dismal performance, 95 minutes of grotesque posturing, inaudible chat and bits of banal dance. [...] If perpetrators of this infantile nonsense are really interested in 'the power' of women, I suggest they study the careers of Anna Pavlova, Tamara Karsavina, Isadora Duncan, Ninette de Valois, Alicia Markova, Martha Graham, Margot Fonteyn, Nora Kaye, Maria Tallchief, Lynn Semour... the list is a long one, but it takes talent, hard work and humility to be included.
>
> (Thorpe, October 21, 1987)

Without wanting to negate his extensive critical knowledge, and without giving space here to critique his review, perhaps suffice to say that Thorpe's list of admirable and inspiring solo artists, prima ballerinas and unique visionaries – roles from which contemporary dance artists worked to disentangle themselves – were raised on pedestals by patrons, critics and admiring audiences of traditions of spectacle. For artists such as Margot Fonteyn and Lyn Seymour, without denying the well-earned status of these ballerinas, their artistry and brilliance was nurtured through many years of working within hierarchical (usually male) choreographer-led structures and oppressive regimes of balletic fetishistic training – from which feminist dancers had worked so hard to disentangle themselves. And although culturally diverse, *are not all these women white?* If a lonely white pedestal is the goal achieved with talent, hard work and humility, then we were content to do without claim to those worthy attributes.[12] As a collaboratively devised performance, exploring race politics, women's ownership of production, relational 'here and now' contact between performers in performance – I suggest this work was out of range of Thorpe's knowledge, if not his wit.

Back then, in my hierarchically defined role as artistic director of Extemporary, I felt the tensions of success and failure as they are embedded within an individualistic model of self that traces back through Western civilization. Gordon Wheeler, writing on the dyad of self and shame from a Gestalt psychotherapy perspective, describes this model of (my) self as one of alone-ness, in a world which is 'simply there, already organized and divided up into separate "things" (including other people)' (Wheeler, 1996: p. 29–30). In this context, the *other* requires organization, not the individual self, who is a 'given thing, preexistent and predefined, a font of life force' (Wheeler, 1996: p. 32). Within this individualistic shame-based world, failure/losing, is inseparable from its binary opposite – success/winning. Both sides of the binary imply judgment, and to judge, 'one' must stand outside the event being judged. Conventional dance training nurtured this binary, encouraging narcissistic needs for success where 'shame is pride's cloke' (Blake, 1790).[13]

Ok – here goes – I am eyeing *G&G* as critics expecting modern dance spectacle might have viewed it. *G&G* was messily designed, lacking slick polish, tight structures or technical brilliance. It was too slow at times and too long. The elements did not hang together, periods of time passed when 'nothing' spectacular happened, there was too much 'being with' one another on stage, too much unrehearsed dancing and undeveloped ideas. It was entertaining, it made people laugh, it was low art, lacking depth, and issues were obvious and stereotypically stated. Spatial patterns of movement were scarce and there was no expressive dancing reaching outwards to the back of theatres. It was framed by feminism – just the thought of which was gloomily non-seductive in its rejection of fetishistic entertainment.

Let's wear the shame mantle a little longer! By 1987, innovation in UK dance performance was happening through live art, physical theatre and independent dance frameworks, rather than repertory companies. I was clinging to a vision for Extemporary that had worked 'successfully' in the past – to bring innovative ideas into a conventional framework. What neo-liberal optimism! This was a vision well past its sell-by date. Lauren Berlant – a professor of English who writes about queer theory and affect theory – would name this as cruel optimism (2011). That is optimism as an attachment to things or ideas that at first appear as a way to realize potential, yet in the end become a stuck-ness. Attachments that no longer achieve their promised ideals becoming 'impediments to personal and social change' – empty attachment (Berlant, 2011: p.18). During *G&G* I was hovering on a tightrope between collaborative ways of working and cumbersome hierarchical machinery. The hover could not be sustained. I was fired from Extemporary two years later and that's failure within a shame-based paradigm.

Maybe all I am doing here, emphasizing shame-based failure, is laying the ground for how certain fragments got cut from *G&G*, one of which continues to haunt me almost 30 years later as a subversive statement in our collaborative process. Here I align myself again with Etchells' writing on collaborative theatre making:

> Disconnected from its 'original' place, lacking context, lacking 'beginning' or 'end', lacking place in an argument, lacking 'reason' – the fragment is both statement and question.
>
> (cited in Heddon and Milling, 2006: p. 196)

## Creative Failure

Before I unearth and unravel Dawn's moment I want to come into the present and outline my current thinking about failing in collaborative performance-making processes, a valuable example being my experience of *What_Now 2014*, held at Siobhan Davies Studios in London.[14] Twenty artists were invited to take up residency at the studios for five days, with no goal other than to question how we might dialogue with each other, over an extended period of time without external influences and without a set agenda. *What_Now 2014* 're-imagined itself as a public residency, taking as its starting point the suggestion that artists need to construct new conditions for the realization of community'.[15]

To begin to consider new conditions required us to slow down to notice how we relate to one another in the here and now. Similar to X6 Collective 40 years previously, this required us to let go of how we conventionally identify ourselves through our attachments to artistic identities and products and instead, just meet each other. Although this brought uncertainty and 'the fear... that the loss of the promising object/scene itself will defeat the capacity to have any hope about anything' (Berlant, 2011: p. 24), it allowed us to slip out of familiar systems of dance production with which we may be attached but become disillusioned.[16] We spent time sitting in a circle pondering collectively how to proceed through the day without making decisions, as each decision might take us back into familiar conditions of artistic practice. Frustrating perhaps, yet this is where failure emerges with a positive voice.

> The maps of desire that render the subject incoherent, disorganized, and passive provide a better escape route than those that lead inexorably to fulfillment.
>
> (Halberstam, 2011: p.130)

Improvisations and small acts of doing emerged out of nowhere rather than being led by anybody with a particular goal. One morning I set up to do some writing in a space on the ground floor, then realized I had forgotten a pen, which was three floors up in the dance studio. It took me the entire morning to retrieve my pen and return to the ground floor because of the interactions I encountered along the way.

My notes written later that day:

> Work here seems to be about shedding individual identities, to see what emerges, or not, through collective waiting. Perhaps not making at all, but unmaking, failing to make. Each day we are being-in-relation with one another – to notice, to experience, to pause. Collaborative practice used to be about making something however fractured that might be, now I am experiencing simply an in-between-ness and outer frames are slipping away. I accept this messiness. What else is there now but to let go into nothing together? All has been done. All has been packaged up and sold. We meet with nothing, in urgency, because we have to, because only through slowing down the production of dance can any potential for change be noticed. This challenge to let go of fixing things happens in times of crisis, and uncertainty is necessary.
>
> Claid, 2014)[17]

I am arguing here for a strategy of failure, not as the binary opposite of success, but as a tool for undoing, displacing and stepping aside from conventional systems of individualistic production. Halberstam offers a queer feminist parallel:

> I explore a feminist politics that issues not from a doing but from an undoing, not from a being or becoming women but from a refusal to be or to become woman as she has been defined and imagined within Western philosophy.
>
> (Halberstam, 2011: p.124)

Looking at feminist achievements in retrospect Halberstam claims a 'shadow feminism', rejecting the matriarchal lineage, suggesting that

> [f]ailure has often been a better bet than success. Where feminine success is always measured by male standards, and gender failure often means being relieved of the pressure to measure up to patriarchal ideals, not succeeding at womanhood can offer unexpected pleasures.
>
> (Halberstam, 2011: p.4)

This strategy for creative failure echoes across a range of theoretical and artistic perspectives. Rebecca Schneider, in her critique of solo performance, writes how originality, so preciously nurtured as individual success, is a 'modernist masculinist myth' now 'displaced as the central paradigm of Western artistic creation' (2005: p.26).

> Feminist art historians, as well as post-structuralist writers in general, have deconstructed the myth of greatness and its relation to genius for both male and female artists.
>
> (Schneider 2005 p.24)[18]

Collaborative practice, such as *What_Now 2014*, undoes individual claims to success. Informed by my practice of interweaving Gestalt existential relational therapy with choreographic processes, I suggest that at the core of a collective gathering of artists such as *What_Now 2014*, burns an experiential understanding of intersubjectivity, embracing uncertainty and un-knowing between us. Meeting intersubjectively offers a relational practice that dissolves notions of original artistic achievement and unique subjectivity. Intersubjective encounters exercise between-ness 'in which subjective realms of experience interpenetrate one another, so that identity and individuality are relative rather than absolute matters' (Midgley, 2006: p. 104). Coming to know myself through relation with you is an existential phenomenological perspective taken up by Van Deurzan as she discusses Buber's philosophy of 'I-Thou' (1937).

> I only become myself as I relate to the other. There is never purely an I on its own. There is only ever the 'I' of the I-Thou or the 'I' of the I-It. The hyphen between us is crucial. Everything takes place in relationship and encounter.
>
> (Van Deurzan, 2005: p.165)

To give up on an individual 'I', is to fail at authorship and ownership within Western cultural ideology, yet is welcomed by many artists working collaboratively. This is a core theme of Bourriaud's writing about 1990s relational arts practice.

> As part of a 'relationist' theory of art, inter-subjectivity does not only represent the social setting for the reception of art, which is its 'environment', its 'field' (Bourdieu), but also becomes the quintessence of artistic practice.
>
> (Bourriaud, 2002: p.22)

Although relational art theory might seem to have little in common with queer feminist debate, I suggest that both fields advocate for an acceptance of failure, queer through an undoing of fixed objects of desire, and relational art aesthetics through emphasis on between-ness of process and product, artist and witness.

My experience at *What_Now 2014* was an embrace of messiness in collaborative arts process, allowing uncertainties of intersubjective relations, encouraging dialogues of between-ness and un-knowing, attending to improvisations that undo original intentions, committing to nothing happening, respecting misunderstandings and welcoming failure as a creative tool. I suggest, in this way, we begin to engage with arts processes that slip through the nets of a neo-liberal market economy, avoid dominant ideologies and spectacle and resist having to name things or sell uniqueness. A collaborative process 'points to a radical upheaval of aesthetic, cultural and political goals introduced by modern art' (Bourriaud, 2002: p.14) and as such holds failure at its heart as a subversive tool for change. I knew this at X6 in the 1970s as I know it now. I lost it at Extemporary.

## Dawn's Moment

Juggling past and present experiential knowledge of failing, I now return to Dawn's moment in *G&G,* offering this fragment as a provocative illustration of paradoxical failure. In writing this chapter I needed to refresh my memory of *G&G,* to bring my past more fully into the present. So I visited the National Resource Centre for Dance at the University of Surrey. Here I found three grainy VHS videos of *G&G*: a rehearsal video and two performances, at The Place Theatre in London (September 1987) and at Performing Arts Studio at Surrey University (November 1987). I watched the Surrey performance first and did not find Dawn's moment. Confusion – perhaps I had imagined this moment. I then watched The Place performance and there it was... here it is.

Lindsey pushes a supermarket shopping trolley on stage. Lying lengthways over the trolley is Dawn, with her legs stiffly protruding out front. She is wearing roller skates. Lindsey pauses center stage and tips the trolley forwards so Dawn slides off onto her skates. She wobbles, her body falls forward, legs splayed like a newborn deer. Splat, she is down on her bum. Back on her legs, swinging her arms wildly, she rolls slowly downstage to bump into Saoirse headfirst. Saoirse pushes her backwards to center stage. Slowly Dawn attempts to stretch one leg out sideways, fails, tips precariously backwards, arms stretched out sideways to regain her balance. She is unsure how to proceed without falling, so she shunts herself forward without lifting her feet, and in this way, faltering and fluttering, falling and flailing, she slowly makes her way to the side of the stage. I laugh now as I did back then, not *at* Dawn, but at her effortful absurdity, her task-like determination and focus to get nowhere. The moment is delightful in its raw inelegance, engaging in its here and now-ness, its randomness and serious clowning.

This scene is part of a series of fragments, happening fast, in succession, single images created from a writing task. Maggie and I had asked performers to recall and write childhood memories, which we developed into performance sketches. Moments of the performers' lives juxtaposed one to another. Dawn's flailing moment happens in a cluster of short sketches: Lindsey repeatedly saying 'I love you' to Kaye snoring in an armchair; Saoirse as school teacher leading an exam session at school; a game of cards; Chantal, Dawn and Fin wrapped in scarves like burkas, swaying slightly with their back to the audience; Kaye miming a monologue about the miners' strike and food parcels while Fin tries to interpret her mime in words. Etchells echoes my thinking about these sketches as he describes the ad hoc nature of collaboratively devised acts.

> None of them in the same show really, or the same world, battling it out for space and the right to speak or own what is happening... Collaboration... was never about perfect unity but about difference, collisions, incompatibilities.
>
> (Etchells, 1999: p.56)

What catches me now is how this chaotic, nonsensical cluster of fragments was cut, between the London and Surrey University performances. Back then, in 1987, as Artistic Director of Extemporary, I saw these as uncrafted and disconnected sketches. As I watch them now on the video, I find the raw-ness of these moments intriguing and subversive for exactly the same qualities. Nothing needed to be done with them. They were just there, enough in themselves.

Dawn's roller-skating in *G&G* epitomizes paradoxical failure, as I hope to demonstrate here by flipping from one side of the paradox to the other, from failure as a fixed binary judgment to failure as a creative source. *It was a mess* – yet its spontaneity, task-based improvisational quality and 'here-and-now action' was alive with awkward surprises. *It was indulgent* – yet, it was emerging from a collective encouragement of laughter, which we employed as a subversive group tactic in our process. This chapter does not allow space for ruminating on laughter; suffice to say that shared laughter can be another strategy for failing individual ideals. 'There is no possessing here, no conserving or hoarding, laughter can be no one's property'.[19] Laughter offers a release from traditional constraints of philosophical thought. Laughing is an infectious affect of relational practice where we are out of control, a physical expression of uncertainty, a falling into liminal space that can simultaneously be infused with wit, satire, irreverence, irony, contradiction and anecdote. Laughing together we fail in serious intention, becoming 'whole, free, sane and fully alive'.[20] Laughing during *G&G* process, we experienced a state of physical falling out of uprightness, which Dawn personified in her courageous attempt to 'un-roller skate' on stage in front of an audience. Her actions playfully illustrate failure as a resource, which 'preserves some of the wondrous anarchy of childhood and disturbs the supposedly clean boundaries between adults and children, winner and losers' (Halberstam, 2011: p. 3). *It was not dance and it lacked skill* – yet Dawn displayed precise physical skill to balance uncertainly on her skates in a perpetual act of falling. *This moment did nothing to promote the theme of identity for black women performers.* This is perhaps the most significant point. With Dawn's concentration on her task of falling and catching herself falling, her image was unfixable within the worthy politically correct white Western feminist arena of contemporary dance. Dawn's moment is a performance 'outside of success' (Halberstam, 2011: p.93), implying that 'to fall short, to get distracted, to take a detour, to find a limit, to lose our way, to forget, to avoid mastery' (Halberstam, 2011: p.120) can be a subversive strategy, one that owes much to 'queer, postcolonial and black feminism' (Halberstam, 2011: p.126).

## Resisting Visibility

With that last point, I slide sideways to acknowledge current thinking in British dance about issues of black identity. *The British Dance and the African Diaspora Research Project* is facilitated by Ramsay Burt and Christy Adair and is a project that 'explores the memories of British-based dancers who are black and celebrates their contributions to British dance' (Adair & Burt, 2014).[21] The aim of this project is to write black British dancers and dances back into history, to make visible black artists' contribution to history and:

> address the nexus of aesthetic and institutional problems that have stopped British-based dance artists who are black gaining the appreciation and support they deserve.
>
> (Adair & Burt, 2014)[22]

The project supports visibility and identity within British dance culture for a wide range of different black dance artists and dance forms.

Yet tensions regarding identity emerge in this project. A *British Dance and the African Diaspora Study Day* was held in London (2014), attended by a number of young contemporary black dance artists.[23] Introducing the day, Adair and Burt told us how, during their research, three characteristics were identified to describe the distinctive voice of a 'British approach to African People's Dance', these being 'rhythm, spirituality and community' (Adair & Burt, 2014). However, a young artist responded saying she did not have rhythm or spirituality and did that mean she was not a black artist – a dilemma shared by Alexandrina Hemsley and Jamilla Johnson-Small who see themselves as part of a contemporary struggle for black women to undo and resist any identifiable statement about British black dance. These artists describe their performance *Project 'O'* as 'a lawless rubbing of everyone's faces in cultural shit about who and what young black women can be' (Hemsley and Johnson-Small, 2013).[24] With its blatant ironic twists on sexuality, academia and gender *Project 'O'* suggests a performance that draws more from Halberstam's writing about:

> Antihumanist, and counterintuitive feminism that arises out of queer, postcolonial, and black feminisms and that thinks in terms of the negation of the subject rather than her formation... the undoing of self rather than its activation.
>
> (Halberstam, 2011: p.126)

Although happening so many years previously, in a different era of gender and racial politics, I can now witness Dawn's moment from a similar perspective to Halberstam. Teetering off balance Dawn's uncertain skating acts as 'a shadow archive of resistance, [...] that [...] articulates itself in terms of evacuation, refusal, passivity, unbecoming, unbeing' (Halberstam, 2011: p.129).

Bringing this fragment to light into the present does not pronounce Dawn's actions as proving or fixing something. Flailing, falling and sliding about, Dawn, as a black woman, slips between definitions, she disables me from defining her, as she falls out of line in an act of un-skilling.

*G&G* was a moment in time and Dawn's roller-skating a lost fragment in that moment. In this writing I have gone back with tools now to re-envision this lost fragment, which was violently erased yet remains memorably vibrant. Erasure then evokes this writing now. Revealing this miniscule sketch, until now hidden away on an old VHS tape of bad quality in a university archive, has offered me an opportunity to reflect on feminist and racial politics in late-twentieth-century dance, and, more importantly, to consider a paradox of failure. At X6 and *What_Now 2014*, I experienced collaboration as an urgent, necessary and messy process, missing a defined focus, stumbling to find a consensus, letting go of fixed ideas and surrendering to a multitude of clamorous possibilities. What I mislaid during the Extemporary years was a trust in the relational practice and intersubjective uncertainty of collaboration. As artistic director uncertainty appeared to me as a negative state rather than a source of creativity and inspiration. I was caught in the world of counting 'bums-on-seats', economic viability, where messy process somehow had to become clean product – and where failure was measured in a binary with success, as judgment external to the project.

Dawn's moment – that disappeared from view – was an unkempt off kilter fragment, caught within frames of performance product, a messy morsel expressing a satirical lightness of our un-becoming dance process. Dawn's skating offered a statement of in/visibility as a subversive tool of agency that, during its short existence, resisted white Western audience expectations of dance product and black identity.

## Notes

1. *Extemporary Dance Theatre* (1975–91). The company archives are held at National Resource Centre for Dance at University of Surrey. http://www.surrey.ac.uk/library/nrcd/index.htm
2. G&G toured to Newcastle, Bristol, Bracknel, Canterbury, Norwich, Mold, Clyde, Guildford, Selwyn, Sheffield, Manchester, Crew & Alsager, London and Lisbon (Portugal).
3. When X6 collective dissolved and I took the job with Extemporary I frequently turned sideways to observe the collaborative work of Forced Entertainment and Goat Island. I felt a strong connection to Forced Entertainment in particular, whose performance work seemed to bring to fruition our early cross-disciplinary collaborative struggles in the 1970s.
4. Adair provided a written context for the work for educational and publicity purposes, which took into account the political drive, ideas and movement vocabulary of the collaborators. She was particularly interested in the discussions on race and gender between the directors Maggie Semple and myself. The writing preceded her book *Women and Dance* (1992) the front cover photograph of which features Chantal and Kaye from *G&G*.
5. Davies worked with Cecilia MacFarlane, Helen Roberts, Maggie Simple and Ginny Wollaston on education projects linked to Grace & Glitter.
6. Tash Fairbanks' text can be found in the programme notes for Grace & Glitter, available from National Resource Centre for Dance.
7. Written between 1969–1986, Angelou's autobiographical novels include *I Know Why the Caged Bird Sings* (1962) and *The Heart of a Woman* (1981).

8. This quote forms part of a paper written by Adair as a core element of the educational pack for *G&G*, distributed to participating schools (1987). Available to reference at National Resource Centre for Dance
9. In the 1970s and 1980s:

> Black artists strove for *visibility* as practitioners of a range of different black dance forms – within the same European culture that white artists were attempting to reject. While white artists were busy rejecting the European aesthetics and colonial heroism of dance culture, black British artists were working to establish individual and different identities of presence that would be recognized within that context.
>
> (Claid, 2006: p. 152)

10. My dis-ease is noticeably documented in an interview with Maggie Semple and Christy Adair in *New Dance* magazine (1987, no. 41, pp. 17–19)
11. Feedback from audience members collated by education team during the tour.
12. See Yolanda Snaith in *Blue Whiteness Rhapsody* 1986. Reviewed in 'Getting There. A profile of Yolande Snaith' (Briginshaw & Burt in *New Dance* (1986) No. 37 pp. 13–15).
13. Marriage of Heaven and Hell (Blake) *http://www.blakearchive.org/exist/blake/archive/work.xq?workid=mhh* (accessed August 2013).
14. http://www.independentdance.co.uk
15. http://www.independentdance.co.uk/film-and-video/ *What_Now* was envisioned by Gill Clarke as a yearly run festival where invited speakers/artists consider questions of dance and about dance. *What_Now* 2014 was co-facilitated by Frank Bock, Hamish Macpherson and Efrosini Protopapa. The event included talks with invited speakers, which were open to general public who could also, at these times, observe us 'in residence'.
16. For Berlant 'all attachments are optimistic', (2011 p.22) as a 'cluster of promises' (2011 p.22) we hope to fulfill or have fulfilled for us, but remain consistently unfulfilled.
17. Unpublished notes from *What_Now* 2014.
18. In a postmodern performance world that embraces double acts, triple plays, hyper copy, repetition, representation, Schneider is asking – where is the place for solo performance?
19. 'Philosophy, literature, and laughter: notes on an ontology of the moment' (p.7) http://www.trinity.edu/departments/philosophy/Philosophy,%20Literature,%20and%20Laughter.pdf (accessed October 2014).
20. 'Philosophy, literature, and laughter: notes on an ontology of the moment' (p.9) http://www.trinity.edu/departments/philosophy/Philosophy,%20Literature,%20and%20Laughter.pdf (accessed October 2014).
    For writing on laughter see Bergson, H. (1986, ebook 2009) *Laughter: An Essay on the Meaning of the Comic*: http://www.gutenberg.org/files/4352/4352-h/4352-h.htm (accessed October 2014).
21. http://www.dmu.ac.uk/research/research-faculties-and-institutes/art-design-humanities/dance/british-dance-african-diaspora/british-dance-and-the-african-diaspora-research-project.aspx (accessed August 2014).
22. http://www.dmu.ac.uk/research/research-faculties-and-institutes/art-design-humanities/dance/british-dance-african-diaspora/british-dance-and-the-african-diaspora-research-project.aspx (accessed August 2014).

23. http://www.dmu.ac.uk/research/research-faculties-and-institutes/art-design-humanities/dance/british-dance-african-diaspora/study-day-2014.aspx (accessed August 2014).
24. *Project 'O'* http://www.acontemporarystruggle.com/#!thedance/cjg9 (accessed August 2014).

## Bibliography


Adair, C. (1987) Programme notes for Grace & Glitter Extemporary Dance Theatre.

———. (1987) 'Interview with Emilyn Claid and Maggie Semple' in *New Dance* No. 41 pp. 17–19.

———. (1992) *Women and Dance* London: MacMillan Press.

———. & Burt, R. (2013) *The British Dance and the African Diaspora Research Project* http://www.dmu.ac.uk/research/research-faculties-and-institutes/art-design-humanities/dance/british-dance-african-diaspora/british-dance-and-the-african-diaspora-research-project.aspx (accessed August 2014).

Angelou, M. (1962) *I Know Why the Caged Bird Sings* London: Virago.

———. (1981) *The Heart of a Woman* London: Virago.

Berlant, L. (2011) *Cruel Optimism* Durham, London: Duke University Press.

Bergson, H. (1986, ebook 2009) *Laughter: An Essay on the Meaning of the Comic*: http://www.gutenberg.org/files/4352/4352-h/4352-h.htm (accessed October 2014).

Blake, W. (1790) *The Marriage of Heaven and Hell http://www.blakearchive.org/exist/blake/archive/work.xq?workid=mhh* (accessed August 2013).

Bourriaud, N. (2002) *Relational Aesthetics* France: Les Presses du réel.

Briginshaw, V. & Burt, R. (1986) 'Getting There. A Profile of Yolande Snaith'. in *New Dance* No. 37 pp. 13–15.

Bryan, B., Dadzie, S., Scafe, S. (1985) *The Heart of the Race – Black Women's Lives in Britain* London: Virago.

Buber, M. (1999) *Martin Buber on psychology and psychotherapy: Essays, letters, and dialogue* (J. Buber Agassi, Ed). New York: Syracuse University Press.

Claid, E. (2006) *Yes? No! Maybe…* London: Routledge.

———. (2014) Unpublished notes from *What_Now 2014*.

Etchells, T. (1999) *Certain Fragments* London: Routledge.

———. (2004) 'A text on 20 years, with 66 footnotes' in J. Helmer and F. Malzacher (eds), *Not Even a Game Anymore: The Theatre of Forced Entertainment* Berlin: Alexander Berlag pp. 269–90.

Fairbanks, T. (1987) Unpublished writings for Grace & Glitter for Extemporary Dance Theatre Access from National Resource Centre for Dance, University of Surrey.

Halberstam, J. (2011) *The Queer Art of Failure* Durham, London: Duke University Press.

Hedden D. & Milling J. (2006) *Devising performance a critical history* New York, Hampshire: Palgrave Macmillan.

Hemsley A. & Johnson-Small, J. (2013) *Project 'O'* http://www.acontemporarystruggle.com/#!thedance/cjg9 (accessed August 2014).

Independent Dance http://www.independentdance.co.uk (accessed July 2014).

Lorde, A. (1984) Uses of the Erotic: Erotic as Power in *Sister Outsider essays and speeches* by Audre Lorde, Berkley California: The Crossing Press

Midgley D. (2006) Intersubjectivity and collective consciousness. *Journal of Consciousness Studies*, 13 (5) pp. 99–109.

National Resource Centre for Dance at University of Surrey. http://www.surrey.ac.uk/library/nrcd/index.htm (accessed July 2014).

Philosophy, literature, and laughter: notes on an ontology of the moment http://www.trinity.edu/departments/philosophy/Philosophy,%20Literature,%20and%20Laughter.pdf (accessed October 2014).

Schneider, R. (2005) Solo Solo Solo in *After Criticism new Responses to Art and Performance* ed. Gavin Butt, pub. Blackwell pp. 23–47.

Soper, K. (1993) 'Productive Contradictions' in *Up Against Foucault: Explorations of some tensions between Foucault and Feminism* ed. Caroline Ramazanoglu, New York: Routledge.

Thorpe, E. (1987) 'Women's Glib' in *The London Evening Standard* (21 October) Access through Durrant's, 103 Whitecross Street, London EC1y 8QT.

Van Deurzan, E. & Arnold-Baker, C. (2005) *existential perspectives on human issues* (eds.) New York & Hampshire: Palgrave Macmillan.

What_Now 2014 http://www.independentdance.co.uk/film-and-video/ (accessed July 2014).

Williams, F. (1996) 'Postmodern, feminism and the question of difference' in *Social Theory, Social Change and Social Work* ed. Nigel Parton, London: Routledge.

Wheeler Gordon & Lee, Robert (eds.) (1996) *The Voice of Shame Silence and Connection in Psychotherapy* Gouldsboro: Gestalt Press.

# 14
# Productive Misapprehensions: Artscross as a Cross-Cultural Collaborative Zone of Contestation of Contemporary Dance Practice

*Stefanie Sachsenmaier*

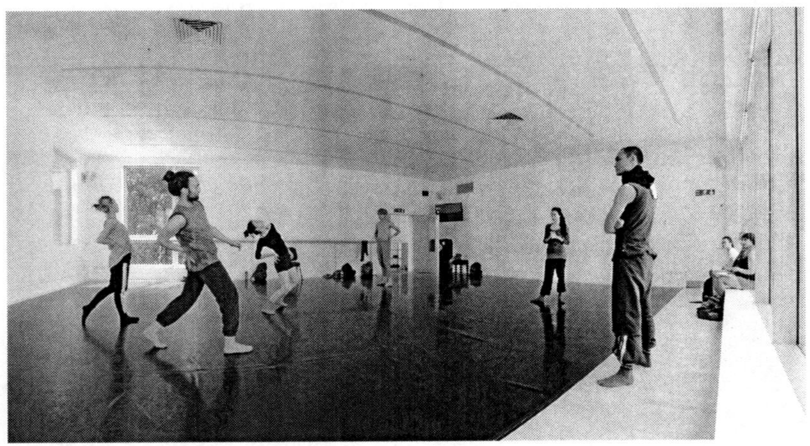

*Fig. 26* Rehearsals *Gloves*, Dam Van Huynh – Photograph Andrew Lang

The present chapter presents an enquiry into how cross-cultural collaborations in creative practice might be constructively conceived, by specifically discussing an international collaborative project in dance-making. Artscross, organized by project partners Beijing Dance Academy (BDA), ResCen at Middlesex University London, Queen Mary University of London and Taipei National University of the Arts (TNUA),[1] is defined as:

> a long-term initiative which brings together academics and artists across cultural, national and artistic borders. It is designed to

> enhance the prospects of stronger, more productive debate between East and West at a strategically critical moment. It seeks to harness the transformative power of the arts and art-making, to further intercultural dialogue and understanding, and to develop professional, personal and institutional exchange.
>
> (Artscross, 2013)

Further, Artscross is more specifically presented as aiming to 'engage in intercultural dialogue and exchange *in and through* the performing arts' (Artscross London 2013, my emphasis). Concurrently, over a phase of three years (2011–13), choreographers from the cities of Beijing, London and Taipei were invited to create work with dancers from each place in open rehearsals attended by academics, with the intention to discuss issues that would arise both in organized debates and conferences, as well as on a project blog.[2] In the present chapter I draw on aspects of my specific engagement as one of the academics invited to take part in observing the practice-led research that Artscross facilitated.

While ongoing to date (2014), a recent cycle of the project comprised a first encounter in Taipei at TNUA in 2011, a second in Beijing at BDA in 2012, and a third in London at The Place in 2013. Each phase of the project has been influential to my thinking on 'cross-cultural' collaboration in the performing arts,[3] and I need to state here clearly that the encounters that took place as part of Artscross were first and foremost facilitated by the inter-institutional collaboration of the parties involved. I propose to deal in this context with the concept of 'collaboration' in the arguably broad sense of 'co-laborating' or *working together* as the Latin root prescribes,[4] and specifically the 'working together across cultures', that took place on behalf of the participants involved, in order to enquire into the challenges, limitations and possibilities that the encounters highlighted.

Based on my observation of the creative processes of choreography-making that took place as part of Artscross, I have identified different ways of working to be at stake in given projects, instigated by individual choreographers. For the present context I have chosen to address a selection of choreographic processes in which I identified collaborative approaches to performance-making to have been foregrounded, and propose to recount and review those experiences of choreography-making through a number of theoretical frames.

The Artscross theme for 2013 was *Leaving Home, Being Elsewhere*, where previous thematic foci had been *Uncertain... Waiting...* in Taipei (2011) and *Light and Water* in Beijing (2012) for the respective encounters.

The title of the most recent event suggests a double challenge, a leaving of one's 'comfort zones' or familiar ways of doing, and most of all discoveries of and encounters with things previously unknown. In the specific context of the cross-cultural collaborations that were instigated as part of this project, in my role of observing the creative processes, I have been sensitive to a range of issues regarding thresholds or 'zones of encounter' that have emerged in the dance studios and performance works presented, as well as in the debates that unfolded.

Due to the set-up that invites practitioners and academics from different regions of the world to create work together and engage in debates around the encounter, Artscross by definition engages with questions around different 'identities', the contested concepts of 'self' versus the 'other', or 'home' and 'elsewhere', as the 2013 thematic focus directly propagated. In its premise, as cited above, the project seeks to enhance debates between 'East and West'. The pitfall is one that is well-known, yet challenging to overcome: any conceptions that entail a quest to understand 'differences' between East and West, or any binary thinking in terms of an East 'versus' West in terms of ways of thinking and doing are highly problematic approaches, and the warnings of Edward Said's *Orientalism* (Said, 1978, 1995) and further writers from the field of intercultural studies[5] ought to be constantly and carefully negotiated.

Hence, in a quest to move beyond thinking in terms of a conventional but problematic geographically-relative binary (East/West), and given the preoccupation with 'languages', communication and translation that was, in my view, very central to the creative processes I observed, in this chapter I draw – necessarily briefly – on research from the areas of Translation Studies, Cultural Studies as well as Philosophy in my focus as privileged observer on the spaces and possibilities of collaboration that the project facilitated. I give particular emphasis on the productive possibilities tied to the idea of 'failure' in communication, highlighting issues of dealing with 'ways of understanding' each other both in terms of language and dance practice.

The questions I address here relate to how the collaborative encounters that took place as part of Artscross, not only in the rehearsal spaces but also in the many discussions that unfolded between academics and practitioners – while interweaved with misunderstandings and misapprehensions – were, and arguably still are, productive in the sense of being transformative to each individual practitioner engaged, and also formative to the works that have arisen as part of this process. Moreover, I want to suggest that the concept of what 'dance' or what a 'dancer' may be has been renegotiated in this zone of encounter, which

I understand as a zone of contestation and re-negotiation, worked out in and through a 'co-laborating' in the context of choreography-making.

## Artscross – a set-up for 'working (dance) out'

How might Artscross be positioned amongst cross-cultural collaborations in the professional dance world, which are not in the least uncommon? Major productions that emphasize the collaborative relation between practitioners from different regions of the world continue to be presented on renowned stages, where the performance works in terms of their thematics tend to be inextricably intertwined in the cross-cultural encounter, worked out in processes of collaboration. How might the project for instance be positioned in relation to the collaboration between Belgian dancer and choreographer Sidi Larbi Cherkaoui, who is of Moroccan descent, British artist Antony Gormley and the Shaolin Monks from China for the piece *Sutra* (premièred in 2008)?[6] Or, to provide a further example, how might Artscross relate to the collaboration between dancer and choreographer Akram Khan, who is British-born of Bangladeshi descent and trained in Indian kathak as well as Western contemporary dance, with South African dancer and choreographer Gregory Maqoma as well as South Korean dancer, Young Jin Kim, for the piece *variations for vibes, strings & pianos* (premièred in 2006)?[7]

In the light of this professional backdrop, my suggestion is that the project Artscross might be better understood as an experiment rather than participating in the professional sphere. By applying the term 'experiment' I intend to highlight that while a series of performances were staged at The Place in London in August 2013, these were crucially arranged and created according to the rules set out by Artscross on behalf of the London-based project partners. Nine choreographers – three each from the cities of Beijing, London and Taipei, selected by invitation by the respective participating institutions – agreed to create a new choreographic work, according to the following outline:

> [T]o create work that is contained within a ten-minute performance allocation, to address the theme [*Leaving Home, Being Elsewhere*], to use up to six performers from the three geographical locations. The last stipulation is frequently the most demanding as it involves working with interpreters and with performers whose training in and understanding of performance may vary widely.
>
> (Artscross, London, 2013)

Prior to the events in London, each participating institution had pre-selected and provided a certain number of choreographers and also dancers, some of which, by the way, were still in training and who were then further selected by the choreographers in a one-day group audition process at the start of the project.[8] As part of the auditioning process, in which the choreographers were asked to select dancers from each of the participating cities, the dancers were asked to perform free group improvisations – crucially in their 'home' groups. In my view this supported the building of a heightened awareness of watching for different qualities and abilities in relation to notions of 'home and elsewhere', as well as how these might be negotiated in working together across cultures. The project, then, in its central premise of seeking 'to further intercultural dialogue and understanding' (Artscross, 2013) set up a heightened awareness on behalf of all parties involved (dance practitioners and academics) towards differences in terms of dance practices and practitioner identities. Concurrently, many of the blog entries that were created during and after the project as well as conference presentations and debates I witnessed, indeed foregrounded a thematization of issues around cultural differences and specificities as well as ways of relating across cultures.[9]

Such questions of differing identities were directly tied up with a sense of place, or more specifically the varying locations of 'home'. (Interestingly, the dancers from the 'London group' had a very mixed international background.) Yet the question arises as to how might identities have been negotiated in the choreographic works that were created as part of Artscross, by the different groups that had been formed? Manuel Castells, in *The Power of Identity* conceives of identity as 'people's source of meaning and experience' and further states:

> By identity, as it refers to social actors, I understand the process of construction of meaning on the basis of a cultural attribute, or a related set of cultural attributes, that is given priority over other sources of meaning. For a given individual, or for a collective actor, there may be a plurality of identities. Yet, such a plurality is a source of stress and contradiction in both self-representation and social action.
>
> (Castells, 2010: 6)

Castells further ties processes of internalization to the formation of identities and conceives of the latter as 'sources of meaning for the actors themselves, and by themselves, constructed through a process of individuation' (Castells 2010: 7). What is of explicit interest in the present context are questions around the ways those different identities are accessed and drawn on in the choreographic processes, as well as how these are being negotiated by the dancers and choreographers in the works created.

A further crucial requirement that Artscross set out was for the participating choreographers to create the work with the dancers in rehearsals through a process that I might loosely call 'collaboration', in the sense that rather than preconceiving the work in its detail before the rehearsal process was underway, the material would be created within and through the encounter with the different practitioners – relating to practices that are an arguably prominent feature in contemporary Western choreography-making.[10] Moreover, the context and organizational set-up was, in my view, determining with regard to the practices that evolved. While most choreographers did not watch others' rehearsals, there was still a general sense of 'other' work being made, in parallel, alongside each different project, to be presented in public together on a fixed date, producing a heightened sense of otherness in relation to what is culturally one's own, of shared and different aspects of 'home' and 'belonging'.

It is in this sense that I want to underline the importance of Artscross having operated according to the logics of experimentation[11] rather than to conditions of professional choreographic practice that prevail in the wider performing arts contexts, despite the project explicitly involving professional choreographers, who worked with professional dancers as well as dancers-in-education and graduate dancers. The distinction is an important one in my view, since the choreographic works created were conditioned by the respective parameters set out by the larger framework that Artscross provided, bearing an impact on the 'expert decision-making processes' (see indicatively Melrose, 2009) of each choreographer involved to greater or lesser degree, depending on each practitioner's ongoing professional signature practice.

I propose to conceive the collaborative events that took place as 'zones of encounter', within which a number of abstractions – issues for example of 'newness' and 'actuality' – were being worked out; in each instance what was proposed was a negotiation of different practitioner identities with a heightened set of attention around the familiar versus the strange. In this sense, the act of working together in performance-making involved a negotiation of different practitioner subjectivities, which, in my view, are inextricably tied up with particularities in terms of histories, training systems and conceptions of agencies in dance-making. What the project highlighted, in particular through its set-up of rehearsal processes being observed and discussed, was the processual dealings with these encounters, tied up with a committed sense of working through misunderstandings, misapprehensions and prejudices as part of choreography-making.

## Locating culturally sensitive perspectives

I have hinted above at the difficulty and delicacy of undertaking practices that bring cultural identity into relief. However, as a European, I do need to raise the issue of how we might conceive of these encounters without applying the connotations that accrue to a Western perspective, which in this context at least, would be strictly limiting. We need to bear in mind that due to its particular history, collaboration in the Western sense is largely defined by its emergence in the 1960s and its subsequent developments, yet performance culture in China and Taiwan both have their respective unique histories, and Western conceptions of collaboration might not reflect Chinese and Taiwanese contemporary performance practices.[12] Considering Dipesh Chakrabarty's publication *Provincializing Europe: Postcolonial Thought and Historical Difference*, setting out from the premise that 'thought is related to places' (Chakrabarty, 2000: xvii), one of the prevalent debates that took place as part of Artscross worth considering here dealt with the varying conceptions of the 'modern' and the 'contemporary' that accrue to the different contexts of the performing arts cultures represented.

Furthermore, not only does Artscross deal with highly particular histories of the localities involved, but crucially there are also complex historical relations between these that would arguably bear an impact on the project. Great Britain's colonial history with China, as well as the ongoing precarious relations between China and Taiwan,[13] by way of example, were necessarily intertwined in the encounters that took place, respectively, in Taipei, Beijing and London. Moreover, the history of problematic historicizations between different societies needs to be considered in the present context.

As such, in his seminal work *Time and the Other: How Anthropology Makes its Object*, Johannes Fabian highlights the fact that historically, knowledges produced between different cultures, and more specifically by predominantly Western anthropologists about 'others', tended to be defined by distancing processes, crucially involving different perspectives that would apply and produce a temporal distancing in the false name of objectivity:

> Beneath their bewildering variety, the distancing devices that we can identify produce a global result. I will call it *denial of coevalness*. By that I mean *a persistent and systematic tendency to place the referent(s) of anthropology in a Time other than the present of the producer of anthropological discourse.*
>
> (Fabian, 2002, 1983: 31, emphasis in original)

Instead of a temporal distancing, as we see above, Fabian argues for 'coevalness' to be applied in human communication and exchange; the term is taken from the German term 'Gleichzeitigkeit' or 'contemporaneity' (Fabian, 2002, 1983: 31), which he defines as 'a mode of temporal relations' that produces an epistemological condition (Fabian, 2002, 1983: 31), by which I understand him to mean that it is an approach to knowledge production that needs to be actively set up and applied. In the many discussions that took place as part of Artscross about conceptions of the 'contemporary' in choreographic practice, especially when comparisons were drawn between existing practices in different places, on several occasions I identified biases towards a 'further developed' dance culture over another. Hence my own understanding of the project's ethos – how the *working together* of dance practitioners from the respective places, might research and newly define what contemporary dance might be – was on occasion countered by the views of the practitioner participants.

Where views were in contention, Doreen Massey's writing from the perspective of geography on the representation of space in the age of globalization is of interest. Following Fabian, she problematizes the effects of what she terms 'aspatial globalisation' in her publication *For Space*. She emphasizes the 'multiplicities of the spatial' and challenges the concept of globalization as a movement that is understood as inevitable and all-embracing. Instead, Massey suggests an understanding of globalization as:

> a making of space(s), an active reconfiguration and meeting-up through practices and relations of a multitude of trajectories, and it is there that lies the politics.
>
> (Massey, 2005: 83)

The notions of reconfiguration and meeting-up are of particular interest in the present context, in that Artscross, from my perspective as a participating academic observing the creative processes of choreography-making, presented an opportunity not only for a 'meeting-up' of multiple dance practices, but also a questioning and reconfiguring what contemporary dance may be, from the multiple perspectives applied by the participants involved. Through an actual engagement in dance-making the following questions became crucial in my view: 1. How would specific practices be negotiated and preferred over others, by choreographers and dancers respectively, when practitioners from different localities came to work together in a group, according to the rules set out? 2. What assumptions do the rules themselves, set out by the organizers of Artscross, entail and produce? 3. What aspects of performance practice and what thought models would be negotiated in the encounter? 4. How would respective misunderstandings and misapprehensions of the 'other', or the inability to find ways of understanding each other, be dealt with? And, crucially, 5. How might we conceive of the encounter in a way that acknowledges but also transcends a focus on differences and allows for a conception of transformation that arguably has taken place?

## Feeling each other move – or – moving 'forward'

The specific rehearsal processes, in which collaborative approaches to choreography-making were at stake in my view, might be said to have been facilitated through the respective choreographers' setting up of improvisation structures in which the contributions of individual dance practitioners were demanded in terms of their creative decision-making with regard to choices of timing, development of movement as well as the establishing of an idiosyncratic performance quality. Taking up Massey's views on globalization, my argument is that this collaborative zone of encounter forms a site of negotiation of dance practice.

In her keynote speech entitled 'Collaborative Practices and the Elephant in the (Rehearsal) Room' at the first Symposium on Collaboration at Middlesex University in 2013, Susan Melrose addressed the experience of the performer in collaborative performance-making processes. She emphasized the 'transformative' aspect of such processes, in which a 'confrontation with difference' is at stake, in relation to the performers' 'ability to work productively the other'. Questions of 'selfhood', 'identity' and 'individuality' are at stake here for the practitioner who engages in a 'powerful experience as other' to fellow performers (Melrose 2013).

As part of Artscross, specifically the creative processes of choreographers Vera Tussing, Dam Van Huyn and Zhao Liang seemed to me to work according to the principle of 'activating' their dancers to work in inventive terms. My argument is that something beyond dance technique was at stake for the dancers in these processes, which not only relates to the subjective in that individual decision-making and development of highly idiosyncratic movement qualities were desired from the dancers. But further, given the framework and set-up of the larger project Artscross, the negotiations of issues of different 'cultural identities' remained a central preoccupation in the given dance works produced.

These selected choreographic processes were arguably facilitated by each choreographer, yet in the specific instances addressed here, aspects of collaborative creation were integrated, in that the respective choreographers set up their making processes in ways that stimulated the individual dancers to actively inform the emerging choreographies through their idiosyncratic negotiations of the processual operations. Moreover, these processes involved decision-making processes that would be responsive and flexible as to the spontaneous work that would arise with the dancers in the studios day-by-day. In other words, these creative processes were not clearly outlined and planned in their detail before their beginning, but instead worked according to the logics of experimentation referred to earlier. In this regard these processes relied on an investment of the 'practitioner personal' and subjectivity, which, as I propose to argue, is directly tied up with questions around cultural identity.

In the context of enquiring into the sets of negotiations that took place in the creative processes of performance-making, Jean-François Lyotard's writing entitled 'Obedience' is of interest, in particular his use of the German term *Durcharbeitung* in a somewhat different but related context: his conception of 'perlaborare' (Lyotard, 1991: 173), of 'working through' something, seems to me highly relevant in the present context which involved a disciplinary 'working through' a complex array of issues within the space of 'working out' a choreography.[14]

How were the encounters set in motion in the studio? My proposition is that one of the most important aspects of these processes of contestation or re-negotiation was a 'feeling each other move' on behalf of the practitioners involved. Teresa Brennan's publication *The Transmission of Affect* is applicable in this context since her research into 'subjectivity' provides insights into the feeling of atmospheres as well as others' affects. According to Brennan, 'affects have an energetic dimension. This is why they can enhance or deplete', and moreover she underlines that humans are not 'self-contained in terms of [their] energies' (Brennan 2004: 6). Applied to the present context, the level of interaction that takes place between dancers when collaborating in processes of choreography-making involves a 'moving together', which produces a tight, energetic interplay.

Before I discuss in more detail how notions of 'working through' and affect transmission were at stake in the operations of the processes of choreography-making I observed, as I signal above, rather than focusing on identifying common grounds and differences, I proceed here to enquire into the possibilities for 'newness' and 'actuality' that might be produced through the act of working together and of working through something. In this context Brian Massumi's work on 'movement, affect and sensation' is insightful: when writing about the 'connection between movement and sensation' (Massumi 2002: 1), Massumi highlights 'qualitative difference' in relation to 'change'. In setting up a focus on movement, change and the processual, he puts forward the idea that 'social and cultural determinations' are positionings that result out of 'fields of emergences' characterized by 'passage and indeterminacy' (8). Massumi introduces the concept of *ontogenesis* – a term previously applied by Fabian (Fabian, 2002, 1983: 61) – which he defines as process concepts that are 'equal to emergence' (8). Referring to Gilbert Simondon, Massumi equates 'ontogenesis' with a 'becoming of culture and the social' (Massumi, 2002: 9). In this context Massumi also draws attention to 'interaction-in-the-making' (9) and states that '[t]he world is in a condition of constant qualitative growth', further observing that 'with every move, with every change, there is something new to the world, an added reality. The world is self-augmenting' (12).

It is this zone of 'becoming of culture' that is of interest to me in the present context where practitioners from different places 'moved together' in processes of performance-making. Taking the lead from Massumi's observations (9), rather than giving priority through a focus in ontological terms on cultural positionings, which implies a 'gridlocking' in terms of their signification, an alternative emphasis may be placed on spatializing processes of 'formation', which crucially function, potentially at least, in *relational* terms. This relational formation, in performance-making terms, may offer precisely that site for a 'becoming of culture and the social', that the various writers cited above allude to, in their different ways.

Can we think, then, of the collaborations between practitioners that were drawn together as part of Artscross as a dynamic process, which is actively forming in terms of the experiences of the participants involved? A connection presents itself here between Brennan's research on affect and Massumi's identification of 'sensory surfaces' in relation to the 'incorporeal dimension' of the body, which he equates with 'intensities' and 'experiences'. In other words he sets up a 'corporeal' aspect or a 'materiality' of the body on the one hand, and an 'incorporeal' dimension, or 'events', from which the 'subject' can emerge (Massumi, 2002: 14). This 'subject', an area to which Massumi consistently returns, can be related to the dance practitioner who works inventively by applying their sometimes idiosyncratic 'ways of doing and thinking' in actively shaping the performance material.

Massumi further mentions the appealing notion of 'the feeling of having a feeling' (14) and sets up the concept of 'tendency' in this context, which he relates to 'futurity' (15). He further discusses the capacity for 'change' and the issue 'in what sense the body coincides with its own transitions and in its transitioning with its potential' (15).

If we apply the elements of Massumi's thinking that I have briefly sketched out to the productive encounters of Artscross, it might allow us to avoid some of the many traps of cultural stereotyping that I highlighted above in thinking through the cross-cultural collaborations that took place.

## Issues of misapprehensions, miscommunication and misunderstandings in collaborative set-ups as a productive zone of creativity

Within the collaborations that have emerged in the various rehearsal processes as part of Artscross the aspect of productivity deserves further elaboration and, more specifically, how the encounters between the different practitioners have been 'worked through' and 'worked into' the performances that were created over the three weeks, and finally presented to a public audience.

One of the zones of encounter that needed to be constantly negotiated was the issue of different languages and their translation within each of the creative processes, and the more general question of the role of language itself in choreographic practices. Daily rehearsals were framed by questions of how practitioners would verbally communicate when working together, and in each rehearsal process of the nine choreographies that were created in London, languages and communication were negotiated in unique terms. In every rehearsal a Mandarin Chinese/English translator was at hand, which highlighted in many instances the different roles that verbal communication can play in choreography-making. Depending on the first languages of the choreographers and the differing language skills of the given dancers in each rehearsal process, as well as the particular skills and sensibilities of the translators, there were idiosyncratic permutations with regard to how choreographers and dancers communicated. Communication and miscommunication, respectively, remained an issue throughout the project. I would argue that it was a fertile one.

Lydia Liu, in the area of translation studies and specifically in the context of mapping out the field of 'translingual practice' in her publication *Translingual Practice: Literature, National Culture, and Translated Modernity – China 1900–1937*, emphasizes the danger of searching for direct translations and of imposing theories or concepts in a comparative way, where, however, different languages also entail different ways of thinking. Liu argues:

> To me it seems sheer folly to wield an analytical concept or category indifferently anywhere as if that which makes sense in one place must necessarily obtain elsewhere.
>
> (Liu, 1995: 6)

Following Liu, it might be useful to work with the idea that the world can be understood in multiple ways, rather than understanding the incommensurability of different languages as a 'problem', as research from the discipline of translation studies has revealed to be an ongoing bias (see Liu 1999: 13). We also need to bear in mind that acts of translation run the risk of reproducing certain historical power relations between nations.

Umberto Eco's work on *Serendipities: Language and Lunacy* (Eco, 1998) is relevant in this context, in that he stresses the positive aspect of errors, miscomprehensions and false beliefs, perhaps about an 'elsewhere' or an 'other', or what an 'elsewhere' might be about, or indeed what the 'other' might be thinking, saying, or doing. In the chapter 'From Marco Polo to Leibniz: Stories of Intellectual Misunderstandings', Eco states that a shock occurs when people from different cultures encounter each other, which is 'a result of their reciprocal diversity' (Eco, 1998: 69). His specific focus is on the 'perspectives' that are applied when such encounters take place and misapprehensions and misconceptions, such as Leibniz' misunderstanding of the *I Ching* led, in this instance, to a development of his mathematical discoveries. Two issues that Eco highlights in this text seem useful to me with regard to the present context: on the one hand, in cross-cultural encounters people tend to try to see what they already know (Eco, 1998: 96), and on the other hand misreadings, misconceptions and misunderstandings can lead to productive developments and must not necessarily be seen as negative.

## Differences at work together

This final section serves to set out some of the details of practices I was able to observe in this complex undertaking, testing as I did so the pertinence of some of the theoretical perspectives I have introduced above. I have identified respective relevant aspects in the creative processes of London-based choreographer Vera Tussing (German by nationality) for her choreographic work *Moving Relations: Research,* of Beijing-based choreographer Zhao Liang for *Infinite Connections* as well as of London-based choreographer Dam Van Huyn (born in Southern Vietnam and raised in the United States) for *Gloves* (Artscross London, 2013).[15]

At the beginning of the project Vera Tussing explained that her background in dance-making was in working through collaboration. In an interview[16] before the rehearsal processes of Artscross began, Tussing stated that she was very interested in issues regarding communication that would arise due to English not being the working language of all dancers. From the very first rehearsals Tussing introduced what might be described as a game, or set of rules that she asked the dancers to follow, according to which they had to negotiate space and relations amongst each other, in their interactions. Her piece, for a long time in the creative process, was noticeably *not* choreographed in a fixed way in space, but would, in theory at least, 'choreograph itself' through the dancers' physical and spatial negotiations that were facilitated by the rules set up.

In rehearsals I witnessed Tussing trying various combinations of pre-set structures, and it was here that the piece needed to be 'worked out', through a shared holding of the structure and the rules on behalf of each dancer, who had to learn to be able to negotiate these, live, in the moment. It put great demands on an intellectual processing of the structure of the piece, and each dancer needed to work at the level of holding the piece together conceptually. Specific tasks and rules needed to be constantly negotiated with the others.

Tussing stated that her creative process was based on creating 'encounters' between the dancers, and she specifically worked with 'weight' – the taking of each other's weight. Her focus was on 'relations' and more specifically 'spatial relations'. In the interview mentioned above she further discussed her interest in creating a more specific 'collaborative body' through working with interactions between dancers:

> What I was interested in was to find a way of setting something up that would allow all dancers to contribute to the research. So rather

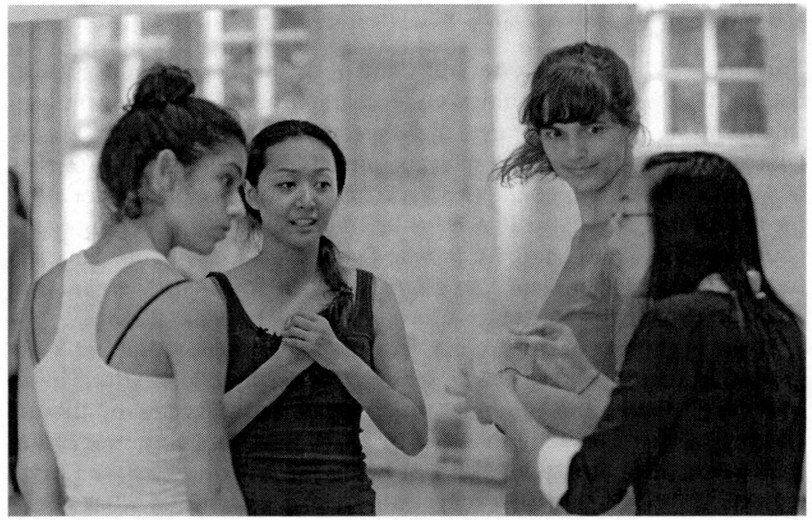

*Fig. 27* Rehearsals *Moving Relations: Research,* Vera Tussing – Photograph Andrew Lang

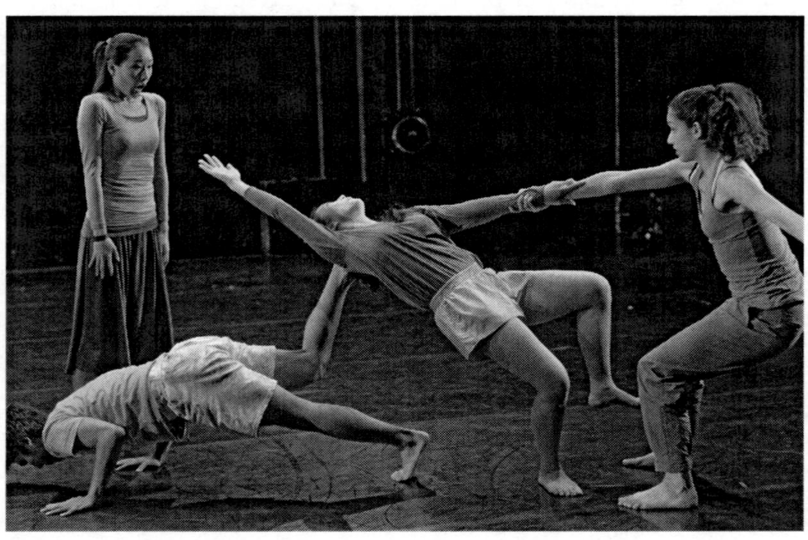

*Fig. 28* Performance *Moving Relations: Research,* Vera Tussing – Photograph Andrew Lang

> than having individual bodies, I was trying to find a way to work with all bodies towards a collaborative body. I guess you could see the basis of the research as a type of game where all participants know the rules and are able to contribute to the way it develops.
>
> (Tussing in: Artscross, 2013)

Tussing typically gave the dancers physical and spatial instructions, focusing in her process of choreography-making on how the dancers related to these. The choreographer specified that her intention was to give the dancers something to 'feel', which would make them 'grow in a different way'. She further stated that she remained unsure about how well the translation process in the studio worked, and brought in pictures to share with her dancers.

Following Tussing, as indicated above, further creative processes took place as part of Artscross, in which the respective choreographers set up *ways of functioning* of rehearsals that demanded from the dancers an active engagement in a 'working each other out' as well as a 'working through' occurring issues (cf Lyotard, 1977) as part of the 'working out of the performance material'.

Beijing-based choreographer Zhao Liang stated in an interview at the outset of the rehearsal process that he felt a strong connection and interest in the theme of 'leaving home'. At the centre of this creative process he located issues around 'identities' and self-understanding, highlighting the three questions 'Where are you from? Who are you? Where are you going?' (Artscross, 2013) as highly important in his work with the dancers.

Zhao's rehearsal process created what I propose to call a 'common zone of encounter' and exchange between the dancers, in that it demanded from them a negotiation of their movement in relation to a large elastic band which could be seen as a concrete metaphor for the thematics of home and elsewhere: in several rehearsal sessions at the start of the creative process the dancers were asked to create their own movement in relation to these large elastic bands stretched across the space. I observed Zhao watching dancers improvise over hours, at times approaching them individually, feeding back about specific movements that stood out to him. In no way did Zhao seem to look for a conformity in terms of the movement vocabulary created – on the contrary, many comments he gave to the dancers seemed to be part of a search to establish an idiosyncratic quality to each dancer's movements.

It was less here about moving from 'home' to a pre-existing or predefined 'elsewhere', but about negotiating a collaboratively created

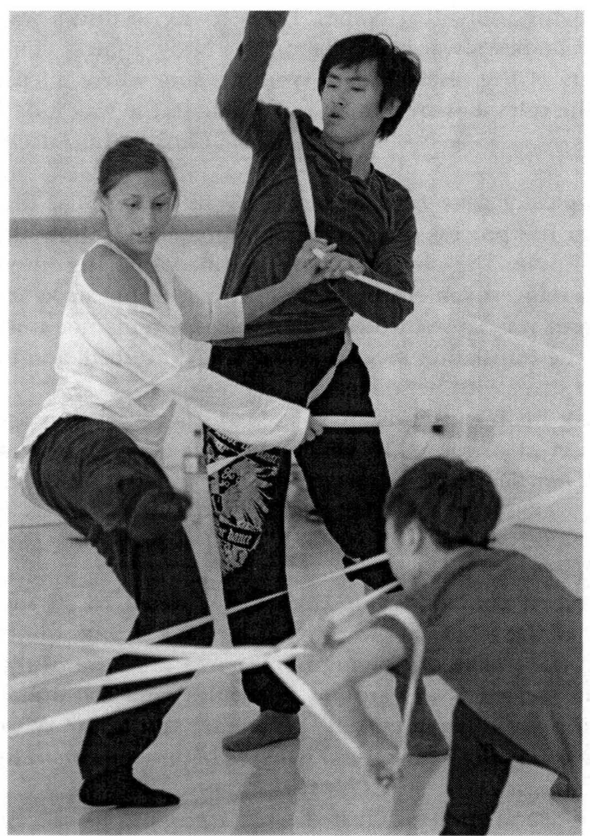

*Fig. 29* Rehearsals *Infinite Connections*, Zhao Liang – Photograph Andrew Lang

space, that introduced its own set of rules and possibilities. The elastic band would occasionally be tied into a tight knot that could not be undone, or else be accidentally lost by the dancers, which meant they had to start all over again, as there was no way of retracing and undoing any mistake.

London-based choreographer Dom Van Huyn (born in Southern Vietnam and raised in the United States) stated in an introductory interview at the beginning of the project that he enjoys and feels comfortable 'being lost' in his processes of choreography-making (Artscross London, 2013). He further explained that his rehearsal process was based on the concept that 'the movement itself is not that important',

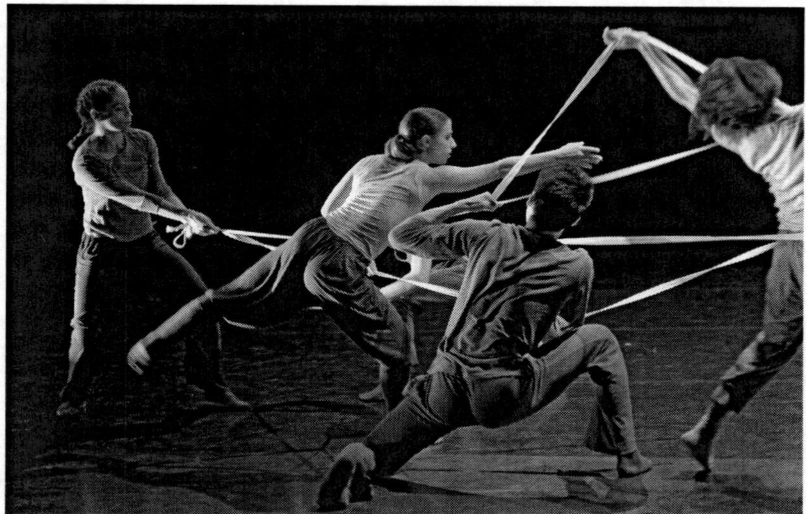

*Fig. 30* Performance *Infinite Connections*, Zhao Liang – Photograph Andrew Lang

however, 'how it is translated back and forth, how the dancer is describing it' is what in his view provides the audience with the possibility of different 'readings' of the material. Early in the rehearsal process Van Huyn emphasized the need for the dancers to understand 'who they are' and 'how they gut feel', as well as 'how they experience their bodies'. His aim was to 'find a balance between his and the dancers' thoughts' (Author's Rehearsal Notes, 2013).

In a specific rehearsal Van Huyn presented a movement phrase to the dancers and asked them to practise it while engaging with the following questions: Where are you? What is unique to you? – emphasizing that the dancers could address these questions in cultural terms; however, as he stated, he was also interested in personal preferences, such as liking ice cream. His instruction was clear: 'Mess that phrase up, please! Dissect it, open it up! [...] I need to know you by the end of this exercise. Surprise me!' He also stated that no movement should be seen as more 'beautiful' than any other, asking his dancers not to make an aesthetic judgement in their interpretation of the given phrase (Author's Rehearsal Notes 2013) – although plainly this instruction might be seen as also involving an aesthetic judgement.

Towards the end of the rehearsal phase, Van Huyn stated in a further interview that the creative process had been challenging in terms of 'the diverse information coming from the different dance artists involved' (Artscross, 2013). He further explained that due to translation processes in the studio taking much more time than the regular communication with dancers he is used to, he experienced difficulties to gage the development of the process. At a specific moment he decided to try working without a translator altogether, and tested whether this decision would allow 'the physical self to convey what it needed to convey', hoping that over time the dancers and himself would 'connect through this kinaesthetic sense', concluding: 'And I found that more effective in terms of the rhythm in the process' (Artscross, 2013).

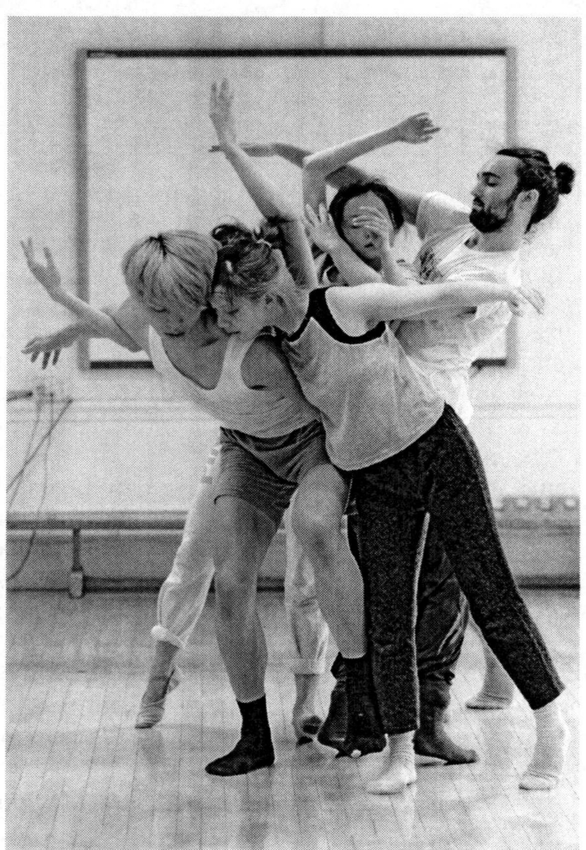

*Fig. 31* Rehearsals *Gloves*, Dam Van Huynh – Photograph Andrew Lang

Van Huyn further stated that he identified special and unique qualities in the dancers from the different regions in terms of the information they provided, the life experiences they had, finding that they produced very diverse elements of movements, which in his view were unique and which he was able to 'capture and harness', 'enriching the process and the vocabulary' in contrast with what he himself could create.[17]

The working together that took place in each piece, due to the set-up that Artscross created – i.e. of each choreographer working with dancers from the cities of Beijing, London and Taipei – meant a 'going elsewhere', in their different ways, for each practitioner involved. This 'elsewhere', in the events I observed, did not mean adapting ways of doing that exist in another place, which might have meant learning skills that were as yet unknown. Instead, what I understood this 'elsewhere' to be, following Liu's insights cited briefly above, was a working out in collaboration, in an actively created space which was, in the event, a zone of encounter with the other. What I want to add here, however, is the observation that 'home', in this critical sense, belongs to the framework and the actions selected and retained first and foremost by the choreographers and to an arguably lesser degree by the dancers, however 'collaboratively' the latter were called upon to contribute.

## Drawing Conclusions from Practices

Van Huyn, Tussing and Zhao have arguably produced very different final choreographic works, yet, in my view, these choreographers clearly sought to 'find' a specific 'identity' of their work in and through working with the set-up of the productive encounters that Artscross facilitated. Each of these creative processes involved a 'working each other out', which has also meant a 'working out' of how the work is being 'worked out' – inevitably entailing negotiations of the issues of miscommunication between the practitioners from different localities.

Several London-based dancers I spoke to conveyed a shared admiration for the technical ability of their colleagues from Taipei and Beijing, while on the other hand the London-based dancers' ability to express their individuality in the ways they moved has been highlighted as a strong skill by the dancers from Taipei and Beijing. Hence one might say that regardless of the collaborative imperative, and regardless of the evident success of this research-driven, collaborative exploration of choreographic potential in the face of cultural difference, judgements clearly emerged that singled out not so much the blurring of cultural boundaries, but the strength of particular cultural identities. Yet coupled with an establishing of differences, crucially through the process of working together, the practitioners involved also learned from and influenced each other.

As I point out above, each performance piece that was created, set up its highly specific parameters in terms of a measurement of what it means to be 'good' at 'dancing something', where that judgement was mediated by the choreographers selected. Different training systems and traditions entail their own judgements as to what might be 'right', and these are always mediated by a choreographer who simultaneously seeks to work in a distinctive, 'signature-specific' manner. The many individual practitioners involved in this project from the three cities Beijing, London and Taipei brought with themselves different skill sets and sensibilities, and each appeared to be driven by the urge to self-delineate the practices involved. Yet these very sensibilities seemed to me to have perceptively widened in the Artscross project in London in 2013.

*With thanks to Susan Melrose for detailed comments on this chapter.*

## Notes

1. The project also involved UK arts partners Step Out Arts, Confucius Institute and The Place, as well as academics from a range of institutions. For further details see Artscross London 2013.
2. Artscross London 2013 Blog: http://rescen.net/blog5/
3. For a discussion of various definitions of performing 'across' cultures see the introduction of Pavis 1996.
4. See Oxford Dictionary http://www.oxforddictionaries.com/definition/english/collaboration Accessed September 2014.
5. See indicatively Liu (1999) and Bhabha (1994). Homi Bhabha, in *The Location of Culture*, addresses 'the overlap and displacement of domains of difference' as a space in which 'intersubjective and collective experiences of *nationness*, community interest, or cultural value are negotiated' (Bhabha, 1994: 2).
6. See http://www.east-man.be/en/35/Sidi-Larbi-Cherkaoui Accessed September 2014.
7. Khan describes the work on the website as 'collaborating with a South African choreographer/dancer, and a South Korean dancer and together the three male artists/dancers wish to use the process as a melting pot for exchanging and developing movement vocabulary unique from their individual personal experiences. The starting points are based on the concept of 'corners' – the corners of our bodies, the corners within our movements, the corners in our space, and most importantly the corners within our stories' (http://www.akramkhancompany.net/html/akram_production.php?productionid=11 Accessed September 2014).

8. This meant that some dancers were performing in more than one production, and not every choreographer was able to work with the dancers of their first choice.
9. See Artscross London 2013.
10. Creative processes that are arranged according to a methodology of 'discovery', in which the performance material is created through a set of methods that are characterized by improvisation and crucially depend on the creative (and not merely technical) input of the individual performer, are a prominent phenomenon in Western contemporary performance practice.
11. In using the term 'logics of experimentation' I lean on the term 'logics of production' that Susan Melrose has widely used (see indicatively Melrose (2009)) to refer to stabilized sets of production modes in professional performance practice. My proposition is that there are likewise stabilized parameters to experimental performance practice, in which a testing of processual givens are foregrounded over the working towards a performance product that is characterized by interpretation of pre-arranged performance material (i.e. a pre-written play in theatre or a pre-written choreography in dance).
12. For a historical overview of contemporary trends in Western choreography-making see for instance Burt (2006). For a discussion of the development of contemporary performance in China and Taiwan see Wetmore, Liu, Mee (2014) as well as Ferrari (2012). It is beyond the scope and direct interest of this chapter to trace definitions and conceptions of collaboration in the different localities that Artscross involves.
13. For a discussion of the development of the dance scene in Taiwan in relation to changes in the political environment see Lin (1998, 2010).
14. Lyotard's conception of 'working through' in the context of choreography-making has previously been discussed in Melrose, Sachsenmaier, Butcher (2013).
15. I want to underline that my selection of these particular creative processes of choreography-making is slightly arbitrary in that further processes of different choreographers might also have served as useful examples here.
16. See Artscross London 2013.
17. See Artscross London 2013.

## Bibliography

Akram Khan Company http://www.akramkhancompany.net/html/akram_production.php?productionid=11 (Accessed September 2014).

Artscross (2013) http://rescen.net/events/ArtsCross_index.html (Accessed 29 November 2014).

Artscross London (2013) http://www.rescen.net/events/ArtsCross_13/ArtsCross_13_1.html#.VGTU1VesXkI (home page), (Accessed 18 April 2014).

Bhabha, Homi K. (1994) *The Location of Culture*. (London and New York: Routledge).

Brennan, Teresa (2004) *The Transmission of Affect*. (Ithaca and London: Cornell University Press).

Burt, Ramsay (2006) *Judson Dance Theater: Performative Traces* (Abingdon and New York: Routledge).

Castells, Manuel (2010) *The Power of Identity*, 2nd ed. (Malden, Oxford, Chichester: Wiley-Blackwell).

Chakrabarty, Dipesh (2000) *Provincializing Europe: Postcolonial Thought and Historical Difference.* (Princeton and Oxford: Princeton University Press).

Eco, Umberto (1998) *Serendipities: Language and Lunacy.* Transl. William Weaver. (New York and London: Phoenix).

Fabian, Johannes (2002, 1983) *Time and the Other: How Anthropology Makes its Object.* (New York and Chichester: Columbia University Press).

Ferrari, Rosella (2012) *Pop Goes the Avant-Garde: Experimental Theatre in Contemporary China.* (London, New York, Calcutta: Seagull Books).

Lin, Yatin (1998, 2010) 'Choreographing a Flexible Taiwan: Cloud Gate Dance Theatre and Taiwan's changing identity' in: Carter, Alexandra and O'Shea, Janet *The Routledge Dance Studies Reader.* 2nd ed. (London and New York: Routledge), pp. 250–60.

Liu, Lydia (1995) *Translingual Practice: Literature, National Culture, and Translated Modernity – China 1900–1937.* (Stanford: Stanford University Press).

Liu, Lydia (ed.) (1999) *Tokens of Exchange.* (Durham and London: Duke University Press).

Lyotard, Jean-François ([1973] 2006) 'Painting as Libidinal Set-up (Genre: Improvised Speech)', in Keith Crome and James Williams (eds) *The Lyotard Reader.* (Edinburgh: Edinburgh University Press), pp. 302–29.

———. (1991) 'Obedience' in: *The Inhuman: Reflections on Time.* Transl. Geoffrey Bennington and Rachel Bowlby. (Stanford: Stanford University Press), pp. 165–81.

Massey, Doreen (2005) *For Space.* (Los Angeles, London, New Delhi, Singapore, Washington DC: SAGE Publications).

Massumi, Brian (2002) *Parables for the Virtual: Movement, Affect, Sensation.* (Durham and London: Duke University Press).

Melrose, Susan (2005) 'just intuitive...' URL http://www.sfmelrose.org.uk/justintuitive/. (Accessed 13 November 2014).

———. (2009) 'Expert-intuitive processing and the logics of production: struggles in (the wording of) creative decision-making in dance' In: *Contemporary Choreography: A Critical Reader.* Butterworth, Jo and Wildschut, Liesbeth, eds., (London and New York: Routledge), pp. 23–37.

———. (2013) unpublished keynote event, Symposium on Collaboration, Middlesex University.

Melrose, Susan and Sachsenmaier, Stefanie, with Butcher, Rosemary (2013) 'Just in Time – 'Momentary' Events in the Making of Rosemary Butcher's Signature Practices'. (Unpublished conference paper, Performance Studies International #19, Stanford University).

Oxford Online Dictionaries. URL: http://www.oxforddictionaries.com (Accessed September 2014).

Pavis, Patrice (ed.) (1996) *The Intercultural Performance Reader.* (Oxon and New York: Routlegde).

Said, Edward (1978, 1995) *Orientalism: Western Conceptions of the Orient.* (London, New York, Victoria, Ontario, New Delhi, Auckland, Johannesburg: Penguin Books).

Sutra – Sidi Larbi Cherkaoui and collaborators. URL: http://www.east-man.be/en/ (Accessed September 2014).

Wetmore Jr, Kevin J., Liu Siyuan and Mee, Erin B. (2014) *Modern Asian Theatre and Performance 1900–2000.* (London, New Delhi, New York, Syndey: Bloomsbury).

# Index

UNIVERSITY OF W[illegible]ESTER
LIBRARY

Lightning Source UK Ltd.
Milton Keynes UK
UKOW01n0005281215

265381UK00005B/114/P